The Portable Kristeva

EUROPEAN PERSPECTIVES

European Perspectives

A Series in Social Thought and Cultural Criticism
Lawrence D. Kritzman, Editor

European Perspectives presents English translations of books by leading European thinkers. With both classic and outstanding contemporary works, the series aims to shape the major intellectual controversies of our day and to facilitate the tasks of historical understanding.

The Portable Kristeva

Kelly Oliver, Editor

Columbia University Press
New York

Columbia University Press
Publishers Since 1893
New York   Chichester, West Sussex
Copyright © 1997 Columbia University Press
All rights reserved

Library of Congress Cataloging-in-Publication Data
Kristeva, Julia, 1941–
    The portable Kristeva / Kelly Oliver, editor.
        p.   cm. — (European perspectives)
    Collection selected from previously published material, 1974–1993.
    Includes bibliographical references (p. 397) and index.
    Partial Contents: "My memory's hyperbole" — Revolution in poetic
    language — Desire in language — Time and sense — Tales of love —
    Black sun — New maladies of the soul — Powers of horror —
    Strangers to ourselves — Desire in language — Julia Kristeva in
    conversation with Rosalind Coward — Interview with Elaine Hoffman
    Baruch on feminism in the United States and France.
        ISBN 0–231–10504–5. — ISBN 0–231–10505–3 (pbk.)
        1. Semiotics.   2. Language and languages—Philosophy.
    3. Psychoanalysis.   4. Feminism.   I. Oliver, Kelly, 1959–
    II. Title.   III. Series.
    P99.K694   1997
    302.2—dc20   96–34403
                                                                      CIP

Casebound editions of Columbia University Press books are printed on permanent and durable acid-free paper.
Printed in the United States of America
c 10 9 8 7 6 5 4 3 2 1
p 10 9 8 7 6 5

Contents

Preface: About This Collection

This collection of Julia Kristeva's writings is designed to give the reader a representative selection from all her major works over the last two decades. The selections were chosen to reflect Kristeva's most significant contributions to the human sciences, including philosophy, literary theory, linguistics, cultural studies, psychoanalytic theory, and feminist theory. In these selections, Kristeva introduces the terminology and conceptual framework with which she goes on to analyze texts, music, visual arts, language, and culture. These selections, then, include her most important theoretical innovations, but they do not include her fiction or detailed applications of her techniques to art and literature. Still, this volume will introduce the reader to the methodology and terminology that inform all Kristeva's writings.

The selections are ordered topically but the original publication dates are included in the table of contents for readers who prefer to read chronologically. I have divided the texts under five topics: 1. Kristeva's Trajectory; 2. The Subject in Signifying Practice; 3. Psychoanalysis of Love: A Counterdepressant; 4. Individual and National Identity; and 5. Maternity, Feminism, and Female Sexuality. Much of Kristeva's writing, however, touches on several issues at once, so many of these selections could have been placed under different topics. For example, the discussion of the semiotic chora from *Revolution in Poetic Language*, in part 2, focuses on the relationship between poetic language and the maternal body. And one of the selections from *Powers of Horror*, in part 4, includes an important discussion of abjection and the maternal body, which informs Kristeva's later writings on female sexuality. In addition, the selections from *Tales of Love*, in part 3, and the selections from *Powers of Horror*, in part 4, include Kristeva's ongoing formulations of subjectivity and signification. The reader may want to refer to the introduction before each part to get a sense of some of the issues addressed in each selection.

In addition to the five introductions, I have included a general introduction in which I discuss one of Kristeva's most revolutionary contributions to the human sciences as it evolves throughout her writings, her attempt to bring the speaking body back into theoretical discourse. *The Portable Kristeva* begins with Kristeva's autobiographical essay "My Memory's Hyperbole," originally published as "Mémoires" in 1983. In this provocative essay, Kristeva describes her intellectual trajectory since her arrival in Paris in December 1965. The introduction before each part also gives more information about Kristeva's intellectual trajectory.

Julia Kristeva was born in Bulgaria in 1941. Although her education in Eastern Europe familiarized her with Marxism and Russian, she was introduced to Western thought and French in her early education by French nuns. Before leaving Bulgaria to continue her education in Paris, Kristeva worked as a journalist for a communist newspaper. She went to Paris in December 1965 on a doctoral research fellowship to work with Lucien Goldmann in Hautes Etudes at the Sorbonne, where she also worked with Roland Barthes. Within one year Kristeva's articles were being published in *Critique*, *Langages*, and *Tel Quel*. She became involved with the *Tel Quel* group and later married the head of the group, novelist Philippe Sollers. They had a son in 1976. In 1970 she was appointed to the editorial board of *Tel Quel*, where she served until the journal was disbanded in 1983 and became the journal *Infini*.

Since her first book, *Semeiotiké: Recherches pour une semanalyse*, was published in 1969, Julia Kristeva has become one of the most prolific theorists in France. The importance of her writing over the past two decades has been felt across the human sciences. The impact of her doctoral dissertation, published as *La Révolution du langage poétique* in 1974, is still being felt. Although the influence of psychoanalysis is manifest in her earliest work, which includes *Semeiotiké* (1969), *Le Texte du roman* (1970), *Révolution* (1974), and *Polylogue* (1977), this work is centered around linguistic analysis, including empirical studies. Her interest in psychoanalytic theory led her to complete training in psychoanalysis in 1979. While interest in language still motivates her work, her writings of the 1980s and 1990s reflect her training and practice as a psychoanalyst. She still maintains her psychoanalytic practice.

After Kristeva defended her dissertation, she was appointed to the faculty of the Department of Science of Texts and Documents at the University of Paris VII, where she continues to teach in the Department of Literature and Humanities. She also holds a regular visiting appointment at Columbia University in the French Department and at the University of Toronto.

Recently, Kristeva became a novelist with the publication of her first novel, *Les Samouraïs*, in 1990, her second, *Le vieil homme et les loups*, in 1991, and her third, *Possessions*, in 1996. Her writing is unique in that it skillfully brings together psychoanalytic theory and clinical practice, literature, linguistics, and philosophy.

Kelly Oliver

Introduction: Kristeva's Revolutions

Meaning has become the central problem of philosophy and the human sciences. I am thinking of two general senses in which this is true. Contemporary theorists ask, "What does our language mean, to what does it refer?" And this question stands upon another, larger, question that has been the subject of philosophy since its inception—"What is the meaning of life?" Meaning operates on various interconnected levels simultaneously. For example, the ordinary language philosopher determines precisely what we mean when we use a particular word by looking at how the word is used. The philologist traces the etymological history of a particular word, whereas the philosopher of language or linguist determines how words have meaning at all; how does language work so that individual words, phrases, and sentences have meaning? Linguists and psychologists might also be concerned with what kinds of meaning language has for the addressee and the addressed. This kind of analysis leads to general questions about the meaning of human experience and perception and the relation of language to life. The multivalent meaning of *meaning* is reflected in the various ways in which the problem of meaning is presented in the human sciences.

Traditionally, philosophers have tried to describe human experience by abstracting from their own experience and articulating the essential characteristics of that experience. As philosophy has become more aware of itself and its methodologies, it has become concerned with the relation between experience itself and its articulation of experience. This kind of philosophical reflection leads to the question "What might get lost in the translation from experience as it is lived to the philosopher's articulation of it?" With the so-called linguistic turn in philosophy, and poststructuralists' attention to language and metaphor, the connection between lived experience and the language in which we articulate that experience has become complicated. The relation between experience and language is no longer seen as the relation between the original and its vessel, mirror image, or inferior copy. Yet what do we mean when we describe the essential characteristics of experience? What do we mean when we make philosophical or theoretical statements? What is the relationship between the theory and what it purports to describe? Can we mean what we say and say what we mean? What is the relationship between language and meaning?

The linguistic turn in philosophy might be said to begin with Hegel, who maintains that, through the dialectical movement of consciousness, the meaning of the world is realized in its philosophical articulation. For Hegel there is a necessary relationship between conceptualization, which he insists is necessary to self-consciousness and articulation. In *Phenomenology of Spirit*, the highest level of consciousness is reached when we can describe our experience—when we mean what we say and say what we mean—when there is no gap between language and our experience. Reality is what is rational, and what is rational can be articulated.

Nietzsche seems to assert that if there is no gap between language and our experience, it is not because the real is rational and therefore articulable. Rather, language and grammar produce a rational reality. In *On the Genealogy of Morals* he maintains that grammar divides sentences into nouns, verbs, and objects, and is therefore responsible for our belief in subjects and substance that transcend activities. In "On Truth and Lies in the Ultramoral Sense," he describes the meaning of words as the result of an arbitrary process of sedimentation and coagulation over time, a history which we forget when we use words.

Influenced by Nietzsche, especially in his later work, Heidegger insists that language is not a mere instrument for the communication of information. Rather, language is the unfolding of meaning itself, including the meaning of human experience. We do not speak language; rather, language speaks us. Heir to both Nietzsche and Heidegger, Jacques Derrida also follows Ferdinand de Saussure's notion that words have meaning only in their differential relation to other words. Saussure proposed that reference is not a necessary relationship between a word and a thing, but an arbitrary relationship between a word and a concept; the signifier (sound pattern of a word) and the signified (concept) have an arbitrary relationship. Meaning is the result of a system of differences without any positive terms. Derrida goes one step further to assert that the signified itself is also the product of differential relationships between signifiers; meaning is produced through an endless chain of signifiers. He introduces the term *différance* to refer to the difference through which meaning is produced, a difference that can never be articulated or conceptualized. The operations of difference and differentiation that make meaning and thought possible can never themselves be thought; the difference of difference itself must always be deferred in our attempts to articulate it or think it.

In spite of the pessimism about the possibility of articulating our experience, and the professionalization of the disciplines, in some sense, philosophy is still held accountable for the meaning of life. Philosophers try to coordinate not only words and their meanings but also the meaning of this activity for life. This larger question of meaning moves us from the questions "What is our experience?" or "How do we articulate it?" to "Why . . . why bother?" "Why do we do what we do?" "Why should we?" These questions return us to a more specific sense of meaning with Nietzsche's question in *On the Genealogy of Morals*, "Why ask why?" Why do we need to ask these questions? What is the experience that gives rise to such questions, and how does this experience become articulated in these questions? What is the relationship between life and meaning?

The advent of psychoanalysis further complicates these questions. Like the Nietzschean genealogist, the psychoanalyst is concerned to diagnose displaced meanings that lurk behind the apparent meaning of our articulation of experience. The concern is no longer whether language can adequately capture, reflect, or copy experience but how we can interpret the meaning of this language as it points to that which necessarily escapes it. Now we are concerned with the hidden, veiled, or unconscious meanings of our language use; we are concerned precisely with the way in which our language does *not* re-present our conscious experience.

Bringing linguistics to Freudian psychoanalytic theory, Jacques Lacan claims that the unconscious is structured like a language. Like language, we need to interpret unconscious processes in terms of syntax and semantics. More than this, the effects of the unconscious are seen as breaks in language—slips of the tongue, jokes, misreadings—and the unconscious is formed in relation to language. Language and signification become signs that point to, rather than represent, our unconscious motivations.

Language provides clues to discovering the key to the mystery of all our questions of "why?"—especially the question "Why do we speak?"

I rehearse these questions of meaning here because I think that Julia Kristeva addresses them in a unique way. Where others have seen an impasse, Kristeva has imagined an adventurous journey, though certainly not without its dangers and pitfalls. In an age of theoretical pessimism on all sides, Kristeva brings together the two questions of meaning, the meaning of language and the meaning of life, to provide hopeful answers that are more than mere theoretical exercises. Taking up the question "Why do we speak?" in all its ambiguities, Kristeva addresses the issues of the relationship of meaning to language, the relationship of meaning to life, and the relationship of language to life. In fact, Kristeva's most famous contribution to language theory, the distinction between the symbolic and the semiotic elements of signification, speaks to these questions in a revolutionary way, opening pathways rather than resigning us to an impasse.

Kristeva maintains that all signification is composed of two elements, the symbolic and the semiotic. The symbolic element is what philosophers might think of as meaning proper. That is, the symbolic is the element of signification that sets up the structures by which symbols operate. The symbolic is the structure or grammar that governs the ways in which symbols can refer. The semiotic element, on the other hand, is the organization of drives in language. It is associated with rhythms and tones that are meaningful parts of language and yet do not represent or signify something. In *Revolution in Poetic Language* (1974), Kristeva maintains that rhythms and tones do not *represent* bodily drives; rather bodily drives are *discharged* through rhythms and tones. In *New Maladies of the Soul* (1993), she discusses different ways of representing that are not linguistic in a traditional sense. There, Kristeva says that the meaning of the semiotic element of language is "translinguistic" or "nonlinguistic" (pp. 32–33, 31); she explains this by describing these semiotic elements as irreducible to language because they "turn toward language even though they are irreducible to its grammatical and logical structures" (p. 35). This is to say that they are irreducible to the *symbolic element* of language. The symbolic element of language is the domain of position and judgment. It is associated with the grammar or structure of language that enables it to signify something.

The symbolic element of language should not, however, be confused with Lacan's notion of the Symbolic, which includes the entire realm of signification whereas Kristeva's symbolic is one element of that realm.

While Lacan's Symbolic refers to signification in the broadest possible sense, including culture in general, Kristeva's symbolic is a technical term that delimits one element of language associated with syntax. In addition, Kristeva's semiotic element (*le sémiotique*) should not be confused with semiotics (*la sémiotique*), the science of signs.

The dialectical oscillation between the semiotic and the symbolic is what makes signification possible. Without the symbolic element of signification, we have only sounds or delirious babble. But without the semiotic element of signification, signification would be empty and we would not speak, for the semiotic provides the motivation for engaging in signifying processes. We have a bodily need to communicate. The symbolic provides the structure necessary to communicate. Both elements are essential to signification. And it is the tension between them that makes signification dynamic. The semiotic both motivates signification and threatens the symbolic element. The semiotic provides the movement or negativity, and the symbolic provides the stasis or stability that keeps signification both dynamic and structured.

Kristeva compares her dialectic between semiotic and symbolic, or negativity and stasis, to Hegel's dialectic; but for her, unlike Hegel, there is no synthesis of the two elements, no *Aufhebung* (sublation or cancellation with preservation). In *Revolution*, she maintains that negativity is not merely the operator of the dialectic but the fourth term of the dialectic. There, she replaces the Hegelian term *negativity* with the psychoanalytic term *rejection*, which adds the connotation of connection to bodily drives. Because they indicate the drive force in excess of conscious thought, Kristeva prefers the terms *expenditure* and *rejection* "for the movement of material contradictions that generate the semiotic function" (p. 119). For Kristeva, unlike Hegel, negativity is never canceled and the contradiction between the semiotic and the symbolic is never overcome.

While the symbolic element gives signification its meaning in the strict sense of reference, the semiotic element gives signification meaning in a broader sense. That is, the semiotic element makes symbols matter; by discharging drives in symbols, it makes them significant. Even though the semiotic challenges meaning in the strict sense, meaning in the terms of the symbolic, it gives symbols their meaning for our lives. Signification makes our lives meaningful, in both senses of meaning—signifying something and having significance—through its symbolic and semiotic elements. The interdependence of the symbolic and semiotic elements of signification guarantees a relationship between language and life, signification and experience; the interdependence between the symbolic and semiotic guarantees a relationship between body (*soma*) and soul (*psyche*).

One of Kristeva's most important contributions to contemporary theory is her attempt to bring the speaking body back into the discourses of the human sciences. Her writing challenges theories that rely on unified, fixed, stagnant theories of subjectivity; she insists on semiotic negativity, which produces a dynamic subjectivity. Yet she challenges theories that would reduce subjectivity to chaotic flux; she also insists on symbolic stasis and identity. Her writing stages the oscillation between the semiotic and the symbolic elements in signification. In order to bring the body back into theories of language, she develops a science that she calls "semanalysis," which is a combination of semiotics, taken from Charles Pierce and Ferdinand de Saussure, and psychoanalysis, taken from Sigmund Freud, Jacques Lacan, and Melanie Klein.

Following Lacan, Kristeva maintains that subjectivity is formed in conjunction with language acquisition and use. All Kristeva's writing has addressed the relationship between language and subjectivity. Kristeva is concerned with the places where self-identity is threatened, the limits of language. As a result, her work is focused between the two poles of language acquisition and psychotic babble. She is interested both in how the subject is constituted through language acquisition and in how the subject is demolished with the psychotic breakdown of language. These limits of language point to the delicate balance between semiotic and symbolic, between affects and words. The motility of the subject and the subject's ability to change are the result of the interplay of semiotic drive force and symbolic stasis. Because of the relationship between language and subjectivity, the psychoanalyst can work backward from language in order to diagnose the analysand's problems with self-image. Freud called psychoanalysis the "talking cure" because the analysand's articulation of his or her malaise is the fulcrum of clinical practice.

Kristeva attempts to bring the speaking body back into discourse by arguing both that the logic of language is already operating at the material level of bodily processes and that bodily drives make their way into language. She postulates that signifying practices are the result of material bodily processes. Drives make their way into language through the semiotic element of signification, which does not *represent* bodily drives but *discharges* them. In this way, all signification has material motivation. All signification discharges bodily drives. Drives move between *soma* and *psyche*, and the evidence of this movement is manifest in signification.

Kristeva takes up Freud's theory of drives as instinctual energies that operate between biology and culture. Drives have their source in organic tissue and aim at psychological satisfaction. Drives are heterogeneous; that is, there are several different drives that can conflict with each other. In *Revolution*, Kristeva describes drives as "material, but they are not solely biological since they both connect and differentiate the biological and symbolic within the dialectic of the signifying body invested in practice" (p. 167). Nearly two decades later, Kristeva emphasizes the same dialectical relationship between the two spheres—biological and social—across which the drives operate. In *New Maladies of the Soul*, she describes the drives as "a pivot between 'soma' and psyche,' between biology and representation" (p. 30). Drives can be reduced neither to the biological nor to the social; they operate in between these two realms and bring one realm into the other. Drives are energies or forces that move between the body and representation. This notion of drives challenges the traditional dualism between the biological and the social, the body and the mind. Kristeva's attempts to bring the body back to theory also challenge traditional notions of the body; for her, the body is more than material.

By insisting that language expresses bodily drives through its semiotic element, Kristeva's articulation of the relationship between language and the body circumvents the traditional problems of representation. The tones and rhythms of language, the materiality of language, is bodily. Traditional theories, which postulate that language represents bodily experience, fall into an impossible situation by presupposing that the body and language are distinct, even opposites. Some traditional theories postulate that language is an instrument that captures, mirrors, or copies bodily experience. The problem, then, becomes how to explain the connection between these two distinct realms of language, on the one hand, and material, on the other.

Since traditional theories have not been able to explain adequately how language is related to the material world, some contemporary theorists have proposed that language does not refer to some extralinguistic material world; rather, language refers only to itself. Words have their meaning in relation to other words and not in relation to things in the world. We can discern the meaning of words by analyzing the structures within which words operate rather than examining the correspondence between words and things. Whereas Husserlian phenomenology describes words as windows onto the meaning constituted by the transcendental subject, structuralism describes words as elements operating within systems that constitute their meanings, and poststructuralism describes words as traces of the processes of difference and deferral that constitute the illusion of their stable meaning and determinant references, Kristeva describes the meaning of words as combinations of dynamic bodily drive force or affect and stable symbolic grammar.

Kristeva criticizes Husserlian phenomenology for taking one stage of the process of subjectivity and fetishizing it. The stasis and stability of the transcendental ego is but one element of subjectivity. In addition, for Kristeva meaning is not the unified product of a unified subject; rather, meaning is Other and as such makes the subject other to itself. Meaning is not constituted by a transcendental ego; meaning is constituted within a biosocial situation. Infants are born into a world where words already have meanings. Meaning is constituted through an embodied relation with another person. In this sense, meaning is Other; it is constituted in relation to an other and it is beyond any individual subjectivity. Insofar as meaning is constituted in relationships—relationships with others, relationships with signification, relationships with our own bodies and desires—it is fluid. And the subject for whom there is meaning is also fluid and relational.

Kristeva maintains that any theory of language is also a theory of the subject. In "From One Identity to an Other" and *Revolution,* against Husserl's transcendental ego Kristeva postulates her notion of a subject-in-process/on trial (*le sujet en procès*). Taking poetic language as emblematic, Kristeva argues, in *Desire in Language,* that signification is "an undecidable process between sense and nonsense, between *language* and *rhythm*" (p. 135). The Husserlian transcendental ego cannot account for nonsense or rhythm within signification; it cannot account for the unconscious. But heterogeneity within signification points to heterogeneity within the speaking subject; if language is a dynamic process then the subject is a dynamic process. Like signification, the subject is always in a constant process of oscillation between instability and stability or negativity and stasis. The subject is continually being constituted within this oscillation between conscious and unconscious as an open system, subject to infinite analysis. The Cartesian *cogito* and the Husserlian transcendental ego, then, are only moments in this process; they are neither chronologically nor logically primary.

Although structuralism does not posit a Husserlian transcendental ego, it does silence the speaking body in favor of bloodless structures. Kristeva describes these theories as necrophiliac. She begins *Revolution in Poetic Language:*

Our philosophies of language, embodiments of the Idea, are nothing more than the thoughts of archivists, archaeologists, and necrophiliacs. Fascinated by the remains of a process which is partly discursive, they substitute this fetish for what actually produced it. . . . These static thoughts, products of a leisurely cognition removed from historical turmoil, persist in seeking the truth of language by formalizing utterances that hang in midair, and the truth of the subject by listening to the narrative of a sleeping body—a body in repose, withdrawn from its socio-historical imbrication, removed from direct experience.

(p. 13)

Feminism has levied similar criticisms against ahistorical theories that ignore or silence the body, particularly women's bodies. Some feminists have been concerned to articulate a feminine sexuality and subjectivity. Luce Irigaray maintains that feminine sexuality and women's bodies have been defined as the other of masculine sexuality and men's bodies, that women are not subjects but the other against which men become subjects. Many feminists argue that women's experiences have been silenced by cultures whose governments and intellectual lives have been controlled by men. Conceptions of subjectivity that once were thought to apply universally—the Cartesian *cogito,* the Kantian autonomous subject, the Husserlian trancendental ego—have been challenged as gender-specific conceptions of man. Feminists have rejected ahistorical notions of subjectivity, which privilege characteristics historically associated with men and masculinity.

While poststructuralist theories generally do not propose formalizing utterances or subjectivity in terms of ahistorical structures or concepts, few of them suggest ways to articulate the body. Kristeva's best-known poststructuralist colleague, Jacques Derrida, struggles with the relationship between language and the living, speaking body. In the most reductionistic and hostile readings, Derrida's critics take a phrase from *Of Grammatology,* "there is nothing outside of the text," out of context to claim that Derrida is a linguistic monist or a nominalist who does not believe in the reality of anything other than language itself (p. 158). A careful reading of Derrida makes this position difficult to defend. As Derrida says in an interview with Richard Kearney: "It is totally false to suggest that deconstruction is a suspension of reference. Deconstruction is always deeply concerned with the 'other' of language. I never cease to be surprised by critics who see my work as a declaration that there is nothing beyond language, that we are imprisoned in language; it is, in fact, saying the exact opposite" (*Dialogues,* p. 123).

Derrida's work is a continual struggle to articulate the "other" of language, which, as he reminds us, is impossible (see "Psyche," p. 60). The other of language is antithetical to language even if it is the call from this other that gives language its meaning. Still, language always only points to that which is absent; it is this absence that makes signification possible. Words can do no more than point to, or conjure, the absence of that about which they speak. That about which they speak—life, love, the material world, even language itself—is other to words.

In Derrida's account in *Of Grammatology*, language does violence to this other (p. 135). At best, language gives us traces of something beyond language, homicidal traces that turn life into death. Although in "Circumfessions" Derrida dreams of a writing that could directly express the living body without violence, for him, language is always the dead remains of a living body: "If I compare the pen to a syringe, and I always dream of a pen that would be a syringe, a suction point rather than that very hard weapon with which one must inscribe, incise, choose, calculate, take ink before filtering the inscribable, playing the keyboard on the screen, whereas here, once the right vein has been found, no more toil, no responsibility, no risk of bad taste nor of violence, the blood delivers itself all alone, the inside gives itself up" (p. 12). Even as Derrida imagines writing that is like a transfusion of the living body into language, he resigns himself to the violence of trying to inscribe the uninscribable. The living body is this uninscribable.

Kristeva's theory more optimistically addresses the problem of the relationship between language and bodily experience by postulating that, through the semiotic element, bodily drives manifest themselves in language. Instead of lamenting what is lost, absent, or impossible in language, Kristeva marvels at this other realm that makes its way into language. The force of language is living drive force transferred into language. Signification is like a transfusion of the living body into language. This is why psychoanalysis can be effective; the analyst can diagnose the active drive force as it is manifest in the analysand's language. Language is not cut off from the body. And while for Kristeva bodily drives involve a type of violence, negation, or force, this process does not merely necessitate sacrifice and loss. The drives are not sacrificed to signification; rather, bodily drives are an essential semiotic element of signification.

In addition to proposing that bodily drives make their way into language, Kristeva maintains that the logic of signification is already present in the material of the body. Once again combining psychoanalytic theory and linguistics, Kristeva relies on both Lacan's account of the

infant's entrance into language and Saussure's account of the play of signifiers. Lacan points out that the entrance into language requires separation, particularly from the maternal body. Saussure maintains that signifiers signify in relation to one another through their differences.
Combining these two theses, it seems that language operates according
to principles of separation and difference, as well as identification and
incorporation. Kristeva argues that the principles or structures of separation and difference are operating in the body even before the infant
begins to use language.

In *Revolution in Poetic Language*, Kristeva proposes that the
processes of identification or incorporation and differentiation or rejection that make language use possible are operating within the material of
the body. She maintains that before the infant passes through what Freud
calls the oedipal phase, or what Lacan calls the mirror stage, the patterns
and logic of language are already operating in a preoedipal situation. In
Revolution she focuses on differentiation or rejection and the oscillation
between identification and differentiation. She identifies material rejection (for example, the expulsion of waste from the body) as part of the
process that sets up the possibility of signification.

She calls the bodily structures of separation the "logic of rejection."
For Kristeva the body, like signification, operates according to an oscillation between instability and stability, or negativity and stases. For
example, the process of metabolization is a process that oscillates
between instability and stability: food is taken into the body and metab-
olized and expelled from the body. Because the structure of separation is
bodily, these bodily operations prepare us for our entrance into language.
From the time of birth, the infant's body is engaging in processes of separation; anality is the prime example. Birth itself is also an experience of
separation, one body separated from another.

Part of Kristeva's motivation for emphasizing these bodily separations
and privations is to provide an alternative to the Lacanian model of language acquisition. Lacan's account of signification and self-consciousness begins with the mirror stage and the paternal metaphor's substitu-
tion of the law of the father for the desire of the mother. In the traditional
psychoanalytic model of both Freud and Lacan, the child enters the
social realm and language out of fear of castration. The child experiences
its separation from the maternal body as a tragic loss and consoles itself
with words instead. Paternal threats make words the only, if inadequate,
alternative to psychosis. Kristeva insists, however, that separation begins
prior to the mirror or oedipal stage and that this separation is not only

painful but also pleasurable. She insists that the child enters the social realm and language not just because of paternal threats but also because of paternal love.

At bottom, Kristeva criticizes the traditional account because it cannot adequately explain the child's move to signification. If what motivates the move to signification are threats and the pain of separation, then why would anyone make this move? Why not remain in the safe haven of the maternal body and refuse the social realm and signification with its threats? Kristeva suggests that if the accounts of Freud and Lacan were correct, then more people would be psychotic (see *Revolution*, p. 132; *Tales*, pp. 30, 31, 125). The logic of signification is already operating in the body, and therefore the transition to language is not as dramatic and mysterious as traditional psychoanalytic theory makes it out to be.

Reconnecting bodily drives to language is the project not only of her theoretical work but also of her clinical psychoanalytic practice and one aspect of her fiction. Since *Tales of Love* (1983), Kristeva has been including notes from analytic sessions in her theory and fiction. In her theory she uses these notes to further substantiate her diagnosis of literary texts and culture. She often diagnoses a gap between her analysand's words and his or her affects. Affects are physical and psychic manifestations of drive energy; recall that drive energy has its source in bodily organs and its aim in satisfaction of desires. Kristeva describes a phenomenon whereby it seems that words become detached from their affects and the corresponding drive energy, and the job of the analyst is to try to help the analysand put them back together again.

A fragile connection between words and affects is set up during a child's acquisition of language and simultaneous acquisition of a sense of self or subjectivity. If this connection between words and affects is broken or never established, borderline psychosis can be the result. Kristeva suggests that in contemporary culture more slippage, or a different kind of slippage, seems to occur than in the past between words and affects, between who we say we are and our experience of ourselves. Perhaps the abyss between our fragmented language and our fragmented sense of ourselves is the empty soul or psyche of the postmodern world. Kristeva's writing attempts to negotiate this impasse by bringing the body back into language and bringing language back into the body, by reconnecting bodily drives to language.

Her discussion of the need to reconnect words and affects, language and the body, is punctuated with quotations from her analysands' speech. Not only does this strategy address the absence of the speaking body from traditional theoretical discourse but also the transcripts stand as examples of the practical consequences of traditional dualistic theoretical positions on the relationship between language and life, symbols and experience, mind and body. Her strategy of including her notes from analytic sessions, peppered with the words of her analysands, brings the speaking body into theoretical discourse. These speaking bodies are articulating the pain of living in worlds where symbols have been detached from affect, where the meaning of words has been detached from the meaning of life, from what matters.

The affective or semiotic element of language matters in the double sense of giving language its raison d'être and its material element. In *New Maladies of the Soul* Kristeva suggests that the loss of meaning and the emptiness of contemporary life are related to an uncoupling of affect and language that is encouraged by the very remedies contemporary society proposes for dealing with the problem. Contemporary society offers two primary ways of addressing the malaise caused by the disconnection of affect and language: drugs (narcotics, psychotropic drugs, and antidepressants) and media images. Kristeva suggests that both drugs and media images do nothing to treat the cause of our malaise; rather, they can be seen as symptoms of the problem itself. The problem, as she articulates it in *New Maladies of the Soul*, is that contemporary culture has left behind the psyche or soul. The soul is empty or nonexistent, and without it our lives, our words, have no meaning.

With the scientific revolution in the seventeenth and eighteenth centuries, religion lost its power to provide language and life with meaning. In the nineteenth and twentieth centuries, we have become suspicious of science and technology to the extent that they no longer provide language and life with meaning. After Nietzsche's proclamations that God is dead and that scientific and philosophical Truth have been clinging to His stinking corpse, where can we find meaning? At one extreme, contemporary theories that propose dogmatic and fixed notions of meaning seem artificial and desperate. At the other, theories that propose that ultimately there is no meaning and anything goes seem equally artificial and frustrating. Neither extreme can provide an anchor for meaning. Neither extreme can reconnect meaning to our language and lives. In fact, these extremes might be symptoms of the separation of meaning from our language and our lives. Theories that propose the meaninglessness of life or the impossibility of connecting language and life can been seen as symptoms of a general malaise caused by a feeling of emptiness.

Working between what she identifies as the extremes of totalitarianism and delirium, Kristeva diagnoses this emptiness as a lack of psyche or soul. In *New Maladies of the Soul*, she suggests that our souls (*psyche*) have been flattened and emptied by the rhythms and images of our culture, which are two-dimensional. Life takes place on the screen—movie screens, TV screens, computer screens. Yet these media images merely cover over the surface of the emptiness that we feel facing the loss of meaning. Psychotropic drugs and antidepressants flatten the psyche. They relieve the feeling of crisis caused by a loss of meaning but leave a feeling of emptiness; they flatten or empty the patient's affects. Both drugs and media images provide false or artificial selves, which only temporarily smooth over the surface of an otherwise empty psyche. By substituting surface images for psychic depth, drugs and media images close psychic space.

Psychic space is the space between the human organism and its aims; it is the space between the biological and the social. It is the space through which drives move energy between these two interconnected spheres. It is within this psychic space that affects materialize between bodily organs and social customs. Our emotional lives depend on this space. Meaning is constituted in this space between the body and culture. Our words and our lives have meaning by virtue of their connection to affect. The meaning of words (in the narrow sense of the symbolic element of language) is charged with affective meaning (in the broader sense of the semiotic element of language) through the movement of drive energy within psychic space.

As Kristeva says in *Tales of Love*, we are extraterrestrials wandering and lost without meaning because of this abolition of psychic space: "What analysands are henceforth suffering from is *the abolition of psychic space*. Narcissus in want of light as much as of a spring allowing him to capture his true image, Narcissus drowning in a cascade of false images (from social roles to the *media*), hence deprived of substance or place" (p. 373). We experience somatic symptoms cut off from their psychic or affective meaning. The goal of the analyst, then, is to reconnect *soma* and *psyche*, body and soul. The "talking cure" involves giving meaning to language by reconnecting words and affects and thereby giving meaning to life. Psychoanalysis is unique in that it tries to open up psychic space and provide various interpretations with which to give meaning to both language and life.

In *Tales of Love*, Kristeva identifies meaning—both the meaning of life and the meaning of language—with love. "Today Narcissus is an exile, deprived of his psychic space, an extraterrestrial with a prehistory bearing, wanting for love. An uneasy child, all scratched up, somewhat disgusting, an alien in a world of desire and power, he longs only to reinvent love" (pp. 382–83). The analysand is a child with no adequate images of a loving mother or a loving father. Kristeva suggests that in the West Christianity has traditionally provided images of a loving mother and a loving father, as problematic as those images might be. But with contemporary suspicions of religion, she seems to ask, where can we find images of loving mothers and fathers? And without images of loving mothers and fathers, how can we love ourselves?

For Kristeva, love provides the support for fragmented meanings and fragmented subjectivities. Love provides the support to reconnect words and affects. She says that "love is something spoken, and it is only that" (p. 277). Our lives have meaning for us, we have a sense of ourselves, through the narratives we prepare to tell others about our experience. Even if we do not tell our stories, we live our experience through the stories that we construct in order to "tell ourselves" to another, a loved one. As we wander through our days, an event takes on its significance in the narrative that we construct for an imaginary conversation with a loved one as we are living it. The living body is a loving body, and the loving body is a speaking body. Without love we are nothing but walking corpses. Love is essential to the living body, and it is essential in bringing the living body to life in language.

Psychoanalysis is a love relationship that builds spoken spaces through transferential love, "that summons the ability to idealize at the very core of desire and hatred" (p. 382). Psychoanalysis addresses this ability to idealize and, through the power of transference and the articulation or elaboration of that transference, calls forth the analysand's imaginary or idealized relations. The way in which relations are structured in the imaginary determines how the analysand relates to others. The transference love of the analytic session provides a space within which those structures can safely be examined and altered. Insofar as the psychoanalytic relationship operates according to transference love, the ethics of psychoanalysis is an ethics of love. Transference and countertransference provide the safety net that supports the redirection and reconnection of affective drive force and signification. Transference and countertransference are love relations that can spark the imagination and open up the possibility of re-imaging and thus re-signifying affects. In *Time and Sense* (1994), Kristeva suggests that transference in the psychoanalytic session inscribes flesh in words. Psychoanalysts "transform the patient's flesh, which [they] have shared with [their] own, into word-presentations." In this way psychoanalysis can treat somatic symptoms by transforming the body through words. The connection between flesh and words conjured and refigured in analytic transference opens up the space for idealization that Kristeva associates with love and psychic space. And this space for idealization gives the analysand a renewed image of self.

In *Black Sun* (1987), Kristeva claims that while religious rituals and literature are cathartic, psychoanalysis goes further as an *elaboration* of the drive processes and their relation to the signifying process. This elaboration is crucial in treating the causes and not just the symptoms of neurosis. While the semiotic drive force is powerful when discharged in signifying practices, the position of judgment made possible by the symbolic element of signification is necessary not only to direct but also redirect that discharge. While there are various discourses that engage theories of subjectivity and many types of cathartic practices that can rejuvenate meaning, for Kristeva psychoanalysis is the only place where *theories* of subjectivity and the dynamic *practice* of the subject-in-process come together so dramatically. The psychoanalytic session is an attempt to come to terms with the dynamic nature of the subject while opening onto its fluidity.

Some of Kristeva's critics have argued that psychoanalysis does not provide an adequate ethics or politics. One concern is that Kristeva seems to suggest that individual psychoanalytic treatment is necessary to counteract everything from melancholy and depression to xenophobia and ethnic violence. The idea that we all need to seek the professional services of psychoanalysts is not only impractical but also politically suspect: psychoanalysis is expensive and time-consuming and can be elitist. Psychoanalysis is also a relationship between two individuals, one in the employ of the other. As such, a politics that privileges psychoanalysis seems to foreclose the importance and possibility of social movements and group initiatives. All social problems are analyzed in terms of individual psychological problems rather than social and institutional problems. This recalls some feminists' criticisms of Freudian psychoanalysis for reducing women's oppression and silence to individual neurosis and hysteria.

Although Kristeva does maintain that psychoanalysis brings together theory and practice in a unique way and that it can elaborate psychic dynamics that other forms of signification manifest, she does not restrict these operations to psychoanalysis. Rather, she justifies the continued use of psychoanalysis. More than this, her elaboration of psychoanalysis works to emphasize the role of the imagination or imaginary realm in the construction of our sense of ourselves and others. Kristeva suggests that we cannot change our practice until we change the way that we imagine ourselves and others. Significant political change and policy reform can result only from changes in our individual and cultural imaginary.

In *Strangers to Ourselves* (1991) and *Nations Without Nationalism* (1993), Kristeva uses psychoanalysis as a model for analyzing relations between peoples of different nations and ethnic backgrounds. Just as she brings the speaking body back into language by putting language into the body, she brings the subject into the place of the other by putting the other into the subject. Just as the pattern or logic of language is already found within the body, the pattern or logic of alterity is already found within the subject. In a Hegelian move, Kristeva makes the social relation interior to the psyche. This is why the subject is never stable but always in process/on trial. Kristeva suggests that if we can learn to live with the return of the repressed other within our own psyches, then we can learn to live with others. With her notions of the subject-in-process, and the other within, she attempts to articulate an ethical relationship between conscious and unconscious, self and other, citizen and foreigner, identity and difference, that rather than relying on sacrifice and violence, is built on acceptance and love.

TEXTS CITED IN INTRODUCTION

Derrida, Jacques. Interview with Richard Kearney. In *Dialogues with Contemporary Continental Thinkers*. Richard Kearney, ed. Manchester: Manchester University Press, 1984.
Of Grammatology. Gayatri Spivak, tr. Baltimore: Johns Hopkins University Press, 1976.
"Psyche: Inventions of the Other." In *Reading DeMan Reading*. Catherine Porter, tr., L. Waters and W. Godzich, eds. Minneapolis: University of Minnesota Press, 1989, pp. 25–65.
"Circumfession." In *Jacques Derrida*. Geoffrey Bennington, tr. Chicago: University of Chicago Press, 1993.

NOTES

Thanks to Tamsin Lorraine, Noëlle McAfee, Benigno Trigo, and Ewa Ziarek for helpful comments on earlier versions of this introduction.

1. The three terms of the Hegelian dialectic are commonly referred to as thesis, antithesis, and synthesis, which correspond to Universal, Particular, Individual.

2. In the history of philosophy, the distinction between body and soul has also been discussed as a distinction between body and mind, or the mind-body problem.

3. For a more developed account of Kristeva's theory of drives, see my *Womanizing Nietzsche: Philosophy's Relation to the "Feminine,"* ch. 6, "Save the Mother" (New York: Routledge, 1995).

4. Kristeva's theory also challenges the narrow conception of material as it is opposed to social or linguistic.

5. Traditional theories have tried to address these problems in various ways. Referential theories of meaning have held that the meaning of a word is its reference to something extralinguistic, something in the world. The meaning of a word is either what it refers to (some thing) or the relationship between the word and its referent. But as Frege pointed out, meaning and reference are not the same since there are many different ways of referring to the same thing; and not all these linguistic expressions necessarily have the same meaning even if they have the same referent. The most famous example is the reference to Venus as both the morning star and the evening star. Some theorists (e.g., Locke, Husserl, Saussure) have tried to avoid some of the problems of referential theories by supposing that the meaning of a word is determined by the thought that corresponds to that word. The referent in this case becomes an idea or concept and not a material thing in the world. These theories, however, merely displace the problems of reference from the material world to the world of ideas. All the problems of correspondence still obtain. Some contemporary theorists (Austin, Wittgenstein, Searle) propose that meaning is determined by the use of words and that the use of words must be analyzed as a type of activity with certain rules and regulations. The way in which words are used, however, varies as much as the thoughts or ideas associated with them and their possible material referents.

6. For a feminist criticism of Descartes, see Susan Bordo, *The Flight to Objectivity* (Albany, N.Y.: SUNY Press, 1987). For a feminist criticim of Kant, see Robin Schott's *Cognition and Eros: A Critique of the Kantian Paradigm* (Boston: Beacon Press, 1988). Kristeva's relationship to feminism is complex. For a discussion of these issues, see Kelly Oliver, *Reading Kristeva: Unraveling the Doublebind* (Bloomington: Indiana University Press, 1993).

7. For a detailed analysis of the relationship between language and the living body in Derrida's "Circumfessions," see my article "The Maternal Operation" in Mary Rawlinson et al., eds., *Derrida and Feminism* (New York: Routledge, 1996).

8. Kristeva's writings themselves can be read as an oscillation between an emphasis on separation and rejection and an emphasis on identification and incorporation. In *Revolution* (1974) and *Powers of Horror* (1980) she focuses on separation and rejection; in *Tales of Love* (1983) and *Black Sun* (1987) she focuses on identification and incorporation. In *Strangers to Ourselves* (1989) she again analyzes separation and rejection. And in *New Maladies of the Soul* (1993) she returns to identification and incorporation. In an interview with Rosalind Coward in 1984 at the Institute of Contemporary Arts, Kristeva claims that for this reason *Powers of Horror* and *Tales of Love* should be read together; alone each provides only half of the story.

9. Starting with *Tales of Love* and continuing through *New Maladies of the Soul*, Kristeva begins to insert what appear as her notes from analytic sessions into her texts.

10. See some of the essays in *Ethics, Politics, and Difference in Julia Kristeva's Writing*, ed. Kelly Oliver (New York: Routledge, 1993), especially Graybeal, Rose, McAfee, Moruzzi, Lowe, Butler, and Edelstein.

The Portable Kristeva

PART 1

Kristeva's Trajectory: In Her Own Words

My Memory's Hyperbole

"My Memory's Hyperbole," translated by Athena Viscusi, was published in a special issue of the *New York Literary Forum* on "The Female Autograph" in 1984. This autobiographical essay first appeared as "Mémoires" in 1983 in the journal that replaced *Tel Quel*, *Infini*. In this essay Kristeva situates her own work in relation to existential philosophy, linguistics, literature, structuralism, and deconstruction. She describes the most important influences on her thinking and writing, including her involvement with the *Tel Quel* group and her friendship with Emile Benveniste. She traces *Tel Quel*'s association with the French Communist Party (PCF). And she describes her movement away from politics and feminism after her trip to China in 1974. In addition, she anticipates some of her latest writing on nationalism.

My Memory's Hyperbole

Hyperbole! from my memory . . .
—Mallarmé,
"Prose pour des esseintes"

When the *New York Literary Forum* asked me to contribute an autobiographical text for this special issue, I had just finished reading *La Cérémonie des adieux* by Simone de Beauvoir. One must surely be endowed with the naive cruelty of this exceptional woman to create such a myth or, at the very least, to make it exist by giving it a narrative thread. In spite of the legend that surrounds the author of *Mandarins*, I am convinced that she has still not been properly evaluated as a chronicler who knew how to construct an entire cultural phenomenon. And isn't it the same austere and cutting pen of this feminist in search of rationalism that gave *Les Temps modernes* its true erotic consistency? Before Marxian rationalizing turned this journal into an idol for the international Left, from the postwar period to today, Beauvoir's cold account of a sexuality more contained than unveiled gave the publication its well-known aura.

My own history and, perhaps most of all, the disturbing abyss that the psychoanalytic experience shapes between "what is said" and undecidable "truth" prevent me from being a good witness. Moreover, *making history* now appears to me, as I will try to show in the course of this essay, a task that, if it has not become impossible, has now been displaced. Rather than compiling "archives" or "annals," other questions make us stretch meaning into fiction. I say "us" because it seems to me that a profound turmoil has occurred in the last few years, still barely visible but operating in all spheres of culture.

What follows, then, will be an autobiography in the first person plural, a "we" of complicity, friendship, love. This "we" is the setting commonly recommended by the social contract for illusions, idealizations, errors, constructions. To write the autobiography of this "we" is surely a paradox that combines the passion for truth of the "I" with the absolute logical necessity of being able to share this truth only in part. To share it, first of all, between "us," so that this "we" survives. To share it also with you, so that an account, a report, a scheme remains (autobiography is a narration), rather than have speech fall into the fervor of dreams or poetry. Being hyperbolic, this "we" will retain from the problem-ridden paths of "I"s only the densest image, the most schematic, the one closest to a cliché. Should I shy away from it? I think of Canto III of Dante's *Paradiso* where the writer, having had visions, hurries to push them aside for fear of becoming a new Narcissus. But Beatrice herself shows him that such a denial would be precisely a mistake comparable to the narcissistic error. For if an immediate vision is possible and must be sought, then it is necessarily accompanied by visionary constructions that are imperfect . . . fragmentary, schematic. . . . Truth can only be partially spoken. And it is enough to begin. . . . Common sense notwithstanding, this hyperbolic "we" is, in effect, only a part of "me." It is merely a temporary stability in which projections and identifications are settled among some and allow the history of a perpetually changing whole to be written. A "we" is alive only if it is never the same. As the chief locus of the image, it thrives only on the change of images. What the "I" loses in delegating itself to the group is partially regained in the metamorphoses of the "we." It is by transforming itself, by changing itself totally that the collective image, the group portrait, proves it is a momentarily fixed passion. To speak of "us" is not an analysis; it is a history that analyzes itself. But isn't any autobiography, even if it doesn't involve "us," a desire to make a collective public image exist, for "you," for "us"?

If you watch newsreels from World War II through the Algerian War on French television, you will find the same rhetoric of the image (technical improvements don't really affect the televised aesthetic of this period). The same verbal rhetoric lasts until 1962–1963: romanticism, bombast, bathos doled out by the slightly nasal voice of an anchorman adept at intoning war bulletins. In the shadow of political events, a fundamental change of outlook was necessary for us to regard this verbal edema as obsolete, to realize it belonged to another era. I see the written trace of this change in the austere paring down of the *nouveau roman*, in its obsession with precision and details, for example, as well as the whole intellectual trend centered on the study of forms. This formalism was the purging of that subjective or rhetorical edema that our parents had set up to protect themselves against the devastating suffering of wars, or that they had used to construct their martyrdom. Fundamentally, May '68, despite its romantic airs, functioned like the fever of this process—an *analytic* process (in the etymological sense of the term, that is, dissolving, abrasive, lucid) that leads us to a modernity that is, of course, mobile, eccentric, and unpredictable, but that breaks with the preceding years and that, or so it seems, must leave its mark on the end of our century.

In short, an account of the intellectual path of this period should primarily be an account of change—and for some it was an explosion—of bodies, of discourses, of ways of being. A sexuality freed from moral constraints, an image of the body no longer merely captured in a fine narcissistic surface but vaporized and sonorized with the help of drugs or rock or pop music if need be. . . . These mutations, these revolutions, contained as many delights as dramas, which had to be confronted, displaced and sublimated at each bend. Women with the pill, free love in broad daylight, assaults on the family, but also, the quest for complicity, tenderness, the security of a childhood always begun anew. . . . The adventure of ideas should be read against the background of a revolution in the reproduction of the species that attacks the classic conception of the sexual difference, makes women emerge aggressively, and finally leads to erotic ties around a new calm and civilizing secular cult of the child. . . . Political demands, of course! But also something beyond demands, with their explosiveness integrated into the fabric of time, of ethics.

The *Tel Quel* Experience As It Was

During Christmas '65, in a bleak and rainy Paris, I would have been completely disappointed with the "city of lights" had I not attended midnight mass at Notre Dame, the ultimate meeting place for tourists. When I arrived in the French capital, I met people who were rather poor, whereas the elegant little restaurants and the chic little boutiques seemed to me to belong to a prewar movie. Between the technical brilliance of America and the leveling radicalisms of East European societies (which embodied, for me, two aspects of "modernity"), France seemed stuck in a pleasant archaicness, attractive and unreal. However, the social discontent that was brewing reached me through newspapers and conversations I overheard—even among people who seemed to be well off. I then realized that this country of shopkeepers wished to become the most developed of East European countries, as if its occult, unspoken goal was transforming itself into a society such as the one I had just left, a society that was criticized in Paris, only in fascinated, hushed tones.

My scholarship, in the framework of Franco-Bulgarian cultural agreements, encouraged my meeting writers and academics. I was, therefore, immediately immersed in an intellectual universe that both partook of this climate (by its interest in critical Marxism, in détente, in what was to become "socialism with a human face," etc.) and, at the same time, was wholly outside of it. I saw intellectuals as forming a real citadel within the state, without, however, burning their bridges to politics. They seemed to be engaged in a unique task: a subtle (even esoteric) and generous task, which not only was specifically French in its refinement and predisposition to formulas but also had universal aims and stakes. Having come to France under the auspices of the Gaullist dream of a "Europe from the Atlantic to the Urals," I felt I had found in this territory that stretched from the publishing house of Le Seuil to the EHESS (then EPHE) a cosmopolitanism that transcended the socialist and the European domains and that constituted a continent of thought, speculation, and writing corresponding to the high points of the universalistic legend of Paris.

I had received a francophile and francophone education. Since I had been trained as an intellectual in the French sense of the word, the *Marseillaise*, and Voltaire, Victor Hugo, Anatole France—authors in no way incompatible, so it was said, with Marxist-Leninism—had been my language but also my moral textbooks. I was then in no way out of my element in the intellectual climate of Paris. I even had the impression, when I wasn't viewed as a more or less monstrous anomaly, that people saw in me, aside from my Stalinism, a perfect product of the French system projected into the future. Moreover, the Hautes Etudes was the ideal place for me: a structure of meeting and greeting similar to the one that served wandering scholastics in the best periods of the Middle Ages.

As soon as I arrived, I found in this environment a hospitality that, though cold and suspicious, was nonetheless functional and reliable; besides, it never contradicted itself. Despite the xenophobia, antifeminism, or anti-Semitism of one person or another, I maintain that French cultural life, as I have known it, has always been marked by a curiosity, discreet but generous, reticent but essentially receptive to nomadisms, oddities, to graftings and exogamies of all kinds. The great tolerance of the English or the enormous capacity for assimilation among Americans surely provides more existential opportunities. But they are, finally, because of their lesser *resistance*, less conducive to the production of new thoughts.

The particular climate of France at that time can be understood in sociological terms. The chasm between social archaism and intellectual advances gave the latter an autonomy that helped them grow. Furthermore, the independence of Gaullist nationalism gave freedom of thought a power unequalled elsewhere: outside of France, there was nowhere else in the world where one could, in the heart of the most official institutions and in the spotlight of the media, draw simultaneously on Marx, Saint Augustine, Hegel, Saussure, and Freud. Finally, the genius of French institutions knew how to accommodate safety valves or precarious loop-holes alongside bureaucratic or bureaucratized bastions: the Ecole des Hautes Etudes counterbalancing the Sorbonne, *Tel Quel* developing despite the NRF or *Temps Modernes*. It is banal to say that this universalistic cosmopolitan climate belongs to a tradition, one that probably dates back to the eminence of clerks and that established intellectuals of the eighteenth century as an autonomous force, beyond but not outside the city-state. However, this tradition also has an intrapsychic, sexual basis.

When thought admits its indebtedness to language—which was the case of the French "essayist" tradition long before structuralism—the speaking being is thrown into the infinite conceived as the power and cunning of the verb. From this locus, the intellectual acquires a transpolitical and transmoral function. Without belonging to any particular group or sect, yet giving the appearance of belonging to one, he thus reaches, by the very range of his search, the key zones, the most sensitive areas of social understanding. Modern art, madness, subjective experience, various marginal phenomena then became not mere objects of observation but actual fields of *study*, as well as of *implication*, which allow for an oblique grappling with "the social." In this way, the dilemma of "engagement" was reworked and displaced for us. It had become an implication, wholly comprised within the intellectual adventure that we lived as a *practice*, subverting the distinctions between the individual/society, subject/group, form/content, style/meaning. With Michel Foucault and Jacques Lacan we didn't have to attack Jean-Paul Sartre's walls. The labyrinths of the *speaking subject*—the microcosm of a complex logic whose effects had only partially surfaced in society—led us directly toward regions that were obscure but crucial, specific but universal, particular but transhistorical, far from society's policed scenarios.

In any event, at the end of '65, I landed at Lucien Goldmann's and Roland Barthes's doors at the Hautes Etudes. Lucien Goldmann welcomed me to his seminar on the "sociology of the novel" with fraternal distraction, convinced that I was a congenital Marxist, since I came from Eastern Europe. At the time, he was settling scores with existentialism, which was of little interest to me (I had arrived in Paris with two modern authors, Maurice Blanchot and Ferdinand Céline, in my suitcase), but the immeasurable practical help he gave me ensured my survival in France in the beginning. It was a kind of help that only those exiled from any country know how to give. With much liberalism and understanding, he directed my thesis on the origins of novelistic discourse, a thesis I defended, not without insolence, amid the generalized commotion of May '68. The atmosphere of a Goldmann seminar was very cosmopolitan: Marxism had already become a Third World matter, but it was also a refuge for young Germans and Italians rebelling against the legacy of families that had been more or less accomplices of the nazi or fascist regimes. . . . In addition, the Vietnam War was raging, and it simply seemed natural for us to side with the victims, that is, with the Marxists. Invoking this war, I thus refused René Girard's invitation to work in an American university. I found Goldmann's objection to my decision candid at the very least: "one has to go there in order to defeat capitalism from the inside," he said to me.

At the same time, at the Hautes Etudes, located in the same C section of the Sorbonne, the teaching of Roland Barthes attracted me because of its capacity to make formalism, which I had found reductive, extremely appealing. His audience, which was more exclusively French in those days (except for a few, Todorov among them who had come to France before), was astounded by the suicide of Lucien Sebag, which remained a mystery beyond all words, all comments. On my arrival, the only topic of conversation was the presentation on Stéphane Mallarmé that Philippe Sollers had just given. I thus read a few issues of *Tel Quel*, and I met Sollers in May '66 through Gérard Genette, who was then attending the same seminar though he was an established literary critic.

Our first conversations with Sollers, in the office at 27 rue Jacob, at the Deux Magots, later at the Coupole, and at the Rose-Bud (Montparnasse soon became our neighborhood) were full of intellectual passion. I can still see us discussing *L'Expérience intérieure* of Georges Bataille, a still vilified author whom Sollers had helped me discover. We also spoke of nationalism, for a quarrel divided East European intellectuals: should Sovietization be resisted with cosmopolitanism or nationalism? Lastly, there was feminism: "We women, like the proletariat, have nothing to lose but our chains," I used to say, with a simplicity that could only have been disarming. Soon after, our friend Sarah George-Picot, who was later in the Psychépo group with me, filmed an interview on this theme—a precocious feminist document that I believe is lost. . . .

These details would have a personal meaning only if they did not reveal an important aspect of a period soon labeled "structuralist."

For us, structuralism (insofar as one can make generalizations about studies that range from Roman Jakobson's to Claude Lévi-Strauss's, or to certain works of Emile Benveniste, as well as of Barthes or Algirdas J. Greimas) was already accepted knowledge. To simplify, this meant that one should no longer lose sight of the real constraints, "material," as we used to say, of what had previously and trivially been viewed as "form." For us, the logic of this formal reality constituted the very meaning of phenomena or events that then became structures (from kinship to literary texts) and thus achieved intelligibility without necessarily relying on "external factors." From the outset, however, our task was to take this acquired knowledge and immediately do something else.

For some, the important task was to "deconstruct" phenomenology and structuralism as a minor form of a hidden metaphysics. Among these was Jacques Derrida, whose Introduction to Husserl's *Origins of Geometry* had been discovered by Sollers, and who was involved in *Tel Quel* for a time, when he already considered literature the privileged object of desire and analysis. For others, among whom I place myself, it was essential to "dynamize" the structure by taking into consideration the speaking subject and its unconscious experience on the one hand and, on the other, the pressures of other social structures. I seized upon Saussure's *Anagrammes*, parts of which Jakobson and Starobinski had published. From this starting point, I tried to establish a "paragrammatical" conception of the literary text as a distortion of signs and their structures that produces an infinitesimal overdetermination of meaning in literature. From the same perspective, I reinterpreted a writer just republished in the U.S.S.R., whom we often read in Eastern Europe, seeing in his work a synthesis of formalism and history: Mikhail Bakhtin. A post-formalist, he had introduced, through the carnival, Rabelais, Dostoyevsky, and the polyphonics of the modern novel, the notion of *alterity and dialogism* into the arsenal of studies inspired by formalism. My conception of dialogism, of ambivalence, or what I call "intertextuality"—notions heavily indebted to Bakhtin and Freud—were to become gadgets that the American university is now in the process of discovering.

This compelling interest in the outer limits of a structure or subjective identity was stimulated by contact with modern literary texts: Bataille first, Mallarmé, Lautréamont, Artaud, Joyce, as well as the publications of my friends at *Tel Quel*. In their writings they aimed at reworking and enriching the technique of the *nouveau roman*, to make it incorporate a painful, dramatic, or ecstatic internal experience, which its somewhat protestant austerity had rejected. Bataille, Joyce, and Artaud were the initiators of this writing technique, which we often reread and discussed. Sollers's *Requiem*, with its traces of the military hospital and the Algerian War, is a good indication of the change of direction imposed on the formalist legacy.

Concern with style as experience or as subjective symptomatology was to lead me to an increasingly *clinical* way of viewing language: acquisition of language by children, on the one hand, dissolution and pathology of discourse, on the other. Little by little, my "semiolotic" mode of thinking (which I already called "semanalysis") expanded to include a truly psychoanalytic approach.

Psychoanalysis—as the locus of extreme abjection, the refuge of private horror that can be lifted only by an infinite-indefinite displacement in speech and its effects—represents for me today the logical consequence of my initial questioning, which it still allows me to pursue. Leaving aside the uncertainties or the perversities of analytic institutions, I see psychoanalysis as the lay version, the only one, of the speaking being's quest for truth that religion symbolizes for certain of my contemporaries and friends. My own prejudice would lead me to think that God is analyzable. Infinitely. . . .

My friendship with Emile Benveniste holds an important place in this period dominated by my participation in *Tel Quel*. This austere scholar, who used to read to me from the *Rigveda* directly from Sanskrit into French and whose name appears below a *Surrealist Manifesto*, borrowed the "Rodez Letters" from me so he could read them during the constitutional congress of the International Semiology Association, held in Warsaw in 1968. He secretly confided in me his belief that there were only two great French linguists: Mallarmé and Artaud. I can see him, some time later, at the hospital in Saint-Cloud, then later in Créteil, stricken with aphasia but surprisingly warm toward me, tracing with a trembling hand on a white sheet of paper the enigmatic letters T-H-E-O.

. . . *Tel Quel* became, I think, the privileged link where the structuralist advance turned into an analysis of subjectivity. For the first time in modern history, except for the very brief futurist-formalist alliance shattered by the Stalinist regime in the U.S.S.R., a kind of thought was emerging that had as its foundation—as its object of analysis but especially its primary stimulant—the practice of writing in the process of production. A devaluated or simply ornamental zone, also far removed from the large art market that benefits painting, film, theater, and music—*l'écriture limite* became the symptom around which a new theoretical discourse on language as subjective experience was constituted. This was not a mere "theory of literature" that remains, by its imaginary uncertainties, the weak link in the social sciences, but a testing point for psychoanalysis, one that is called upon to measure itself against a social creation, the text, rather than a private delirium. Finally, this writing is a site where the "sacred" is subverted, insofar as it is the discourse of a crisis in identity.

As I see it, this latter point, fundamental because of the breadth of the tradition it touches on (in France, largely Catholicism) and because of the interest it holds for the post-May '68 generation, is often misunderstood. It is interpreted as a manifestation of distress, the fad of a generation bereft of revolutionary ideas, even a joke. If it is true that Maurice Clavel ostensibly waived the post-'68 banner of this movement, then *Tel Quel* bears the responsibility for its nocturnal emergence, like that of an old mole gnawing through the basements of mechanistic rationalism. Without the flair of the "nouveaux philosophes"—who are, all in all, fellow travelers closer to the media than to our research—our own thoughts on writing and the various mythemes of the sacred (from the sacrificial rite that institutes the symbolic to the Virgin, and the topos of the incarnation) have had a swift and artful dissemination whose toughness and corrosiveness have not always been appreciated. In short, these thoughts, as various articles and works of fiction published in *Tel Quel* demonstrate, have nothing to do with a religious psychology or ideology but rather with certain phantasmic and linguistic knots on which the power of the sacred is built.

I remember the visit to the offices of *Tel Quel* of an editor from the Soviet journal *Voprossi Filosoffi*. A specialist, I think, in aesthetics and modern literature, she was shocked by the formalism of the novels published in the series and by critics who left no room for the "soul," for the *doucha*, as she said. This provoked great hilarity on Sollers's part, who was astonished to hear a "dialectical materialist" express herself in such a way. I am convinced that this laughter lives on in the author of *Paradis* and *Eloge à Jean Paul II*.

The plurality, the diversity of these orientations—literature, psychoanalysis, history of religions—is disconcerting. Some readers have exhibited a tendency to see decided reversals in this phenomenon. It is true that the dominant concerns have not always been the same. "Semantic materialism" may have been overtaken by the "subject on trial," but it was never eclipsed. The names of Bataille, Sade, Artaud, and Joyce have remained fixed references, attesting not only that our aim has not been principally, even exclusively, literary, but that an experiment was involved even though personal or circumstantial limitations led to highlighting only one aspect of a palette of possibilities.

Obviously, each person who has worked, or who does work, with, for, or against *Tel Quel* has his or her own profile, his or her own limit. From Barthes, Todorov, Genette, Derrida, from Deguy, Hallier, Faye, Ricardou, Baudry, Henric, etc., to those—such as Sollers, Pleynet, Risset, Devade, Houdebine, and Scarpetta, who continue to be involved or, more indirectly, B.-H. Levy first of all but also Benoist, Muray, and Jambet—the epistemological, ideological, stylistical options clearly vary (even diverge) among the writers. Is public opinion wrong to associate these irreducible diversities, somehow and in spite of everything, to the myth of a poststructuralism or to *Tel Quel*? It seems to me that the common denominator among these divergences, which perhaps hinge on a question of generation or "the spirit of the times," nevertheless lies in a postphenomenological or postanalytical vigilance. We set forth as pioneers—some of us cautiously, others recklessly—against what must be termed the phobic discretion of phenomenology and analysis before the contemporary aesthetic experience and what we have called the modern religion, that is, politics. One day, we will have to accept, or dare to think, that we are responsible for a certain position in language from which the meaning of the human adventure, bordering on the insane, is deciphered with an involvement that is decidedly risky (this has nothing to do with neutral "scientific" description).

In fact, a future historian of ideas will be able to discern the harbinger of the present insurrection against political reductionism in a specific lecture at a Milan colloquium when we criticized "politics as common measure." That historian will be able to decipher in our readings of Hegel, during our memorable "theoretical groups" at 44 rue de Rennes not simply "the only initiation to speculative philosophy appealing to today's youth" (as a journalist recently said) but also, and above all, the never abandoned effort to take transcendence seriously and to track down its premises in the innermost recesses of language. We will also be able to see, for instance, how certain brilliant students from my courses on Céline became journalists expert in the subtleties of right-wing aesthetics, or in the diffuse spirituality of our times.

I am not trying to have laurels bestowed upon us as precursors of the movement of vulgarization peculiar to contemporary cultural life. I would rather reestablish differences. Whether we came from a Catholic education or a frankly atheist one, or from an exquisite blend of the two, familiarity with Freud and with style in modern art and literature modified for us the enigma of Faith as well as the omnipotence of universal reason. Without rejecting their appeal, their economy was transformed into an inquiry on the dynamics of the speaking Subject and of Meaning. More than the convivial embroidery of Heidegger on the canvas of Logos, it was *Lacan's* insolence in daring to introduce the "great Other" into the very heart of the speaking structure that propelled us on this course. We were attempting, in our own fashion, to circumscribe the unavoidable necessity of this Other and to analyze its crises, which determine the transformations, the life, and the history of discourses. That there is meaning, which is "One" and polyphonic nevertheless; that it exists but only in the irreducible multiplicities, that it follows the whims of desires and games of languages—these are surely views common to artists and analysts. In holding to these views, we necessarily felt far removed from both the antioedipals and the "deconstructionists." In a margin, irreducible and constructive, such as it is: *tel quel*.

What's the Use of Politics in Times of Distress?

Clarté, the journal of communist students, had published, at the end of 1965, I think, a large picture of Sollers along with a text in which he explained, in essence, that only the socialist Revolution could provide a social setting propitious to avant-garde writing. This was, before the mediation of Genette, my first encounter with *Tel Quel*. And the first seduction. The theme Sollers elaborated had struck me. Not that the romantics or the surrealists hadn't proclaimed it before him. But it seemed to me completely unrealistic from the standpoint of the socialism I had experienced. I knew to what extent a regime born of a Marxist social mutation rejected not merely all aesthetic formalism deemed individualistic or antisocial, but also all individual stylistic experience that could question or explore the common code and its stereotypes in which ideology must seek shelter in order to dominate. Nevertheless, the logical firmness and the existential assurance of this young star in a *nouveau roman*, rewritten by the painful adventure of the Algerian War and the Bataillian mystique, led me, as well as those who were to become my friends at *Tel Quel*, to think that "in France, it would be different." In addition, hadn't Louis Althusser, whom we met soon after, taken the toughest (for me, the most "Stalinist") points of Marxism in order to instill new hope in the French Communist Party and all of French society, the harbinger of a worldwide Marxist spring? I remained, then, less sensitive to the arguments of the director of studies of the rue d'Ulm than to the revolutionary aestheticism of *Tel Quel*, which seemed, after all, to bode well for the success of the futurist utopia.

Our attitude, which many termed scandalous at the time and which I now regard as illusory, still constitutes the national wager in France today. Were we, then, in the avant-garde on this level as well?

An important point must be emphasized to understand our boarding the Communist Party vessel. The French Communist Party (PFC) was, and still remains to a large extent, the only French party to have a cultural politics. The fact that today this party has lost its intellectuals of national and international renown does little to change its impact upon the cultural workers at the base. Even more—and in my mind this is essential—the PFC is the only party in France to have drawn a lesson (often machiavellically subtle thought for the most part clumsily and dogmatically applied) from having closely witnessed the great adventures of twentieth-century thought and art. The Socialist Party has only followed this course somewhat belatedly. Scorched by Stalinist social realism and shaken by détente, the Kremlin, with Aragon (like the Vatican with Mauriac), had already hailed the work of the young Sollers. But starting in 1966, the entire machine of the PFC awakened to the experiments of the avant-garde. Let's not forget that in France, institutional recognition of Russian formalism, futurism, and, by analogy, contemporary writing, with literary theory as one of its facets, first came with the publications of the PFC, *Les Lettres Françaises* and the *Nouvelle Critique*, and the colloquia it organized (Cluny I and Cluny II). In fact, I recently saw Japanese academics in Kyoto initiated into semiology through the published acts of these colloquia.

It is clear that without the fomentation of the militant base (schoolteachers and professors), the "social sciences" in their structuralist hue, and this includes Lacanian psychoanalysis, would not have invaded the university. Although the Edgar Faure reform provided a helping hand in this assault, these disciplines and methodologies nevertheless get their clientele from the audience of the PFC—notwithstanding the protests of leftists declaring "war unto death against the Communist Party." This may seem paradoxical on the part of a party devoted—if one is to believe its programs—to Marxist-Leninism. Those were times for "revisionism," however, and I'll always remember the words of comrade Juquin, during a luncheon of the *Nouvelle Critique* colloquium, explaining to my companions, young bourgeois recently interested in the doctrine, that "Leninism is obsolete." The PFC was trying to take a social-democrat turn which, as we know, failed. The Socialist Party profited from this failure and gained ground, thus pushing the Communist Party toward its present decline.

But to remain on the cultural level, the narrow-minded battle of Mme Saunié-Seite against all forms of noninstitutionalized thought was nevertheless correct on this point: the Communist Party certainly appropriated, on behalf of the establishment, those currents of thought and aesthetic creation that would have remained marginal without it. From the moment of institutionalization, however, we ceased to believe in the permanent subversiveness of the Communist Party and ceased to see ourselves in what we had briefly believed was fated to mark the explosive beginnings of a revolutionary party.

Before coming to this moment of divorce, though, I cannot help but emphasize the scandal that our attitude caused in the moderate intelligentsia. I will pass over the first greeting I received from French public opinion: an insulting article in the magazine *Minute*, claiming to unmask me, on the basis of an article on Bakhtin I had published in *Critique*, as a Soviet spy. It was brought to me at Cochin hospital, where I was suffering from viral hepatitis in the spring of 1967, and I think it aided my recovery.

More spectacular in my view were articles in the *Nouvel Observateur*, in which, after publication in the *Tel Quel* series of a book by Pierre Daix, then still a member of the French Communist Party, we were labeled "Jdanovians" and "catatonics." I admit that I still find the connection between the rigidity of Jdanov and our baroque readings of Sade, Bataille, Freud, or the materialism of Lucretius to be rather tenuous. What I think I understand, however, is the feeling of betrayal, of a truly narcissistic injury, that an essentially Trotskyist—as it should be in the West—left must have felt in seeing our rapprochement to the Communist Party.

What, in fact, were we doing on this galley? Can one discern a general reason, a common denominator in this provisional attraction to the PFC beyond our very diverse psychological motivations, linked to each of our personal histories?

The generation of our elders, which should reproach itself for its dogmatic words and deeds and the more or less tragic consequences that occurred during its stint in the Communist Party, typically explains or, better yet, stigmatizes our behavior as "religious." As if religion were unanalyzable, the fascinating and indescribable enigma before which reason must lay down its arms.

For us, on the contrary, religion, I repeat, was not an enemy to flee, a target for reinvestment beneath the facade of a lay institution. It had already become a discourse for analysis. Since we were neither guilty of terrorist words and deeds, nor even secretly religious, what were we looking for in the PCF? My hypothesis, I think, far from exempting us, casts a less violent but more cruel light on the cynicism that binds the individual to politics, on the perversion that lies at the heart of the political institution, regardless of its nature.

As a state within the state, having considerable powers of dissemination and propaganda distinct from the traditional circuits saturated with more conventional products, the PCF was the best mouthpiece for experimental literary or theoretical work. To make this work public, in order to continue it, seemed to us imperative in an era of mass media. Indeed, an interview with Jean Paulhan, published at the time, compared the surrealists to *Tel Quel*, emphasizing that we were a "mass movement." It was true, and to a large extent thanks to the Communist Party; but, on the whole, the idea was to use the Communist Party, not to be used by it.

To be sure, we did not deliberately exploit this misunderstanding. If there was any cynicism on our part, it can be derived from what must rightly be called our exaggerated regard for theory. Dialectical materialism, which, in our view, represented Hegel overturned by Lucretius, Mallarmé, and Freud (to cite only three parameters of a nonmechanistic materialism), gave us some hope, if not of modifying the bureaucratic defects of an oppressive machine—we didn't have the pragmatic soul of law-enforcers or founders of morally pure communities—at least of bracketing them.

I identify as political perversion a coherent structure determined by an ideal (this ideal was *theoretical* for us; perhaps it has been *moral* for others), which nevertheless uses the abjections of a reality, one that is neglected or even foreclosed, on behalf of libidinal or sublimated gratifications. (Our own gratification was essentially the development and appreciation of our work.) During the anarchic eruptions of May '68 (in which we participated around the clock), we kept from the beginning a foot on the barricades (that romantic intoxication corresponded to our erotic rhythms and our thoughts, which had broken with convention) and an eye in search of something that could ensure cultural transmission, something in the party that could be useful (to us).

Does this mean that I consider the intellectual essentially ambivalent, torn, treacherous? Not at all. Not only because others were, at the time, greater anarchists or conformists, depending on the logic of their own history. Not only because the principal result of May '68 was to accelerate the revisionism of the PCF, leading to a general social-democratization of French society—a process during which communist sensibility swerved to the center left, while Gaullist sensibility engendered a powerful center right, creating a bipartyism in the face of which any revolutionary stance was, ipso facto, transformed into an archaically oedipal attitude. But most of all, because this shift to the outskirts of the PCF gave us a clear view of the reality of a machine, of a group of human beings constituting itself to serve as the conveyor between, on the one hand, the ideal (be it murderous) and, on the other, the individual (whatever that person's value).

Rejected by both the perverted and the "political" animal, this machine is the killer mechanism of individual difference. "Society is a crime committed in common": in congresses and articles, in courses and theses, we have never ceased observing the truth of Freud's famous statement.

Because I brushed against this perverse experience in its cultural manifestation, I still cannot discard the idea that it is the central problem of modern social life, one we still need to analyze. My *Essai sur l'abjection* is probably indirectly linked to this notion. One thing is certain: it is because we saw what was perverse in our relation to the Communist Party that we kept aloof, from then on, from any other political perversion, even a left-wing one. Our Maoism was an antiorganizational, antipartisan antidote, a utopia in pure form, which had nothing to do with the sects of the left (which were wary of us, and rightly so), proletarian or not, all of whom were rejects fascinated by or love-hating the Communist Party. In this light, the PCF itself does not appear an oddity. More radically, more somberly, it is the essence of the political tie: popular common sense, radical rationalization, the banal hideout, the orthodox lining of perversion.

What about the schisms, anathemas, persecutions, exclusions that checkered our game with these intrinsically perverse institutions? When they did not grow out of individual psychoanalysis, they were based on the wounds that our child's play with the (red) fire of politics reopened in the flesh of phobic adults. At times, reading articles in which some Parisian writer labeled me a Bogdanov, enemy of the wise Lenin, along with metaphors unleashed from the cellars of Bolshevism, I felt immersed in the universe of *The Possessed*. The sleepwalking fascination exerted by the clichés of the October Revolution on intellectuals weaned on the French Revolution seemed to illustrate a demonic and inevitable eternal return, in which it is impossible to distinguish between cause and effect, living spark and apocalyptic debacle.

As this period was ending, at least for me personally, my Czech friend Antonin Liehm arrived in Paris. An editor of the journal *Literarni Listi*, Liehm was at the center of the "Prague spring" and had been expelled from his country after the arrival of Soviet tanks. He and I resumed our conversations on "liberty and Marxism" in jest, with an irony that only the phoenix people of Central and Eastern Europe can keep alive. About the same time, Louis Althusser, a leader with a great following, was proclaiming the necessity of maintaining the "dictatorship of the proletariat" but in a state of tension that seemed on the verge of breaking down. For the liberal press, however, the myth of the "Stalinist dogmatism" of *Tel Quel* was in full swing. It was time to flee.

Peking-Shanghai-Louoyang-Nanking-Xian-Peking . . . New York

When we left, in the spring of 1974, for the first great voyage of Western intellectuals to China after the Cultural Revolution, many considered the trip a pilgrimage to the Mecca of dogmatism. It was impossible for me to make French intellectuals and my friends from Eastern Europe recognize that the China of the Cultural Revolution represented hope for national and libertarian socialism. For some of us, this gesture of friendship and adherence to the Chinese revolution was a way of associating with a left-wing political movement devoid of the Communist Party legacy. For others such as myself, who were not interested in political discourse, it was a means of finding another set of social and historical roots for "internal experience."

What we were looking for in the spasms of Chinese antibureaucratism at a moment when the party machinery had exploded and women, after the young, were suddenly pushed to the front line was Taoist culture, Chinese writing, and poetry, like jade, bland but subtle.

Joseph Needham, whom I had met in the chapel of Caius College, in Cambridge, and to whom we owe the monumental *Science and Civilisation in China*, had no trouble convincing me that Mao, poet and writer, was the most faithful modern version of ancestral Taoism. I loved—I still love—to lose myself, as in a dream, in the characters of Chinese texts that my professor at Jussieu had rudimentarily taught me. In short, it was classical China, dressed in the worker's blue suit of socialism, that we had gone to find, more interested in Ming tombs or Buddhist steles than in the stories ("bricks, as information theory uses the term," said Roland Barthes) of the friendly Chinese activist comrades. I myself was alarmed by the profound, unflagging, sly presence of the Soviet model, the only sign of the twentieth century in this land of peasants, and all the more evident because it was violently resisted. This led me to write an awkward book, *Des Chinoises* [1974], in which I tried to convey the strangeness of China and to explain the fascination we Occidentals feel for it, a fascination unquestionably involved with our own strange, foreign, feminine, psychotic aspects.

Politically, I saw nothing that might possibly prevent the Cultural Revolution from becoming a national and socialist variation, whose basic reference point remains the province of the Soviets. It marked my farewell to politics, including feminism.

The eruptions, encounters, loves, passions, as well as the more or less liberated or controlled eroticism that have shaped each person's biography constitute, I am convinced, the deepest influences on an individual path. In this essay, I simply present visible surface effects. Only a diary, a novel, could perhaps one day restore the wild indecency of it.

I can say, however, that for most of the Paris-Peking-Paris travelers (Roland Barthes, Philippe Sollers, Marcelin Playnet, François Wahl, and myself), this arduous journey, one that from the outset was more cultural than political, definitively inaugurated a return to the only continent we had never left: internal experience.

The psychoanalytic adventure on which my inquiries into infantile language, psychotic discourse, and style had started me finally led me to the Institute of Psychoanalysis. Lacan, whose seminar I attended until 1974 and whose baroque genius sometimes upset me as much as an actual session with an analyst, had not managed to free himself of the constraints his entourage imposed on him to follow us to China, as he wished to do. Even then, I thought I could discern signs of age in him— and signs of imposture in his school. I therefore avoided following him to his painful end.

The psychoanalytic experience struck me as the only one in which the wildness of the speaking being, and of language, can be heard. Political adventures, against the background of desire and hate that analysis openly unveils, appeared to me the way distance changes them: like a power of horror, like abjection. The sublime and horribly compromised work of Céline gave me the opportunity to speak of this.

Tel Quel—never a whole, but rather a provisional association of individuals as they were, *tel quels*—continued to develop, more than ever emphasizing the irreducible nature of writing, style, passion. Barthes's *Fragments d'un discours amoureux* became the best-seller of a formalism altered in its very core: the pleasure of the text. Sollers, after *Nombres* and *Lois* and *H*, which explore oneiric and vocal writing, published the first part of *Paradis*, a saga in which the impact of sexual and political reality is bound to an apocalyptic lyricism that he was able, like a bard, to voice and stage in an excessive, magical performance that traveled from Beaubourg to Greenwich Village.

An unavoidable stage of our journey was our discovery of America. Pleynet, who sought out all forms of modern painting, had for some time been a frequent visitor. Since the early 1970s, I had been, in turn, warmly welcomed by a generous American university, free and encouraging in its curiosity and intellectual naiveté. The Alexandrine, cosmopolitan, decadent climate of New York City always gives me (this despite the archaisms of the American left) the impression of a latter-day Rome; I find nothing more stimulating to my work than those sojourns across the Atlantic. It seems to me that the Western individual, whose "hecceite" we, with Duns Scotus, unearthed in the last few issues of *Tel Quel*, simultaneously enjoys, in the United States, a barbaric youth and an exquisite exhaustion.

To view my skeptical appreciation for this state of mind—of which the United States is clearly only an emblem—merely as a fad would be to ignore the individualist and universalist, desperate and jubilant aloofness, with its solitary atomism and its neutralized polyglotism, which substitutes for a community in this country of immigrants. They are traits specific to this *fin de siècle* culture; jazz and rock are their popular manifestations. The United States is a culture in which you write a novel as though you were playing jazz or rock, where you can hear or think discourses, beginning with the convulsive excesses of individuals in the modern megalopolis, whose words seem to be mere provisional and inessential masks. It could be that they represent inordinate ambitions that often disturb editors, analysts, and academics alike. What is clear is that in this inordinacy there is no adherence to a culture, be it local, regional, French, Latin, or Mediterranean. It is perhaps a quest, in form and meaning, for these limits, which have become the reality, the *tel quel*, of our time.

While the Latin American or Arab Marxist revolution is brewing on the doorstep of the United States, I feel closer to truth and liberty when

I work within the space of this challenged giant, which may, in fact, be on the point of becoming a David before the growing Goliath of the Third World.

I dream that our children will prefer to join this David, with his errors and impasses, armed with our erring and circling about the Idea, the Logos, the Form: in short, the old Judeo-Christian Europe.

If it is only an illusion, I like to think it may have a future.

PART 2

The Subject in Signifying Practice

Revolution in Poetic Language

Revolution in Poetic Language is probably Julia Kristeva's best-known text, for the central themes of her work over the last two decades have their beginnings here. Kristeva presented *La Révolution du langage poétique*, 646 pages, for her State Doctorate in July 1973 in Paris. It was originally published in 1974 by Editions du Seuil. Columbia University Press published Margaret Waller's translation of just one-third of the original text in 1984. The following selection is part of that translation. The portions of *Révolution* that have not been translated contain detailed analyses of texts by Lautréamont and Mallarmé. Those translated into English form the theoretical framework that Kristeva uses to analyze these texts. Here I have included the Prolegomenon and the following chapters from part 1, "The Semiotic and the Symbolic"—

1. The Phenomenological Subject of Enunciation
2. The Semiotic Chora Ordering the Drives
5. The Thetic: Rupture and/or Boundary
6. The Mirror and Castration
8. Breaching the Thetic: Mimesis
9. The Unstable Symbolic
10. The Signifying Process
12. Genotext and Phenotext

And from part 2, "Negativity: Rejection"—

1. The Fourth "Term" of the Dialectic
7. Freud's Notion of Expulsion: Rejection.

Kristeva's thesis is that nineteenth-century post-Symbolist avant-garde literature performs a revolution in language that transforms the structure of literary representation—a revolution in poetic language is analogous to a political revolution. The writings of Lautréamont and Mallarmé are examples of the revolution in language staged by the disruption of what Kristeva calls the "semiotic chora" in language. In the first part of *Revolution*, "The Semiotic and the Symbolic," Kristeva describes what she means by semiotic chora and how this semiotic element of language differs from the symbolic element of language. Kristeva takes the term *chora* from *Timeaus*, where Plato used it to refer to a receptacle. For the ancient Greeks chora meant space, area, or land. Kristeva uses it to mean the space in which drives enter language. The semiotic chora is associated with the maternal body because the infant's drives are structured around the mother's body. Following Lacan, Kristeva describes the infant's movements through the mirror stage and castration to signification. Yet she insists that the semiotic chora, with its regulation and motility, prefigures the specular realm of the mirror stage. The semiotic chora is associated with sounds and rhythms that set up the possibility of signification before the infant (mis)recognizes itself in the mirror image.

Poetic language can reactivate the semiotic drive force in language through its sounds and rhythms. Poetic language performs what Kristeva calls a *reversed reactivation* of the contradiction between semiotic and symbolic. Recall from the introduction to this collection, "Kristeva's Revolutions," that the semiotic is the element of signification associated with drives and affects, while the symbolic is the element of signification associated with position and judgment. The tension or contradiction between the semiotic and the symbolic elements is what makes language signify and significant. Poetic language does not represent the semiotic chora or drives in language; rather, poetic language reactivates the contradiction between the semiotic and the symbolic. By reactivating the drives in language, poetic language displays the process through which all signification is possible: all signification is possible through the dialectical movement between semiotic and symbolic, negativity and stases. Kristeva calls the founding moment of stasis in this dialectical process "the thetic" or a "thetic break."

Poetic language plays between what Kristeva calls the "genotext" and the "phenotext." The genotext is the underlying drive force in language.

The phenotext is structured and grammatical; it makes communication possible. The genotext is a space that can be mapped in a topology but is not calculable. The phenotext, on the other hand, is a structure that can be calculated in an algebra. Whereas the genotext is a process, the phenotext is static. The distinction between genotext and phenotext corresponds to the distinction between semiotic and symbolic. The distinctions set up in *Revolution* inform all Kristeva's writing.

In the second part of *Revolution*, "Negativity: Rejection," Kristeva argues that poetic language is unique in that it displays the process through which signification is possible. Like poetic language, all signification is the result of a dialectical movement between semiotic and symbolic elements. In poetry, however, this dialectical tension is on display because of the poet's attention to the rhythms of words. The contradiction between semiotic and symbolic elements in language is never overcome through some kind of Hegelian dialectical synthesis. Rather, in Kristeva's description of the dialectical oscillation between these two elements, the contradiction itself is reactivated. In this way, negativity, or what, following Freud, she calls "rejection," makes its way into signification. Negativity is not sublimated into a higher level of stasis in the signifying process; rather, semiotic negativity is a necessary element of the signifying process that cannot be incorporated into symbolic stasis.

"From One Identity to an Other"

"D'une identité l'autre" was originally read at a seminar organized by Jean-Marie Benoist and directed by Claude Lévi-Strauss at the Collège de France, January 27, 1975. It first appeared in print in *Tel Quel* in the summer of 1975. It was reprinted in *Polylogue* in 1977. "D'une identité l'autre" was translated as "From One Identity to an Other" by Thomas Gora, Alice Jardine, and Leon Roudiez in *Desire in Language: A Semiotic Approach to Literature and Art*, edited by Roudiez and published by Columbia University Press in 1980.

In this essay, Kristeva takes up some of the themes from *Revolution in Poetic Language* (1974). She further elaborates the revolutionary aspect of poetic language, especially the relationship between poetic language and the speaking subject. Poetic language puts the speaking subject in crisis. Here she proposes that the rhythms of poetic language not only violate the grammar of language but also render syntax indeterminate. Syntactical elisions in recent literature make it impossible to determine or distinguish basic syntactical categories like object or verb. The rhythms

of language allow phonemes to function apart from the symbolic register of meaning and reference. Poetic language operates between sense
and nonsense, meaning and nonmeaning. Moreover, poetic language
shows how all signification operates between these two realms. All signification is undeterminable in this way.

Poetic language makes it clear that signification is a process that is not
completely controlled by a unified subject. The two registers, semiotic
and symbolic, of poetic language suggest a split subject, the split subject
of psychoanalysis who always operates between unconscious and conscious realms. The semiotic and the symbolic elements of language
become associated with the unconscious and consciousness. Kristeva
challenges the Husserlian notion of a transcendental ego and postulates
a subject-in-process or on trial (*le sujet en procès*). The speaking subject
is never fully developed or unified; rather the subject is a precarious
process. In "From One Identity to an Other," as in *Powers of Horror*
(1980), Kristeva applies her analysis of the questionable subject-in-
process of poetic language to the writing of Louis-Ferdinand Céline.

Time and Sense

Le temps sensible: Proust et l'experience littéraire was originally published in Paris by Gallimard in 1994. Ross Guberman's translation, *Time
and Sense: Proust and Literary Experience* was published by Columbia
University Press in 1996. Part of chapter 6, "Is Sensation a Form of
Language?" and one section, "Freudian Time," of chapter 10, "Losing
Impatience," are reprinted here. *Time and Sense* is a lengthy, in-depth
study of Proust's writings. For the first time, Kristeva devotes an entire
book to the work of one writer. She analyzes everything from Proust's philosophy of time to the sentence structure and phonemes in his writings.

In "Is Sensation a Form of Language?" Kristeva analyzes the relationship between sensation and thought and sensation and language in the
history of philosophy and psychoanalysis from Plato to Melanie Klein.
She suggests that the practice of psychoanalysis, through transference
and countertransference, attempts to reconnect sensation and language.
She maintains that writing is also a process that moves back and forth
between signs and flesh. In the section from chapter 10, Kristeva
describes the time of transference as the time in which the unconscious
(which operates outside of time) is inscribed.

Revolution in Poetic Language

Prolegomenon

Our philosophies of language, embodiments of the Idea, are nothing more than the thoughts of archivists, archaeologists, and necrophiliacs. Fascinated by the remains of a process that is partly discursive, they substitute this fetish for what actually produced it. Egypt, Babylon, Mycenae: we see their pyramids, their carved tablets, and fragmented codes in the discourse of our contemporaries and think that by codifying them we can possess them.

These static thoughts, products of a leisurely cogitation removed from historical turmoil, persist in seeking the truth of language by formalizing utterances that hang in midair and the truth of the subject by listening to the narrative of a sleeping body—a body in repose, withdrawn from its sociohistorical imbrication, removed from direct experience: "To be or not to be . . . To die, to sleep . . . To sleep—perchance to dream."

And yet, this thinking points to a truth, namely, that the kind of activity encouraged and privileged by (capitalist) society represses the *process* pervading the body and the subject, and that we must therefore break out of our interpersonal and intersocial experience if we are to gain access to what is repressed in the social mechanism: the generating of significance.

The archivistic, archaeological, and necrophilic methods on which the scientific imperative was founded—the building of arguments on the basis of empirical evidence, a systematizable given, and an observable object—in this case, language—are an embarrassment when applied to modern or contemporary phenomena. These methods show that the capitalist mode of production has stratified language into idiolects and divided it into self-contained, isolated islands—heteroclite spaces existing in different temporal modes (as relics or projections), and oblivious of one another.

These random discursive instances have yet to be assigned a typology corresponding to the subjective and socioeconomic typologies in society as a whole. Instead, as agents of totality, in positions of control, science and theory intervene to make such discursive instances intelligible, each within its separate domain, even though they may lose them and have to start unifying them over and over again, if only provisionally—for that is their Long March. Linguistics, semiotics, anthropology, and psychoanalysis reveal that the thinking subject, the Cartesian subject who defines his being through thought or language, subsumes within that being and the operations which supposedly structure it, all translinguistic practice—a practice in which language and the subject are merely moments. From this perspective, the philosophy of language and the "human sciences" that stem from it emerge as reflections on moments. Whether they are viewed as simply linguistic, subjective, or more largely socioeconomic—depending on the "discipline"—such moments are nevertheless fragments, remains; their individual articulation is often examined, but rarely their interdependence or inception.

The critical question is not whether one can do otherwise. One clearly cannot if the object chosen is a human universe of full subjects who simply make systematic combinations in language and are themselves implicated in communication. Nor is it a question of calculating the pyramid's base and slant height and miming traces on Babylonian tablets or letters in Cretan linear writing. Such refinements in economics, phenomenology, and psychoanalysis de-structure finite systems and show that they are produced by a random albeit necessary causality. But one must still posit an "outside" that is in fact internal to each closed set, since otherwise the set would remain enclosed, even if internal differentiation could be extended indefinitely. One must, then, decenter the closed set and elaborate the dialectic of a process within plural and heterogeneous universes.

We will make constant use of notions and concepts borrowed from Freudian psychoanalytic theory and its various recent developments in order to give the advances of *dialectical logic* a *materialist founda-*

tion—a theory of signification based on the subject, his formation, and his corporeal, linguistic, and social dialectic. Our purpose is not to adhere to the orthodoxy of any particular school, but rather to select those aspects of analytic theory capable of rationalizing the signifying process as it is practiced within texts. Does this dialectic itself avoid archivism? At least it indicates its own position, and renounces both the totalizing fragmentation characteristic of positivist discourse, which reduces all signifying practices to a formalism, and a reductive identification with other (discursive, ideological, economic) islands of the social aggregate.

From this position, it seems possible to perceive a signifying practice which, although produced in language, is only intelligible *through* it. By exploding the phonetic, lexical, and syntactic object of linguistics, this practice not only escapes the attempted hold of all anthropomorphic sciences, it also refuses to identify with the recumbent body subjected to transference onto the analyzer. Ultimately, it exhausts the ever tenacious ideological institutions and apparatuses, thereby demonstrating the limits of formalist and psychoanalytic devices.[1] This signifying practice—a particular type of modern literature—attests to a "crisis" of social structures and their ideological, coercive, and necrophilic manifestations. To be sure, such crises have occurred at the dawn and decline of every mode of production: the Pindaric obscurity that followed Homeric clarity and community is one of many examples. However, with Lautréamont, Mallarmé, Joyce, and Artaud, to name only a few, this crisis represents a new phenomenon. For the capitalist mode of production produces and marginalizes, but simultaneously exploits for its own regeneration, one of the most spectacular shatterings of discourse. By exploding the subject and its ideological limits, this phenomenon has a triple effect and raises three sets of questions:

1. Because of its specific isolation within the discursive totality of our time, this shattering of discourse reveals that linguistic changes constitute changes in the *status of the subject*—his relation to the body, to others, and to objects; it also reveals that normalized language is just one of the ways of articulating the signifying process that encompasses the body, the material referent, and language itself. How are these strata linked? What is their interrelation within signifying practice?

2. The shattering further reveals that the capitalist mode of production, having attained a highly developed means of production through science and technology, no longer need remain strictly within linguistic

and ideological *norms*, but can also integrate their *process qua process*. As art, this shattering can display the productive basis of subjective and ideological signifying formations—a foundation that primitive societies call "sacred" and modernity has rejected as "schizophrenia." What is the extent of this integration? Under what conditions does it become indispensable, censured, repressed, or marginal?

3. Finally, in the history of signifying systems and notably that of the arts, religion, and rites, there emerge, in retrospect, fragmentary phenomena that have been kept in the background or rapidly integrated into more communal signifying systems but point to the very process of significance. Magic, shamanism, esoterism, the carnival, and "incomprehensible" poetry all underscore the limits of socially useful discourse and attest to what it represses: the *process* that exceeds the subject and his communicative structures. But at what historical moment does social exchange tolerate or necessitate the manifestation of the signifying process in its "poetic" or "esoteric" form? Under what conditions does this "esoterism," in displacing the boundaries of socially established signifying practices, correspond to socioeconomic change, and, ultimately, even to revolution? And under what conditions does it remain a blind alley, a harmless bonus offered by a social order that uses this "esoterism" to expand, become flexible, and thrive?

If there exists a "discourse" that is not a mere depository of thin linguistic layers, an archive of structures, or the testimony of a withdrawn body, and is, instead, the essential element of a practice involving the sum of unconscious, subjective, and social relations in gestures of confrontation and appropriation, destruction and construction—productive violence, in short—it is "literature," or, more specifically, the *text*. Although simply sketched out, this notion of the text (to which we shall return) already takes us far from the realm of "discourse" and "art." The text is a practice that could be compared to political revolution: the one brings about in the subject what the other introduces into society. The history and political experience of the twentieth century have demonstrated that one cannot be transformed without the other—but could there be any doubt after the overturning [*renversement*] of the Hegelian dialectic[2] and especially after the Freudian revolution? Hence, the questions we will ask about literary practice will be aimed at the political horizon from which this practice is inseparable, despite the efforts of aestheticizing esoterism and repressive sociologizing or formalist dogmatics to keep them apart.

We shall call this heterogeneous practice *signifiance* to indicate, on the one hand, that biological urges are socially controlled, directed, and organized, producing an excess with regard to social apparatuses; and, on the other, that this instinctual operation becomes a *practice*—a transformation of natural and social resistances, limitations, and stagnations—if and only if it enters into the code of linguistic and social communication. Laing and Cooper, like Deleuze and Guattari, are right to stress the destructuring and a-signifying machine of the unconscious.[3] Compared with the ideologies of communication and normativeness, which largely inspire anthropology and psychoanalysis, their approach is liberating. What is readily apparent, however, is that their examples of "schizophrenic flow" are usually drawn from modern literature, in which the "flow" itself exists only through language, appropriating and displacing the signifier to practice *within it* the heterogeneous generating of the "desiring machine."

What we call *signifiance*, then, is precisely this unlimited and unbounded generating process, this unceasing operation of the drives toward, in, and through language; toward, in, and through the exchange system and its protagonists—the subject and his institutions. This heterogeneous process, neither anarchic, fragmented foundation nor schizophrenic blockage, is a structuring and de-structuring *practice*, a passage to the outer *boundaries* of the subject and society. Then—and only then—can it be jouissance and revolution.

NOTES

1. "Device" is Kristeva's own choice for the translation of *dispositif*: "dispositif," something devised or constructed for a particular purpose.—Trans.

2. The expression *le renversement de Hegel* refers to a complex series of visions and revisions of the materialist debt to Hegel's dialectic. Kristeva's use of the term would seem to be informed by Althusser's "symptomatic reading" of Marx. In "Contradiction and Overdetermination," Althusser questions Marx's ambiguous and metaphorical statement that the Hegelian dialectic is "standing on its head" and "must be turned right side up again," and he argues that the materialist "inversion" of Hegel is no inversion at all. *For Marx*, Ben Brewster (New York: Random House, 1969), pp. 89–116. I have therefore translated *renversement* as "overturning" to convey the notion of a radical transformation that may or may not consist in a "reversal" of Hegel's dialectic.—Trans.

3. Gilles Deleuze and Félix Guattari, *Anti-Oedipus: Capitalism and Schizophrenia*, Robert Hurley et al., tr. (New York: Viking Press, 1977).

The Semiotic and the Symbolic

Further determine [the] object for itself, [a] logic
behind consciousness
—Hegel, Autumn 1831

1. The Phenomenological Subject of Enunciation

We must specify, first and foremost, what we mean by the *signifying process* vis-à-vis general theories of meaning, theories of language, and theories of the subject.

Despite their variations, all modern linguistic theories consider language a strictly "formal" object—one that involves syntax or mathematicization. Within this perspective, such theories generally accept the following notion of language. For Zellig Harris, language is defined by: (1) the arbitrary relation between signifier and signified, (2) the acceptance of the sign as a substitute for the extralinguistic, (3) its discrete elements, and (4) its denumerable, or even finite, nature.[1] But with the development of Chomskyan generative grammar and the logico-semantic research that was articulated around and in response to it, problems arose that were generally believed to fall within the province of "semantics" or even "pragmatics," and raised the awkward question of the *extralinguistic*. But language [*langage*]—modern linguistics' self-assigned object[2]—lacks a subject or tolerates one only as a *transcendental ego* (in Husserl's sense or in Benveniste's more specifically linguistic sense),[3] and defers any interrogation of its (always already dialectical because translinguistic) "externality."

Two trends in current linguistic research do attend to this "externality" in the belief that failure to elucidate it will hinder the development of linguistic theory itself. Although such a lacuna poses problems (which we will later specify) for "formal" linguistics, it has always been a particular problem for semiotics, which is concerned with specifying the functioning of signifying practices such as art, poetry, and myth that are irreducible to the "language" object.

1. The first of these two trends addresses the question of the so-called arbitrary relation between signifier and signified by examining signifying

systems in which this relation is presented as "motivated." It seeks the principle of this motivation in the Freudian notion of the unconscious insofar as the theories of drives [*pulsions*] and primary processes (displacement and condensation) can connect "empty signifiers" to psychosomatic functionings, or can at least link them in a sequence of metaphors and metonymies; though undecidable, such a sequence replaces "arbitrariness" with "articulation." The discourse of analysands, language "pathologies," and artistic, particularly poetic, systems are especially suited to such an exploration.[4] Formal linguistic relations are thus connected to an "externality" in the psychosomatic realm, which is ultimately reduced to a fragmented substance [*substance morcelée*] (the body divided into erogenous zones) and articulated by the developing ego's connections to the three points of the family triangle. Such a linguistic theory, clearly indebted to the positions of the psychoanalytic school of London and Melanie Klein in particular, restores to formal linguistic relations the dimensions (instinctual drives) and operations (displacement, condensation, vocalic and intonational differentiation) that formalistic theory excludes. Yet for want of a dialectical notion of the *signifying process* as a whole, in which significance puts the subject in process/on trial [*en procès*], such considerations, no matter how astute, fail to take into account the syntactico-semantic functioning of language. Although they rehabilitate the notion of the fragmented body—pre-Oedipal but always already invested with semiosis—these linguistic theories fail to articulate its transitional link to the post-Oedipal subject and his always symbolic and/or syntactic language. (We shall return to this point.)

2. The second trend, more recent and widespread, introduces within theory's own formalism a "layer" of *semiosis*, which had been strictly relegated to pragmatics and semantics. By positing a *subject of enunciation* (in the sense of Benveniste, Culioli, and others), this theory places logical modal relations, relations of presupposition, and other relations between interlocutors within the speech act, in a very deep "deep structure." This *subject of enunciation*, which comes directly from Husserl and Benveniste (see n. 3), introduces, through categorical intuition, both *semantic fields* and *logical*—but also *intersubjective—relations*, which prove to be both intra- and translinguistic.[5]

To the extent it is assumed by a subject who "means" (*bedeuten*), language has "deep structures" that articulate *categories*. These categories are semantic (as in the semantic fields introduced by recent developments in generative grammar), logical (modality relations, etc.), and intercommunicational (those that Searle called "speech acts" seen as bestowers of meaning).[6] But they may also be related to historical linguistic changes, thereby joining diachrony with synchrony.[7] In this way, through the subject who "means," linguistics is opened up to all possible categories and thus to philosophy, which linguistics had thought it would be able to escape.

In a similar perspective, certain linguists, interested in explaining semantic constraints, distinguish between different types of *styles* depending on the speaking subject's position vis-à-vis the utterance. Even when such research thereby introduces stylistics into semantics, its aim is to study the workings of signification, taking into account the subject of enunciation, which always proves to be the phenomenological subject.[8] Some linguistic research goes even further: starting from the subject of enunciation/transcendental ego and prompted by the opening of linguistics onto semantics and logic, it views signification as an ideological and therefore historical production.[9]

We shall not be able to discuss the various advantages and drawbacks of this second trend in modern linguistics except to say that it is still evolving and that, although its conclusions are only tentative, its epistemological bases lead us to the heart of the debate on phenomenology which we can only touch on here—and only insofar as the specific research we are at present undertaking allows.[10]

To summarize briefly what we shall elucidate later, the two trends just mentioned designate *two modalities* of what is, for us, the same signifying process. We shall call the first *the semiotic* and the second *the symbolic*. These two modalities are inseparable within the *signifying process* that constitutes language, and the dialectic between them determines the type of discourse (narrative, metalanguage, theory, poetry, etc.) involved; in other words, so-called natural language allows for different modes of articulation of the semiotic and the symbolic. On the other hand, there are nonverbal signifying systems that are constructed exclusively on the basis of the semiotic (music, for example). But, as we shall see, this exclusivity is relative, precisely because of the necessary dialectic between the two modalities of the signifying process, which is constitutive of the subject. Because the subject is always *both* semiotic *and* symbolic, no signifying system he produces can be either "exclusively" semiotic or "exclusively" symbolic, and is instead necessarily marked by an indebtedness to both.

2. The Semiotic *Chora*: Ordering the Drives

We understand the term "semiotic" in its Greek sense: σημεῖον = distinctive mark, trace, index, precursory sign, proof, engraved or written sign, imprint, trace, figuration. This etymological reminder would be a mere archaeological embellishment (and an unconvincing one at that, since the term ultimately encompasses such disparate meanings), were it not for the fact that the preponderant etymological use of the word, the one that implies a *distinctiveness*, allows us to connect it to a precise modality in the signifying process. This modality is the one Freudian psychoanalysis points to in postulating not only the *facilitation* and the structuring *disposition* of drives, but also the so-called *primary processes*, which displace and condense both energies and their inscription. Discrete quantities of energy move through the body of the subject who is not yet constituted as such and, in the course of his development, they are arranged according to the various constraints imposed on this body—always already involved in a semiotic process—by family and social structures. In this way the drives, which are "energy" charges as well as "psychical" marks, articulate what we call a *chora*: a nonexpressive totality formed by the drives and their stases in a motility that is as full of movement as it is regulated.

We borrow the term *chora*[11] from Plato's *Timaeus* to denote an essentially mobile and extremely provisional articulation constituted by movements and their ephemeral stases. We differentiate this uncertain and indeterminate *articulation* from a *disposition* that already depends on representation, lends itself to phenomenological, spatial intuition, and gives rise to a geometry. Although our theoretical description of the *chora* is itself part of the discourse of representation that offers it as evidence, the *chora*, as rupture and articulations (rhythm), precedes evidence, verisimilitude, spatiality, and temporality. Our discourse—all discourse—moves with and against the *chora* in the sense that it simultaneously depends upon and refuses it. Although the *chora* can be designated and regulated, it can never be definitively posited: as a result, one can situate the *chora* and, if necessary, lend it a topology, but one can never give it axiomatic form.[12]

The *chora* is not yet a position that represents something for someone (i.e., it is not a sign); nor is it a *position* that represents someone for another position (i.e., it is not yet a signifier either); it is, however, generated in order to attain to this signifying position. Neither model nor copy, the *chora* precedes and underlies figuration and thus specularization, and is analogous only to vocal or kinetic rhythm. We must restore this motility's gestural and vocal play (to mention only the aspect relevant to language) on the level of the socialized body in order to remove motility from ontology and amorphousness[13] where Plato confines it in an apparent attempt to conceal it from Democritean rhythm. The theory of the subject proposed by the theory of the unconscious will allow us to read in this rhythmic space, which has no thesis and no position, the process by which signifiance is constituted. Plato himself leads us to such a process when he calls this receptacle or *chora* nourishing and maternal,[14] not yet unified in an ordered whole because deity is absent from it. Though deprived of unity, identity, or deity, the *chora* is nevertheless subject to a regulating process [*réglementation*], which is different from that of symbolic law but nevertheless effectuates discontinuities by temporarily articulating them and then starting over, again and again.

The *chora* is a modality of signifiance in which the linguistic sign is not yet articulated as the absence of an object and as the distinction between real and symbolic. We emphasize the regulated aspect of the *chora*: its vocal and gestural organization is subject to what we shall call an objective *ordering* [*ordonnancement*], which is dictated by natural or sociohistorical constraints such as the biological difference between the sexes or family structure. We may therefore posit that social organization, always already symbolic, imprints its constraint in a mediated form that organizes the *chora* not according to a *law* (a term we reserve for the symbolic) but through an *ordering*.[15] What is this mediation?

According to a number of psycholinguists, "concrete operations" precede the acquisition of language, and organize preverbal semiotic space according to logical categories, which are thereby shown to precede or transcend language. From their research we shall retain not the principle of an operational state[16] but that of a preverbal functional state that governs the connections between the body (in the process of constituting itself as a body proper), objects, and the protagonists of family structure.[17] But we shall distinguish this functioning from symbolic operations that depend on language as a sign system—whether the language [*langue*] is vocalized or gestural (as with deaf-mutes). The kinetic functional stage of the *semiotic* precedes the establishment of the sign; it is not, therefore, cognitive in the sense of being assumed by a knowing, already constituted subject. The genesis of the *functions*[18] organizing the semiotic process can be accurately elucidated only within a theory of the subject that does not reduce the subject to one of understanding, but instead opens up within the subject this other scene of presymbolic functions. The Kleinian theory expanding upon Freud's positions on the drives will momentarily serve as a guide.

Drives involve pre-Oedipal semiotic functions and energy discharges that connect and orient the body to the mother. We must emphasize that "drives" are always already ambiguous, simultaneously assimilating and destructive; this dualism, which has been represented as a tetrad[19] or as a double helix, as in the configuration of the DNA and RNA molecule,[20] makes the semiotized body a place of permanent scission. The oral and anal drives, both of which are oriented and structured around the mother's body,[21] dominate this sensorimotor organization. The mother's body is therefore what mediates the symbolic law organizing social relations and becomes the ordering principle of the semiotic *chora*,[22] which is on the path of destruction, aggressivity, and death. For although drives have been described as disunited or contradictory structures, simultaneously "positive" and "negative," this doubling is said to generate a dominant "destructive wave" that is drive's most characteristic trait: Freud notes that the most instinctual drive is the death drive.[23] In this way, the term "drive" denotes waves of attack against stases, which are themselves constituted by the repetition of these charges; together, charges and stases lead to no identity (not even that of the "body proper") that could be seen as a result of their functioning. This is to say that the semiotic *chora* is no more than the place where the subject is both generated and negated, the place where his unity succumbs before the process of charges and stases that produce him. We shall call this process of charges and stases a *negativity* to distinguish it from negation, which is the act of a judging subject.

Checked by the constraints of biological and social structures, the drive charge thus undergoes stases. Drive facilitation, temporarily arrested, marks *discontinuities* in what may be called the various material supports [*matériaux*] susceptible to semiotization: voice, gesture, colors. Phonic (later phonemic), kinetic, or chromatic units and differences are the marks of these stases in the drives. Connections or *functions* are thereby established between these discrete marks, which are based on drives and articulated according to their resemblance or opposition, either by slippage or by condensation. Here we find the principles of metonymy and metaphor indissociable from the drive economy underlying them.

Although we recognize the vital role played by the processes of displacement and condensation in the organization of the semiotic, we must also add to these processes the relations (eventually representable as topological spaces) that connect the zones of the fragmented body to each other and also to "external" "objects" and "subjects," which are not yet constituted as such. This type of relation makes it possible to specify the *semiotic* as a psychosomatic modality of the signifying process; in other words, not a symbolic modality but one articulating (in the largest sense of the word) a continuum: the connections between the (glottal and anal) sphincters in (rhythmic and intonational) vocal modulations, or those between the sphincters and family protagonists, for example.

All these various processes and relations, anterior to sign and syntax, have just been identified from a genetic perspective as previous and necessary to the acquisition of language, but not identical to language. Theory can "situate" such processes and relations diachronically within the process of the constitution of the subject precisely because *they function synchronically within the signifying process of the subject himself*, that is, the subject of *cogitatio*. Only in *dream* logic, however, have they attracted attention, and only in certain signifying practices, such as the *text*, do they dominate the signifying process.

It may be hypothesized that certain semiotic articulations are transmitted through the biological code or physiological "memory" and thus form the inborn bases of the symbolic function. Indeed, one branch of generative linguistics asserts the principle of innate language universals. As it will become apparent in what follows, however, the *symbolic*—and therefore syntax and all linguistic categories—is a social effect of the relation to the other, established through the objective constraints of biological (including sexual) differences and concrete, historical family structures. Genetic programmings are necessarily semiotic: they include the primary processes such as displacement and condensation, absorption and repulsion, rejection and stasis, all of which function as innate preconditions, "memorizable" by the species, for language acquisition.

Mallarmé calls attention to the semiotic rhythm within language when he speaks of "The Mystery in Literature" ["Le Mystére dans les lettres"]. Indifferent to language, enigmatic and feminine, this space underlying the written is rhythmic, unfettered, irreducible to its intelligible verbal translation; it is musical, anterior to judgment, but restrained by a single guarantee: syntax. As evidence, we could cite "The Mystery in Literature" in its entirety.[24] For now, however, we shall quote only those passages that ally the functioning of that "air or song beneath the text" with woman:

And the instrument of Darkness, whom they have designated, will not set down a word from then on except to deny that she must have been the enigma; lest she settle matters with a wisk of her skirts: "I don't get it!"
. . . .
—They [the critics] play their parts disinterestedly or for a minor gain: leaving our Lady and Patroness exposed to show her dehiscence or lacuna, with respect to certain dreams, as though this were the standard to which everything is reduced.[25]

To these passages we add others that point to the "mysterious" functioning of literature as a rhythm made intelligible by syntax: "Following the instinct for rhythms that has chosen him, the poet does not deny seeing a lack of proportion between the means let loose and the result." "I know that there are those who would restrict Mystery to Music's domain; when writing aspires to it."[26]

What pivot is there, I mean within these contrasts, for intelligibility? a guarantee is needed—
    Syntax—
    . . . an extraordinary appropriation of structure, limpid, to the primitive lightning bolts of logic. A stammering, what the sentence seems, here repressed [. . .]
. . . .
The debate—whether necessary average clarity deviates in a detail—remains one for grammarians.[27]

Our positing of the semiotic is obviously inseparable from a theory of the subject that takes into account the Freudian positing of the unconscious. We view the subject in language as decentering the transcendental ego, cutting through it, and opening it up to a dialectic in which its syntactic and categorical understanding is merely the liminary moment of the process, which is itself always acted upon by the relation to the other dominated by the death drive and its productive reiteration of the "signifier." We will be attempting to formulate the distinction between *semiotic* and *symbolic* within this perspective, which was introduced by Lacanian analysis, but also within the constraints of a practice—the *text*—which is only of secondary interest to psychoanalysis.

5. The Thetic: Rupture and/or Boundary

We shall distinguish the semiotic (drives and their articulations) from the realm of signification, which is always that of a proposition or judgment, in other words, a realm of *positions*. This positionality, which Husserlian phenomenology orchestrates through the concepts of *doxa*, *position*, and *thesis*, is structured as a break in the signifying process, establishing the *identification* of the subject and its object as preconditions of propositionality. We shall call this break, which produces the positing of signification, a *thetic* phase. All enunciation, whether of a word or of a sentence, is thetic. It requires an identification; in other words, the subject must separate from and through his image, from and through his objects. This image and objects must first be posited in a space that becomes symbolic because it connects the two separated positions, recording them or redistributing them in an open combinatorial system.

The child's first so-called holophrastic enunciations include gesture, the object, and vocal emission. Because they are perhaps not yet sentences (NP-VP), generative grammar is not readily equipped to account for them. Nevertheless, they are already thetic in the sense that they separate an object from the subject and attribute to it a semiotic fragment, which thereby becomes a signifier. That this attribution is either metaphoric or metonymic ("woof-woof" says the dog, and all animals become "woof-woof") is logically secondary to the fact that it constitutes an *attribution*, which is to say, a positing of identity or difference, and that it represents the nucleus of judgment or proposition.

We shall say that the thetic phase of the signifying process is the "deepest structure" of the possibility of enunciation, in other words, of signification and the proposition. Husserl theologizes this deep logic of signification by making it a productive *origin* of the "free spontaneity" of the Ego:

> Its *free spontaneity and activity* consists in positing, positing on the strength of this or that, positing as an antecedent or a consequent, and so forth; it does not live within the theses as a passive indweller; the theses radiate from it as from a primary source of generation [*Erzeugungen*]. Every thesis begins with a *point of insertion* [*Einsatzpunkt*] with a point at which *the positing has its origin* [*Ursprungssetzung*]; so it is with the first thesis and with each further one in the synthetic nexus. This "inserting" even belongs to the thesis as such, as a remarkable *modus* of original actuality. It somewhat resembles the *fiat*, the point of insertion of will and action.[28]

In this sense, *there exists only one signification*, that of the thetic phase, which contains the object as well as the proposition, and the complicity between them.[29] There is no sign that is not thetic and every sign is already the germ of a "sentence," attributing a signifier to an object through a "copula" that will function as a signified.[30] Stoic semiology, which was the first to formulate the matrix of the sign, had already established *this complicity between sign and sentence*, making them proofs of each other.

Modern philosophy recognizes that the right to represent the founding *thesis* of signification (sign and/or proposition) devolves upon the transcendental ego. But only since Freud have we been able to raise the question not of the origin of this thesis but rather of the process of its production. To brand the thetic as the foundation of metaphysics is to risk serving as an antechamber for metaphysics—unless, that is, we specify the way the thetic is produced. In our view, the Freudian theory of the unconscious and its Lacanian development show, precisely, that thetic signification is a stage attained under certain precise conditions during the signifying process and that it constitutes the subject without being reduced to his process precisely because it is the threshold of language. Such a standpoint constitutes neither a reduction of the subject to the transcendental ego, nor a denial [*dénégation*] of the thetic phase that establishes signification.

6. The Mirror and Castration: Positing the Subject as Absent from the Signifier

In the development of the subject, such as it has been reconstituted by the theory of the unconscious, we find the thetic phase of the signifying process, around which signification is organized, at two points: the mirror stage and the "discovery" of castration.

The first, the mirror stage, produces the "spatial intuition" which is found at the heart of the functioning of signification—in signs and in sentences. From that point on, in order to capture his image unified in a mirror, the child must remain separate from it, his body agitated by the semiotic motility we discussed above, which fragments him more than it unifies him in a representation. According to Lacan, human physiological immaturity, which is due to premature birth, is thus what permits any permanent positing whatsoever and, first and foremost, that of the image itself, as separate, heterogeneous, dehiscent.[31] Captation of the image and the drive investment in this image, which institute primary narcissism, permit the constitution of objects detached from the semiotic *chora*. Lacan maintains, moreover, that the specular image is the "prototype" for the "world of objects."[32] Positing the imaged ego leads to the positing of the object, which is, likewise, separate and signifiable.

Thus the two separations that prepare the way for the sign are set in place. The sign can be conceived as the voice that is projected from the agitated body (from the semiotic *chora*) onto the facing *imago* or onto the object, which simultaneously detach from the surrounding continuity. Indeed, a child's first holophrastic utterances occur at this time, within what are considered the boundaries of the mirror stage (six to eighteen months). On the basis of this positing, which constitutes a *break*, signification becomes established as a digital system with a double articulation combining discrete elements. Language learning can therefore be thought of as an acute and dramatic confrontation between positing-separating-identifying and the motility of the semiotic *chora*. Separation from the mother's body, the *fort-da* game, anality and orality, all act as a permanent negativity that destroys the image and the isolated object even as it facilitates the articulation of the semiotic network, which will afterwards be necessary in the system of language where it will be more or less integrated as a *signifier*.

Castration puts the finishing touches on the process of separation that posits the subject as signifiable, which is to say, separate, always confronted by an other: *imago* in the mirror (signified) and semiotic process (signifier). As the addressee of every demand, the mother occupies the place of alterity. Her replete body, the receptacle and guarantor of demands, takes the place of all narcissistic, hence imaginary, effects and gratifications; she is, in other words, the phallus. The discovery of castration, however, detaches the subject from his dependence on the mother, and the perception of this lack [*manqué*] makes the phallic function a symbolic function—*the* symbolic function. This is a decisive moment fraught with consequences: the subject, finding his identity in the symbolic, *separates* from his fusion with the mother, *confines* his jouissance to the genital, and transfers semiotic motility onto the symbolic order. Thus ends the formation of the thetic phase, which posits the gap between the signifier and the signified as an opening up toward every desire but also every act, including the very jouissance that exceeds them.[33]

At this point we would like to emphasize, without going into the details of Lacan's argument, that the phallus totalizes the effects of signifieds as having been produced by the signifier: the phallus is itself a signifier. In other words, the phallus is not given in the utterance but instead refers outside itself to a precondition that makes enunciation possible. For there to be enunciation, the *ego* must be posited in the signified, but it must do so as a function of the *subject* lacking in the signifier; a system of finite positions (signification) can only function when it is supported by a subject and on the condition that this subject is a want-to-be [*manque à être*].[34] Signification exists precisely because there is no subject in signification. The gap between the imaged ego and drive motility, between the mother and the demand made on her, is precisely the break that establishes what Lacan calls the place of the Other as the place of the "signifier." The subject is hidden "by an ever purer signifier";[35] this want-to-be confers on an *other* the role of containing the possibility of signification; and this other, who is no longer the mother (from whom the child ultimately separates through the mirror stage and castration), presents itself as the place of the signifier that Lacan will call "the Other."

Is this to say, then, that such a theoretical undertaking transcendentalizes semiotic motility, setting it up as a transcendental Signifier? In our view, this transformation of semiotic motility serves to remove it from its autoerotic and maternal enclosure and, by introducing the signifier/signified break, allows it to produce signification. By the same token, signification itself appears as a stage of the signifying process—not so much its base as its boundary. Signification is placed "under the sign of the preconscious."[36] Ultimately, this signifier/signified transformation, constitutive of language, is seen as being indebted to, induced, and imposed by the social realm. Dependence on the mother is severed, and transformed into a symbolic relation to an other; the constitution of the Other is indispensable for communicating with an other. In this way, the signifier/signified break is synonymous with social sanction: "the first social censorship."

Thus we view the thetic phase—the positing of the *imago*, castration, and the positing of semiotic motility—as the place of the Other, as the precondition for signification, that is, the precondition for the positing of language. The thetic phase marks a threshold between two heterogeneous realms: the semiotic and the symbolic. The second includes part of the first and their scission is thereafter marked by the break between signifier and signified. *Symbolic* would seem an appropriate term for this always split unification that is produced by a rupture and is impossible without it. Its etymology makes it particularly pertinent. The σύμβολον is a sign of recognition: an "object" split in two and the parts separated, but, as eyelids do, σύμβολον brings together the two edges of that fissure. As a result, the "symbol" is any joining, any bringing together that is a contract—one that either follows hostilities or presupposes them—and, finally, any exchange, including an exchange of hostility.

Not only is symbolic, thetic unity divided (into signifier and signified), but this division is itself the result of a break that put a heterogeneous functioning in the position of signifier. This functioning is the instinctual semiotic, preceding meaning and signification, mobile, amorphous, but already regulated, which we have attempted to represent through references to child psychoanalysis (particularly at the pre-Oedipal stage) and the theory of drives. In the speaking subject, fantasies articulate this irruption of drives within the realm of the signifier; they disrupt the signifier and shift the metonymy of desire, which acts within the place of the Other, onto a jouissance that divests the object and turns back toward the autoerotic body. That language is a defensive construction reveals its ambiguity—the death drive underlying it. If language, constituted as symbolic through narcissistic, specular, imaginary investment, protects the body from the attack of drives by making it a place—the place of the signifier—in which the body can signify itself through positions; and if, therefore, language, in the service of the death drive, is a pocket of narcissism toward which this drive may be directed, then fantasies remind us, if we had ever forgotten, of the insistent presence of drive heterogeneity.[37]

All poetic "distortions" of the signifying chain and the structure of signification may be considered in this light: they yield under the attack of the "residues of first symbolizations" (Lacan), in other words, those drives that the thetic phase was not able to sublate [relever, aufheben] by linking them into signifier and signified. As a consequence, any disturbance of the "social censorship"—that of the signifier/signified break—attests, perhaps first and foremost, to an influx of the death drive, which no signifier, no mirror, no other, and no mother could ever contain. In "artistic" practices the semiotic—the precondition of the symbolic—is revealed as that which also destroys the symbolic, and this revelation allows us to presume something about its functioning.

Psychoanalysts acknowledge that the pre-Oedipal stages Melanie Klein discusses are "analytically unthinkable" but not inoperative; and, furthermore, that the relation of the subject to the signifier is established and language learning is completed only in the pregenital stages that are set in place by the retroaction of the Oedipus complex (which itself brings about initial genital maturation).[38] Thereafter, the supposedly characteristic functioning of the pre-Oedipal stages appears only in the complete, postgenital handling of language, which presupposes, as we have seen, a decisive imposition of the phallic. In other words, the subject must be firmly posited by castration so that drive attacks against the thetic will not give way to fantasy or to psychosis but will instead lead to a "second-degree thetic," that is, a resumption of the functioning characteristic of the semiotic *chora* within the signifying device of language. This is precisely what artistic practices, and notably poetic language, demonstrate.

Starting from and (logically and chronologically) after the phallic position and the castration that underlies it—in other words, after the Oedipus complex and especially after the regulation of genitality by the retroactive effect of the Oedipus complex in puberty—the semiotic *chora* can be read not as a failure of the thetic but instead as its very precondition. Neurotics and psychotics are defined as such by their relationship to what we are calling the thetic. We now see why, in treating them, psychoanalysis can only conceive of semiotic motility as a disturbance of language and/or of the order of the signifier. Conversely, the refusal of the thetic phase and an attempt to hypostasize semiotic motility as autonomous from the thetic—capable of doing without it or unaware of it—can be seen as a resistance to psychoanalysis. Some therefore even contend that one can find in poetry the unfolding of this refusal of the thetic, something like a direct transcription of the genetic code—as if practice were possible without the thetic and as if a text, in order to hold together as a text, did not require a completion [*finition*], a structuration, a kind of totalization of semiotic motility. This completion constitutes a synthesis that requires the thesis of language in order to come about, and the semiotic pulverizes it only to make it a new device—for us, this is precisely what distinguishes a text as *signifying practice* from the "drifting-into-non-sense" [*dérive*] that characterizes neurotic discourse. The distinction cannot be erased unless one puts oneself outside "monumental history" in a transcendence which often proves to be one of the reactionary forces combining that history's discrete blocks.[39]

In this way, only the subject, for whom the thetic is not a repression of the semiotic *chora* but instead a position either taken on or undergone, can call into question the thetic so that a new disposition may be articulated. Castration must have been a problem, a trauma, a drama, so that the semiotic can return through the symbolic position it brings about. This is the crux of the matter: both the completion of the Oedipus complex and its reactivation in puberty are needed for the *Aufhebung* of the semiotic in the symbolic to give rise to a signifying *practice* that has a sociohistorical function (and is not just a self-analytical discourse, a substitute for the analyst's couch). At the same time, however, this completion of the Oedipal stage and the genitality it gives rise to should not repress the semiotic, for such a repression is what sets up metalanguage and the "pure signifier." No pure signifier can effect the *Aufhebung* (in the Hegelian sense) of the semiotic without leaving a remainder, and anyone who would believe this myth need only question his fascination or boredom with a given poem, painting, or piece of music. As a traversable boundary, the thetic is completely different from an imaginary castration that must be evaded in order to return to the maternal *chora*. It is clearly distinct as well from a castration imposed once and for all, perpetuating the well-ordered signifier and positing it as sacred and unalterable within the enclosure of the Other.[40]

8. Breaching[41] the Thetic: Mimesis

Signification in literature implies the possibility of denotation. But instead of following denotative sequences, which would lead, from one judgment to another, to the knowledge of a real object, literary signification tends toward the exploration of grammaticality and/or toward enunciation. *Mimesis* is, precisely, the construction of an object, not according to truth but to *verisimilitude*, to the extent that the object is posited as such (hence separate, noted but not denoted); it is, however, internally dependent on a subject of enunciation who is unlike the transcendental ego in that he does not suppress the semiotic *chora* but instead raises the *chora* to the status of a signifier, which may or may not obey the norms of grammatical locution. Such is the *connoted* mimetic object.

Although mimesis partakes of the symbolic order, it does so only to reproduce some of its constitutive rules, in other words, grammaticality. By the same token, it must posit an object, but this "object" is merely a result of the drive economy of enunciation; its true position is inconsequential.[42] What is more, when poetic language—especially modern poetic language—transgresses grammatical rules, the *positing* of the symbolic (which mimesis has always explored) finds itself subverted, not only in its possibilities of *Bedeutung* or denotation (which mimesis has always contested), but also as a possessor of *meaning* (which is always grammatical, indeed more precisely, syntactic). In imitating the constitution of the symbolic as *meaning*, poetic mimesis is led to dissolve not only the denotative function but also the specifically thetic function of *positing* the subject. In this respect, modern poetic language goes further than any classical mimesis—whether theatrical or novelistic—because it attacks not only denotation (the positing of the object) but meaning (the positing of the enunciating subject) as well.

In thus eroding the verisimilitude that inevitably underlay classical mimesis and, more important, the very position of enunciation (i.e., the positing of the subject as absent from the signifier), poetic language puts the subject in process/on trial through a network of marks and semiotic facilitations. But the moment it stops being mere instinctual glossolalia and becomes part of the linguistic order, poetry meets up with denotation and enunciation—verisimilitude and the subject—and, through them, the social.

We now understand how the thetic conditions the possibilities of truth specific to language: all transgressions of the thetic are a crossing of the boundary between true and false—maintained, inevitably, whenever signification is maintained, and shaken, irremediably, by the flow of the semiotic into the symbolic. Mimesis, in our view, is a transgression of the thetic when truth is no longer a reference to an object that is identifiable outside of language; it refers instead to an object that can be constructed through the semiotic network but is nevertheless posited in the symbolic and is, from then on, always verisimilar.

Mimetic verisimilitude does not, therefore, eliminate the unique break Frege saw presiding over signification. Instead it maintains that break because it preserves meaning and, with it, a certain object. But neither true nor false, the very status of this verisimilar object throws into question the absoluteness of the break that establishes truth. Mimesis does not actually call into question the unicity of the thetic; indeed it could not, since mimetic discourse takes on the structure of language and, through narrative sentences, posits a signified and signifying object. Mimesis and the poetic language inseparable from it tend, rather, to prevent the thetic from becoming theological; in other words, they prevent the imposition of the thetic from hiding the semiotic process that produces it, and they bar it from inducing the subject, reified as a transcendental ego, to function solely within the systems of science and monotheistic religion.

To note that there can be no language without a thetic phase that establishes the possibility of truth, and to draw consequences from this discovery, is quite a different matter from insisting that every signifying practice operate uniquely out of the thetic phase. For this would mean that the thetic, as origin and transcendence, could only produce (in the Husserlian sense) a tautological discourse, which, having originated in a thesis, can only be a synthesis of theses. We maintain therefore that science and theological dogma are doxic. By repressing the *production* of doxy, they make the thetic a belief from which the quest for truth departs; but the path thus programmed is circular and merely returns to its thetic point of departure.[43] If mimesis, by contrast, pluralizes denotation, and if poetic language undermines meaning, by what specific operations are these corruptions of the symbolic carried out?

As we know, Freud specifies two fundamental "processes" in the work of the unconscious: *displacement* and *condensation*. Kruszewski and Jakobson[44] introduced them, in a different way, during the early stages of structural linguistics, through the concepts of *metonymy* and *metaphor*, which have since been interpreted in light of psychoanalysis.[45]

To these we must add a third "process"—the *passage from one sign system to another*. To be sure, this process comes about through a combination of displacement and condensation, but this does not account for its total operation. It also involves an altering of the thetic *position*—the destruction of the old position and the formation of a new one. The new signifying system may be produced with the same signifying material; in language, for example, the passage may be made from narrative to text. Or it may be borrowed from different signifying materials: the transposition from a carnival scene to the written text, for instance. In this connection we examined the formation of a specific signifying system—the novel—as the result of a redistribution of several different sign systems: carnival, courtly poetry, scholastic discourse.[46] The term *intertextuality* denotes this transposition of one (or several) sign system(s) into another; but since this term has often been understood in the banal sense of "study of sources," we prefer the term *transposition* because it specifies that the passage from one signifying system to another demands a new articulation of the thetic—of enunciative and denotative positionality. If one grants that every signifying practice is a field of transpositions of various signifying systems (an intertextuality), one then understands that its "place" of enunciation and its denoted "object" are never single, complete, and identical to themselves, but always plural, shattered, capable of being tabulated. In this way polysemy can also be seen as the result of a semiotic polyvalence—an adherence to different sign systems.

Along with condensation (*Verdichtung*) and displacement (*Verschiebung*), Freud also speaks of *considerations of representability* (*die Rücksicht auf Darstellbarkeit*), which are essential to dream work (*die Traumarbeit*). Representability comes about through a process, closely related to displacement but appreciably different from it, that Freud calls "ein Vertauschung des sprachlichen Ausdruckes." We shall call *transposition* the signifying process' ability to pass from one sign system to another, to exchange and permutate them; and *representability* the specific articulation of the semiotic and the thetic for a sign system. Transposition plays an essential role here inasmuch as it implies the abandonment of a former sign system, the passage to a second via an instinctual intermediary common to the two systems, and the articulation of the new system with its new representability.[47]

Poetic mimesis maintains and transgresses thetic unicity by making it undergo a kind of anamnesis, by introducing into the thetic position the stream of semiotic drives and making it signify.[48] This telescoping of the symbolic and the semiotic pluralizes signification or denotation: it pluralizes the thetic doxy. Mimesis and poetic language do not therefore disavow the thetic; instead they go through its truth (signification, denotation) to tell the "truth" about it. To be sure, the latter use of the term "truth" is inappropriate, since it no longer refers to denotative truth in Frege's sense. This "second truth" reproduces the path which was cleared by the first truth (that of *Bedeutung*) in order to posit itself. Both mimesis and poetic language with its connotations assume the right to enter into the social debate, which is an ideological debate, on the strength of their confrontation with *Bedeutung* (signification and denotation) but also with all meaning, and hence all enunciation produced by a posited subject.

But mimesis and poetic language do more than engage in an intraideological debate; they question the very principle of the ideological because they unfold the *unicity* of the thetic (the precondition for meaning and signification) and prevent its theologization. As the place of production for a subject who transgresses the thetic by using it as a necessary boundary—but not as an absolute or as an origin—poetic language and the mimesis from which it is inseparable, are profoundly a-theological. They are not critics of theology but rather the enemy within and without, recognizing both its necessity and its pretensions. In other words, poetic language and mimesis may appear as an argument complicitous with dogma—we are familiar with religion's use of them—but they may also set in motion what dogma represses. In so doing, they no longer act as instinctual floodgates within the enclosure of the sacred and become instead protestors against its posturing. And thus, its complexity unfolded by its practices, the signifying process joins social revolution.

9. The Unstable Symbolic: Substitutions in the Symbolic—Fetishism

The thetic permits the constitution of the symbolic with its vertical stratification (referent, signified, signifier) and all the subsequent modalities of logico-semantic articulation. The thetic originates in the "mirror stage" and is completed, through the phallic stage, by the reactivation of the Oedipus complex in puberty; no signifying practice can be without it. Though absolutely necessary, the thetic is not exclusive: the semiotic, which also precedes it, constantly tears it open, and this transgression brings about all the various transformations of the signifying practice that are called "creation." Whether in the realm of metalanguage (mathematics, for example) or literature, what remodels the symbolic order is always the influx of the semiotic. This is particularly evident in poetic language since, for there to be a transgression of the symbolic, there must be an irruption of the drives in the universal signifying order, that of "natural" language which binds together the social unit. That the subject does not vanish into psychosis when this transgression takes place poses a problem for metaphysics, both the kind that sets up the signifier as an untransgressable law and the kind for which there exists no thetic and therefore no subject.

The semiotic's breach of the symbolic in so-called poetic practice can probably be ascribed to the very unstable yet forceful positing of the thetic. In our view, the analysis of texts shows that thetic lability is ultimately a problem with imaginary captation (disorders in the mirror stage that become marked scopophilia, the need for a mirror or an identifying addressee, etc.) and a resistance to the discovery of castration (thereby maintaining the phallic mother who usurps the place of the Other). These problems and resistances obstruct the thetic phase of the signifying process. When they fail to prevent the constitution of the symbolic (which would result in psychosis), they return in and through its position. In so doing, they give rise to "fantasies"; more importantly, they attempt to dissolve the first social censorship—the bar between signifier and signified—and, simultaneously, the first guarantee of the subject's position—signification, then meaning (the sentence and its syntax). Language thus tends to be drawn out of its symbolic function (sign-syntax) and is opened out within a semiotic articulation; with a material support such as the voice, this semiotic network gives "music" to literature.

But the irruption of the semiotic within the symbolic is only relative. Though permeable, the thetic continues to ensure the position of the subject put in process/on trial. As a consequence, musicality is not without signification; indeed it is deployed within it. Logical syntheses and all ideologies are present, but they are pulverized within their own logic before being displaced toward something that is no longer within the realm of the idea, sign, syntax, and thus Logos, but is instead simply semiotic functioning. The precondition for such a heterogeneity that alone posits and removes historical meaning is the thetic phase: we cannot overemphasize this point.

Without the completion of the thetic phase, we repeat, no signifying practice is possible; the negation/denial [*dénégation*] of this phase leads the subject to shift the thetic, even though he is determined by it, onto one of the places that the signifying process must cross on its way to fulfillment. Negating or denying the symbolic, without which he would be incapable of doing anything, the subject may imagine the thetic at the place of an object or a partner. This is a fetishist mechanism, which consists in denying the mother's castration, but perhaps goes back even further to a problem in separating an image of the ego in the mirror from the bodily organs invested with semiotic motility. Negation-as-denial (*Verneinung*) or disavowal (*Verleugung*) in perversion, which may go so far as the foreclosure (*Verwerfung*) of the thetic phase, represent different modalities capable of obscuring castration and the sexual difference underlying it as well as genital sexuality. Further on we shall see how a marked investment in anal eroticism leads to this rejection of the thetic because it allows a questioning of the symbolic order; but by this very process it shifts the *thesis* onto *objects*. The prototype of such objects is excrement since it is midway between an autoerotic body, which is not yet autonomous from its eroticized sphincters, and the pleasure the mother's body or her supposed phallus would procure—a belief that is disclaimed but maintained, behind, as a compromise.

Since there can be no signifying practice without a thetic phase, the thetic that does not manage to posit itself in the symbolic order necessarily places itself in the objects surrounding the body and instinctually linked to it. Fetishism is a compromise with the thetic; although erased from the symbolic and displaced onto the drives, a "thesis" is nevertheless maintained so that signifying practice can take place. Therefore we shall contend that it is the thetic, and not fetishism, that is inherent in every cultural production, because fetishism is a displacement of the thetic onto the realm of drives. The instinctual *chora* articulates facilitations and stases, but fetishism is a telescoping of the symbolic's characteristic thetic moment and of one of those instinctually invested stases (bodies, parts of bodies, orifices, containing objects, and so forth). This stasis thus becomes the ersatz of the sign. Fetishism is a stasis that acts as a thesis.

We might then wonder whether the semiotic's dismantling of the symbolic in poetry necessarily implies that the thetic phase is shifted toward the stases of the semiotic *chora*. Doesn't poetry lead to the establishment of an object as a substitute for the symbolic order under attack, an object that is never clearly *posited* but always "in perspective."[49] The object may be either the body proper or the apparatuses erotized during vocal utterance (the glottis, the lungs), objects that are either linked to the addressee of desire or to the very material of language as the predominant object of pleasure. Moreover, since the symbolic is corrupted so that an object—the book, the work—will result, isn't this object a substitute for the thetic phase? Doesn't it take the thetic's place by making its symbolicity opaque, by filling the thetic with its presence whose pretension to universality is matched only by its very finite limits? In short, isn't art the fetish par excellence, one that badly camouflages its archaeology? At its base, isn't there a belief, ultimately maintained, that the mother is phallic, that the ego—never precisely identified—will never separate from her, and that no symbol is strong enough to sever this dependence? In this symbiosis with the supposedly phallic mother, what can the subject do but occupy her place, thus navigating the path from fetishism to autoeroticism? That indeed is the question.

In order to keep the process signifying, to avoid foundering in an "unsayable" without limits, and thus posit the subject of a practice, the subject of poetic language clings to the help fetishism offers. And so, according to psychoanalysis, poets as individuals fall under the category of fetishism; the very practice of art necessitates reinvesting the maternal *chora* so that it transgresses the symbolic order; and, as a result, this practice easily lends itself to so-called perverse subjective structures. For all these reasons, the poetic function therefore converges with fetishism; it is not, however, identical to it. What distinguishes the poetic function from the fetishist mechanism is that it maintains a "signification" (*Bedeutung*). All its paths into, indeed valorizations of, presymbolic semiotic stases, not only require the ensured maintenance of this signification but also serve signification, even when they dislocate it. No text, no matter how "musicalized," is devoid of meaning or signification; on the contrary, musicalization pluralizes meanings. We may say therefore that the text is not a fetish. It is, moreover, just like "natural" language in this regard, if the abstract word is thought of as a correlate for the fetish in primitive societies. The text is completely different from a fetish because it *signifies*; in other words, it is not a *substitute* but a *sign* (signifier/signified), and its semantics is unfurled in sentences.[50] The text signifies the un-signifying: it assumes [*relève*] within a signifying practice this functioning (the semiotic), which ignores meaning and operates before meaning or despite it. Therefore it cannot be said that everything signifies, nor that everything is "mechanistic." In opposition to such dichotomies, whether "materialist" or "metaphysical," the text offers itself as the dialectic of two heterogeneous operations that are, reciprocally and inseparably, preconditions for each other.[51]

We understand, then, that this heterogeneity between the semiotic and the symbolic cannot be reduced to computer theory's well-known distinction between "analog" and "digital."[52] An analog computer is defined as any device that 'computes' by means of an analog between real, physical, *continuous* quantities and some other set of variables," whereas the digital computer presupposes "*discrete* elements and discontinuous scales."[53] Certain linguists have wanted to transpose this distinction—which arose with the development of computers and perhaps applies to "natural" codes (nerve cell codes or animal communication, for example)—onto the functioning of language. But in making this transposition, one quickly forgets not only that language is simultaneously "analog" and "digital" but that it is, above all, a doubly articulated system (signifier and signified), which is precisely what distinguishes it from *codes*. We therefore maintain that what we call the semiotic can be described as both analog and digital: the functioning of the semiotic *chora* is made up of continuities that are segmented in order to organize a digital system as the *chora*'s guarantee of survival (just as digitality is the means of survival both for the living cell and society);[54] the stases marked by the facilitation of the drives are the discrete elements in this digital system, indispensable for maintaining the semiotic *chora*.

Yet this description (which itself is possible only on the basis of a highly developed symbolic system) does not account for what produces the *qualitative leap* between a code and a double articulation.[55] But this essential phase is precisely what we are examining when we distinguish between the semiotic and the symbolic, and when we assign the thetic phase the role of boundary between the two heterogeneous domains. Because of the human being's prematurity, his semiotic "code" is cut off from any possible identification unless it is assumed by the other (first the mother, then the symbolic and/or the social group). Making the analog digital is thus not enough to ensure our bodily survival because it cannot check the drives' endless facilitations. An *alteration* must be made, making the *other* the regulator between the semiotic *chora* and the totality called the *ecosystem*. This alteration makes it possible to gather together the analog and digital "code" and, through a break prepared by the mirror stage, posit it as unified, mastered, dominated, and in another space—imaginary, representational, symbolic. Through this alteration, the "code" leaves the place of the body and the ecosystem and, freed from their constraints, acquires the variability characteristic of a system of "arbitrary" signs—human language—the later development of which forms the immense edifice of signifying practices.

The *semiotic* (analog and digital) thereby assumes the role of a linguistic signifier signifying an *object* for an *ego*, thus constituting them both as thetic. Through its thetic, altering aspect, the signifier *represents* the subject—not the thetic ego but the very process by which it is posited. A signifier indebted in this manner to semiotic functioning tends to return to it. In all its various vacillations, the thetic is displaced toward the stages previous to its positing or within the very stases of the semiotic—in a particular element of the digital code or in a particular continuous portion of the analog code. These movements, which can be designated as fetishism, show (human) language's characteristic tendency to return to the (animal) code, thereby breaching what Freud calls a "primal repression." The thetic—that crucial place on the basis of which the human being constitutes himself as signifying and/or social—is the very place textual experience aims toward. In this sense, textual experience represents one of the most daring explorations the subject can allow himself, one that delves into his constitutive process. But at the same time and as a result, textual experience reaches the very foundation of the social—that which is exploited by sociality but which elaborates and can go beyond it, either destroying or transforming it.

10. The Signifying Process

Once the break instituting the symbolic has been established, what we have called the semiotic *chora* acquires a more precise status. Although originally a precondition of the symbolic, the semiotic functions within signifying practices as the result of a transgression of the symbolic. Therefore the semiotic that "precedes" symbolization is only a *theoretical supposition* justified by the need for description. It exists in practice only within the symbolic and requires the symbolic break to obtain the complex articulation we associate with it in musical and poetic practices. In other words, symbolization makes possible the complexity of this semiotic combinatorial system, which only theory can isolate as "preliminary" in order to specify its functioning. Nevertheless, the semiotic is not solely an abstract object produced for the needs of theory.

As a precondition of the symbolic, semiotic functioning is a fairly rudimentary combinatorial system, which will become more complex only after the break in the symbolic. It is, however, already put in place by a biological setup and is always already social and therefore historical. This semiotic functioning is discernible before the mirror stage, before the first suggestion of the thetic. But the semiotic we find in signifying practices always comes to us after the symbolic thesis, after the symbolic break, and can be analyzed in psychoanalytic discourse as well as in so-called artistic practice. One could not, then, limit oneself to representing this semiotic functioning as simply "analog" or "digital" or as a mere scattering of traces. The thetic gathers up these facilitations and instinc-tual semiotic stases within the positing of signifiers, then opens them out in the three-part cluster of referent, signified, and signifier, which alone makes the enunciation of a truth possible. In taking the thetic into account, we shall have to represent the semiotic (which is produced recursively on the basis of that break) as a "second" return of instinctual functioning within the symbolic, as a negativity introduced into the sym-bolic order, and as the transgression of that order.

This transgression appears as a breach [*effraction*] subsequent to the thetic phase, which makes that phase negative and tends to fuse the lay-ers of signifier/signified/referent into a network of traces, following the facilitation of the drives. Such a breach does not constitute a positing. It is not at all thetic, nor is it an *Aufhebung* of "original doxy" through a synthesizing spiral movement and within the pursuit of the exhaustion of truth undertaken by Hegelian absolute knowledge. On the contrary, the transgression breaks up the thetic, splits it, fills it with empty spaces, and uses its device only to remove the "residues of first symbolizations" and make them "reason" [*raisonner*] within the symbolic chain. This explo-sion of the semiotic in the symbolic is far from a negation of negation, an *Aufhebung* that would suppress the contradiction generated by the thetic and establish in its place an ideal positivity, the restorer of presymbolic immediacy.[56] It is, instead, a *transgression* of position, a reversed reacti-vation of the contradiction that instituted this very position.

The proof is that this negativity has a tendency to suppress the thetic phase, to de-syn-thesize it. In the extreme, negativity aims to foreclose the thetic phase, which, after a period of explosive semiotic motility, may result in the loss of the symbolic function, as seen in schizophrenia.

"Art," on the other hand, by definition, does not relinquish the thetic even while pulverizing it through the negativity of transgression. Indeed, this is the only means of transgressing the thetic, and the difficulty of maintaining the symbolic function under the assault of negativity indi-cates the risk that textual practice represents for the subject. What had seemed to be a process of fetishizing inherent in the way the text functions now seems a structurally necessary protection, one that serves to check negativity, confine it within stases, and prevent it from sweeping away the symbolic position.

The regulation of the semiotic in the symbolic through the thetic break, which is inherent in the operation of language, is also found on the various levels of a society's signifying edifice. In all known archaic societies, this founding break of the symbolic order is represented by murder—the killing of a man, a slave, a prisoner, an animal. Freud reveals this founding break and generalizes from it when he emphasizes that society is founded on a complicity in the common crime.[57] We indicated earlier how language, already as a semiotic *chora* but above all as a symbolic system, is at the service of the death drive, diverts it, and confines it as if within an isolated pocket of narcissism. The social order, for its part, reveals this confinement of the death drive, whose endless course conditions and moves through every stasis and thus every structure, in an act of murder. Religions, as we know, have set themselves up as specialists on the discourse concerning this radical, unique, thetic event.

Opposite religion or alongside it, "art" takes on murder and moves through it. It assumes murder insofar as artistic practice considers death the inner boundary of the signifying process. Crossing that boundary is precisely what constitutes "art." In other words, it is as if death becomes interiorized by the subject of such a practice; in order to function, he must make himself the bearer of death. In this sense, the artist is comparable to all other figures of the "scapegoat." But he is not just a scapegoat; in fact, what makes him an artist radically distinguishes him from all other sacrificial murderers and victims.[58]

In returning, through the event of death, toward that which produces its break; in exporting semiotic motility across the border on which the symbolic is established, the artist sketches out a kind of second birth. Subject to death but also to rebirth, his function becomes harnessed, immobilized, represented, and idealized by religious systems (most explicitly by Christianity), which shelter him in their temples, pagodas, mosques, and churches. Through themes, ideologies, and social meanings, the artist introduces into the symbolic order an asocial drive, one not yet harnessed by the thetic. When this practice, challenging any stoppage, comes up, in its turn, against the produced object, it sets itself up as a substitute for the initially contested thetic, thus giving rise to the aesthetic fetishism and narcissism supplanting theology.

12. Genotext and Phenotext

In light of the distinction we have made between the semiotic *chora* and the symbolic, we may now examine the way texts function. What we shall call a *genotext* will include semiotic processes but also the advent of the symbolic. The former includes drives, their disposition, and their division of the body, plus the ecological and social system surrounding the body, such as objects and pre-Oedipal relations with parents. The latter encompasses the emergence of object and subject, and the constitution of nuclei of meaning involving categories: semantic and categorial fields. Designating the genotext in a text requires pointing out the transfers of drive energy that can be detected in phonematic devices (such as the accumulation and repetition of phonemes or rhyme) and melodic devices (such as intonation or rhythm), in the way semantic and categorial fields are set out in syntactic and logical features, or in the economy of mimesis (fantasy, the deferment of denotation, narrative, etc.). The genotext is thus the only transfer of drive energies that organizes a space in which the subject is not *yet* a split unity that will become blurred, giving rise to the symbolic. Instead, the space it organizes is one in which the subject will be *generated* as such by a process of facilitations and marks within the constraints of the biological and social structure.

In other words, even though it can be seen in language, the genotext is not linguistic (in the sense understood by structural or generative linguistics). It is, rather, a *process*, which tends to articulate structures that are ephemeral (unstable, threatened by drive charges, "quanta" rather than "marks") and nonsignifying (devices that do not have a double articulation). It forms these structures out of: (a) instinctual dyads, (b) the corporeal and ecological continuum, (c) the social organism and family structures, which convey the constraints imposed by the mode of production, and (d) matrices of enunciation, which give rise to discursive "genres" (according to literary history), "psychic structures" (according to psychiatry and psychoanalysis), or various arrangements of "the participants in the speech event" (in Jakobson's notion of the linguistics of discourse).[59] We may posit that the matrices of enunciation are the result of the repetition of drive charges (a) within biological, ecological, and sociofamilial constraints (b and c), and the stabilization of their facilitation into stases whose surrounding structure accommodates and leaves its mark on symbolization.

The genotext can thus be seen as language's underlying foundation. We shall use the term *phenotext* to denote language that serves to communicate, which linguistics describes in terms of "competence" and "performance." The phenotext is constantly split up and divided, and is irreducible to the semiotic process that works through the genotext. The phenotext is a structure (which can be generated, in generative grammar's sense); it obeys rules of communication and presupposes a subject of enunciation and an addressee. The genotext, on the other hand, is a process; it moves through zones that have relative and transitory borders and constitutes a *path* that is not restricted to the two poles of univocal information between two full-fledged subjects. If these two terms—genotext and phenotext—could be translated into a metalanguage that would convey the difference between them, one might say that the genotext is a matter of topology, whereas the phenotext is one of algebra. This distinction may be illustrated by a particular signifying system: written and spoken Chinese, particularly classical Chinese. Writing represents/articulates the signifying process into specific networks or spaces; *speech* (which may correspond to that writing) restores the diacritical elements necessary for an exchange of meaning between two subjects (temporality, aspect, specification of the protagonists, morpho-semantic identifiers, and so forth).[60]

The signifying process therefore includes both the genotext and the phenotext; indeed it could not do otherwise. For it is in language that all signifying operations are realized (even when linguistic material is not used), and it is on the basis of language that a theoretical approach may attempt to perceive that operation.

In our view, the process we have just described accounts for the way all signifying practices are generated.[61] But every signifying practice does not encompass the infinite totality of that process. Multiple constraints—which are ultimately sociopolitical—stop the signifying process at one or another of the theses that it traverses; they knot it and lock it into a given surface or structure; they discard *practice* under fixed, fragmentary, symbolic *matrices*, the tracings of various social constraints that obliterate the infinity of the process: the phenotext is what conveys these obliterations. Among the capitalist mode of production's numerous signifying practices, only certain literary texts of the avant garde (Mallarmé, Joyce) manage to cover the infinity of the process, that is, reach the semiotic *chora*, which modifies linguistic structures. It must be emphasized, however, that this total exploration of the signifying process generally leaves in abeyance the theses that are characteristic of the social organism, its structures, and their political transformation: the text has a tendency to dispense with political and social signifieds.

It has only been in very recent years or in revolutionary periods that signifying practice has inscribed within the phenotext the plural, heterogeneous, and contradictory process of signification encompassing the flow of drives, material discontinuity, political struggle, and the pulverization of language.

Lacan has delineated four types of discourse in our society: that of the hysteric, the academic, the master, and the analyst.[62] Within the perspective just set forth, we shall posit a different classification, which, in certain respects, intersects these four Lacanian categories and, in others, adds to them. We shall distinguish between the following signifying practices: narrative, metalanguage, contemplation, and text-practice.

Let us state from the outset that this distinction is only provisional and schematic, and that although it corresponds to actual practices, it interests us primarily as a didactic implement [*outil*]—one that will allow us to specify some of the modalities of signifying dispositions. The latter interest us to the extent that they give rise to different practices and are, as a consequence, more or less coded in modes of production. Of course narrative and contemplation could also be seen as devices stemming from (hysterical and obsessional) transference neurosis; and metalanguage and the text as practices allied with psychotic (paranoid and schizoid) economies.

NOTES

1. See Zellig Harris, *Mathematical Structures of Language* (New York: Interscience Publishers, 1968). See also Maurice Gross and André Lentin, *Introduction to Formal Grammars*, M. Salkoff, tr. (Berlin: Springer-Verlag, 1970); M.-C. Barbault and J.-P. Desclés, *Transformations formelles et théories linguistiques*, Documents de linguistique quantitative, no. 11 (Paris: Dunod, 1972).

2. On this "object" see *Langages* 24 (December 1971), and, for a didactic, popularized account, see Julia Kristeva, *Le Langage, cet inconnu* (Paris: Seuil, 1981).

3. Edmund Husserl, in *Ideas: General Introduction to Pure Phenomenology*, W. R. Boyce Gibson, tr. (London: Allen & Unwin, 1969), posits this subject as a subject of intuition, sure of this universally valid unity (of consciousness), a unity that is provided in *categories* itself, since transcendence is precisely the immanence of this "Ego," which is an expansion of the Cartesian *cogito*. "We shall consider conscious experiences," Husserl writes, "*in the concrete fullness and entirety with which they figure in their concrete context—the stream of experience—and to which they are closely attached through their own proper essence. It then becomes evident that every experience in the stream which our reflexion can lay hold on has its own essence open to intuition, a 'content' which can be considered in its singularity in and for itself.* We shall be concerned to grasp this individual

content of the *cogitatio* in its *pure* singularity, and to describe it in its general features, excluding everything which is not to be found in the *cogitatio* as it is in itself. We must likewise describe the *unity of consciousness* which is demanded *by the intrinsic nature of the cogitationes*, and so necessarily demanded that they could not be without this unity" (p. 116). From a similar perspective, Benveniste emphasizes language's dialogical character, as well as its role in Freud's discovery. Discussing the I/you polarity, he writes: "This polarity does not mean either equality or symmetry: 'ego' always has a position of transcendence with regard to *you.*" In Benveniste, "Subjectivity in Language," *Problems in General Linguistics*, Miami Linguistics Series, no. 8, Mary Elizabeth Meek, tr. (Coral Gables, Fla.: University of Miami Press, 1971), p. 225. In Chomsky, the subject-bearer of syntactic synthesis is clearly shown to stem from the Cartesian *cogito*. See his *Cartesian Linguistics: A Chapter in the History of Rationalist Thought* (New York: Harper & Row, 1966). Despite the difference between this Cartesian-Chomskyan subject and the transcendental ego outlined by Benveniste and others in a more clearly phenomenological sense, both these notions of the act of understanding (or the linguistic act) rest on a common metaphysical foundation: consciousness as a synthesizing unity and the sole guarantee of Being. Moreover, several scholars—without renouncing the Cartesian principles that governed the first syntactic descriptions—have recently pointed out that Husserlian phenomenology is a more explicit and more rigorously detailed basis for such description than the Cartesian method. See Roman Jakobson, who recalls Husserl's role in the establishment of modern linguistics, "Linguistics in Relation to Other Sciences," in *Selected Writings*, 2 vols. (The Hague: Mouton, 1971), 2:655–96; and S.-Y. Kuroda, "The Categorical and the Thetic Judgment: Evidence from Japanese Syntax," *Foundations of Language* 9 (November 1972): 153–85.

4. See the work of Ivan Fónagy, particularly "Bases pulsionnelles de la phonation," *Revue Française de Psychanalyse* 34 (January 1970): 101–36, and 35 (July 1971): 543–91.

5. On the "subject of enunciation," see Tzvetan Todorov, spec. ed., *Langages* 17 (March 1970). Formulated in linguistics by Benveniste ("The Correlations of Tense in the French Verb" and "Subjectivity in Language," in *Problems*, pp. 205–16 and 223–30), the notion is used by many linguists, notably Antoine Culioli, "A propos d'opérations intervenant dans le traitement formel des langues naturelles," *Mathématiques et Sciences Humaines* 9 (Summer 1971): 7–15; and Oswald Ducrot, "Les Indéfinis et l'énonciation," *Langages* 5 (March 1970): 91–111. Chomsky's "extended standard theory" makes use of categorial intuition but does not refer to the subject of enunciation, even though the latter has been implicit in his theory ever since *Cartesian Linguistics* (1966); see his *Studies on Semantics in Generative Grammar*, Janua Linguarum, series minor, no. 107 (The Hague: Mouton, 1972).

6. See John R. Searle, *Speech Acts: An Essay on the Philosophy of Language* (London: Cambridge University Press, 1969).

7. See Robert D. King, *Historical Linguistics and Generative Grammar* (Englewood Cliffs, N.J.: Prentice-Hall, 1969); Paul Kiparsky, "Linguistic Uni-

versals and Linguistic Change," in *Universals of Linguistic Theory*, Emmon Bach and Robert T. Harms, eds. (New York: Holt, Rinehart & Winston, 1968), pp. 170–202; and Kiparsky, "How Abstract Is Phonology?" mimeograph reproduced by Indiana University Linguistics Club, October 1968.

8. S.-Y. Kuroda distinguishes between two styles, "reportive" and "non-reportive." "Reportive" includes first-person narratives as well as those in the second and third person in which the narrator is "effaced"; "non-reportive" involves an omniscient narrator or "multi-consciousness." This distinction explains certain anomalies in the distribution of the adjective and verb of sensation in Japanese. (Common usage requires that the adjective be used with the first person but it can also refer to the third person. When it does, this agrammaticality signals another "grammatical style": an omniscient narrator is speaking in the name of a character, or the utterance expresses a character's point of view.) No matter what its subject of enunciation, the utterance, Kuroda writes, is described as representing that subject's *Erlebnis* ("experience"), in the sense Husserl uses the term in *Ideas*. See Kuroda, "Where Epistemology, Style, and Grammar Meet," mimeographed, University of California, San Diego, 1971.

9. Even the categories of dialectical materialism introduced to designate a discourse's conditions of production as essential bestowers of its signification are based on a "subject-bearer" whose logical positing is no different from that found in Husserl (see above, n. 3). For example, Cl. Haroche, P. Henry, and Michel Pêcheux stress "the importance of linguistic studies on the relation between utterance and enunciation, by which the 'speaking subject' situates himself with respect to the representations he *bears*—representations that are put together by means of the linguistically analyzable 'preconstructed.'" They conclude that "it is undoubtedly on this point—together with that of the syntagmatization of the characteristic substitutions of a discursive formation—that the contribution of the theory of discourse to the study of ideological formation (and the theory of ideologies) can now be most fruitfully developed." "La Sémantique et la coupure saussurienne: Langue, langage, discours," *Langages* 24 (December 1971): 106. This notion of the subject as always already there on the basis of a "preconstructed" language (but how is it constructed? and what about the subject *who constructs* before *bearing* what has been constructed?) has even been preserved under a Freudian cover. As a case in point, Michel Tort questions the relation between psychoanalysis and historical materialism by placing a subject-bearer between "ideological agency" and "unconscious formations." He defines this subject-bearer as "the biological specificity of individuals (individuality as a biological concept), inasmuch as it is the material basis upon which individuals are called to function by social relations." "La Psychanalyse dans le matérialisme historique," *Nouvelle Revue de Psychanalyse* 1 (Spring 1970): 154. But this theory provides only a hazy view of how this subject-bearer is produced through the unconscious and within the "ideological" signifier, and does not allow us to see this production's investment in ideological representations themselves. From this perspective, the only thing one can say about "arts" or "religions," for example, is that they are "relics." On language

and history, see also Jean-Claude Chevalier, "Langage et histoire," Langue Française 15 (September 1972): 3–17.

10. On the phenomenological bases of modern linguistics, see Kristeva, "Les Epistémologies de la linguistique," *Langages* 24 (December 1971): 11; and especially Jacques Derrida, "The Supplement of Copula: Philosophy before Linguistics," Josué V. Harari, tr., *Textual Strategies*, Josué V. Harari, ed. (Ithaca, N.Y.: Cornell University Press, 1979), pp. 82–120; *Of Grammatology*, Gayatri Chakravorty Spivak, tr. (Baltimore: Johns Hopkins University Press, 1976), pp. 27–73; and *Speech and Phenomena, and Other Essays on Husserl's Theory of Signs*, David B. Allison, introd. and tr. (Evanston, Ill.: Northwestern University Press, 1973).

11. The term *chora* has recently been criticized for its ontological essence by Jacques Derrida, *Positions*, Alan Bass, annotator and tr. (Chicago: University of Chicago Press, 1981), pp. 75 and 106, n. 39.

12. Plato emphasizes that the receptacle (ὑποδοχεῖον), which is also called space (χώρα) vis-à-vis reason, is necessary—but not divine since it is unstable, uncertain, ever changing, and becoming; it is even unnameable, improbable, bastard: "Space, which is everlasting, not admitting destruction; providing a situation for all things that come into being, but itself apprehended without the senses by a sort of bastard reasoning, and hardly an object of belief. This, indeed, is that which we look upon as in a dream and say that anything that is must needs be in some place and occupy some room." (*Timaeus*, Francis M. Cornford, tr., 52a–52b). Is the receptacle a "thing" or a mode of language? Plato's hesitation between the two gives the receptacle an even more uncertain status. It is one of the elements that antedate not only the *universe* but also *names* and even *syllables*: "We speak . . . positing them as original principles, elements (as it were, letters) of the universe; whereas one who has ever so little intelligence should not rank them in this analogy even so low as syllables" (ibid., 48b). "It is hard to say, with respect to any one of these, which we ought to call really water rather than fire, or indeed which we should call by any given name rather than by all the names together or by each severally, so as to use language in a sound and trustworthy way. . . . Since, then, in this way no one of these things ever makes its appearance as the same thing, which of them can we steadfastly affirm to be *this*—whatever it may be—and not something else, without blushing for ourselves? It cannot be done" (ibid., 49b–d).

13. There is a fundamental ambiguity: on the one hand, the receptacle is mobile and even contradictory, without unity, separable and divisible: presyllable, preword. Yet, on the other hand, because this separability and divisibility antecede numbers and forms, the space or receptacle is called *amorphous*; thus its suggested rhythmicity will in a certain sense be erased, for how can one think an articulation of what is not yet singular but is nevertheless necessary? All we may say of it, then, to make it intelligible, is that it is amorphous but that it "is of such and such a quality," not even an index or something in particular ("this" or "that"). Once named, it immediately becomes a container that takes the place of infinitely repeatable separability. This amounts to saying that this repeated

separability is "ontologized" the moment a *name* or a *word* replaces it, making it intelligible: "Are we talking idly whenever we say that there is such a thing as an intelligible Form of anything? Is this nothing more than a word?" (ibid., 51c). Is the Platonic *chora* the "nominability" of rhythm (of repeated separation)?

Why then borrow an ontologized term in order to designate an articulation that antecedes positing? First, the Platonic term makes explicit an insurmountable problem for discourse: once it has been named, that functioning, even if it is presymbolic, is brought back into a symbolic position. All discourse can do is differentiate, by means of a "bastard reasoning," the receptacle from the motility, which, by contrast, is not posited as being "a *certain* something" [*une telle*]. Second, this motility is the precondition for symbolicity, heterogeneous to it, yet indispensable. Therefore what needs to be done is to try to differentiate, always through a "bastard reasoning," the specific arrangements of this motility, without seeing them as recipients of accidental singularities, or a *Being* always posited in itself, or a projection of the *One*. Moreover, Plato invites us to differentiate in this fashion when he describes this motility, while gathering it into the receiving membrane: "But because it was filled with powers that were neither alike nor evenly balanced, there was no equipoise in any region of it; but it was everywhere swayed unevenly and shaken by these things, and by its motion shook them in turn. And they, being thus moved, were perpetually being separated and carried in different directions; just as when things are shaken and winnowed by means of winnowing baskets and other instruments for cleaning corn ... it separated the most unlike kinds farthest apart from one another, and thrust the most alike closest together; whereby the different kinds came to have different regions, even before the ordered whole consisting of them came to be ... but were altogether in such a condition as we should expect for anything when deity is absent from it" (ibid., 52d–53b). Indefinite "conjunctions" and "disjunctions" (functioning, devoid of Meaning), the *chora* is governed by a necessity that is not God's law.

14. The Platonic space or receptacle is a mother and wet nurse: "Indeed we may fittingly compare the Recipient to a mother, the model to a father, and the nature that arises between them to their offspring" (ibid., 50d); "Now the wet nurse of Becoming was made watery and fiery, received the characters of earth and air, and was qualified by all the other affections that go with these ..."; ibid., 52d; translation modified.

15. "Law," which derives etymologically from *lex*, necessarily implies the act of judgment whose role in safeguarding society was first developed by the Roman law courts. "Ordering," on the other hand, is closer to the series "rule," "norm" (from the Greek γνώμων, meaning "discerning" [adj.], "carpenter's square" [noun]), etc., which implies a numerical or geometrical necessity. On normativity in linguistics, see Alain Rey, "Usages, jugements et prescriptions linguistiques," *Langue Française* 16 (December 1972): 5. But the temporary ordering of the *chora* is not yet even a *rule*: the arsenal of geometry is posterior to the *chora*'s motility; it fixes the *chora* in place and reduces it.

16. Operations are, rather, an act of the subject of understanding.

Hans G. Furth, in *Piaget and Knowledge: Theoretical Foundations* (Engle-wood Cliffs, N.J.: Prentice-Hall, 1969), offers the following definition of "con-crete operations": "Characteristic of the first stage of operational intelligence. A concrete operation implies underlying general systems or 'groupings' such as classification, seriation, number. Its applicability is limited to objects considered as real (concrete)" (p. 260).—Trans.

17. Piaget stresses that the roots of sensorimotor operations precede language and that the acquisition of thought is due to the symbolic function, which, for him, is a notion separate from that of language per se. See Jean Piaget, "Language and Symbolic Operations," in *Piaget and Knowledge*, pp. 121–30.

18. By "function" we mean a dependent variable determined each time the independent variables with which it is associated are determined. For our pur-poses, a function is what links stases within the process of semiotic facilitation.

19. Such a position has been formulated by Lipot Szondi, *Experimental Diagnostic of Drives*, Gertrude Aull, tr. (New York: Grune & Stratton, 1952).

20. See James D. Watson, *The Double Helix: A Personal Account of the Discovery of the Structure of DNA* (London: Weidenfeld & Nicholson, 1968).

21. Throughout her writings, Melanie Klein emphasizes the "pre-Oedipal" phase, i.e., a period of the subject's development that precedes the "discovery" of castration and the positing of the superego, which itself is subject to (paternal) Law. The processes she describes for this phase correspond, *but on a genetic level*, to what we call the semiotic, as opposed to the symbolic, which underlies and conditions the semiotic. Significantly, these pre-Oedipal processes are organized through projection onto the mother's body, for girls as well as for boys: "at this stage of development children of both sexes believe that it is the body of their mother which contains all that is desirable, especially their father's penis." *The Psycho-analysis of Children*, Alix Strachey, tr. (London: Hogarth Press, 1932), p. 269. Our own view of this stage is as follows: Without "believing" or "desiring" any "object" whatsoever, the subject is in the process of constituting himself vis-à-vis a nonobject. He is in the process of separating from this nonobject so as to make that nonobject "one" and posit himself as "other": the mother's body is the not-yet-one that the believing and desiring subject will imagine as a "receptacle."

22. As for what situates the mother in symbolic space, we find the phallus again (see Jacques Lacan, "La Relation d'objet et les structures freudiennes," *Bulletin de Psychologie*, April 1957, pp. 426–30), represented by the mother's father, i.e., the subject's maternal grandfather (see Marie-Claire Boons, "Le Meurtre du Père chez Freud," *L'Inconscient* 5 [January–March 1968]: 101–29).

23. Though disputed and inconsistent, the Freudian theory of drives is of interest here because of the predominance Freud gives to the death drive in both "living matter" and the "human being." The death drive is transversal to iden-tity and tends to disperse "narcissisms" whose constitution ensures the link between structures and, by extension, life. But at the same time and conversely, narcissism and pleasure are only temporary positions from which the death drive blazes new paths [*se fraye de nouveaux passages*]. Narcissism and pleasure are therefore inveiglings and realizations of the death drive. The semiotic *chora*, con-

verting drive discharges into stases, can be thought of both as a delaying of the death drive and as a possible realization of this drive, which tends to return to a homeostatic state. This hypothesis is consistent with the following remark: "at the beginning of mental life," writes Freud, "the struggle for pleasure was far more intense than later but not so unrestricted: it had to submit to frequent interruptions." *Beyond the Pleasure Principle*, in *The Standard Edition of the Works of Sigmund Freud*, James Strachey, ed. (London: Hogarth Press and the Institute of Psychoanalysis, 1953), 18:63.

24. Mallarmé, *Oeuvres complètes* (Paris: Gallimard, 1945), pp. 382–87.

25. Ibid., p. 383.

26. Ibid., pp. 383 and 385.

27. Ibid., pp. 385–86.

28. Husserl, *Ideas*, p. 342.

29. In *Ideas*, posited meaning is "the unity of meaning and thetic character." "The concept of proposition (*Satz*)," Husserl writes, "is certainly extended thereby in an exceptional way that may alienate sympathy, yet it remains within the limits of an important unity of essence. We must constantly bear in mind that for us the concepts of meaning (*Sinn*) and posited meaning (or position) (*Satz*) contain nothing of the nature of expression and conceptual meaning, but on the other hand include all explicit propositions and all propositional meanings" (*Ideas*, p. 369). Further on, the inseparability of posited meaning, meaning, and the object is even more clearly indicated: "According to our analyses these concepts indicate an abstract stratum belonging to the *full tissue of all noemata* [emphasis added]. To grasp this stratum in its all-enveloping generality, and thus to realize that it is represented in *all act-spheres*, has a wide bearing on our way of knowledge. Even in the plain and simple *intuitions* the concepts meaning (*Sinn*) and posited meaning (*Satz*) which belong inseparably to the concept of object (*Gegenstand*) have their necessary application." (pp. 369–70).

30. On the matrix of the sign as the structura of a logical proof, see Emile Bréhier, *La Théorie des incorporels dans l'ancien stoicisme* (Paris: J. Vrin, 1970).

31. "The fact is that the total form of the body by which the subject anticipates in a mirage the maturation of his power is given to him only as *Gestalt*, that is to say, in an exteriority in which this form is certainly more constituent than constituted, but in which it appears to him above all in a contrasting size (*un relief de stature*) that fixes it and in a symmetry that inverts it, in contrast with the turbulent movements that the subject feels are animating him." Lacan, "The Mirror Stage as Formative of the Function of the I," in *Ecrits/A Selection*, Alan Sheridan, tr. (New York: Norton, 1977), p. 2.

32. "The Subversion of the Subject and the Dialectic of Desire in the Freudian Unconscious," *Ecrits/A Selection*, p. 319.

33. In Lacan's terminology, castration and the phallus are defined as "position," "localization," and "presence": "We know that the unconscious castration complex has the function of a knot: . . . (2) in a regulation of the development that gives its *ratio* to this first role: namely, the *installation* in the subject of an unconscious *position* without which he would be unable to identify himself

with the ideal type of his sex . . . " ("The Signification of the Phallus," *Ecrits/A Selection*, p. 281; emphasis added). "We know that in this term Freud specifies the first genital maturation: on the one hand, it would seem to be characterized by the imaginary dominance of the phallic attribute and by masturbatory *jouissance* and, on the other, it *localizes* this *jouissance* for the woman in the clitoris, which is thus raised to the function of the phallus" (p. 282; emphasis added). "[The phallus] is the signifier intended to *designate* as a whole the effects of the signified, in that the signifier conditions them by its *presence* as a signifier" (p. 285; emphasis added).

34. Lacan himself has suggested the term "want-to-be" for his neologism (*manque à être*). Other proposed translations include "want-of-being" (Leon S. Roudiez, personal communication) and "constitutive lack" (Jeffrey Mehlman, "The 'Floating Signifier': From Lévi-Strauss to Lacan," *Yale French Studies* 48 (1972): 37).—Trans.

35. *Ecrits/A Selection*, p. 299.

36. Ibid.

37. Our definition of language as deriving from the death drive finds confirmation in Lacan: "From the approach that we have indicated, the reader should recognize in the metaphor of the return to the inanimate (which Freud attaches to every living body) that margin beyond life that language gives to the human being by virtue of the fact that he speaks, and which is precisely that in which such a being places in the position of a signifier, not only those parts of his body that are exchangeable, but this body itself" ("The Subversion of the Subject and the Dialectic of Desire in the Freudian Unconscious," *Ecrits/A Selection*, p. 301). We would add that the symbolism of magic is based on language's capacity to store up the death drive by taking it out of the body. Lévi-Strauss suggests this when he writes that "the relationship between monster and disease is internal to [the patient's] mind, whether conscious or unconscious: It is a relationship between symbol and thing symbolized, or, to use the terminology of linguists, between signifier and signified. The shaman provides the sick woman with a *language*, by means of which unexpressed and otherwise unexpressible psychic states can be immediately expressed. And it is the transition to this verbal expression—at the same time making it possible to undergo in an ordered and intelligible form a real experience that would otherwise be chaotic and inexpressible—which induces the release of the physiological process, that is, the reorganization, in a favorable direction, of the process to which the sick woman is subjected." Claude Lévi-Strauss, "The Effectiveness of Symbols," in *Structural Anthropology*, 2 vols., Claire Jacobson and Brooke Grundfest Schoepf, trs. (New York: Basic Books, 1963), 1:197–98; translation modified.

38. See Lacan, "On a Question Preliminary to Any Possible Treatment of Psychosis," in *Ecrits/A Selection*, p. 197.

39. "The theory of textual writing's history may be termed 'monumental history' insofar as it serves as a 'ground' [*fait fond*] in a literal way, in relation to a 'cursive,' figural (teleological) history which has served at once to constitute and dissimulate a written/exterior space. . . . Writing 'that recognizes the rupture' is

therefore irreducible to the classical (representational) concept of 'written text': what it writes is never more than one part of itself. It makes the rupture the intersection of two sets (two irreconcilable states of language)," Philippe Sollers writes, "Program," in *Writing and the Experience of Limits*, David Hayman, ed., Philip Barnard and David Hayman, trs. (New York: Columbia University Press, 1983), p. 7. Our reading of Lautréamont and Mallarmé will attempt to follow these principles; see *La Révolution du langage poétique* (Paris: Seuil, 1974), pp. 361–609.

40. Indeed, even Lacanian theory, although it establishes the signifier as absolute master, makes a distinction between two modalities of the signifier represented by the two levels of the "completed graph" (*Ecrits/A Selection*, p. 314). On the one hand, the *signifier* as "signifier's treasure," as distinct from the *code*, "for it is not that the univocal correspondence of a sign with something is preserved in it, but that the signifier is constituted only from a synchronic and enumerable collection of elements in which each is sustained only by the principle of its opposition to each of the others" (p. 304). Drives function within this "treasure of the signifiers" (p. 314), which is also called a signifying "battery." But from that level on, and even beforehand, the subject submits to the signifier, which is shown as a "punctuation in which the signification is constituted as finished product" (p. 304). In this way the path from the treasure to punctuation forms a "previous site of the pure subject of the signifier," which is not yet, however, the true place [*lieu*] of the Other. On that level, the psychotic "dance" unfolds, the "pretense" [*feinte*] that "is satisfied with that previous Other," accounted for by game theory. The fact remains that this *previous site* does not exhaust the question of signification because the subject is not constituted from the code that lies in the Other, but rather from the message emitted by the Other. Only when the Other is distinguished from all other partners, unfolding as signifier and signified—and, as a result, articulating himself within an always already sentential signification and thus transmitting messages—only then are the preconditions for language ("speech") present.

At this second stage, the signifier is not just a "treasure" or a "battery" but a *place* [*lieu*]: "But it is clear that Speech begins only with the passage from 'pretense' to the order of the signifier, and that the signifier requires another locus—the locus of the Other, the Other witness, the witness Other than any of the partners—for the Speech that it supports to be capable of lying, that is to say, of presenting itself as Truth" (p. 305). Only from this point will the ego start to take on various configurations. What seems problematic about this arrangement, or in any case what we believe needs further development, is the way in which the "battery," the "treasure" of the signifier, functions. In our opinion, game theory cannot completely account for this functioning, nor can a signification be articulated until an alterity is *distinctly posited* as such. One cannot speak of the "signifier" before the positing or the thesis of the Other, the articulation of which begins only with the mirror stage. But what of the previous processes that are not yet "a site," but a *functioning*? The thetic phase will establish this functioning as a signifying *order* (though it will not stop it) and will return in this order.

41. *Effraction*, in French, is the juridical term for "breaking and entering"; in Kristeva's sense it also means a "breaking into" or "breaking through." I have translated it as "breach": the act or result of breaking and, more significantly, an infraction or violation as of a law.—Trans.

42. It has recently been emphasized that *mimesis* is not an imitation of an object but a reproduction of the trajectory of enunciation; in other words, *mimesis* departs from denotation (in Frege's sense) and confines itself to meaning. Roland Barthes makes this explicit: "The function of narrative is not to 'represent,' it is to constitute a spectacle still very enigmatic for us . . . Logic has here an emancipatory value—and with it the entire narrative. It may be that men ceaselessly re-inject into narrative what they have known, what they have experienced; but if they do, at least it is in a form which has vanquished repetition and instituted the model of a process of becoming. Narrative does not show, does not imitate; the passion which may excite us in reading a novel is not that of a 'vision' (in actual fact, we do not 'see' anything). Rather it is that of meaning . . . ; 'what happens' is language alone, the adventure of language, the unceasing celebration of its coming." Barthes, "Introduction to the Structuralist Analysis of Narratives," in *Image, Music, Text*, Stephen Heath, tr. (New York: Hill & Wang, 1977), pp. 123–24. This is also what Goethe means when he writes: "In your own mode of rhyme my feet I'll find, / The repetitions of pleasures shall incite: / At first the sense and then the words I'll find [Erst werd ich Sinn, sodann auch Worte finden], / No sound a second time will I indite / Unless thereby the meaning is refined / As you, with peerless gifts, have shown aright!" But this analysis of meaning through sounds must result in a new device that is not just a new meaning but also a new "form": "Measured rhythms are indeed delightful, / And therein a pleasing talent basks; / But how quickly they can taste so frightful, / There's no blood nor sense in hollow masks [Hohle Masken ohne Blut und Sinn]. / Even wit must shudder at such tasks / If it can't, with new form occupied, / Put an end at last to form that's died." "Imitation" [*Nachbildung*], *West-Eastern Divan/West-Oestlicher Divan*, J. Whaley, tr. (London: Oswald Wolff, 1974), pp. 34–37.

43. This is why Lacan stated in his spring 1972 seminar that the expression *Die Bedeutung des Phallus* is a tautology.

44. See Jakobson, "L'importanza di Kruszewski per lo sviluppo della linguistica generale," *Ricerche Slavistiche* 14 (1967): 1–20.

45. See Lacan, *Ecrits/A Selection*, pp. 156–57, et passim.

46. See Kristeva, *Le Texte du roman: Approche sémiologique d'une structure discursive transformationnelle* (The Hague: Mouton, 1970).

47. "We have not yet referred to any other sort of displacement [*Verschiebung*]. Analyses show us, however, that another sort exists and that it reveals itself in a change in the *verbal expression* of the thoughts concerned . . . One element is replaced by another [ein Element seine Wortfassung gegen eine andere vertauscht]. . . . Any one thought, whose form of expression may happen to be fixed for other reasons, will operate in a determinant and selective manner on the possible forms of expression allotted to the other thoughts, and it may do so, per-

haps, from the very start—as is the case in writing a poem [Der eine Gedanke, dessen Ausdruck etwa aus anderen Gründen feststeht, wird dabei verteilend und auswählend auf die Ausdrucksmöglichkeiten des anderen einwirken, und dies vielleicht von vorneherein, ähnlich wie bei der Arbeit des Dichters]." *The Interpretation of Dreams, Standard Edition*, 5:339–40; *Gesammelte Werke* (London: Imago, 1942), 2–3:344–45. See "La Transposition, le déplacement, la condensation," *La Révolution du langage poétique*, pp. 230–39.

48. Goethe speaks of this when, describing the Arabic tradition, he calls to mind the poet whose role is to express "Undeniable truth indelibly: / But there are some small points here and there / Which exceed the limits of the law [Ausgemachte Wahreit unauslöschlich: / Aber hie und da auch Kleinigkeiten / Ausserhalb der Grenze des Gesetzes]." "Fetwa," *West-Eastern Divan*, pp. 30–33.

49. "Yet this 'object of perspective,' may be handled in different ways. In fetishism (and, in my view, in art works), it pushes itself into the great ambiguous realm of disavowal, and materializes . . . As a result, we see . . . that all scientific or esthetic observation or activity has a part to play in the fate reserved for the 'perspective object,'" writes Guy Rosolato, "Le Fétishisme dont se 'dérobe' l'objet," *Nouvelle Revue de Psychanalyse* 2 (Autumn 1970): 39.

For a more complete account of this concept in English, see Rosolato, "Symbol Formation," *International Journal of Psychoanalysis* 59 (1978): 303–13.—Trans.

50. As Jean Pouillon remarks, "if words were merely fetishes, semantics would be reduced to phonology." "Fétiches sans fétichisme," *Nouvelle Revue de Psychanalyse* 2 (Autumn 1970): 147.

51. By contrast, discourse in Molière's "Femmes savantes" is an exemplary case of the fetishizing process since it focuses exclusively on the signifier. "It is indeed the sign that becomes an erotic object and not the 'erotic' signified of discourse, as is usual in simple cases of repression (obscene talk or graffiti). It is not obsession but perversion." Josette Rey-Debove, "L'Orgie langagière," *Poétique* 12 (1972): 579.

52. See John von Neumann, *The Computer and the Brain* (New Haven: Yale University Press, 1958).

53. Anthony Wilden, "Analog and Digital Communication," *Semiotica* 6, no. 1 (1972): 50–51.

Kristeva gives a loose translation of these passages in French. I have restored the original English quotation. Wilden, it should be noted, uses "computer" in the broad sense, whether the device actually computes in the strict sense or not.—Trans.

54. Ibid., p. 55.

55. Benveniste has taught us not to confuse these two operations, but rather to call something a language only when it has a double articulation; the distinction between phonemes devoid of meaning and morphemes as elements—for which no code is pertinent—is a *social*, specifically human occurrence. See "Animal Communication and Human Language," *Problems*, pp. 49–54.

56. This is what Hegel believes. At the end of the "Larger Logic," describing negativity as that which constructs absolute knowledge, he writes: "This negativity, as self-transcending contradiction, is the *reconstitution of the first immediacy*, of simple universality; for, immediately, the Other of the Other and the negative of the negative is the *positive, identical*, and *universal*." *Hegel's Science of Logic*, W. H. Johnston and L. G. Struthers, trs., 2 vols. (London: Allen & Unwin, 1929; 1966), 2:478; emphasis added.

57. *Moses and Monotheism, Standard Edition*, 23:7–137.

58. The two roles have often merged, as Georges Dumézil reminds us in *Mitra-Varuna* (Paris: Gallimard, 1948). See "Deux conceptions de la souveraineté," *La Révolution du langage poétique*, pp. 545–52.

59. See "Shifters, Verbal Categories, and the Russian Verb," in Jakobson, *Selected Writings*, 2:130–47.

60. See Joseph Needham, *Science and Civilisation in China*, 4 vols. (Cambridge: Cambridge University Press, 1960), vol. 1.

61. From a similar perspective, Edgar Morin writes: "We can think of magic, mythologies, and ideologies both as mixed systems, making affectivity rational and rationality affective, and as outcomes of combining: a) fundamental drives, b) the chancy play of fantasy, and c) logico-constructive systems. (To our mind, the theory of myth must be based on triunic syncretism rather than unilateral logic.)" He adds, in a note, that "myth does not have a single logic but a synthesis of three kinds of logic." "Le Paradigme perdu: La Nature humaine," paper presented at the "Invariants biologiques et universaux culturels" Colloquium, Royaumont, September 6–9, 1972.

62. Lacan presented this typology of discourse at his 1969 and 1970 seminars.

Negativity: Rejection

> *The negative having been in all probability greatly strengthened by the "struggle," a decision between insanity and security is imminent.*
> —*Kafka*, Diaries, *February 2, 1922*

1. The Fourth "Term" of the Dialectic

The notion of *negativity* (*Negativität*), which may be thought of as both the cause and the organizing principle of the *process*, comes from Hegel.[1] The concept of negativity, distinct from that of nothingness (*Nichts*) and negation (*Negation*), figures as the indissoluble relation between an "ineffable" mobility and its "particular determination." Negativity is the mediation, the supersession of the "pure abstractions" of being and nothingness in the concrete where they are both only moments. Although *negativity* is a concept and therefore belongs to a contemplative (theoretical) system, it reformulates the static *terms* of pure abstraction as a process, dissolving and binding them within a mobile law. Thus, while still maintaining their dualism, negativity recasts not only the theses of *being* and *nothingness*, but all categories used in the contemplative system: universal and particular, indeterminate and determinate, quality and quantity, negation and affirmation, and the like. Negativity constitutes the logical impetus beneath the thesis of negation and that of the negation of negation, but is identical to neither since it is, instead, the logical functioning of the movement that produces the theses.

Lenin noted Hegel's statement that the "triplicity" of the dialectic is its "external, superficial side."[2] By contrast, negativity is the liquefying and dissolving agent that does not destroy but rather reactivates new organizations and, in that sense, affirms. As transition (*Übergang*), negativity constitutes an *enchaînement in the choreographical sense, "the necessary connection" and "the immanent emergence of distinctions." Here Lenin writes:*

> Very important!! This is what it means, in my opinion:
>
> 1) *Necessary* connection, the objective connection of all the aspects, forces, tendencies, etc., of the given sphere of phenomena;
> 2) The "immanent *emergence* of distinctions"—the inner objective logic of evolution and of the struggle of the differences, polarity.

Lenin underscores and accepts the notion of "inherent negativity" as an *objective* principle—the principle of all physical and spiritual life—and not as a simple "subjective craving to shake and break down what is fixed and true."[3] In the final analysis, dialectical materialism will inherit from Hegel's dialectic this and only this founding principle; it will reinstate materialist dualism and see negativity at work in and through two differentiated and heterogeneous orders.

Before returning to this heteronomy, we would like to stress that the Hegelian conception of negativity already prepared the way for the very possibility of thinking a materialist *process*. While remaining an intraspeculative notion, Hegelian negativity bursts, as it were, from within its conceptual unity since it links [*enchaîne*]—unleashes [*déchaîne*]—the "real" and the "conceptual," the objective and the subjective, and, if one wished to find its representation, culminates in the ethical order: although it is *objectivity* itself, negativity is at the same time and for that very reason the "free subject." The *ethics* that develops in the process of negativity's unfolding is not the kind of "ethics" that consists in obedience to laws. It amounts instead to the corruption and absorption of laws by what Hegel calls the aesthetic. The subject of that Hegelian aesthetic—the free subject par excellence—reveals the diremption [*épuisement*] of the ethical subject and effects its *Aufhebung* in order to reintroduce him into a process of transformation of community relations and discursive strata.[4] The logical definition given to this negativity is freedom "for itself": "The highest form of nothingness [taken] for itself is *freedom*, but it is negativity to the extent that it goes as deep into itself as possible, and is itself affirmation."[5]

As the logical expression of the objective process, negativity can only produce a subject in process/on trial. In other words, the subject, constituted by the law of negativity and thus by the law of an objective reality, is necessarily suffused by negativity—opened onto and by objectivity, he is mobile, nonsubjected, free. A subject submerged in negativity is no longer "outside" objective negativity as a transcendent unity or a specifically regulated monad; instead he positions himself as the "*innermost* and *most objective* moment of Life and Spirit." This Hegelian principle is the ferment of dialectical materialism, where it becomes both the concept of *human activity* as revolutionary activity and that of the *social and natural laws* this activity shows to be objective. Hegel writes:

> The negativity which has just been considered is the *turning-point* of the Notion. It is the simple point of negative self-relation, the internal source of all activity, vital and spiritual self-movement, the dialectic soul which all truth has in it and through which it alone is truth; for the transcendence of the opposition between the Notion and Reality, and that unity which is the truth, rest upon this subjectivity alone.— The second negative, the negative of the negative, which we have reached, is this transcendence of the contradiction but is no more the *activity* of *an* external reflection than the contradiction is; it is the *innermost* and *most objective* moment of Life and Spirit, by virtue of which a subject, the person, the free, has being.

Lenin notes in the margins of this passage: "the kernel of dialectics," "the criterion of truth (the unity of the concept and reality)."[6]

But the materialist dialectic will retain only one element of the subject's negativation: his subordination, as a unit, to the social and natural process. Inheriting the weak points of dialectical materialist logic, dog-matico-revisionism will either dismiss the very problem of the subject and retain only the process of substance in a Spinozistic sense or the process of modes of production (as in dogmatism); or else it will hyposta-size a psychological "subject" that has no process and only an external negativity (as in revisionism).

Let us take a closer look at the vicissitudes and dead ends of Hegelian negativity. If "the truth is, not either Being or Nothing, but that Being—not passes—but *has passed over* into Nothing, and Nothing into Being" (emphasis added), and if "their truth is therefore this *movement*, this immediate disappearance of the one into the other, in a word, *Becoming*; a movement wherein both are distinct, but in virtue of a distinction which has equally immediately dissolved itself,"[7] then we see that this supersession amounts to the erasing of heterogeneity within the Hegelian dialectic. Nothing, posited as such or active as a *relation* in negativity, can only be a *Becoming* or an *abstract negation*: the "absolute void" in Oriental systems. When negativity is considered a logical operation, it becomes reified as a void, as an absolute zero—the zero used in logic and serving at its base—or else as a connective in the logical Becoming. Yet what the dialectic represents as negativity, indeed Nothing, is precisely that which remains outside logic (as the signifier of a subject), what remains heterogeneous to logic even while producing it through a move-ment of separation or rejection, something that has the necessary objec-tivity of a law and can be seen as the logic of matter. This notion is pos-sible because of and in spite of Hegel because he maintains, in opposition to Spinoza, the inseparability, the interpenetration, indeed the contradic-tion of "Being" and "Nothing" even if only within the sphere of the Idea:

> Those who assert the proposition that Nothing is just Nothing, and even grow heated in its defence, do not know that in so doing they are subscribing to the abstract Pantheism of the Eleatics and, in essentials, of Spinoza. That view in philosophy which takes for principle that Being is merely Being, and Nothing merely Nothing, deserves the name of system of identity: this abstract identity is the essence of Pantheism.[8]

To those surprised by this thesis of the inseparability of Being and Nothing, Hegel objected that such "wonderment . . . forgets that in this Science [philosophy] there occur determinations quite different from those of ordinary consciousness and so-called common-sense,—which is not exactly sound understanding, but understanding educated up to abstractions and the faith, or rather superstition, of abstractions."[9]

A *negativity* inseparable from the Hegelian notion of *Being* is thus precisely what splits and prevents the closing up of Being within an abstract and superstitious understanding. It points to an outside that Hegel could only think of as something inherent in belief, and which his phenomenological descendants would posit as a negative theology. We nevertheless maintain that Hegelian negativity prevents the immobilization of the thetic, unsettles doxy, and lets in all the semiotic motility that prepares and exceeds it. Hegel, moreover, defines this negativity as the *fourth term* of the true dialectic: triplicity is only an appearance in the realm of the Understanding.[10]

The logic exposed above will become materialist when, with the help of Freud's discovery, one dares think negativity as the *very movement of heterogeneous matter*, inseparable from its differentiation's symbolic function. Although in Kant this material movement of scission, of rejection (to which we shall return), remains a "negative" term for the understanding, it is conceived dialectically, *because it is considered inseparable from Being*, as a fundamental *positivity*: "In this respect therefore mere Unseparateness or Inseparability would be a good substitute for Unity; but these would not express the affirmative nature of the relation of the whole."[11]

Thus, even while maintaining Kantian oppositions, the Hegelian dialectic moves toward a fundamental reorganization of these oppositions—one that will establish an *affirmative negativity*, a *productive dissolution* in place of "Being" and "Nothing." The theology inherent in this reorganization will, however, leave its mark in an implicit teleology: namely, the *Becoming* that subordinates, indeed erases, the moment of rupture.

7. Freud's Notion of Expulsion: Rejection

Rejection, or expenditure, constitutes the key moment shattering unity, yet it is unthinkable outside unity, for rejection presupposes thetic unity as its precondition and horizon, one to be always superseded and exceeded. Rejection serves to bind only to the extent that it is the *precondition* of the binding that takes place on another scene. To posit rejection as fundamental and inherent in every thesis does not mean that we posit it as origin. Rejection rejects origin since it is always already the repetition of an impulse that is itself a rejection. Its law is one of returning, as opposed to one of becoming; it returns only to separate again immediately and thus appear as an impossible forward movement.

Of the terms "rejection," "scission," and "separation," *rejection* is the one that best designates, archaeologically, the instinctual, repetitive, and transsignifying aspect of the dynamics of signifiance. It implies a preverbal "function," one that is prelogical and a-logical in the sense that the *logos* signifies a "relation," a "connection." *Scission* and *separation* are more appropriate terms for that rupture when it is considered from the point of view of the subject and already constituted meaning, which is to say, within a perspective that takes into account language and the unity of the subject—a signifying sociality dependent on norms. We shall stress the first term (*rejection*) because it suggests the heterogeneity of signifiance we are attempting to demonstrate, and because, within the text, it opens up an a-signifying, indeed prelinguistic, crucible. But we shall use the other terms (*scission* and *separation*) as well because they emphasize the underlying unity which withdraws and is reconstituted in the return of rejection. They also signal the permanent logical constraint of an insurmountable *consciousness*, which ensures the reactivation of rejection in a process, thus saving it from foundering in inarticulable instinctuality, where signifying production would be impossible. Our conception of rejection will oscillate between the two poles of drives and consciousness, and this ambiguity will reveal the ambiguity of process itself, which is both divided and unitary. But to the extent that these two threads (drives and consciousness) intersect and interweave, the *unity of reason* which consciousness sketches out will always be shattered by the *rhythm* suggested by drives: repetitive rejection seeps in through "prosody," and so forth, preventing the stasis of One meaning, One myth, One logic.

In Freud's article on *Verneinung* [negation], expulsion (*Ausstossung*) is what constitutes the real object as such; it also constitutes it as lost, thus setting up the symbolic function. For the pleasure-ego, the oral ego of incorporation and unification (*Einbeziehung*), the outside does not matter. Expulsion (*Ausstossung*) establishes an outside that is never definitively separate—one that is always in the process of being posited. But in doing so, it already runs counter to the unifying pleasure principle and sets up the most radical exteriority: the struggle with the latter will represent the recipient *topos*, the mobile *chora* of the subject in process/on trial. The pleasure principle, which unifies and identifies, seems to have been conceived by Freud as an aid to repression. Expulsion (and its symbolic representation in the sign of negation), acting against the pleasure principle, acts against the consequences of repression. "The performance of the function of judgement is not made possible," writes

Freud, "until the creation of the symbol of negation has endowed think-ing with a first measure of freedom from the consequences of repression and, with it, from the compulsion of the pleasure principle."[12]

Significantly, in thinking the establishment of the symbolic function through the symbol of negation, Freud remarks that the symbolic func-tion is instituted on the basis of *expulsion* (*Ausstossung*, referred to as *Verwerfung* [foreclosure] in "Wolf Man"),[13] but says nothing about the "drive bases" of this "act," or about the drive that activates this "kineme": in other words, he says nothing about rejection. As a result of this omission, Freud sets up an opposition, via expulsion, between the symbolic function and *Einbeziehung*—unification, incorporation—which refers to orality and pleasure. The symbolic function is thereby dissociated from all pleasure, made to oppose it, and is set up as the paternal place, the place of the superego. According to this view, the only way to react against the consequences of repression imposed by the com-pulsion of the pleasure principle is to renounce pleasure through sym-bolization by setting up the sign through the absence of the object, which is expelled and forever lost.

What this interpretation seems to rule out is the pleasure underlying the symbolic function of expulsion, a pleasure which this function represses but that can return to it and, when combined with oral plea-sure, disturb, indeed dismantle, the symbolic function. In any case, it can transform ideation into an "artistic game," corrupt the symbolic through the return of drives, and make it a semiotic device, a mobile *chora*. This pleasure derives from the anal drive—anal rejection, anality—in which Freud sees the sadistic component of the sexual instinct and which he identifies with the death drive. We would like to stress the importance of anal rejection or anality, which precedes the establishment of the sym-bolic and is both its precondition and its repressed element. Because the process of the subject involves the process of his language and/or of the symbolic function itself, this implies—within the economy of the body bearing it—a reactivation of anality. The texts of Lautréamont, Jarry, and Artaud—among others—explicitly point to the anal drive that agi-tates the subject's body in his subversion of the symbolic function.

Freud's silence, both on the subject of anality and in front of Signor-elli's frescoes, is not just the symptom of a certain blindness toward homosexuality, which, to his credit, he nevertheless sees at the basis of social institutions. His silence is also bound up with psychoanalysis' silence about the way the literary function subverts the symbolic function and puts the subject in process/on trial. Although psychoanalysis may speak of fantasies in literature, it never mentions the economy of the subject bound up with those fantasies that dissolves the symbolic and language. If the return of rejection, by corrupting both the symbolic and sublimation in modern texts, attests to the presence of the death drive—a destruction of both the living being and the subject—how can we neglect the jouissance harbored by this "aggressivity," this "sadistic component"? The jouissance of destruction (or, if you will, of the "death drive"), which the text manifests through language, passes through an unburying of repressed, sublimated anality. In other words, before arranging itself in a new semiotic network, before forming the new structure which will be the "literary work," the not yet symbolized drive and the "residues of first symbolizations" attack, through unburied anality and fully cognizant of homosexuality, all the stases of the signifying process: sign, language, identifying family structure.

It will now be helpful to recall in more detail the role that rejection and jouissance play in the symbolic function and in putting that function in process/on trial. Although the sadistic component of the sexual instinct makes a veiled appearance in both the oral and genital phase, it dominates the anal phase and is so essential to libidinal economy that Freud recognizes that there might be such a thing as a primary sadism, one "that has been turned round upon the subject's own ego" before any object has been isolated, and would hence constitute primary masochism.[14] What we mean by *rejection* is precisely the semiotic mode of this permanent aggressivity and the possibility of its being *posited*, and thus *renewed*. Although it is destructive—a "death drive"—rejection is the very mechanism of reactivation, tension, life; aiming toward the equalization of tension, toward a state of inertia and death, it *perpetuates* tension and life.

The anal phase designated by psychoanalysis comes before the Oedipus conflict and the separation of the ego from the id in Freudian topography. This phase concludes a more extensive and more fundamental period for the infantile libido: the period called *sadistic*, which predominates before the Oedipus complex begins and constitutes an oral, muscular, urethral, and anal sadism. In all these forms, of which the anal is the last to be repressed and hence the most important, energy surges and discharges erotize the glottic, urethral, and anal sphincters as well as the kinetic system. These drives move through the sphincters and arouse pleasure at the very moment substances belonging to the body are separated and rejected from the body. This acute pleasure therefore coincides with a loss, a separation from the body, and the isolating of objects outside it. Before the body itself is posited as a detached alterity, and hence the real object, this expulsion of objects is the subject's fundamental experience of separation—a separation which is not a lack, but a discharge, and which, although privative, arouses pleasure. The psychoanalyst assumes that this jubilant loss is simultaneously felt as an attack against the expelled object, all exterior objects (including father and mother), and the body itself.

The problem then becomes how to hold this "aggressivity" in check. In other words, how does one curb the pleasure of separation caused by rejection, the ambivalence of which (the body's jouissance plus the loss of body parts) constitutes a nexus of the pleasure and threat that characterizes drives. The "normal," Oedipal way of curbing this pleasure consists in identifying the body proper with one of the parents during the Oedipal stage. At the same time, the rejected object definitively separates and is not simply rejected but suppressed as a material object; it is the "opposite other" [*l'autre en face*] with whom only one relation is possible—that of the sign, symbolic relation *in absentia*. Rejection is thus a step on the way to the object's becoming-sign, at which the object will be detached from the body and isolated as a real object. In other words, rejection is a step on the way to the imposition of the *superego*.

However, as cases of child schizophrenia prove, the violence of rejection and of the anal pleasure it produces is sometimes so powerful that Oedipal identification cannot absorb and symbolize them by setting up a signifiable, real object. In such instances, the body is unable to "defend" itself against rejection through suppression or repression and the pleasure aroused by the return of rejection immobilizes the body there. Rejection and sadism, which is its psychological side, return and disturb the symbolic chains put in place by the Oedipal complex. Melanie Klein interprets the behavior "disturbances" that result as the organism's "defenses" against the danger of aggressivity. But she recognizes that "this defense . . . is of a *violent* character and differs fundamentally from the later mechanism of repression," which symbolism establishes.[15] These "defenses" are resistances, *thetic substitutes* for the "violent" drive process, which, far from having a psychological value of prevention, *arrange* the "sadistic" drive charge, *articulate* rejection in such a way that it is not subsumed by the construction of a *superego* (as is the case in the Oedipus complex). The distortion of words, the repetition of words and syntagms, and hyperkinesia or stereotypy reveal that a *semiotic network*—the *chora*—has been established, one that simultaneously defies both verbal symbolization and the formation of a superego patterned after paternal law and sealed by language acquisition.

Indeed, the acquisition of language and notably syntactic structure, which constitutes its normativeness, is parallel to the mirror stage.[16] Language acquisition implies the suppression of anality; in other words, it represents the acquisition of a capacity for symbolization through the definitive detachment of the rejected object, through its repression under the sign. Every return of rejection and of the erotic pleasure it produces in the sphincters disturbs this symbolic capacity and the acquisition of language that fulfills it. By inserting itself into the signifying system of language, rejection either delays its acquisition or, in the case of the schizoid child, prevents it altogether. In the adult, this return to nonsublimated, nonsymbolized anality breaks up the linearity of the signifying chain, and suffuses it with paragrams and glossolalia.[17] In this sense, interjections—those semiotic devices that run through modern phenotexts[18] and become rhythmic expectorations in Artaud—convey the struggle of a nonsublimated anality against the superego. Ideologically, this transformation of the signifying chain attacks, provokes, and unveils repressed sadism—the anality underlying social apparatuses.

There exist two signifying modalities that seem to permit the survival of rejection to the extent that they harmonize the shattering brought about by rejection, affirm it, and make it positive without suppressing it under paranoid paternal unity. The first of these modalities is *oralization*: a reunion with the mother's body, which is no longer viewed as an engendering, hollow, and vaginated, expelling and rejecting body, but rather as a vocalic one—throat, voice, and breasts: music, rhythm, prosody, paragrams, and the matrix of the prophetic parabola; the Oedipus complex of a far-off incest, "signifying," the real if not reality. The second modality, always inseparable from the first, appears in the reunion with brothers' bodies, in the reconstitution of a *homosexual phratry* that will forever pursue, tirelessly and interminably, the murder of the One, the Father, in order to impose *one* logic, *one* ethics, *one* signified: *one*, but *other*, critical, combatant, revolutionary—the brothers in Freud's primal horde, for example, or Michelangelo's "Battle of the Centaurs" in Florence.

These two modalities—oralization and the homosexual phratry— point to the two sides—"poetic" and "mastering"—of texts, situated on the path of rejection, which carry out the signifying process by making it a production for community use. The "poetic" side of the text can be seen in the supposedly pianistic scansion of sentences in *Maldoror*, Mallarméan rhythmics, the iciness of "Hérodiade," or in the opulent chic of Méry Laurent, coveted by the Parisian poetic inner circle. Examples vary: from preciosity and snobbery (a token of the forbidden, idealized, and oralized mother) to the glottal spasm in Malarmé; or, in Lautréamont, a mother who is oceanic and submissive though she is also the overpossessive lover of the hanged man. The Hegelian philosophy in Mallarmé's A Throw of the Dice and Igitur,[19] the monastic, sacramental, and ritual call of his Le "Livre", and the broken and then restored logic of Lautréamont's Poems show that the second, "mastering" modality is a lining of the first, "poetic" modality.

Oralization can be a mediator between the fundamental sadism of rejection and its signifying sublimation. Melody, harmony, rhythm, the "sweet," "pleasant" sounds and poetic musicality found in "symbolist" poetry and in Mallarmé, for example, may be interpreted as oralization. This oralization restrains the aggressivity of rejection through an attempted fusion with the mother's body, a devouring fusion: Mallarmé's biography documents this attempt. A return to oral and glottal pleasure combats the superego and its linear language, which is characterized by the subject/predicate sequences of its syntagms. Suction or expulsion, fusion with or rejection of the mother's breast seem to be at the root of this erotization of the vocal apparatus and, through it, the introduction into the linguistic order of an excess of pleasure marked by a redistribution of the phonematic order, morphological structure, and even syntax: portmanteau words in Joyce and syntax in Mallarmé, for example.

The oral cavity is the first organ of perception to develop and maintains the nursing infant's first contact with the outside but also with the other. His initial "burrowing" movement, which is meant to establish contact—indeed biologically indispensable fusion—with the mother's body, takes on a negative value by the age of six months. The rotating movement of the head at that age indicates refusal even before the "semantic," abstract word "no" appears at fifteen months.[20] Fusing orality and devouring, refusing, negative orality are thus closely intermingled, as they are in the anal stage that follows. During this stage aggressivity is accentuated, ensuring the body's separation from and always already negative relation to the outside and the other. In addition, even if it is recognized as more archaic than rejection, fusing orality and the libidinal drive it supports are borne by rejection and, in the genesis of the subject's symbolic functioning, determined by it.[21]

If, through a defusion of the drives or for some other reason, rejection as the bearer of drives or, more precisely, their negative discharge, is accentuated, this discharge uses the muscular apparatus as a passageway for discharging energy in brief spurts:[22] pictorial or dancing gesturality may be ascribed to this mechanism. But rejection may pass through the vocal apparatus as well. The oral cavity and the glottis are the only internal organs that do not have the characteristic capacity of muscular apparatuses to restrain bound energy. Instead they free discharges through a finite system of phonemes specific to each language, by increasing their frequency, by accumulating or repeating them, and thus determining the choice of morphemes.[23] They may even condense several "borrowed" morphemes into a single lexeme.[24] In so doing, the rejection that invests the oral cavity awakens in and through it the "libidinal," "unifying," "positive" drive which characterizes, at the earliest stages, this same cavity in its initial "burrowing" movement. Through the new phonematic and rhythmic network it produces, rejection becomes a source of "aesthetic" pleasure. Thus, without leaving the line of meaning, it cuts up and reorganizes that line by imprinting on it the path of drives through the body: from the anus to the mouth.

Rejection therefore constitutes the return of expulsion—*Ausstossung* or *Verwerfung*[25]—within the domain of the constituted subject: rejection *re*constitutes real objects, "creates" new ones, reinvents the real, and resymbolizes it. Although in so doing rejection recalls a schizoid regressive process, it is more important to note that rejection positivizes that process, affirming it by introducing the process into the signifying sphere: the latter thus finds itself separate, divided, put in process/on trial. This symbolization of rejection is the place of an untenable contradiction which only a limited number of subjects can reach. Although rejection includes the moment of "excorporation,"[26] ("expectoration" in Artaud's terms, or "excretion" in Bataille's), this motorial discharge and corporeal spasm are invested in the sign—in language—which is itself already divided, reintroducing and unfolding within it the very mechanics by which the separation between words and things is produced. Rejection thus unfolds, dismantles, and readjusts both the *vocal* register (as in Mallarmé's texts or Lautréamont's *Maldoror*) and the *logical* register (as in Ducasse's *Poems*).[27] Rejection is reintroduced and reiterated in a divided language.

Characteristically, the formalist theory of symbolism simplifies the signifying process by seeing it only as a *text* (in the sense of a coded or deviant distribution of marks), without perceiving the drive rejection that produces it, straddling the corporeal and natural on the one hand, the symbolic and social on the other, and found in each of them specifically. By contrast, recognizing the dialectical heterogeneity of these "orders" means indicating, above all, that rejection—anal, sadistic, aggressive— posits the "object" and the "sign," and that it constitutes the *real* where phantasmatic or objective reality is found. From this standpoint, the subject seems to have two possibilities.

Either he goes elsewhere, which is to say, beyond rejection into reality, forever surpassing the trajectory of separation and scission, living it only as the spin-off or side aspect of a "commitment" to the real where all the logic of *meta-* is reified: *meta*subject, *meta*language, *meta*physics. In this case, he places himself under the law of the father and takes on both this paranoia and the homosexuality connoting paranoia, the sublimation of which is all too fragile: here we see Orestes who murders his mother in the name of the laws of the city-state.

Or else the subject constantly returns to rejection and thus reaches what lies beneath the paranoid homosexuality laid bare by signifying production: the schizoid moment of scission. Mallarmé's suffering body and, later, the shattered and mummified body of Artaud attest to this loss of unity.

The representation of the "character" who becomes the place of this process is one that normative consciousness finds intolerable. For this "character"'s polymorphism is one that knows every perversion and adheres to none, one that moves through every vice without taking up any of them. Unidentical and inauthentic, his is the wisdom of artifice which has no interiority and is constant rejection. He is familiar with the social organism and its paranoid reality but makes light of it and, for them, he is an unbearable monstrosity. This has always been his traditional representation, from Heraclitus' "misanthropy" to the maliciousness of [Diderot's] *Le Neveu de Rameau* and his *Paradoxe du comédien*.

Within the Greek tradition, the extant fragments of Heraclitus seem to have come closest to grasping the process of a simultaneous "hypertrophy of a self"[28] and its separation within maintained reason. Thus, without leaving the domain of reason, Heraclitus makes of reason not a logical unity, as Plato and the Stoics have accustomed us to understanding it, but rather a divided speech, a counterspeech, sanctioning [*homologuant*] what stands separate: words and things, but also things among things and words among words—the word as rejection of both the thing that it utters and another word, said or unsaid. Only the "clever" one who has mastered the technique of saying can achieve this "poetic" wisdom, τὸ σοφόυ, "art." This does not mean that "art," which maintains words within rejection, is a discourse on discourse: the discursive is only one of the phenomenal and linguistic manifestations of the process. Although metalanguage can apprehend this process only through language, by pursuing stylistic, logical, and etymological figures, the separation that discourse replays refers to presymbolic and intrasymbolic rejection, where logos and its sanction disappear. It refers to the a-symbolized and a-symbolizable scission, to the nothing that is neither one nor multiple, but rather the "infinite nothingness" spoken of by speculative philosophy, which we shall posit as matter that is always already split; from it, repeated rejections will generate not only the thetic logos but its shattering.

Heraclitean art is the practice that takes up, through the *logos*, this *separation* without beginning or end, which certain Freudian formulations assign to the unconscious.[29] "Of all the discourses I have heard," states one of the Heraclitean fragments, "not one manages to distinguish the distinct element that makes art what it is."[30] No discourse can identify the distinct element—instinctual matter—that characterizes art. Although it contradicts the One and discourse, instinctual matter is inscribed in them in order to reject them and reject itself from them. Iamblichus echoes Heraclitus, suggesting that the singular and rare man who is able to achieve rejection in reason does so on the basis of matter. Though this man is more than matter, matter is his precondition; it produces him by rejecting itself and rejecting him: "Hence I posit two kinds of sacrifice. On the one hand, those of completely purified men, which, as Heraclitus says, even a singular man can only rarely carry out, or only a numbered few; and on the other hand, those that remain material [*restent dans la matière*]."[31]

Now that we have followed the notion of expulsion [*repoussement*] in Freud, let us pick it up again in Hegel, who opened the way for the notion of *negativity* outlined at the beginning of this chapter.[32] In Hegel, the term *Repulsion* designates a movement within negativity that comes close to what we have called *rejection* yet does not coincide with it. *Repulsion* is the negative relation of the One with itself, as opposed to *Becoming*, which is "a transition of Being into Nothing."[33] Since it is the fundamental determination of the One and its fragmentation, Repulsion both ensures the preservation of the One and produces the plurality of Ones by the Attraction it presupposes. Thus we see that Hegelian Repulsion is always subordinate to Unicity and that, in beginning to act within it, Repulsion calls Unicity into question only *from the outside*, by adding multiple external meanings. There is no doubt, and Hegel himself stresses, that Repulsion fundamentally interiorizes negativity, in opposition to Kantian analytics where the "two basic forces remain, within matter, opposed to one another, external and independent," and where "Kant determines . . . repulsive force . . . as a *superficial force*, by means of which parts of matter can act upon one another only at the common surface of contact."[34] But in internalizing Repulsion within the One itself and in making Repulsion what specifies, determines, and, in sum, identifies the One, Hegel subordinates Repulsion to what we have called the "symbolic function"; whereas Freud, on the other hand, joins dialectical logic by making *expulsion* the essential moment in the constitution of the symbolic function. The difference is that, in Freud, what activates expulsion is "another scene" based on the drives. Since he does not have this heteronomy in view, Hegel can only supercede the exteriority of Repulsion that Freud has sketched out. This comes about because separation in Hegel becomes the explanation of what the One is in itself; it gets exported outside this One, which is always already constructed, becomes exteriorized, and, as a result of the dialectic, ends up in an exteriority:

> The self-repulsion of the One is the explication of that which the One is in itself; but infinity, as split-up, is here infinity which has *passed beyond itself*: and this it has done through the immediacy of the infinite entity, the One. It is a simple relation of One to One, and equally, or rather, the absolute unrelatedness of the One; it is the former according to the simple affirmative self-relation of One, and the latter according to the same as negative. In other words, the plurality of the One is its self-positing; the One is its own negative self-relation and nothing else, and this relation (the One itself) is many Ones. But equally, plurality is merely external to the One; for the *One also is the transcending of Otherness, Repulsion is its self-relation and simple self-identity. The plurality of Ones is infinity, as contradiction which unconcernedly produces itself.*[35]

What Hegel does not envisage is the moment the One is *shattered* in a return of Repulsion onto itself, which is to say, a turning against its own potential power for positing and multiplying the One. Nor does Hegelian logic see the heterogeneous parcelling of the symbolic, which underlies the symbolic's very constitution and constantly undermines it even while maintaining it in process; the simultaneous existence of the *boundary* (which is the One) and the a-reasonable, a-relative, a-mediating *crossing* of that boundary; or the possibility of the constitution-unconstitution of One meaning-nonmeaning, passing through categorial boundaries ("inside," "one," "multiple," etc.), which is precisely what *rejection* brings about in the "schizoid" process of the text.

The ideational closure of the Hegelian dialectic seems to consist in its inability to posit negativity as anything but a repetition of ideational unity in itself. The exteriority to which it is condemned *in fact* is thus bound up with the ideational enclosure, in which, despite many detours, its trajectory ends. Repeated rejection, far from purely and simply restoring the series of many Ones, instead opens up in and through Unity—we are tempted to say beyond "signifying unity" and "subjective unity"— *the material process of repeated* (a-signifying and instinctual) *scissions*; these repeated scissions act with the regularity of objective laws and recall, through the rifts or new arrangements they produce, the pulsation of that process through symbolic unification. These are the conclusions we may draw from a materialist interpretation, opened up by the Freudian position on repetition compulsion.

Indeed, although for Freud *Ausstossung* or *Verwerfung* posits the sign, it already functions beforehand, "objectively" so to speak, in the movement of living matter subject to natural and social constraints. "In order to understand this step forward [the constitution of the real as separate], we must recollect that all presentations originate from perceptions and are repetitions of them."[36]

While establishing the sign, subject, and judgment, *Verwefung* points *at the same time* toward the repeated scissions of a-symbolized living matter and toward the inorganic. The drive that thus takes shape operates in a transsymbolic realm that sends the signifying body back to biological a-signifiance and finally to death. Moreover what is *represented* as a "death" is probably—as a great many "literary" texts show—nothing but the verbalization of this rejection, this multiplied rupture of all unity, including that of the body: "Now we shall have to call it the decorporealization of reality, the kind of rupture intent, it would seem, on multiplying; a rupture between things and the feeling they produce in our mind, the place they must take."[37]

Freud reveals the obstinate and constraining return of rejection, its "repetition compulsion," as one of the "ultimate" mechanisms of psychic functioning—more essential than the "pleasure principle"—and characterizes it as "demonic," as "an urge inherent in organic life" to stop the galloping evolution of organic forms and their symbolizing capacity in order to return to a state of inertia and constancy. Through these formulations and beyond Freud's speculations on death (avowed as such by Freud himself),[38] from observations about "schizophrenia," but, for our purposes, even more so from modern texts, there emerges the confirmation of an objective law. *Rejection*, the specific movement of matter, produces its various forms, including their symbolic manifestations, at the same time that it ensures, by its repetition, a *threshold of constancy*: a *boundary*, a restraint around which difference will be set up—the path toward symbolization. But even as it posits the symbolic and its differentiation, this expenditure of *drives* returns—notably in the text—to shatter difference and introduce, through its play, what silently acts on it: the scissions of matter. Because these scissions—which Freud situates in the *id* or in the *unconscious*—irrupt within the differentiation of symbolic play, we maintain that the signifying process practiced in its infinite totality has no unconscious; in other words, the text has no unconscious. Repeated and returned rejection opposes repression and, in Freudian terms, reintroduces "free energy" into "bound energy."

We have now reached a crucial point in the notion of *signifying process*. Rejection, which is the signifying process' powerful mechanism, is heterogeneous, since it is, from a Freudian standpoint, *instinctual*, which means that it constitutes an articulation [*charnière*] between the "psychical" and the "somatic." So much so that although the dichotomy between these two "orders" is upheld, it is also dialecticized, and the "signifier" appears only as a *thesis*—a positing—of infinite repetitions of material rejections when "free energy," always already splitting, doubling, and rejecting, collides against the walls of natural and social *structures*, which Freud terms "external disturbing forces," crystallizing "unities." Freud notes that "the manifestations of a compulsion to repeat . . . exhibit to a high degree an instinctual character and, when they act in opposition to the pleasure principle, give the appearance of some 'daemonic' force at work." Further on, he continues:

> But how is the predicate of being "instinctual" related to the compulsion to repeat? At this point we cannot escape a suspicion that we may have come upon the track of a universal attribute of drives and perhaps of organic life in general which has not hitherto been clearly recognized or at least not explicitly stressed. *It seems, then, that a drive is an urge inherent in organic life to restore an earlier state of things* which the living entity has been obliged to abandon under the pressure of external disturbing forces; that is, it is a kind of organic elasticity, or, to put it another way, the expression of the inertia inherent in organic life.[39]

Conformist psychoanalysis after Freud has embarked on an attempt to "break down the id's resistances" by interpreting them and thereby suppressing drive rejection within the domain of so-called action in order to "signify" or "nuance" it. When established as a principle, this normalization of rejection contributes to the destruction of the "spearhead" of the signifying process. On the other hand, when rejection is brought back to its essential motor functions, when it necessarily becomes, whether unconsciously or voluntarily, the maintained and reinforced agent of the signifying process, it produces new cultural and social formations which are innovative and—under specific conditions which we shall discuss further on—subversive.

How is this return of rejection—this *surplus of rejection* that puts in process/on trial the symbolic already instituted by *Verwerfung*—represented in discourse? What is the negativity of the text, which is different from symbolic negation in judgment and is sustained by the threatened subject? What is its libidinal organization and discursive economy?

According to Freud in his article "Negation,"[40] symbolization implies a repression of pleasure and erotic drives. But this repression is not absolute. Freud implies that complete repression (if it were possible) would stop the symbolic function. Repression, Lacan explains, is a "*kind of discordance* between the signified and the signifier that is determined by any censorship originating in society."[41] Setting up the symbolic function requires this repression and prevents the removed truth of the real from slipping in anywhere except "between the lines," that is, in the linguistic structure, as "negation" for instance.

"The performance of the function of judgment," Freud continues, "is not made possible until the creation of the symbol of negation has endowed thinking with a first measure of freedom from the consequences of repression." Let us now return to an earlier point in the text on negation. For Freud, "negation is a lifting of the repression [*Aufhebung der Verdrängung*]," which means an "intellectual acceptance of the repressed," but not its discharge or its "consumption." As a consequence, the "intellectual function" is separated from the "affective process," which results in "a kind of intellectual acceptance of the repressed, while at the same time what is essential to the repression persists."

The appearance of the symbol of negation in the signifier thus partially liberates repression and introduces into the signifier a part of what remains outside the symbolic order: what was repressed and what Freud calls "affective." These are instinctual, corporeal foundations stemming from the concrete history of the concrete (biological, familial, social) subject. Although it is true that the "affective" can be grasped only through discursive structuration, it would be semantic empiricism to believe that it does not in some fashion exist outside it. Clearly, negation as a *symbolic function* inherent in judgment (inherent in symbolization) constitutes an intellectual sublimation (*Aufhebung*) of only one part of fore-closure (*Verwerfung*).

Negation-as-denial [*dénégation*] in cases of "obsessive ideas," writes Freud, allows "the ideational content of what is repressed . . . [to] reach consciousness." In analysis, through transference, "we succeed in con-quering the negation as well, and in bringing about a full intellectual acceptance of the repressed; but the repressive process itself is not yet removed by this."

By contrast, in aesthetic productions, which do not involve transfer-ence, negation is not "conquered." Rejection operates in them and does not produce an "intellectual acceptance of the repressed" (in other words, it does not effect the passage of the repressed element into the signified, into the symbolic function). Instead it *marks signifying mater-ial* with the repressed. This observation implies, on the one hand, that setting up the symbolic function (founded on judgment) requires a trans-ference situation. It implies, on the other hand, that the symbolic func-tion already carries out the distinction not only between "objective" and "subjective," but also between "signifier" and "signified." The reintro-duction of the symbol of negation into poetic language (as opposed to the reintroduction of negation as "denial" [*dénégation*] into analysis), *arranges the repressed element in a different way*, one that does not rep-resent an "intellectual acceptance of the repressed," an *Aufhebung*, but instead constitutes a postsymbolic (and in this sense antisymbolic) hall-marking of the material that remained intact during first symbolization. This "material," expelled by the sign and judgment from first symbol-izations, is then withdrawn from the unconscious into language, but is not accepted there in the form of "metalanguage" or any kind of intel-lection. The repeated death drive (negativity, destruction) withdraws from the unconscious and *takes up a position as already positivized and erotized in a language* that, through drive investment, is organized into prosody or rhythmic timbres.[42] If, as Freud writes in the same article, "in analysis we never discover a 'no' in the unconscious and [if] that recognition of the unconscious on the part of the ego is expressed in a negative formula," then the semiotic device constructed by poetic lan-guage through the positing of language as a symbolic system constitutes third-degree negativity. It is neither the lack of a "no" (as in the uncon-scious), nor a negative formula (a sign of the instituted symbolic func-tion), nor negation-as-denial (symptoms of the neurotic ego idealizing the repressed), but instead a *modification of linguistic and logical lin-earity and ideality*, which cannot be located in any ego. Poetic rhythm does not constitute the acknowledgment of the unconscious but is instead its expenditure and implementation.

For psychoanalysis, "the true subject is the subject of the unconscious" who appears only in the phenomenon of transference. Clearly, this is not the poetic subject. Although psychoanalysis and, hence, transference have allowed the (plural) topographies of the subject to emerge for science, the topography of poetic language appears as one that draws out, within a signifying device (which has been called "prosody," "art," and so forth), not the "ideational content" of what remains outside first symbolization, but rather its *economy*: the *movement* of rejection. This rejection may be implied in affirmative judgment (*Bejahung*) (as in Lautréamont), or in linguistic morphology and syntax (as in Mallarmé); in other words, it may appear in the symbol of negation or in morphosyntactic destruction. Poetic negativity is third-degree rejection. As the rejection of symbolic and neurotic negation, it recalls, spatially and musically, the dialectical moment of the generating of signifiance.

In so doing, the text *momentarily* sets right the conflict between signifier and signified established by the symbol of negation and which determines all censorship originating in society—repositing it, of course, but redistributing it as well. The text makes rejection work on and in the very place of symbolic and social censorship, which establishes language as a symbolic system with a double articulation: signifier and signified.

NOTES

1. Hegel's terminology poses a problem. Whereas the French translations Kristeva cites are generally consistent in their rendering of key terms, no such "standards" inform the various English translations of either *Phenomenology of Spirit*—even the title is a point of contention—or *Science of Logic*. Both texts, for example, refer to *Nichts,* commonly translated as *néant* in French but as "Nothing" in Johnston and Struthers's *Hegel's Science of Logic* or as "nothingness" in A. V. Miller's *Phenomenology.* The same problem arises with *le devenir* ("Becoming" or "process of Becoming"), *extériorisation* ("exteriorization" or "expression"), and other such terms. I have not standardized these two different translations. When the discussion of Hegel does not refer to a specific work, I have generally selected French cognates.—Trans.

2. Lenin, "Conspectus of Hegel's Book on *The Science of Logic*," Clemens Dutt, tr., *Collected Works,* Stewart Smith, ed. (Moscow: Foreign Languages Publishing House, 1961), 38:230.

3. Ibid., p. 97.

4. See "Religion in the Form of Art," in Hegel, *Phenomenology of Spirit*, A. V. Miller, tr. (Oxford: Oxford University Press, 1977), pp. 424–53.

5. Hegel, *Encyclopédie des sciences philosophiques*, vol. 1, *Science de la logique* (1817), B. Bourgeois, tr. (Paris: Vrin, 1970), p. 203.

6. Lenin, "Conspectus," *Collected Works* 38:229.

7. *Hegel's Science of Logic*, W. H. Johnston and L. G. Struthers, trs. (London: Allen & Unwin, 1929; 1966), 1:95; emphasis added.

8. Ibid., p. 96.

9. Ibid., p. 97.

10. Ibid., 2:478–79.

11. Ibid., 1:104.

12. Freud, "Negation," *Standard Edition*, 19:239.

13. "Foreclosure," write J. Laplanche and J.-B. Pontalis, is a "term introduced by Jacques Lacan denoting a specific mechanism held to lie at the origin of the psychotic phenomenon and to consist in a primordial *expulsion* of a fundamental 'signifier' (e.g., the phallus as signifier of the castration complex) from the subject's symbolic universe." *The Language of Psychoanalysis*, Daniel Lagache, introd., Donald Nicholson-Smith, tr. (London: Hogarth Press, 1973), p. 166; emphasis added.—Trans.

14. See *Beyond the Pleasure Principle*, *Standard Edition*, 18:54–55.

15. Melanie Klein, "The Importance of Symbol-Formation in the Development of the Ego," in *Contributions to Psychoanalysis* (London: Hogarth Press, 1948), p. 237.

16. Psychoanalysis places the mirror stage between the ages of 6 and 18 months, after which the so-called phallic stage begins. Observations have shown that around the latter period (age 2), language acquisition is inhibited despite the accelerated maturation of the brain and its lateralization. After this period of inhibition until the end of the Oedipus complex, and thus the decline of the phallic stage (between the ages of 4 and 5), the major elements of linguistic competence are acquired at an accelerated rate. After this, in the latency period, the curve of language acquisition becomes less steep, rising only slightly. See Eric H. Lenneberg, *Biological Foundations of Language* (New York: Wiley, 1967), pp. 168, 376.

17. A text is paragrammatic, writes Leon S. Roudiez, "in the sense that its organization of words (and their denotations), grammar, and syntax is challenged by the infinite possibilities provided by letters or phonemes combining to form networks of significations not accessible through conventional reading habits . . . ," "Twelve Points from Tel Quel," *L'Esprit Créateur* 14 (Winter 1974): 300. See Kristeva's essay, "Pour une sémiologie des paragrammes," in Σημειωτιχὴ, pp. 174–207.—Trans.

18. See "Le Dispositif sémiotique du texte," *La Révolution du langage poétique*, pp. 209–358.

19. On Mallarmé, Hegel, and the "wife-concept," see *La Révolution du langage poétique*, pp. 534–40.

20. See René Spitz, *The First Year of Life: A Psychoanalytical Study of Normal and Deviant Development of Object Relations* (New York: International Universities Press, 1965), p. 193.

21. "In my opinion, in the normal state of fusion of the two drives, aggression plays a role which is comparable to that of a carrier wave. In this way the impetus of aggression makes it possible to direct both drives toward the surround. But if the aggressive and libidinal drives do not achieve fusion or, alternately, if a defusion has taken place, then aggression is returned against the own person; and in this case libido also can no longer be directed toward the outside" (ibid., p. 288).

22. See Freud, "The Economic Problem of Masochism," *Standard Edition*, 19:159–70.

23. Alliteration, assonance, etc. See *La Révolution du langage poétique*, pp. 210–19.

24. Portmanteau words, see ibid.

25. Freud on the "Wolf Man" in "Inhibitions, Symptoms and Anxiety," *Standard Edition*, 20:104ff.

26. See André Green, "La Projection."

27. Isidore Ducasse's *Maldoror*, first published in its entirety in 1869, was signed: comte de Lautréamont. The following year, under his own name, Ducasse published *Poems*.—Trans.

28. Jean Bollack and Heinz Wismann, *Héraclite ou la séparation* (Paris: Minuit, 1972), p. 14.

29. The theory of drives, for example.

30. Bollack and Wismann, *Héraclite*, p. 30.

Bollack and Wismann interpret σοφόυ as "ingeniousness and savoir-faire." "Art" therefore refers to "a way of fashioning discourse and the disposition of its material" (p. 306). Compare the English translation by G. S. Kirk: "Of all whose accounts I have heard no one reaches the point of recognizing that wise is separated from all." *Heraclitus: The Cosmic Fragments* (Cambridge: Cambridge University Press, 1954), p. 398.—Trans.

31. Bollack and Wismann, *Héraclite*, p. 226. See also p. 69.

32. Although the French translators use the term *repoussement* for both Freud's *Ausstossung* and Hegel's *Repulsion*, I maintain the standard English translation of these terms, "expulsion," and "Repulsion," respectively.—Trans.

33. See *Hegel's Science of Logic* 1:180–83. Hegel uses the terms *abstossen* (to repulse), *repellieren* (to repel) and *Repulsion* (repulsion). In French, both verbs are translated as *repousser* and the noun as *repoussement*.—Trans. See Hegel, *Science de la logique*, Pierre-Jean Labarrière and Gwendoline Jarczyk, trs. (Paris: Aubier-Montaigne, 1972), vol. 1, Book 1 (1812), pp. 138 f.

34. *Hegel's Science of Logic*, 1:195; emphasis added.

35. Ibid., 182; emphasis added.

36. "Negation," *Standard Edition*, 19:237.

37. Artaud, "Description d'un état physique," *Oeuvres complètes* (Paris: Gallimard, 1956), 1:75. In Part C of *La Révolution du langage poétique* ("L'Etat et le mystère"), we stress the a-theological function of this shattering of the One (notably pp. 579 ff.). We recall the statement noted by Gisela Pankow in the "dream of the 'non-existent God'": "Schizophrenia is synony-

mous with atheism," in *L'Homme et sa psychose* (Paris: Aubier-Montaigne, 1969), p. 220.

38. "In the works of my later years (*Beyond the Pleasure Principle* [1920], *Group Psychology and the Analysis of the Ego* [1921], and *The Ego and the Id* [1923]), I have given free reign to the inclination, which I have kept down for so long, to speculation." "An Autobiographical Study," *Standard Edition*, 20:57.

39. *Beyond the Pleasure Principle*, *Standard Edition*, 18:35 and 36; translation modified.

40. *Standard Edition*, 19:235–39.

41. Lacan, "Introduction au commentaire de Jean Hyppolite," in *Ecrits*, p. 372.

42. See "Rhythmes phoniques et sémantiques," *La Révolution du langage poétique*, pp. 209–63.

Desire in Language, 1975

From One Identity to an Other

I shall attempt, within the ritual limits of a one-hour seminar, to posit (if not to demonstrate) that every language theory is predicated upon a conception of the subject that it explicitly posits, implies, or tries to deny. Far from being an "epistemological perversion," a definite subject is present as soon as there is consciousness of signification. Consequently, I shall need to outline an epistemological itinerary: taking three stages in the recent history of linguistic theory, I shall indicate the variable position these may have required of the speaking subject-support within their object language. This—on the whole, technical—foray into the epistemology of linguistic science will lead us to broach and, I hope, elucidate a problem whose ideological stakes are considerable but whose banality is often ignored. Meaning, identified either within the unity or the multiplicity of subject, structure, or theory, necessarily guarantees a certain transcendence, if not a theology; this is precisely why all human knowledge, whether it be that of an individual subject or of a meaning structure, retains religion as its blind boundaries, or at least, as an internal limit, and at best, can just barely "explain and validate religious sentiment" (as Lévi-Strauss observed, in connection with structuralism).[1]

Second, I shall deal with a particular signifying practice, which, like the Russian Formalists, I call "poetic language," in order to demonstrate that this kind of language, through the particularity of its signifying operations, is an unsettling process—when not an outright destruction—of the identity of meaning and speaking subject,[2] and consequently, of transcendence or, by derivation, of "religious sensibility." On that account, it accompanies crises within social structures and institutions—the moments of their mutation, evolution, revolution, or disarray. For if mutation within language and institutions finds its code through this signifying practice and its questionable subject in process that constitutes poetic language, then that practice and subject are walking a precarious tightrope. Poetic language, the only language that uses up transcendence and theology to sustain itself; poetic language, knowingly the enemy of religion, by its very economy borders on psychosis (as for its subject) and totalitarianism or fascism (as for the institutions it implies or evokes). I could have spoken of Vladimir Mayakovsky or Antonin Artaud; I shall speak of Louis-Ferdinand Céline.

Finally, I shall try to draw a few conclusions concerning the possibility of a *theory* in the sense of an *analytical discourse* on signifying systems, which would take into account these crises of meaning, subject, and structure. This for two reasons: first, such crises, far from being accidents, are inherent in the signifying function and, consequently, in sociality; second, situated at the forefront of twentieth-century politics, these phenomena (which I consider within poetic language, but which may assume other forms in the West as well as in other civilizations) could not remain outside the so-called human sciences without casting suspicion on their ethic. I shall therefore and in conclusion argue in favor of an analytical theory of signifying systems and practices that would search within the signifying phenomenon for the *crisis* or the *unsettling process* of meaning and subject rather than for the coherence or identity of either *one* or a *multiplicity* of structures.

Without referring back to the stoic sage, who guaranteed both the sign's triad and the inductive conditional clause, let us return to the congruence between conceptions of language and of subject where Ernest Renan left them. We are all aware of the scandal he caused among nineteenth-century minds when he changed a theological discourse (the Gospels) not into a *myth* but into the *history* of a man and a people. This conversion of *theological* discourse into *historical* discourse was possible thanks to a tool (for him, scientific) whose omnipotence he never ceased praising—philology. As used by Renan or Eugene Burnouf in Avestic Studies, for example, philology incorporates the *comparativism* of philologists Franz Bopp or August Schleicher. Whatever the difference between comparativists seeking those *laws* unique to *families* of languages and philologists deciphering the *meaning* of *one* language, a common conception of language as an *organic identity* unites them. Little does it matter that, as comparativists believed, this organic identity articulates itself thanks to *a law* that crosses national and historical language borders making of them one family (cf. Jacob Grimm's phonetic laws); or that, as philologists believed, this organic identity articulates itself thanks to *one meaning*—singular and unique—inscribed into a text still undeciphered or whose decipherability is debatable. In both cases this *organic identity* of law or meaning implies that language is the possession of a *homo loquens* within history. As Renan writes in *Averoés et l'Averroïsme*, "for the philologist, a text has only one meaning" even if it is through "a kind of necessary misinterpretation" that "the philosophical and religious development of humanity" proceeds.[3] Closer to the objectivity of the Hegelian "consciousness of self" for the comparativists, embodied in a singularity that, be it concrete, individual, or national, still owes something to Hegel for the philologists; language is always *one* system, perhaps even one "structure," always *one meaning*, and, therefore, it necessarily implies a subject (collective or individual) to bear witness to its history. If one has difficulty following Renan when he affirms that "rationalism is based on philology"—for it is obvious that the two are interdependent—it is no less obvious that philological reasoning is maintained through the identity of a historical subject: a subject in becoming. Why? Because, far from dissecting the internal logic of sign, predication (sentence grammar), or syllogism (logic), as did the universal grammar of Port Royal, the comparativist and philological reason that Renan exemplifies considers the signifying unit in itself (sign, sentence, syllogism) as an unanalyzable given. This signifying unit remains implicit within each description of law or text that philologists and comparativists undertake: linear, unidimensional descriptions—with no analysis of the sign's density, the logical problematic of meaning, etc.—but which, once technically completed, restore structural identity (for the comparativists) or meaning (for the philologists); in so doing they reveal the initial presupposition of the specifically linguistic undertaking as an ideology that posits either the people or an exceptional individual as appropriating this structure or this meaning. Because it is in itself unanalyzable (like the sign, sentence, and syllogism, it has no density, no economy), this subject-support of comparativist laws or of philological analysis does not lend itself to change, that is to say, to shifting from one law to another, from one structure to another, or from one meaning to another, except by postulating the movement of becoming, that is, of history. In the analysis of a signifying function (language or any "human," social phenomenon), what is censured at the level of semantic complexity reemerges in the form of a becoming: that obliteration of the density that constitutes sign, sentence, and syllogism (and consequently, the speaking subject), is compensated for by historical reasoning; the reduction of the complex signifying economy of the speaking subject (though obliquely perceived by Port Royal) produces without fail an opaque "I" that makes history. Thus, philological reasoning, while founding history, becomes a deadlock for language sciences, even though there actually is in Renan, beyond countless contradictions, an appreciation of universal grammar, a call for the constitution of a linguistics for an isolated language (in the manner of the ancient Indian grammarian Pāṇini), and even surprisingly modern proposals that advocate the study of crisis rather than normality, and in his Semitic studies the remarks on "that delirious vision transcribed in a barbaric and undecipherable style" as he calls the Christian gnostic texts, or on the texts of John the Apostle.[4]

Linguistic reasoning, which, through Saussure, succeeded philological reasoning, works its revolution precisely by affecting the constitutive unity of a particular language; a language is not a system, it is a system of signs, and this vertically opens up the famous gap between signifier and signified, thus allowing linguistics to claim a logical, mathematical formalization on the one hand, but on the other, it definitely prevents reducing a language or text to one law or one meaning. Structural linguistics and the ensuing structural movement seem to explore this epistemological space by eliminating the speaking subject. But, on a closer look, we see that the subject they legitimately do without is nothing but the subject (individual or collective) of historico-philological discourse I just discussed, in which the Hegelian consciousness of self became stranded as it was concretized, embodied in philology and history; this subject, which linguistics and the corollary human sciences do without, is the "personal identity, miserable treasure."[5] Nevertheless, a subject of enunciation takes shape within the gap opened up between signifier and signified that admits both structure and interplay within; and structural linguistics ignores such a subject. Moreover, because it left its place vacant, structural linguistics could not become a linguistics of speech or discourse; it lacked a grammar, for in order to move from sign to sentence the place of the subject had to be acknowledged and no longer kept vacant. Of course, generative grammar does reinstate it by rescuing universal grammar and the Cartesian subject from oblivion, using that subject to justify the generative, recursive functions of syntactic trees. But in fact, generative grammar is evidence of what structural linguistics omitted, rather than a new beginning; whether structural or generative, linguistics since Saussure adheres to the same presuppositions, implicit within the structuralist current, explicit in the generative tendency that can be found summed up in the philosophy of Husserl.

I refer modern linguistics and the modes of thought which it oversees within the so-called human sciences back to this founding father from another field, but not for conjunctural reasons, though they are not lacking. Indeed, Husserl was invited to and discussed by the Circle of Prague; indeed, Jakobson explicitly recognized in him a philosophical mentor for post-Saussurian linguists; indeed, several American epistemologists of generative grammar recognize in Husserlian phenomenology, rather than in Descartes, the foundations of the generative undertaking. But it is possible to detect in Husserl the basis of linguistic reasoning (structural or generative) to the extent that, after the reduction of the Hegelian consciousness of self into philological or historical identity, Husserl masterfully understood and posited that any signifying act, insofar as it remains capable of elucidation by knowledge, does not maintain itself by a "me, miserable treasure" but by the *"transcendental ego."*

If it is true that the division of the Saussurian sign (signifier/signified), unknown to Husserl, also introduces the heretofore unrecognized possibility of envisioning language as a free play, forever without closure, it is also true that this possibility was not developed by Saussure except in the very problematic *Anagrammes*.[6] Moreover, this investigation has no linguistic followers, but rather, philosophical (Heideggerian discourse) and psychoanalytic (Lacan's signifier) contemporaries or successors, who today effectively enable us to appreciate and circumscribe the contribution of phenomenological linguistics from a Husserlian perspective. For post-Saussurian structural linguistics still encloses the signifier, even if nonmotivated, within patterns of a signification originally destined for faultless communication, either coinciding with the explicit signified or set off a short distance from it, but still fastened to the unalterable presence of meaning and, similarly, tributary to phenomenological reason.

It is therefore impossible to take up the congruence between conceptions of language and of subject where Renan left off without recalling how Husserl shifted ground by raising it above empiricism, psychologism, and incarnation theories typical of Renan. Let us examine for a moment the signifying act and the Husserlian transcendental ego, keeping in mind that linguistic reason (structural or generative) is to Husserl what philological reason was to Hegel: reduction perhaps, but also concrete realization, that is, failure made manifest.

As early as *Logical Investigations* of 1901, Husserl situates the sign (of which one could have naively thought that it had no subject) within the act of expressing meaning, constituted by a judgment on something: "The articulate sound-complex, the written sign, etc., first becomes a spoken word or communicative bit of speech, when a speaker produces it with the intention of 'expressing himself about something' through its means."[7]

Consequently, the thin sheath of the sign (signifier/signified) opens onto a complex architecture where intentional life-experience captures material (hylic) multiplicities, endowing them first with noetic meaning, then with noematic meaning, so that finally the result for the judging consciousness is the formation of an *object* once and for all signified as real. The important point here is that this real *object*, first signified by means of hylic data, through noesis and noemis, if it exists, can only be transcendental in the sense that it is elaborated in its identity by the judging consciousness of transcendental ego. The signified is transcendent as it is posited by means of certain concatenations within an experience that is always confined to judgment; for if the phenomenologist distinguishes between intuiting and endowing with meaning, then perception is already *cogitation* and the *cogitation* is transcendent to perception.[8] So much so that if the world were annihilated, the signified *res* would remain because they are transcendental: they "refer entirely to a consciousness" insofar as they are signified *res*. The *predicative* (syntactic) operation constitutes this judging consciousness, positing at the same time the signified *Being* (and therefore, the object of meaning and signification) and the *operating consciousness* itself. The ego as support of the predicative act therefore does not operate as the ego-cogito, that is, as the ego of a logically conceived consciousness and "fragment of the world"; rather, the transcendental ego belongs to the constituting operating consciousness, which means that it takes shape within the predicative operation. This operation is *thetic* because it simultaneously posits the thesis (position) of both Being *and* ego. Thus, for every signified transcendental object, there is a transcendental ego, both of which are givens by virtue of thetic operation—predication of judgment.

"Transcendental egology"[9] thus reformulates the question of the signifying act's subject: (1) the operating consciousness, through predication simultaneously constitutes Being, the (transcendent) signified real object, and the ego (in so far as it is transcendental); the problematic of the sign is also bound up in this question; (2) even if intentionality, and with it, the judging consciousness, is already a given in material data and perceptions, as it "resembles" them (which allows us to say that the transcendental ego is always already in a way given), *in fact*, the ego constitutes itself only through the operating consciousness at the time of predication; the subject is merely the subject of predication, of judgment, of the sentence; (3) "belief" and "judgment" are closely interdependent though not identical: "The syntheses of belief (*Glaubenssynthesen*) find their 'expression' in the forms of stated meaning."[10]

Neither a historical individual nor a logically conceived consciousness, the subject is henceforth the operating thetic consciousness positing correlatively the transcendental Being and ego. Thus, Husserl makes clear that any linguistic act, insofar as it sets up a signified that can be communicated in a sentence (and there is no sign or signifying structure that is not already part of a sentence), is sustained by the transcendental ego.

It is perhaps not unimportant that the rigor of Judaism and the persecution it has been subjected to in our time underlie Husserl's extraordinarily firm elucidation of the transcendental ego, just as they are the foundation of the human sciences.

For the purposes of our discussion, we can draw two conclusions from this brief review:

1. It is impossible to treat problems of signification seriously, in linguistics or semiology, without including in these considerations *the subject thus formulated as operating consciousness*. This phenomenological conception of the speaking subject is made possible in modern linguistics by the introduction of logic into generative grammar and, in a much more lucid manner, through a linguistics (developing in France after Benveniste) that is attuned to the *subject of enunciation* and includes in the latter's operating consciousness not only logical modalities, but also interlocutory relationships.

2. If it is true, consequently, that the question of signification and therefore of modern linguistics is dominated by Husserl, the attempts to criticize or "deconstruct" phenomenology bear concurrently on Husserl, meaning, the still transcendental subject of enunciation, and linguistic methodology. These criticisms circumscribe the metaphysics inherent in the sciences of signification and therefore in the human sciences—an important epistemological task in itself. But they reveal their own shortcomings not so much, as some believe, in that they prevent serious theoretical or scientific research, but in that such "deconstructions" refuse (through discrediting the signified and with it the transcendental ego)

what constitutes one function of language though not the only one: to express meaning in a communicable sentence between speakers. This function harbors coherence (which is indeed transcendental) or, in other words, social identity. Let us first acknowledge, with Husserl, this thetic character of the signifying act, which establishes the transcendent object and the transcendental ego of communication (and consequently of sociability), before going beyond the Husserlian problematic to search for that which produces, shapes, and exceeds the operating consciousness (this will be our purpose when confronting poetic language). Without that acknowledgment, which is also that of the episteme underlying structuralism, any reflection on significance, by refusing its thetic character, will continually ignore its constraining, legislative, and socializing elements: under the impression that it is breaking down the metaphysics of the signified or the transcendental ego, such a reflection will become lodged in a negative theology that denies their limitations.

Finally, even when the researcher in the field, beginning with what is now a descriptive if not scientific perspective, thinks he has discovered givens that may escape the *unity* of the transcendental ego (because each identity would be as if flaked into a multiplicity of qualities or appurtenances), the discourse of knowledge that delivers this multiplied identity to us remains a prisoner of phenomenological reason for which the multiplicities, inasmuch as they signify, are givens of consciousness, predicates within the same eidetic unity: the unity of an object signified by and for a transcendental ego. In an interpretive undertaking for which there is no domain heterogeneous to meaning, all material diversities, as multiple attributes, revert to a real (transcendental) object. Even apparently psychoanalytic interpretations (relationship to parents, etc.), from the moment they are posited by the structuring learning as particularities of the transcendental real object, are false multiplicities; deprived of what is heterogeneous to meaning, these multiplicities can only produce a plural identity—but an identity all the same, since it is eidetic, transcendental. Husserl therefore stands on the threshold not only of modern linguistics concerned with a subject of enunciation, but of any science of man as signified phenomenon, whose objecthood, even if multiple, is to be restored.

To the extent that poetic language operates with and communicates meaning, it also shares particularities of the signifying operations elucidated by Husserl (correlation between signified object and the transcendental ego, operating consciousness, which constitutes itself by predication—by syntax—as thetic: thesis of Being, thesis of the object, thesis of the ego). Meaning and signification, however, do not exhaust the poetic function. Therefore, the thetic predicative operation and its correlatives (signified object and transcendental ego), though valid for the signifying economy of poetic language, are only one of its *limits*: certainly constitutive, but not all-encompassing. While poetic language can indeed be studied through its meaning and signification (by revealing, depending on the method, either structures or process), such a study would, in the final analysis, amount to reducing it to the phenomenological perspective and, hence, failing to see what in the poetic function departs from the signified and the transcendental ego and makes of what is known as "literature" something other than knowledge: the very place where social code is destroyed and renewed, thus providing, as Artaud writes, "A release for the anguish of its time" by "animating, attracting, lowering onto its shoulders the wandering anger of a particular time for the discharge of its psychological evil-being."[11]

Consequently, one should begin by positing that there is within poetic language (and therefore, although in a less pronounced manner, within any language) a *heterogeneousness* to meaning and signification. This *heterogeneousness*, detected genetically in the first echolalias of infants as rhythms and intonations anterior to the first phonemes, morphemes, lexemes, and sentences; this heterogeneousness, which is later reactivated as rhythms, intonations, glossalalias in psychotic discourse, serving as ultimate support of the speaking subject threatened by the collapse of the signifying function; this heterogeneousness to signification operates through, despite, and in excess of it and produces in poetic language "musical" but also nonsense effects that destroy not only accepted beliefs and significations, but, in radical experiments, syntax itself, that guarantee of thetic consciousness (of the signified object and ego)—for example, carnivalesque discourse, Artaud, a number of texts by Mallarmé, certain Dadaist and Surrealist experiments. The notion of *heterogeneity* is indispensable, for though articulate, precise, organized, and complying with constraints and rules (especially, like the rule of *repetition*, which articulates the units of a particular rhythm or intonation), this signifying disposition is not that of meaning or signification: no sign, no predication, no signified object and therefore no operating consciousness of a transcendental ego. We shall call this disposition *semiotic* (*le sémiotique*), meaning, according to the etymology of the Greek *sémeion* (σημεῖον), a distinctive mark, trace, index, the premonitory sign, the proof, engraved mark, imprint—in short, a *distinctiveness* admitting of an uncertain and indeterminate articulation because it does not yet refer (for young children) or no longer refers (in psychotic discourse) to a signified object for a thetic consciousness (this side of, or through, both object and consciousness). Plato's *Timaeus* speaks of a *chora* (χώρα), receptacle (ὑποδοχεῖον), unnameable, improbable, hybrid, anterior to naming, to the One, to the father, and consequently, maternally connoted to such an extent that it merits "not even the rank of syllable." One can describe more precisely than did philosophical intuition the particularities of this signifying disposition that I have just named semiotic—a term which quite clearly designates that we are dealing with a disposition that is definitely heterogeneous to meaning but always in sight of it or in either a negative or surplus relationship to it. Research I have recently undertaken on child language acquisition in the prephonological, one could say prepredicative stages, or anterior to the "mirror stage," as well as another concomitant study on particularities of psychotic discourse aim notably at describing as precisely as possible—with the help of, for example, modern phono-acoustics—these semiotic operations (rhythm, intonation) and their dependence vis-à-vis the body's drives observable through muscular constractions and the libidinal or sublimated cathexis that accompany vocalizations. It goes without saying that, concerning a *signifying practice*, that is, a socially communicable discourse like poetic language, this semiotic heterogeneity posited by theory is inseparable from what I shall call, to distinguish it from the latter, the *symbolic* function of significance. The symbolic (*le symbolique*), as opposed to the semiotic, is this inevitable attribute of meaning, sign, and the signified object for the consciousness of Husserl's transcendental ego. Language as social practice necessarily presupposes these two dispositions, though combined in different ways to constitute *types of discourse*, types of signifying practices. Scientific discourse, for example, aspiring to the status of metalanguage, tends to reduce as much as possible the semiotic component. On the contrary, the signifying economy of poetic language is specific in that the semiotic is not only a constraint as is the symbolic, but it tends to gain the upper hand at the expense of the thetic and predicative constraints of the ego's judging consciousness. Thus in any poetic language, not only do the rhythmic constraints, for example, perform an organizing function that could go so far as to violate certain grammatical rules of a national language and often neglect the importance of an ideatory message, but in recent texts, these semiotic constraints (rhythm, phonic, vocalic timbres in Symbolist work, but also graphic disposition on the page) are accompanied by nonrecoverable syntactic elisions; it is impossible to reconstitute the particular elided syntactic category (object or verb), which makes the meaning of the utterance undecidable (for example, the nonrecoverable elisions in *Un Coup de Dés*).[12] However elided, attacked, or corrupted the symbolic function might be in poetic language, due to the impact of semiotic processes, the symbolic function nonetheless maintains its presence. It is for this reason that it is a language. First, it persists as an internal limit of this bipolar economy, since a multiple and sometimes even incomprehensible signified is nevertheless communicated; second, it persists also because the semiotic processes themselves, far from being set adrift (as they would be in insane discourse), set up a new formal construct: a so-called new formal or ideological "writer's universe," the never-finished, undefined production of a new space of significance. Husserl's "thetic function" of the signifying act is thus reassumed, but in different form: though poetic language unsettled the position of the signified and the transcendental ego, it nonetheless posits a thesis, not of a particular being or meaning, but of a signifying apparatus; it posits its own process as an undecidable process between sense and nonsense, between *language* and *rhythm* (in the sense of linkage that the word "rhythm" had for Aeschylus's *Prometheus* according to Heidegger's reading), between the symbolic and semiotic.

For a theory attuned to this kind of functioning, the language object itself appears quite differently than it would from a phenomenological perspective. Thus, a phoneme, as distinctive element of meaning, belongs to language as symbolic. But this same phoneme is involved in rhythmic, intonational repetitions; it thereby tends toward autonomy from meaning so as to maintain itself in a semiotic disposition near the instinctual drives' body; it is a sonorous distinctiveness, which therefore is no longer either a phoneme or a part of the symbolic system—one might say that its belonging to the set of the language is indefinite, between zero and one. Nevertheless, the set to which it thus belongs exists with this indefinition, with this fuzziness.

It is poetic language that awakens our attention to this undecidable character of any so-called natural language, a feature that univocal, rational, scientific discourse tends to hide—and this implies considerable consequences for its subject. The support of this signifying economy could not be the transcendental ego alone. If it is true that there would unavoidably be a speaking *subject* since the signifying set exists, it is nonetheless evident that this subject, in order to tally with its heterogeneity, must be, let us say, a questionable *subject-in-process*. It is of course Freud's theory of the unconscious that allows the apprehension of such a subject; for through the surgery it practiced in the operating consciousness of the transcendental ego, Freudian and Lacanian psychoanalysis did allow, not for (as certain simplifications would have it) a few typologies or structures that might accommodate the same phenomenological reason, but rather for heterogeneity, which, known as the unconscious, shapes the signifying function. In light of these statements, I shall now make a few remarks on the questionable subject-in-process of poetic language.

1. The semiotic activity, which introduces wandering or fuzziness into language and, a fortiori, into poetic language is, from a synchronic point of view, a mark of the workings of drives (appropriation/rejection, orality/anality, love/hate, life/death) and, from a diachronic point of view, stems from the archaisms of the semiotic body. Before recognizing itself as identical in a mirror and, consequently, as signifying, this body is dependent vis-à-vis the mother. At the same time instinctual and maternal, semiotic processes prepare the future speaker for entrance into meaning and signification (the symbolic). But the symbolic (i.e., language as nomination, sign, and syntax) constitutes itself only by breaking with this anteriority, which is retrieved as "signifier," "primary processes," displacement and condensation, metaphor and metonomy, rhetorical figures—but which always remains subordinate—subjacent to the principal function of naming-predicating. Language as symbolic function constitutes itself at the cost of repressing instinctual drive and continuous relation to the mother. On the contrary, the unsettled and questionable subject of poetic language (for whom the word is never uniquely sign) maintains itself at the cost of reactivating this repressed instinctual, maternal element. If it is true that the prohibition of incest constitutes, at the same time, language as communicative code and women as exchange objects in order for a society to be established, *poetic language would be* for its questionable subject-in-process the *equivalent of incest*: it is within the economy of signification itself that the questionable subject-in-process appropriates to itself this archaic, instinctual, and maternal territory; thus it simultaneously prevents the word from becoming mere sign and the mother from becoming an object like any other—forbidden. This passage into and through the forbidden, which constitutes the sign and is correlative to the prohibition of incest, is often explicit as such (Sade "Unless he becomes his mother's lover from the day she has brought him into the world, let him not bother to write, for we shall not read him,"— *Idée sur les romans*; Artaud, identifying with his "daughters"; Joyce and his daughter at the end of *Finnegans Wake*; Céline, who takes as pseu-

donym his grandmother's first name; and innumerable identifications with women, or dancers, that waver between fetishization and homosexuality). I stress this point for three reasons:

(*a*) To emphasize that the dominance of semiotic constraint in poetic language cannot be solely interpreted, as formalist poetics would have it, as a preoccupation with the "sign," or with the "signifier" at the expense of the "message"; rather, it is more deeply indicative of the instinctual drives' activity relative to the first structurations (constitution of the body as self) and identifications (with the mother).

(*b*) To elucidate the intrinsic connection between literature and breaking up social concord: because it utters incest, poetic language is linked with "evil"; "literature and evil" (I refer to a title by Georges Bataille) should be understood, beyond the resonances of Christian ethics, as the social body's self-defense against the discourse of incest as destroyer and generator of any language and sociality. This applies all the more as "great literature," which has mobilized unconsciousnesses for centuries, has nothing to do with the hypostasis of incest (a petty game of fetishists at the end of an era, priesthood of a would-be enigma—the forbidden mother); on the contrary, this incestuous relation, exploding in language, embracing it from top to bottom in such a *singular* fashion that it defies *generalizations*, still has this common feature in all outstanding cases: it presents itself as demystified, even disappointed, deprived of its hallowed function as support of the law, in order to become the cause of a permanent trial of the speaking subject, a cause of that agility, of that analytic "competency" that legend attributes to Ulysses.

(*c*) It is of course possible, as Lévi-Strauss pointed out to Dr. André Green, to ignore the mother-child relationship within a given anthropological vision of society; now, given not only the thematization of this relationship, but especially the mutations in the very economy of discourse attributable to it, one must, in discussing poetic language, consider what this presymbolic and transsymbolic relationship to the mother introduces as aimless wandering within the identity of the speaker and the economy of its very discourse. Moreover, this relationship of the speaker to the mother is probably one of the most important factors producing interplay within the structure of meaning as well as a questioning process of subject and history.

2. And yet, this reinstatement of maternal territory into the very economy of language does not lead its questioned subject-in-process to repudiate its symbolic disposition. Formulator—logothete, as Roland Barthes would say—the subject of poetic language continually but never defini-

tively assumes the thetic function of naming, establishing meaning and signification, which the paternal function represents within reproductive relation. Son permanently at war with father, not in order to take his place, nor even to endure it, erased from reality, as a symbolic, divine menace and salvation in the manner of Senatspräsident Schreber. But rather, to signify what is untenable in the symbolic, nominal, paternal function. If symbolic and social cohesion are maintained by virtue of a sacrifice (which makes of a *soma* a sign toward an unnameable transcendence, so that only thus are signifying and social structures clinched even though they are ignorant of this sacrifice) and if the paternal function represents this sacrificial function, then it is not up to the poet to adjust to it. Fearing its rule but sufficiently aware of the legislation of language not to be able to turn away from this sacrificial-paternal function, he takes it by storm and from the flank. In *Maldoror*, Lautréamont struggles against the Omnipotent. After the death of his son Anatole, Mallarmé writes a *Tombeau*, thanks to which a book replaces not only the dead son, his own father, mother, and fiancée at the same time, but also hallowed humanism and the "instinct of heaven" itself. The most analytical of them all, the Marquis de Sade, gives up this battle with, or for, the symbolic legislation represented by the father, in order to attack the power represented by a woman, Madame de Montreuil, visible figurehead of a dynasty of matrons toward whom he usurps, through writing, the role of father and incestuous son; here, the transgression is carried out and the transsymbolic, transpaternal function of poetic language reaches its thematic end by staging a simultaneously impossible, sacrificial, and orgastic society—never one without the other.

Here we must clearly distinguish two positions: that of the rhetorician and that of the writer in the strongest sense of the word; that is, as Céline puts it, one who has "style." The rhetorician does not invent a language; fascinated by the symbolic function of paternal discourse, he *seduces* it in the Latin sense of the verb—he "leads it astray," inflicts it with a few anomalies generally taken from writers of the past, thus miming a father who remembers having been a son and even a daughter of his father, but not to the point of leaving cover. This is indeed what is happening to the discourse of contemporary philosophers, in France particularly, when, hemmed in by the breakthroughs in social sciences on the one hand, and social upheavals on the other, the philosopher begins performing literary tricks, thus arrogating to himself a power over imaginations: a power which, though minor in appearance, is more fetching than that of the transcendental consciousness. The stylist's adventure is totally different; he no longer needs to seduce the father by rhetorical affectations. As winner of the battle, he may even drop the name of the father to take a pseudonym (Céline signs with his grand-mother's first name), and thus, in the place of the father, assume a different discourse; neither imaginary discourse of the self, nor discourse of transcendental knowledge, but a permanent go-between from one to the other, a pulsation of sign and rhythm, of consciousness and instinctual drive. "I am the father of my imaginative creations," writes Mallarmé at the birth of Geneviève. "I am my father, my mother, my son, and me," Artaud claims. Stylists all, they sound a dissonance within the thetic, paternal function of language.

3. Psychosis and fetishism represent the two abysses that threaten the unstable subject of poetic language, as twentieth-century literature has only too clearly demonstrated. As to *psychosis*, symbolic legality is wiped out in favor of arbitrariness of an instinctual drive without meaning and communication; panicking at the loss of all reference, the subject goes through fantasies of omnipotence or identification with a totalitarian leader. On the other hand, where *fetishism* is concerned, constantly dodging the paternal, sacrificial function produces an objectification of the pure signifier, more and more emptied of meaning—an insipid formalism. Nevertheless, far from thus becoming an unpleasant or negligible accident within the firm progress of symbolic process (which, in the footsteps of science, would eventually find signified elements for all signifiers, as rationalists believe), these borderline experiences, which contemporary poetic language has undergone, perhaps more dramatically than before or elsewhere, show not only that the Saussurian cleavage (signifier/signified) is forever unbridgeable, but also that it is reinforced by another, even more radical one between an instinctual, semioticizing body, heterogeneous to signification, and this very signification based on prohibition (of incest), sign, and thetic signification establishing signified object and transcendental ego. Through the permanent contradiction between these two dispositions (semiotic/symbolic), of which the internal setting off of the sign (signifier/signified) is merely a witness, poetic language, in its most disruptive form (unreadable for meaning, dangerous for the subject), shows the constraints of a civilization dominated by transcendental rationality. Consequently, it is a means of overriding this constraint. And if in so doing it sometimes falls in with deeds brought about by the same rationality, as is, for example, the instinctual determination of fascism—demonstrated as such by Wilhelm Reich—poetic language is also there to forestall such translations into action.

This means that if poetic economy has always borne witness to crises and impossibilities of transcendental symbolics, in our time it is coupled with crises of social institutions (state, family, religion), and, more profoundly, a turning point in the relationship of man to meaning. Transcendental mastery over discourse is possible, but repressive; such a position is necessary, but only as a limit open to constant challenge; this relief with respect to repression—establishing meaning—is no longer possible under the incarnate appearance of a providential, historical, or even rationalist, humanist ego (in the manner of Renan), but through a *discordance* in the symbolic function and consequently within the identity of the transcendental ego itself: this is what the literary experience of our century intimates to theoretical reason, thereby taking its place with other phenomena of symbolic and social unrest (youth, drugs, women).

Without entering into a technical analysis of the economy specific to poetic language (an analysis too subtle and specious, considering the purpose of this specific paper), I shall extract from Céline, first, several procedures and, second, several themes, which illustrate the position of the unsettled, questionable subject-in-process of poetic language. I shall not do this without firmly underlining that these themes are not only inseparable from "style," but that they are produced by it; in other words, it is not necessary "to know" them, one could have heard them by simply listening to Céline's staccato, rhythmic discourse, stuffed with jargon and obscenity.

Thus, going beyond semantic themes and their distributions, one ought to examine the functioning of poetic language and its questionable subject-in-process, beginning with constitutive linguistic operations: syntax and semantics. Two phenomena, among others, will become the focus of our attention in Céline's writing: *sentential rhythms* and *obscene words*. These are of interest not only because they seem to constitute a particularity of his discourse, but also because, though they function differently, both of them involve constitutive operations of the judging consciousness (therefore of identity) by simultaneously perturbing its clarity and the designation of an object (objecthood). Moreover, if they constitute a network of constraints that is added to denotative signification, such a network has nothing to do with classic poeticness (rhythm, meter, conventional rhetorical figures) because it is drawn from the drives' register of a desiring body, both identifying with and rejecting a community (familial or folk). Therefore, even if the so-called poetic codes are not recognizable within poetic language, a constraint that I have termed semiotic functions in addition to the judging consciousness, provokes its lapses, or compensates for them; in so doing, it refers neither to a literary convention (like our poetic canons, contemporary with the major national epics and the constitution of nations themselves) nor even to the body *itself*, but rather, to a signifying disposition, pre- or transsymbolic, which fashions any judging consciousness so that any ego recognizes its crisis within it. It is a jubilant recognition that, in "modern" literature, replaces petty aesthetic pleasure.

Sentential rhythms. Beginning with *Death on the Installment Plan*, the sentence is condensed: not only does Céline avoid coordination and embeddings, but when different "object-phrases" are, for example, numerous and juxtaposed with a verb, they are separated by the characteristic "three dots." This procedure divides the sentence into its constitutive phrases; they thus tend to become independent of the central verb, to detach themselves from the sentence's own signification, and to acquire a meaning initially incomplete and consequently capable of taking on multiple connotations that no longer depend on the framework of the sentence, but on a free context (the entire book, but also, all the addenda of which the reader is capable). Here, there are no syntactic anomalies (as in the *Coup de Dés* or the glossalalias of Artaud). The predicative thesis, constitutive of the judging consciousness, is maintained. By using three dots to space the phrases making up a sentence, thus giving them rhythm, he causes connotation to rush through a predication that has been striated in that manner; the denotated object of the utterance, the transcendental object, loses its clear contours. The elided object in the sentence relates to a hesitation (if not an erasure) of the *real object* for the speaking subject. That literature is witness to this kind of deception involving the object (object of love or transcendental object), that the existence of the object is more than fleeting and indeed impossible: this is what Céline's rhythms and syntactic elisions have recently evidenced within the stern humor of an experiment and with all its implications for the subject. This is also true of Beckett, whose recent play, *Not I*, spoken by a dying woman, sets forth in elided sentences and floating phrases the impossibility of God's existence for a speaking subject lacking any object of signification and/or love. Moreover, beyond and with connotation, with the blurred or erased object, there flows through meaning this "emotion" of which Céline speaks—the nonsemanticized instinctual drive that precedes and exceeds meaning.

The exclamation marks alternating with three dots even more categorically point to this surge of instinctual drive: a panting, a breathlessness, an acceleration of verbal utterance, concerned not so much with finally reaching a global summing up of the world's meaning, as, to the contrary, with revealing, within the interstices of predication, the rhythm of a drive that remains forever unsatisfied—in the vacancy of judging consciousness and sign—because it could not find an other (an addressee) so as to obtain meaning in this exchange. We must also listen to Céline, Artaud, or Joyce, and read their texts in order to understand that the aim of this practice, which reaches us as a language, is, through the signification of the nevertheless transmitted message, not only to impose a music, a rhythm—that is, a polyphony—but also to wipe out sense through nonsense and laughter. This is a difficult operation that obliges the reader not so much to combine significations as to shatter his own judging consciousness in order to grant passage through it to this rhythmic drive constituted by repression and, once filtered by language and its meaning, experienced as jouissance. Could the resistance against modern literature be evidence of an obsession with meaning, of an unfitness for such jouissance?

Obscene words. Semantically speaking, these pivotal words in the Célinian lexicon exercise a *desemanticization* function analogous to the fragmentation of syntax by rhythm. Far from referring, as do all signs, to an object exterior to discourse and identifiable as such by consciousness, the obscene word is the minimal mark of a situation of desire where the identity of the signifying subject, if not destroyed, is exceeded by a conflict of instinctual drives linking one subject to another. There is nothing better than an obscene word for perceiving the limits of a phenomenological linguistics faced with the heterogeneous and complex architectonics of significance. The obscene word, lacking an objective referent, is also the contrary of an autonym—which involves the function of a word or utterance as sign; the obscene word mobilizes the signifying resources of the subject, permitting it to cross through the membrane of meaning where consciousness holds it, connecting it to gesturality, kinesthesia, the drives' body, the movement of rejection and appropriation of the other. Then, it is neither object, transcendental signified, nor signifier available to a neutralized consciousness: around the object denoted by the obscene word, and that object provides a scanty delineation, more than a simple context asserts itself—the drama of a questioning process heterogeneous to the meaning that precedes and exceeds it. Childrens' counting-out rhymes, or what one calls the "obscene folklore of children," utilize the same rhythmic and semantic resources; they maintain the subject close to these jubilatory dramas that run athwart the repression that a univocal, increasingly pure signifier vainly attempts to impose upon the subject. By reconstituting them, and this on the very level of language, literature achieves its cathartic effects.

Several themes in Céline bring to light the relationships of force, at first within the family triangle, and then in contemporary society, that produce, promote, and accompany the particularities of poetic language to which I have just referred.

In *Death on the Installment Plan*, the most "familial" of Céline's writings, we find a paternal figure, Auguste: a man "of instruction," "a mind," sullen, a prohibitor, prone to scandal, full of obsessional habits like, for example, cleaning the flagstones in front of his shop. His anger explodes spectacularly once, when he shuts himself up in the basement and shoots his pistol for hours, not without explaining in the face of general disapproval, "I have my conscience on my side," just before falling ill. "My mother wrapped the weapon in several layers of newspaper and then in a cashmere shawl . . . 'Come, child . . . come!' she said when we were alone [. . .] We threw the package in the drink."[13]

Here is an imposing and menacing father, strongly emphasizing the enviable necessity of his position, but spoiling it by his derisive fury: undermined power whose weapon one could only take away in order to engulf it at the end of a journey between mother and son.

In an interview, Céline compares himself to a "society woman" who braves the nevertheless maintained family prohibition, and who has the right to her own desire, "a choice in a drawing room": "the whore's trade doesn't interest me"; before defining himself, at the end: "I am the son of a woman who restored old lace . . . [I am] one of those rare men who knows how to distinguish batiste from valencienne . . . I do not need to be taught. I know it."

This fragile delicacy, heritage of the mother, supports the language—or if you wish, the identity—of him who unseated what Céline calls the "heaviness" of men, of fathers, in order to flee it. The threads of instinctual drive, exceeding the law of the paternal word's own mastery, are nonetheless woven with scrupulous precision. One must therefore conceive of another disposition of the law, through signified and signifying identity and confronting the semiotic network: a disposition closer to the Greek *gnomon* ("one that knows," "carpenter's square") than to the Latin *lex*, which necessarily implies the act of logical and legal judgment. A device, then, a regulated discrimination, weaves the semiotic network of instinctual drives; if it thus fails to conform to signifying identity, it nevertheless constitutes another identity closer to repressed and gnomic archaisms, susceptible of a psychosis-inducing explosion, where we decipher the relationship of the speaker to a desiring and desired mother.

In another interview, this maternal reference to old lacework is explicitly thought of as an archeology of the word: "No! In the beginning was emotion. The Word came next to replace emotion as the trot replaces the gallop [. . .] They pulled man out of emotive poetry in order to plunge him into dialectics, that is, into gibberish, right?" Anyway, what is *Rigodon* if not a popular dance which obliges language to bow to the rhythm of its emotion.

A speech thus slatted by instinctual drive—Diderot would have said "musicated"—could not describe, narrate, or theatricalize "objects": by its composition and signification it also goes beyond the accepted categories of lyric, epic, dramatic, or tragic. The last writings of Céline, plugged in live to an era of war, death, and genocide, are what he calls in *North*, "the vivisection of the wounded," "the circus," "the three hundred years before Christ."

While members of the Resistance sing in alexandrine verse, it is Céline's language that records not only the institutional but also the profoundly symbolic jolt involving meaning and the identity of transcendental reason; fascism inflicted this jolt on our universe and the human sciences have hardly begun to figure out its consequences. I am saying that this literary discourse enunciates through its formal decentering, more apparent in Artaud's glossalalias, but also through the rhythms and themes of violence in Céline, better than anything else, the faltering of transcendental consciousness: this does not mean that such a discourse is aware of such a faltering or interprets it. As proof, writing that pretends to agree with "circus" and "vivisection" will nonetheless find its idols, even if only provisional; though dissolved in laughter and dominant nonsense, they are nevertheless posited as idols in Hitlerian ideology. A reading of any one of Céline's anti-Semitic tracts is sufficient to show the crudely exhibited phantasms of an analysand struggling against a desired and frustrating, castrating, and sodomizing father; sufficient also to understand that it is not enough to allow what is repressed by the symbolic structure to emerge in a "musicated" language to avoid its traps. Rather, we must in addition dissolve its sexual determinations. Unless poetic work can be linked to analytical interpretation, the discourse that undermines the judging consciousness and releases its repressed instinctual drive as rhythm always turns out to be at fault from the viewpoint of an ethic that remains with the transcendental ego—whatever joys or negations might exist in Spinoza's or Hegel's.

Since at least Hölderlin, poetic language has deserted beauty and meaning to become a laboratory where, facing philosophy, knowledge, and the transcendental ego of all signification, the impossibility of a signified or signifying identity is being sustained. If we took this venture seriously—if we could hear the burst of black laughter it hurls at all attempts to master the human situation, to master language by language—we would be forced to reexamine "literary history," to rediscover beneath rhetoric and poetics its unchanging but always different polemic with the symbolic function. We could not avoid wondering about the possibility, or simultaneously, the legitimacy of a theoretical discourse on this practice of language whose stakes are precisely to render impossible the transcendental bounding that supports the discourse of knowledge.

Faced with this poetic language that defies knowledge, many of us are rather tempted to leave our shelter to deal with literature only by miming its meanderings, rather than by positing it as an object of knowledge. We let ourselves be taken in by this mimeticism: fictional, paraphilosophical, parascientific writings. It is probably necessary to be a woman (ultimate guarantee of sociality beyond the wreckage of the paternal symbolic function, as well as the inexhaustible generator of its renewal, of its expansion) not to renounce theoretical reason but to compel it to increase its power by giving it an object beyond its limits. Such a position, it seems to me, provides a possible basis for a theory of signification, which, confronted with poetic language, could not in any way account for it, but would rather use it as an indication of what is heterogeneous to meaning (to sign and predication): instinctual economies, always and at the same time open to biophysiological socio-historical constraints.

This kind of heterogeneous economy and its questionable subject-in-process thus calls for a linguistics other than the one descended from the phenomenological heavens—a linguistics capable, within its language object, of accounting for a nonetheless articulated *instinctual drive*, across and through the constitutive and insurmountable frontier of *meaning*. This instinctual drive, however, located in the matrix of the sign, refers back to an instinctual body (to which psychoanalysis has turned its attention), which ciphers the language with rhythmic, intonational, and other arrangements, nonreducible to the position of the transcendental ego even though always within sight of its thesis.

The development of this theory of signification is in itself regulated by Husserlian precepts, because it inevitably makes an *object* even of that which departs from meaning. But, even though abetting the law of signifying structure as well as of all sociality, this expanded theory of signification cannot give itself new objects except by positing itself as nonuniversal: that is, by presupposing that a questionable subject-in-process exists in an economy of discourse other than that of thetic consciousness. And this requires that subjects of the theory must be themselves subjects in infinite analysis; this is what Husserl could not imagine, what Céline could not know, but what a woman, among others, can finally admit, aware as she is of the inanity of Being.

When it avoids the risks that lie in wait for it, literary experience remains nevertheless something other than this analytical theory, which it never stops challenging. Against knowing thought, poetic language pursues an effect of *singular truth*, and thus accomplishes, perhaps, for the modern community, this solitary practice that the materialists of antiquity unsuccessfully championed against the ascendance of theoretical reason.

NOTES

"D'une identité l'autre," the original title of Kristeva's essay reflects and makes use of the title of Céline's novel *D'un château l'autre*. Although this has been translated as *Castle to Castle*, the more literal "From One Identity to an Other" has been chosen in order to keep the ambiguous feeling of the French as well as the word "other," an important one in philosophy since Hegel and also in Kristeva's work.—Trans.

1. Claude Lévi-Strauss, *L'Homme nu* (Paris: Plon, 1971), p. 615.

2. Kristeva's French phrase is *mise en procès*, which, like *le sujet en procès*, refers to an important, recurring concept—that of a constantly changing subject whose identity is open to question.

3. Ernest Renan, *Oeuvres complètes*, (Paris: Calmann-Lévy, 1947–58) 3:322.

4. Ernest Renan, *The Future of Science* (Boston: Roberts Bros., 1891), p. 402.

5. Lévi-Strauss, *L'Homme nu*, p. 614.

6. See Jean Starobinski, *Les Mots sous les mots* (Paris: Gallimard, 1971).—Ed.

7. Edmund Husserl, *Logical Investigations*, J. N. Findlay, tr. (London: Routledge & Kegan Paul, 1970), pp. 276–77.

8. Edmund Husserl, *Ideas: General Introduction to Pure Phenomenology*, W. R. Boyce Gibson, tr. (London: Collier-Macmillan, 1962), pp. 93–94 and 101.

9. Edmund Husserl, *Erste Philosophie*, VIII, in *Husserliana* (The Hague: Hrsg. von R. Boehm, 1956).

10. Husserl, *Ideas*, p. 313.

11. Antonin Artaud, "L'Anarchie sociale de l'art," in *Oeuvres complètes* (Paris: Gallimard, 1956), 8:287.

12. See Kristeva, *La Révolution du language poétique* (Paris: Seuil, 1974), pp. 274ff.—Ed.

13. Louis-Ferdinand Céline, *Death on the Installment Plan*, Ralph Manheim, tr. (New York: New Directions, 1966), p. 78.

Time and Sense

Is Sensation a Form of Language?

Freud's View of Perception and Consciousness: Questions of Identity and Difference

We know that the notion of sensation is not central in Freud's writings. Even so, he addresses the concept in his letters to Fliess (1887–1902), in his *Project for a Scientific Psychology* (1895), in his *Interpretation of Dreams* (1900), and finally in his much-discussed *Note upon the "Mystic Writing-Pad"* (1925). Although Freud adapts his notion of sensation to suit his continually developing work, certain points remain consistent throughout these four texts.

First of all, perception is connected to the Perceptual-Conscious system, which lacks memory because it retains no trace of what has occurred.

Yet in the beginning were perceptions. What is a perception? "[It consists of] neurons in which perceptions originate, to which consciousness attaches, but which in themselves retain no trace of what has happened. For *consciousness and memory are mutually exclusive*."[1]

This is followed by the "indication of perception," which is "the *first registration* of the perceptions; *it is quite incapable of consciousness*, and arranged according to associations by simultaneity."

Unconsciousness "is the second registration, arranged according to other (perhaps causal) relations."

It is important to note here that perception "registers" "simultaneity" and the unconscious registers "causal relations."

Unconscious traces "would perhaps correspond to *conceptual memories*; equally inaccessible to consciousness."

The *preconscious* is "the third transcription, attached to word-presentations and corresponding to our official ego. . . . This *secondary thought-consciousness* is subsequent in time, and is probably linked to the hallucinatory activation of word-presentations, so that the neurons of consciousness would once again be perceptual neurons and in themselves without memory."

Freud adds: "I explain the peculiarities of the psychoneuroses by supposing that *the translation has not taken place* in the case of some of the material."[2]

These passages are still worthy of note, not because of the neurological notions they offer (notions that have been challenged by more recent advances in neurological research) but because they propose a *multilayered model* (Perception, Unconsciousness, Consciousness). Each layer is defined by the presence (or absence) of language, memory, or both language and memory. According to Freud's early model, the three layers must be subjected to a sort of "translation" of the subject to function in a psychologically sound manner.

We must not misinterpret the term *perceptual-conscious.*[3] Although Freud may seem to be positing an *identity* between Perception and Consciousness, he also emphasizes their *difference* by stressing that word-presentations in the preconscious and the "secondary thought-consciousness" he associates with the hallucinatory activation of word-presentations are *subsequent.*

What Freud calls the *Wahrnehmung* (ω) system—"perception"—is set into motion by quantities minute enough for quantity to become quality. This third system of neurons (ω-neurons) consists of "neurons of perception." It functions alongside the exogenous ψ-neurons and the endogenous ψ-neurons. The ω-system transmits neither quantity nor quality to the ψ-system, for it can only excite ψ: "In the case of every external perception a qualitative excitation occurs in system ω, which in the first instance, however, has no significance for system ψ. It must be added that the system ω excitation leads to system ω discharge, and information of this . . . reaches system ψ. *The information of this discharge from system ω is thus the indication of quality or of reality for system ψ.*"[4]

In a second logical and chronological stage, during which judgment comes into play, "the perceptions, on account of their possible connection with the wished-for object, [arouse] interest, and their complexes are dissected into an unassimilable component (the thing) and one known to the ego from its own experience (attribute, activity)—what we call *understanding*."[5] Note that the *wished-for* (and unassimilable) object appears at the same time as *understanding*, both of which are placed in sharp contrast to the preceding instance of sensation-perception founded on "information" and "indications."

The implications of this are clear: perception (*Wahrnehmung*) "excites" understanding, which makes understanding a *secondary effect*. This process is contingent on *two sorts* of contact with verbal expression. It is important to note that these are two distinct experiences—and their dissimilarity is what facilitates the passage from perception to expression.

On the one hand, painful objects make us cry out, and these cries endow the object with its character by making it an object of suffering that is capable of leaving us with a conscious memory, whereas perception that is not inscribed through a verbal expression (such as a simple scream) cannot be remembered. Freud associates the objects that make us cry out with pain with a second class of sonorous objects: complex, perceptual objects for which sound plays a pivotal role.

On the other hand, a supplementary process comes into play. "In virtue of the trend towards *imitation*, which emerges during judging, it is possible to find the information of movement attaching to this sound-image."[6] The series of movements can thus become conscious, and one can voluntarily emit sounds that are associated with particular perceptions. By observing these auditory signs of discharge, the subject discovers memories in himself that become conscious perceptions and can be invested by the ψ-system.

"Thus we have found that it is characteristic of the process of *cognitive* thought that during it attention is from the first directed to the *indications* of thought-discharge, to the indications of speech."[7]

Here Freud takes a logical shortcut that is important to note: information of discharged thought *sets into motion* the process of *cognitive thinking*, yet it is not the same as cognitive thinking. Similarly, auditory *imitation* or cries are not the same as *linguistic signs*, as Freud would lead us to believe. Freud forgets, however, that he used the word *index* to describe the perception and its expression. The link between a given sensation (of a pain or of a sound) and a given vocal utterance (expressing distress or imitation and object) places the subject in what Freud calls *thing-presentations*, and not in *word-presentations*.[8] It places them in what Melanie Klein and Hanna Segal call "symbolic equivalencies" (cries, imitation)[9] and in a domain of *signifiance* that is not one of verbal representation or the linguistic signifier. Instead, it is the register of the memory trace, of "representability," of the "container" or the "fetish"— a register that does not separate the thing represented from the representing self. It can grow into or merge with a sign-judgment, or it can remain at its own level without ever reaching that of the representation or of the signifier.

In reality, the *Unconscious* is what enables Freud's model of the psychic apparatus to function as a cognitive apparatus. We see the unconscious at work in the metaphor of the mystic writing-pad.

The psychic apparatus contains two layers: the upper layer (the stimulus-screen) and the lower layer (the surface that receives the stimulus), which is known as the Perceptual-Conscious system. The piece of celluloid is compared to the Perceptual-Conscious system with its stimulus-screen, while the waxed paper on which the trace is engraved is compared to the Unconscious: the Unconscious is a protected receptacle of endogenous or exogenous perceptual excitations, and its traces can be registered such that they imitate motor activity and eventually turn into judgments. Such a model requires several conditions:

- an accumulation and a reactivation of preconscious verbal representations;
- a lessening of the quantity of perceptual excitation through the possible intervention of a psychopharmacological drug; and
- the intervention of a third factor operating within the space between the other two and serving as both a screen for the excitation and a liaison with the world of signs. This third factor would play a pre-Oedipal, paternal role and would be a source of support for primary identification. Freud does not address this third element (which is a precondition for signs and thought) until he addresses the neurological model of perception as he pursues later developments in his discovery of psychoanalysis.

Taken as a whole, Freudian theory offers us a concept of sensation-perception that is *separate* from the strictly psychoanalytic view that identification and the Oedipal complex are essential for mental functioning.

What is more, after Freud isolates the *Wahrnehmung* (ω) system from the φ-exogenous and ψ-endogenous systems, he identifies Perception and Consciousness by relying on a paradox or an impatient logic (that Lacan cultivated) seeking to identify prelanguage and language (cries and imitation = judgment). Freud's notion presents us with two possibilities:

either we take into account logical impatience (or confusion?), which would imply the eradication of the internal hierarchy of the psychic apparatus described in the *Note upon the "Mystic Writing-Pad,"* or we revive the "multilayered" function of the psychic apparatus by trying to return to the logical order of judgment that cloaks the anterior or inferior stages made up of *quasi-signs*. In such stages, we find what I call the "semiotic"[10] and what Freud calls "cries," "imitations," and "perceptions-excitations," which can reach consciousness only if they are linked with language and with unconscious desires (even though they come from a different register).

If we accept the second hypothesis, we understand that the speaking subject's access to sensations requires an expanded and nuanced rhetoric. This rhetoric could name unnameable experiences without becoming reduced to a "pure signifier" but by relying on perceptive and sensory regression. Whether you are a therapist or a writer, if you seek to offer signs and style to this sensory cave, which is for the most part unnameable, you will encounter a true experience (*Erlebnis* and *Erfahrung*).[11] After you identify yourself with what is perceived and who is perceiving, you become not a "decoder" but an "encoder," a "nomothet," as Plato says in the *Cratylus*, a legislator, a creator of a language able to describe a singular experience.

Before returning to this *poiesis* of sensory nomination, let us take a brief detour through the cognitivist approach to sensation-perception.

The Cognitivists' Appropriation of Sensation

Cognitivists are the only contemporary theoreticians who study the sequence of sensation, perception, and emotion. Most of them believe that sensations are either *complementary judgments* (such as statements where the sensation of redness is the same as the clause "I sense redness" and where *red* is an *object*, a *logical complement*) or *adverbial judgments* (such as "I feel as if it were red" when *red* is being used as an adverb). Such judgments may or may not be accompanied by emotions that are themselves evaluating *judgments*. According to the cognitivists, whether *cognitive awareness* is central to perception or simply a precondition for perception, it is intrinsic to the process of sensation.[12]

Some researchers have challenged these claims, basing their criticisms on recorded observations of phylogenetic and ontogenetic phenomena. When animals perceive certain conditions in their environment and react with fear, for example, their fear stems not from an evaluative *judgment* but from their initial *impulse*. Similarly, when children are affected by a color or a sound they have perceived, they show their reaction on their face *before* they have acquired the tools of evaluative logic. In the field of psychology, R. B. Zajonc (in a 1980 article published in *American Psychologist*) has proposed that olfactory and gustatory stimuli (like aural stimuli for infants) prompt immediate emotional responses that do not necessarily entail judgment.[13] We know that certain emotional and sensory states can be induced by various drugs and hormones (valium, for instance, alters the state of the subject's perceptions and emotions without regard for his evaluation of the information he takes in). We also know that in human beings as well as in animals, emotions can be stimulated without implicating the part of the brain used in judgment.

In many species, moreover, a direct line can be traced between the retina and the hypothalamus, and this connection enables the organism to generate an emotional reaction to respond to sensory input. Although we do not know for certain that this line exists in human beings, such a connection might explain why certain tests have revealed our "noncognitive preference" for tones and polygons that we perceive spontaneously even when they are so blurred that they can no longer be distinguished from one another.

For these reasons, several scholars have concluded that although sensations-emotions *can* stem from rational evaluation, the ability to create propositions *is not* a precondition for sensations-emotions.

In response to these findings, scholars such as S. G. Clarke have suggested that we consider both feeling and emotion ("emotion as feeling," as Clarke puts it) to be unities of information that are *not complex enough* to adopt the form of a proposition or to be judgments (of threat, danger, misfortune, and so forth).[14] Although varying degrees of "cognitive (evaluative) penetration" can have a bearing on sensation, the cognitive process itself is not necessarily a precondition for sensation.

In fact, some sensations are "cognitively impenetrable," such as *akrasia* (the term used to describe the phenomenon by which sensations tend either to be delayed or to linger even after our affective judgment has changed). In other words, the rational control of sensations is not enough to change them. Even so, Clarke concludes that the constraints of normalization and signification affect perceptions and emotions before they can be controlled directly. We must remember, however, that these constraints are of another order. They are different from propositional processes such as "belief" or "evaluation" and should not be described in syntactic, semantic, or rhetorical terms.

Plato's Cave and the Sensory Cave

Let us turn briefly to the philosophical debate that asks whether a sensation is a thought. This debate has important ramifications for contemporary philosophical inquiry, but its origins date back to antiquity. The polemics of this debate inform two diametrically opposed conceptions of psychic life.

The trace (or perhaps the scar) of this debate dates back to the well-known episode in book seven of the *Republic*, in which Plato describes a *cave* at the rear of which dance shadows of chained prisoners and people carrying various objects. These "shadow" are "the *symbols of sensory experience,*" which are by the same token intelligible realities. There are two kinds of shadows, one primary and the other secondary. Both are cast by the Fire placed behind the prisoners. Fire being a symbol for the Sun or for Good and Evil. The prisoners see nothing but shadows of the outside world, yet if they leave the cave, they will be blinded by the sun. Thus they must access an intermediate reality that is neither a sensory illusion nor an invisible secret but a mathematical construction of forms providing a path toward true knowledge. Ever since Plato posited this notion, we have found ourselves in an *aporia of sensation*. Sensation, which cannot be reduced to ideas even though it is intrinsically dependent on them, can never be equivalent to Intelligence (because Intelligence is, after all, paramount). Nevertheless, sensation can only exist if it makes itself intelligible. The cave of Plato's "shadows" considers emotion to be a rudimentary stage along the path to representation. Tricked as it is by illusions, sensation is inevitably false, for it is always contingent upon the Intelligible.

The difficulty of defining sensation prompts us to shift our discussion to a disorder that has attracted the attention of psychotherapists, psychiatrists, neurologists, and contemporary psychoanalysts: autism. It has recently been suggested that autistic symptoms are caused by an inability to acquire language despite the existence of a complex sensory life.[15] I refer to this ailment because its specialists have offered a useful theoretical understanding of sensation and of the relationship between sensation and language.

The psychic and technical complexity of autism impels us to expand our philosophical paradigm and to posit what must be called *another cave*, one even more profound and inexpressible than Plato's. Indeed, since this cave is deprived of the intelligible and evaluative Fire-Sun, it is *a sensory cave without any symbols* (without "shadows," as Plato would say). In this sensory cave, a lived Experience (*Erlebnis*) that has not yet been given form by cognitive experience (*Erfahrung*),[16] and that often resists it, can nevertheless encounter thing-presentations that endow its inner workings with form and signification. Sensory experience, which is incited by thing-presentations, plays an important role in the psychic experience of the speaking subject. *Word-presentations* do not necessarily convey this experience. Although everyone has a sensory cave, some of us experience it as a psychic catastrophe (those afflicted with autism being the most extreme example), some attain jouissance from it (hysterics complain that what is felt and what is said are in constant conflict), and some attempt to turn it into a normative discourse generating the coalescence between sensations and linguistic signs that we call literary style.

By hypothesizing that the sensory cavern is ubiquitous and for the most part irreducible to language, am I subscribing to the notion that autism is *universal*, endogenous, occurring before what Melanie Klein calls the "depressive position," and at the fringe of psychic life? Not exactly. If we borrow the terms of what Freud calls an "economic" conception (as opposed to a model that relies on chronological or developmental stages), we may consider the sensory cavern to be an essential part of the psychic apparatus, which is heterogeneous. The psychic apparatus is a stratified *significance* that excessively rigid linguistic and cognitive discourses sometimes conceal or restrict to the dimension of language modeled on the Idea.

The autistic child withdraws into his sensory cave, which he effectively fossilizes and renders inexpressible. F. Tustin has broadened our notion of autism by showing that the neurotic personality contains an element of autism. The neurotic personality is a manifestation of a defeated autism, which may in itself prove to be a sign of its universal and fundamental permanence in the psyche.[17]

Let us examine the problem in another way. Even if sensation-perception, which is an essential and archaic part of psychic experience, cannot be absorbed by—or reduced to—language, the sensory domain's resistance to being reduced to the cognitive domain is not necessarily experienced through the painful form of autism, for it can also be expressed through perversion, art, or psychoanalysis.

Interpretation between Word-Signs and Word-Fetishes: A Source of Beauty

The dynamics of writing in Proust's work are not all that different from the dynamics of listening that characterize psychoanalytic interpretation.

Writing is memory regained from signs to flesh and from flesh to signs through an intense identification (and a dramatic separation from) an other who is loved, desired, hated, and rendered indifferent. Interpretation shares these same qualities, at least during those rare moments of grace when countertransference responds to the logic of transference and reshapes the psychic map of the analyst and the analysand. Yet what exactly occurs when we provide a name for our patients' often inexpressible sensations?

The process of naming sensations requires an *identification* with the analysand that mobilizes my entire psychic apparatus. I identify with his biography, his presumed and even transgenerational memory, and his presumed sensation. The resulting display of countertransference is an imaginary operation, yet it is also a real one. It is a sort of *transubstantiation* (Joyce, another extremely sensitive author, used this Catholic liturgical term to describe the subjective economy of writing as the advent of new signs and a new body).[18] Whether this identification is of the primary, secondary, projective, or any other variety, we should consider it in its paroxysmal intensity, a need that has not been sufficiently addressed by classic psychoanalytic theory (which is too preoccupied with neurosis) but which depressive, psychotic, and especially autistic symptoms have made apparent.

To reach this paroxysmal intensity of identification, which is absolutely essential for certain treatments, a psychoanalyst would do well to consider what Merleau-Ponty says about the way our own bodies affect the outside world as well as the bodies of other people. Merleau-Ponty sees this relationship as *reversible* and *chiasmic*, for touch is always tangible, sight is always visible, substance is body, and the same is other. He wants to challenge the metaphysical dichotomies of philosophy and psychology. Our instincts (which are borne out by science) tell us that an X perceives a Y from whom it is presumed to be always already separated. In the spirit of his radicalization of Husserl, however, Merleau-Ponty challenges the very existence of this separation. I believe it would be legitimate to transpose this *interpenetration* and *reversibility*—which operate between who or what perceives and what is perceived and between who or what feels and what is felt—not only onto psychoanalysis but onto the reading of literary texts. Merleau-Ponty uses the loaded term *flesh* to refer to this process:

> It is said that the colors, the tactile reliefs given to the other, are for me
> an absolute mystery, forever inaccessible. This is not completely true;

for me to have not an idea, an image, nor a representation, but as it were the imminent experience of them, it suffices that I look at a landscape, that I speak of it with someone. Then, through the concordant operation of his body and my own, what I see passes into him, this individual green of the meadow under my eyes invades his vision without quitting my own, I recognize in my green his green, as the customs officer recognizes suddenly in a traveler the man whose description he had been given. There is here no problem of the *alter ego* because it is not I who sees, not he who sees, because an anonymous visibility inhabits both of us, a vision in general, in virtue of that primordial property that belongs to the flesh, being here and now, of radiating everywhere and forever, being an individual, of being an individual, of being also a dimension and a universal.[19]

"Once again, the flesh we are speaking of is not matter. It is the coiling over of the visible upon the seeing body, of the tangible upon the touching body . . . this pact between them and me according to which I lend them my body, in order that they inscribe upon it and give me their resemblance, this fold, this central cavity of the visible which is my vision. . . . We must not think the flesh starting from substances, from body and spirit—for then it would be the union of contradictories—but we must think it, as we said, as an element, as the concrete emblem of a general manner of being."[20]

"We touch here the most difficult point, that is, the bond between the flesh and the idea, between the visible and the interior armature which it manifests and which it conceals. No one has gone further than Proust in fixing the relations between the visible and the invisible."[21]

Merleau-Ponty's remarks, which are problematic and mystically significant, are useful for a reader of Proust: they free up the representability of what is felt, which is torn between world and thought. This two-sided sensoriality is a "way of being" that characterizes the experience of writing in the sense of a "time regained." The philosopher tries to make this sensation surge forth into the world, whereas the psychoanalyst experiences it through transference and countertransference. A *state of flesh* appears to underlie the therapeutic act, but it can become a true *therapeutic act* only if language is led to the reversible and chiasmic sensation that supports it.

Becoming flesh is one element in the analytic process that must be restored, although not at the expense of all the others. Indeed, granting a sign to what is sensed presupposes a distance, and perhaps a split—a distance that explains the professional perversion displayed by psycho-analysts. The act of naming consists of abandoning the pleasure and pain of carnal identification, of carnal texture, in order to dissociate thing-presentations and word-presentations. Interpretation arranges word-presentations in an arbitrary autonomy stemming from their status as signs that are distinct from perception-sensations. Interpretation goes on to constitute these word-presentations as fetishes, to prompt the patient to play with these words-signs-fetishes, and then gives them back to him, like a mother to her child, in the initial form of play-objects. We transform the patient's flesh, which we have shared with our own, into word-presentations. By placing, repeating, and punctuating these word-presentations, however, we give words the consistency of reified symbols and link them to thing-presentations in the same way that the writer repeats, loves, and organizes his text. Thus the analyst uses sensorial *fixations* as a starting point for sensory *play* and then for *words*, but words that are *word-pleasures*, *word-things*, and *word-fetishes*. We could describe the analyst's naming process as the art of making the flesh of signs into transitional objects, an art that is more essential for the treatment of narcissistic disorders than for any other treatment. The reification, or fetishization, of the word plays an important role in the passage from sensation to the idea and to the relaxation of the logical order in which the idea is expected to expand itself into a thought.

Those who have treated autistic children have observed that such children experience a sort of aesthetic pleasure the first time they use words, which are charged with sensations more than ideas.[22] Beauty, then, is needed for psychic growth and the expansion of thought, but it can exist only if the analyst who carries out this process is capable of creating this same beauty and jouissance for himself and the other. For this reason, studying Proustian pleasures permits one not only to share my questionable interest in the excitation that supported the art of the famous writer known as "little Marcel" until his death but to consider the sado-masochistic element of aesthetic performance hidden in *psychoanalytic interpretation* in general, especially when analysts are faced with psychosis or autism. We do experience unconscious sadomasochistic pleasure when we identify with a chained-up soul, with the palpitating and mute sensation that does not know me as an *other* even though it includes me in its touch, its saliva, its breathing, and its blank, fleeing, or persecuting gaze. There is also a violent pleasure stemming from the word that I neither hear nor see but produce. Through a hole in my consciousness, which is temporarily opened as flesh, I see a shackled psyche. I cultivate it with my fusion, yet I know that it needs for me to take some distance from it. In that way, this other flesh, responding to my named pleasure, can perhaps become someone else, a *subject*.

Freud became aware of the commonplace, innocuous way that the protective violence of naming evolves by observing the famous *Fort-Da* game his grandson played with a wooden reel and a piece of string.[23] He emphasized the game's violent side in his analysis of *Die Verneinung*, the well-known and ambiguous "negativity" that rejects eroticism while positing a primary symbolism that operates through a dialectic relying on an incessant rejection of the drives.[24] Parents witness negativity when their children have temper tantrums while acquiring language and/or an Oedipal positioning. Violence is intrinsic to the process of naming the senses, and it is especially useful for ushering along the inner workings of treatment. Indeed, how could we create a discontinuity, how could we break up a *sign* for an *object* that can only be constituted by becoming an object of desire, if we do not disturb the patient's continuous and ana-logical sensoriality or if we fail to impose on him our own desire for a name, for an object? Desire, which takes things away from us, can only hurt and wound us. What is more essential, then, are kindness and tact, especially in treatments that go beyond aesthetic pleasure and depend on the analyst's distance as well as on his own latent sadomasochism.

Psychoanalysts have a long way to go toward perfecting their own art of rhetoric. Reading Proust makes us think of figures who can shape the flesh of our intense identifications with people who neither talk nor think about their sensations. Even so, we should not allow ourselves to be overcome with phenomenological beatitude. Instead, we should strive to remain attentive to the sadomasochistic logic of both sensory *identifica-tion* and *nomination*. And why? So that we might use these sensory processes not as the threshold of our jouissance but as a way to care for the other when the specificity of the human being as a speaking being seems to be lost. Indeed, if we look beyond the autistic symptom of the sensory cave, we shall discover a borderline region in our psyche that is restored by aesthetic experience and that nourishes psychoanalytic inter-pretation without being reduced to it.

NOTES

1. Letter to Fliess, December 6, 1896, in Freud, *Standard Edition*, 1:234.
2. Ibid., pp. 234–35. Italics mine.

3. On several occasions, Freud compared the system, or consciousness, to perception.—Trans.

4. *Project for a Scientific Psychology*, in *Standard Edition*, 1:325.

5. Ibid., p. 366.

6. Ibid., p. 367.

7. Ibid. Italics mine.

8. See the metapsychology papers in appendix C of *Standard Edition*, 14:109–215.

9. See Segal, "Notes on Symbol Formation," *International Journal of Psychoanalysis* 37 (1957).

10. See Kristeva, *Revolution in Poetic Language*, Margaret Waller, tr. (New York: Columbia University Press, 1984).

11. See "Imaginary Experience," in ch. 4. "The Experience of Time Embodied," in Kristeva, *Time and Sense*, Ross Guberman, tr. (New York: Columbia University Press, 1996).

12. W. Sellars subscribes to the adverbial theory, whereas Searle believes that the contents of a perception is a clause. E. Wright claims that sensory processes have a passive component and that they are not of an epistemic or intentional character, contrary to what A. Ben-Zeev has proposed. At the same time, while C. S. Peirce notes that the sensation process, like other phenomena of the mind, relies on an "inference," he prefigured later thinkers who believe that sensation possesses a particularly "irreducible vagueness." See also R. C. Solomon, *The Passions* (New York: Doubleday, 1976) and W. Lyons, *Emotions* (Cambridge: Cambridge University Press, 1980) as well as works by Lazarus and Greenspan.

13. R. B. Zajonc, "Feeling and Thinking Preferences Need No Inferences," *American Psychology* 35 (1980).

14. Clarke, "Emotions: Rationality Without Cognitivism," *Dialogue: The Canadian Philosophical Review* 25, no. 4 (1986): 663–74.

15. See, for instance, Tustin, *Autistic Barriers in Neurotic Patients* (London: Carnac Books, 1986).

16. See Kristeva, *Time and Sense*, p. 376, n. 87.—Trans.

17. Tustin, *Autistic Barriers*.

18. See my "Joyce: The Gracehoper or Orpheus' Return." in *New Maladies of the Soul*, Ross Guberman, tr. (New York: Columbia University Press, 1995), pp. 172–88.

19. M. Merleau-Ponty, *The Visible and the Invisible*, Alphonso Lingis, tr. (Evanston, Ill.: Northwestern University Press, 1968), p. 142.

20. Ibid., pp. 146–47.

21. Ibid., p. 149.

22. See D. Meltzer and M. H. Williams, *The Apprehension of Beauty: The Role of Aesthetic Conflict in Development, Art, and Violence* (N.p.: Clunie Press, Roland Harris, 1988).

23. Freud, *Beyond the Pleasure Principle*, in *Standard Edition*, 1813–64.

24. Freud, "Negation," in *Standard Edition*, 19:233–39.

Freudian Time

According to Freud, the unconscious does not know negatives or contrasts, and it also does not know time. Unbeknownst to us, this provides for a scene consisting of our desires as well as our drives, of which the most "instinctual" is the death drive. Freud offers an unexpected gift to those who subscribe to his beliefs. By relieving us of our anxieties about enduring, the Freudian unconscious throws us into the pure time of what is unbearable, which proves to be a logical space.[1] It is up to us to discover the key to this logic, to write a novel about the interpretation of dreams.

The neurotic seeks to repress the outside-time of the unconscious. The psychotic attempts to tear a hole in it; a specialist of ellipses, he always loses at least one of his logical links, which nonetheless reappears in an act of madness. The pervert plays with outside-time, reifying it in the part-objects that he ritualistically uses to respond to his sexual needs. Yet he becomes exhausted by these needs, primarily because he cannot access their meaning—which is reflected in the poor quality of his discourse and his fantasies. To put it briefly, each psychic structure has its own way of placing the unconscious "outside-time" within temporal duration. What is more, each time the subject fails to absorb this transposition, the different versions of the failure are embodied in the various structures.

When Freud claims, not incorrectly, that he succeeds where the paranoid person fails, he most likely means that psychoanalytic interpretation takes into account the subject's inability to represent his *other*. He hopes, however, that by delineating various levels of representation (primary and secondary processes, fantasies as well as drives, and the entire conceptual framework of psychoanalytic theory), he will be able to inscribe *the outside-time* of the subject and his other's fight to the finish inside *the time of transference*. Although Freud makes this laudable revelation, which leads him to compare the psychoanalytic experience with the psychotic's experience[2] (psychoanalysis obviously overcomes psychosis even though psychosis is present in interpretative countertransference), he says nothing about what perversion has taught him. He also says little about neurosis (the negative of perversion), especially obsessional neurosis.

The fantasy makes the unconscious into a narrative. As a result, when the outside-time of the unconscious is named and recounted, it acquires meaning, a goal, and a value. The fantasy, along with the dream narrative, becomes a narration torn between the atemporality of the unconscious and the forward-moving flight of the story. The fantasy is the novel that Freud asked his patients to bring him. As opposed to the neurotic, who is afraid and ashamed of his fantasies, and the pervert, who acts them out meticulously without being disturbed by what they mean, the analysand is invited to do with words what the pervert does with things (and with people who are reduced to mere things). He is invited to *stage* his unconscious. When the pervert's staging occurs in the form of a metaphor placed in the world of an unmistakably temporal discourse, a *story* is set into motion. Still, the reason that the fantasy is not just any narrative but a novel in miniature is that it is structured like a "catastrophe" in the mathematical sense of the word.[3] The fantasy is at the boundary between the outside-time space of the unconscious (which threatens to consume it by depriving it of words in order to direct it toward drives and acts) and the haste of the narration (which is the hero's seduction of his victim and the narrator's seduction of his addressee).

Because of this "catastrophic" dynamic, the narrative-fantasy is always augmented with interpolations, retracings, signs of childishness or divisions of jouissances that do not necessarily find a style of their own but place the analysand in an amphibious temporality. This two-sided temporality is a source of *jouissance* when the fantasy enacts unconscious desire and of *logic* when the action projected onto the axis of past-present-future takes into account interaction with other people. This sort of double temporality is favorable to analysis, and the speaking being's division works within it. Hence it is entirely prepared to project itself in the sublimations of the imaginary-novel. We read novels with our fantasies, yet novelists transpose their own fantasies onto the supple structure of a genre that seeks only to submit to the fantasies of a given reader. Art begins when a transposition comes into play that consists of rhetorical figures, syntactic structures, and superimposed characters. Still, *sublimation* takes place when the fantasy is put into words. If the analysand is not ever so slightly like a narrator, he is silenced. He occasionally causes gripping or commonplace signs to emanate from the nameless border of his unconscious, but he never tells *his* story. The analyst yields to this scenario by becoming bored or by playfully offering his own fantasies to the analysand. In other words, if transference and countertransference fail to make the analysand a narrator, the analysis breaks down and dies. Did Freud wish for his patients to become budding narrators? Did he transform the subjects of civilization and its discontents into novelists lacking an aesthetic religion?

NOTES

1. See André Green, "Temps et mémoire," *Nouvelle Revue de Psychanalyse* 41 (1990): 176–260, and *Revue française de psychanalyse* 43 (1979), devoted to memory and recollection in psychoanalytic practice.

2. See Julia Kristeva, "Psychoanalysis and the Polis," *Critical Inquiry* 9, no. 1 (September 1982): 77–92.

3. See Thom, *Modèles mathématiques de la morphogenèse. Recueil de textes sur théorie des catastrophes et applications* (Paris: UGE, 1974).

PART 3

Psychoanalysis of Love:
A Counterdepressant

Tales of Love

Histoires d'amour was originally published in Paris by Denoël in 1983. It was translated as *Tales of Love* by Leon Roudiez for Columbia University Press in 1987. In *Tales of Love* Kristeva develops a theory and history of love wherein it operates between need and desire. She substantiates her theory with analyses of love from Plato's eros, through biblical love, Christian Agape, Molière's *Dom Juan*, Shakespeare's *Romeo and Juliet*, Jeanne Guyon the mystic's eroticism, Baudelaire's passion, Stendhal's politics of passion, to Bataille's erotics.

She begins *Tales of Love* with an analysis of Freud's theory of eros. An earlier version of the first chapter "Freud and Love," a portion of which is reprinted here, was published as "L'abjet d'amour" in *Tel Quel* in spring, 1982. In "Freud and Love," against Lacan, Kristeva suggests that the paternal function does not just include castration threats and law. The father is not merely the stern father of the law. Rather, she proposes a loving father, what she calls "the imaginary father." The imaginary father provides the loving support that enables the child to abject, or separate from, its mother and enter the social (see part 4 on abjection in *Powers of Horror*). Following Freud's notion of the father of preindividual history, Kristeva describes the imaginary father as a mother-father conglomerate. In her scenario, the imaginary father performs the function of love. It is the child's feeling that it is loved that allows the child to separate from the safe haven of the maternal body. Threats and laws alone do not provide this necessary support.

On the traditional psychoanalytic model of both Freud and Lacan, the child enters the social or language out of fear of castration. The child experiences its separation from the maternal body as a tragic loss and consoles itself with words. Paternal threats make words the only, if inadequate, alternative to psychosis. Kristeva insists, however, that separation begins prior to the mirror stage or Oedipal situation and that this separation is not only painful but also pleasurable. She insists that the child enters the social and language not only because of paternal threats but also owing to paternal love. She describes the infant's identification with paternal love or the imaginary father as a metaphor of love. In "Throes of Love," she associates the operations of metaphor with the psychoanalytic notion of transference. She suggests that the infant's identification with the imaginary father is actually a type of transference to the place of love. The infant's separation from the maternal body is dependent upon a transference to this supportive love. This transference operation prefigures and sets up the possibility of metaphor and language. And, conversely, as Kristeva says, love is always spoken. She proposes her notion of love and metaphorical transference identification as an alternative to Lacan's notion of desire and metonymical displacement.

Kristeva criticizes the Lacanian scenario because it cannot adequately explain the child's move to signification. If the motivation for the move to signification is threats and the pain of separation, then why would anyone make this move? Why not remain in the safe haven of the maternal body and refuse the social and language with its threats? Why aren't more people psychotic? Kristeva suggests that just as the separations inherent in the material of the body are pleasurable, even if they are also sometimes painful, so too the separations that make signification possible are pleasurable. The logic of signification is already operating in the body, and therefore the transition to language is not as dramatic and mysterious as traditional psychoanalytic theory makes it out to be.

In the last chapter of *Tales of Love*, "Extraterrestrials Suffering for Want of Love," Kristeva prefigures the issues that she takes up again in *New Maladies of the Soul* (1993). Here she diagnoses contemporary analysands' sufferings as the result of the abolition of psychic space. With the break up of Christianity, Kristeva describes a culture caught at a stage in the process of subjectivity between identification and differentiation. No cultural image of a mother is available to offset the horrifying abject mother, and as a result women are denigrated and motherhood disdained. And on the other hand, no cultural image of a loving father who might ease the move away from the abject maternal body is present.

Contemporary analysands are extraterrestrials suffering from the want of love from either mother or father. They are caught in the not-yet of subjectivity that leaves them empty and unsatisfied.

Black Sun

Soleil Noir: Dépression et Mélancolie was originally published in Paris by Gallimard Press in 1987. It was translated by Leon Roudiez as *Black Sun: Depression and Melancholy* for Columbia University Press in 1989. This selection is the first chapter of that translation. In *Black Sun*, Kristeva diagnoses the common structure of depression and melancholy as a structure of mourning for the lost maternal "object" (which she calls a "Thing" since it is not fully an object), and the failure of language to compensate for the loss. It is the inability of signifiers to compensate for the loss of the maternal Thing that leads to a sense of emptiness and meaninglessness; words are meaningless to express the pain of depression and melancholy. Here Kristeva develops and uses her notion of the abject mother from *Powers of Horror* (1980) and her notion of the imaginary father from *Tales of Love* (1983).

Kristeva suggests that whereas antidepressants treat only the symptoms of depression, psychoanalysis can treat the causes and provide a needed counterdepressant. Psychoanalysis can provide the loving support needed to leave the maternal body and to accept the consolation of words and an interpretative framework. The interpretative framework of psychoanalysis provides the psychic meaning necessary to fill the emptiness of psychic space. Psychoanalytic interpretation can help the analysand construct an eroticized maternal body that is as desirable as it is abject (the case of female heterosexuality is more complex; see part 5) and a loving imaginary father who supports the movement from the maternal body into language. This love allows affects to connect with words, drives to connect to language, and re-creates meaning.

New Maladies of the Soul

New Maladies of the Soul was translated by Ross Guberman for Columbia University Press in 1994 from the original published as *Les Nouvelles Maladies de l'âme* in Paris by Fayard in 1993. In *New Maladies of the Soul*, Kristeva powerfully diagnoses the loss of meaning and emptiness of contemporary life. In the first chapter, "The Soul and the Image," she asks whether "in the wake of psychiatric medicines, aerobics, and media zapping, does the soul still exist?" (p. 3). Continuing to challenge the distinction between nature and culture, she situates the contemporary soul between biology and sociology. The soul or psyche mediates between the body, others, and our representations of ourselves. Without an adequate language to express the body or our relation to others, we turn to drugs (antidepressants, tranquilizers, narcotics) and/or media images to fill the void. But drugs and television only postpone the feelings of emptiness and lack of satisfaction. Kristeva maintains that we need new ways to reattach language to affect.

In the second chapter, "In Times Like These, Who Needs Psycho-analysts?" she discusses the relation between drives, affects, and language. She situates Freudian drives between biology and culture and delineates the special role of psychoanalysis in addressing this psychic life that operates between the two realms. She articulates "new maladies of the soul" and psychic emptiness, which she maintains are unique in each analysand. She maps a new terrain for psychoanalysis and suggests new routes to meaning. She extends her thesis from *Black Sun* that perhaps psychoanalysis can provide a counterdepressant that treats the cause of our depression and not just an antidepressant that treats the symptoms.

Tales of Love (1983)

Freud and Love: Treatment and Its Discontents

In his journey through the land of love Freud reaches Narcissus only after having traveled over the dissociated space of hysteria. The latter leads him to establish the "psychic space" that he will explode, first through Narcissus and finally through the death drive, into the impossible spaces of "lovehate,"[1] that is, infinite transference.

Narcissism—a Screen for Emptiness

The hypothesis of Narcissus is crucial to this Freudian course. Before calling itself "death," the libido undergoes a first threat to its omnipotence—one that makes the existence of an *other* for the *self* appear problematic. Freud seems to suggest that it is not Eros but narcissistic primacy that sparks and perhaps dominates psychic life; he thus sets up self-deception as the basis of one's relationship to reality. Such a perpetuation of illusion, however, finds itself rehabilitated, neutralized, normalized, at the bosom of my loving reality. For Freud, as we know, binds the state of loving to narcissism; the choice of the love object, be it "narcissistic" or "anaclitic," proves satisfying in any case if and only if that object relates to the subject's narcissism in one of two ways: either through personal narcissistic reward (where Narcissus is the subject), or narcissistic delegation (Narcissus is the other; for Freud, the woman). A narcissistic destiny would in some way underlie all our object choices, but this is a destiny that society, on the one hand, and the moral rigor of Freud, on the other, tend to thrust aside in favor of a "true" object choice.[2] And yet on closer examination even the Ego Ideal, which insures the transference of our claims and desires toward a true object laden with all the pomp of good and beauty as defined by parental and social codes, is a revival of narcissism, its abeyance, its conciliation, its consolation. Freud's text, one might say, imposes an omnipresence of narcissism which permeates the other realms to the point that one finds it again in the *object* (where it is reflected)—if we assume that an object can be designated, in other words symbolized and loved as such, outside of chaos, rejection, and destruction.

Moreover, the ubiquity of the notion of "narcissism" goes hand in hand with its being far from originary. It is a supplement, and Freud points out that it is the product of a "new action," which we should understand as that of a third realm supplementing the autoeroticism of the mother-child dyad: "The autoerotic drives, however, are there from the very first; so there must be something added to autoeroticism—a new psychical action—in order to bring about narcissism."[3]

That observation endows narcissism with an intrasymbolic status, dependent upon a third party but within a disposition that chronologically and logically precedes that of the Oedipal Ego. It prompts one to conceive of an archaic disposition of the paternal function, preceding the Name, the Symbolic, but also preceding the "mirror stage," whose logical potentiality it would harbor—a disposition that one might call that of the Imaginary Father (a point I shall return to). Lacan takes up Freud's observation only briefly to emphasize the need to stipulate the "mirror stage." He specifies that "The human ego establishes itself on the basis of the imaginary relation."[4]

The questions prompted by the Freudian notion of narcissism would then be the following: What is this narcissistic "identity"? How stable are its borders, its relation to the other? Does the "mirror stage" emerge out of nowhere? What are the conditions of its emergence? A whole *complex structuration* can seemingly be conceived through what is after all a psychiatric term, "narcissism"; it is an already ternary structuration with a different articulation from the Ego-object-Other triangle that is put together in the shadow of the Oedipus complex.

Furthermore, the ubiquity of Freudian narcissism has caused some to suggest that narcissism is no more than a Freudian fantasy—and that nothing else exists but originary mimetism. Such a thesis is probably a paranoid version of what would lie at the basis of social and symbolic relations: it finds its mechanism in the "scapegoat" theory, where Melanie Klein's "projective relationship" unwittingly serves as a cornerstone for society and the sacred. Nevertheless, it is still a fact that narcissism, caught in a play of rebounds within the Freudian text, in a first stage seems to be a mimetic play that would establish psychic identities (Ego/object), until that play finally, and in the dizziness of rebounds, reveals itself as a screen over *emptiness*. That notion has been developed in psychoanalysis by André Green, whose reflections I draw upon for this particular point.[5]

Consequently I shall emphasize this notion of emptiness, which is at the root of the human psyche. It does not reveal itself merely because "psychotic states" have broken forth on psychoanalytic couches or have shown through the low points of many neuroses. One is compelled to note that the aims of psychoanalysis have changed. After psychiatric *semeiology*, Freud had discovered the *symptom* as metaphor, that is, condensation, of fantasy. Now, and thanks to Lacan, one analyzes the symptom as a screen through which one detects the workings of *significance* (the process of formation and de-formation of meaning and the subject); these coextend with the speaking being as such and, consequently, they cut through not only "normal" and "pathological" states but also psychoanalytic symptomatology. In this respect, the arbitrariness of the Saussurian sign has placed us in front of a *bar*, or even an *emptiness*, that constitutes the referent/signified/signifier relationship, of which Lacan has merely taken up the "visible" aspect in the *gaping hole* of the mirror stage. Saussure's *arbitrariness* of the sign and Lacan's *gaping hole* both readily point to what might be understood from the standpoint of representation—given the uneasy uncertainty, ubiquity, and inconsistency of "narcissism" in Freud . . .

Thus, against the background of linguistic theory and language learning, the *emptiness* that is intrinsic to the beginnings of the symbolic function appears as the first separation between what is not yet an *Ego* and what is not yet an *object*. Might narcissism be a means for protecting that emptiness? But against what?—a protection of emptiness (of "arbitrariness," of the "gaping hole") through the display of a decidedly narcissistic parry, so that emptiness can be maintained, lest chaos prevail and borders dissolve. Narcissism protects emptiness, causes it to exist, and thus, as lining of that emptiness, insures an elementary separation. Without that solidarity between emptiness and narcissism, chaos would sweep away any possibility of distinction, trace, and symbolization, which would in turn confuse the limits of the body, words, the real, and the symbolic. The child, with all due respect to Lacan, not only *needs* the real and the symbolic—it signifies itself as child, in other words as the subject that it is, and neither as a psychotic nor as an adult, precisely in that zone where *emptiness and narcissism*, the one upholding the other, constitute the zero degree of imagination.

We have, however, reached the threshold of another question: What is it that preserves this emptiness—a cause for complaint but also an absolute necessity of the so-called narcissistic structures, a fleeting effect of enigmatic as well as creative non-sense—at the heart of childhood narcissism? This is where we need to return to the notion of "identification."

Einfühlung—an Identification with a Metaphorical "Object"

Amatory identification, *Einfühlung* (the assimilation of other people's feelings), appears to be madness when seen in the light of Freud's caustic lucidity: the ferment of collective hysteria in which crowds abdicate their own judgment, a hypnosis that causes us to lose perception of reality since we hand it over to the *Ego ideal*.[6] The object in hypnosis devours or absorbs the ego, the voice of consciousness becomes blurred, "in loving blindness one becomes a criminal without remorse"—*the object has taken the place of what was the ego ideal*.[7]

The identification that provides the support for the hypnotic state known as loving madness rests upon a strange object. This archaic identification, which is characteristic of the oral phase of the libido's organization where what I incorporate is what I become, where *having* amounts to *being*, is not, truly speaking, objectal. I identify, not with an object, but with what offers itself to me as a *model*. That enigmatic apprehending of a *pattern* to be imitated, one that is not yet an object to be libidinally cathected, leads us to wonder whether the loving state is a state without object and reminds us of an archaic *reduplication* (rather than imitation), "possible before any choice of object."[8] This enigmatic, nonobjectal identification might be related to the internal, recursive, redundant logic of discourse, which is accessible within the "afterspeech"; it is an identification that sets up love, the sign, and repetition at the heart of the psyche. For the sake of an object to come, later or never? . . . It does not matter, since I am already in the throes of *Einfühlung*. . . . Later I shall examine the conditions that allow the advent of that uni-fication, that identification, on the basis of autoeroticism and within the pre-Oedipal triad . . .

For the moment let me simply note that becoming *as* the One is imagined by Freud as an oral assimilation; indeed he links the possibility of archaic identification to the "oral phase of the libido's organization,"[9] and he then cites Robertson Smith who, in his *Kinship and Marriage* (1885), describes the communal bonds set up through participation in a common meal as resting upon "the acknowledgment of the possession of a common substance."[10] Ferenczi and his followers would later develop the notions of *introjection* and *incorporation*.

Nevertheless, one might well wonder about the notional slippage that takes place between the "incorporation" of an object, or even its "introjection," and an *Identifizierung* that is not on the level of "having" but locates itself at once on that of "being like." On what ground, within what material does *having* switch over to *being*? While seeking an answer to that question it appeared to me that incorporating and introjecting orality's function is the essential substratum of what constitutes man's being, namely, *language*. When the object that I incorporate is the speech of the other—precisely a nonobject, a pattern, a model—I bind myself to him in a primary fusion, communion, unification. An identification. For me to have been capable of such a process, my libido had to be restrained; my thirst to devour had to be deferred and displaced to a level one may well call "psychic," provided one adds that if there is repression it is quite primal, and that it lets one hold on to the joys of chewing, swallowing, nourishing oneself . . . with words. In being able to receive the other's words, to assimilate, repeat, and reproduce them, I become like him: One. A subject of enunciation. Through psychic osmosis/identification. Through love.

Freud has described the One with whom I fulfill the identification (this "most primitive aspect of affective binding to an object")[11] as a Father. Although he did not elaborate what he meant by "primary identification," he made it clear that this father is a "father in individual prehistory."

An "Immediate" and Objectless Identification

A strange father if there ever was one, since for Freud, because there is no awareness of sexual difference during that period (more accurately: within that disposition), such a "father" is the same as "both parents." Identification with that "father in prehistory," that Imaginary Father, is called "immediate," "direct," and Freud emphasizes again, "previous to any concentration on any object whatsoever": Only with secondary identification does the "libidinal covetousness that is part of the first sexual period and is directed toward the father and the mother appear, in normal instances, to be resolved in a secondary, mediate identification that would come and reinforce the primary, direct identification."[12]

The whole symbolic matrix sheltering emptiness is thus set in place in an elaboration that precedes the Oedipus complex. Indeed, if the primary identification constitutive of the Ego Ideal does not involve libidinal cathexis, drives are dissociated from the psychic realm. Simultaneously, what one can only call the *absolute* existence of *transference* is established, a transference laden with libido. It is a transference rather than an "identification," a transference in the sense of *Verschiebung*, a displacement, as in the *Interpretation of Dreams*, but also and at the same time in the sense of *Übertragung*, as it will show up during treatment and be directed toward the person of the analyst. Finally, such a transference is called *immediate (unmittelbare)* and works in the direction of a complex, composite, and, in short, imaginary realm ("the father in individual prehistory").

We know that, *empirically*, the first affections, the first imitations, and the first vocalizations as well are directed toward the mother; it is thus hardly necessary to stress that one's pointing to the Father as the magnet for primary love, primary identification, is tenable only if one conceives of *identification* as being always already within the symbolic orbit, under the sway of language. Such appears to be, implicitly, the Freudian position, which owes its acuity as much to Freud's sensitivity concerning the dominant place of language in the constitution of *being* as it does to the resurgence of monotheism in his thought. But is there really a difference?

On the contrary, there is Melanie Klein's well-known position, which must be called inexpressible and closer to ordinary common sense. The bold theoretician of the death drive is also a theoretician of gratitude seen as "an important offshoot of the capacity for love," "necessary for the acknowledgment of what is 'good' in others and in oneself."[13] Where does this capacity come from? It is innate and leads to the experience of a "good breast" that sates the child's hunger; it is also apt to convey the feeling of a plenitude that would be the prototype of all subsequent experience of jouissance and happiness. Melanie Klein's gratitude is nevertheless and at the same time directed toward the maternal object in its entirety: "I am not saying that for the child the breast simply represents a physical object."[14]

Yet, along with such innateness, Melanie Klein maintains that the capacity for love is not an activity of the organism (as it would seem to be for Freud, according to Klein) but rather that it is a "primordial activity of the ego." Gratitude would stem from a necessity to confront the forces of death and consist in a "progressive integration born out of the life drive."[15] Without being identical with the "good object," the idealized object reinforces it. "Idealization stems from persecution anguish and constitutes a defense against it," "the ideal breast is a complement of the devouring breast."[16] It is as if those who are unable to set up a "good breast" for themselves naturally manage it by idealizing; now idealization often collapses and reveals its cause, which is the persecution against which it had established itself. But how does one succeed in idealizing? By what miracle is that possible in a Kleinian life where two live without a third party other than a persecuting or fascinating penis?

The problem is not to find an answer to the enigma: Who might be the object of primary identification, daddy or mummy? Such an attempt would only open up the impossible quest for the absolute origin of the capacity for love as a psychic and symbolic capacity. The question is rather: Of what value would the question be when it actually bears on states existing on the border between the psychic and the somatic, idealization and eroticism, within analytic treatment itself? To emphasize transference, the love that founds the analytic process, implies that one hears the discourse that is performed there starting with that limit of advent-and-loss of the subject—which is *Einfühlung*.

Provided one does not forget that in analysis any discourse complies with the dynamics of identification, with and beyond resistances, this entails at least two consequences for interpretation. First, the analyst situates himself on a ridge where, on the one hand, the "maternal" position—gratifying needs, "holding" (Winnicott)—and on the other the "paternal" position—the differentiation, distance, and prohibition that produces both meaning and absurdity—are intermingled and severed, infinitely and without end. Analytic tactfulness—ultimate refuge of an interpretation's relevance—is perhaps no more than the capacity to make use of identification and along with it the imaginal resources of the analyst, in order to accompany the patient as far as the limits and accidents of his object relations. This ability is even more important precisely when the patient has difficulty in establishing, or fails to establish, an object relation.

Metonymic Object and Metaphorical Object

Second, the *Einfühlung* gives the language signifier exchanged during treatment a heterogeneous, drive-affected dimension. It loads it with something preverbal, or even nonrepresentable that needs to be deciphered while taking into account the more precise articulations of discourse (style, grammar, phonetics), and at the same time while cutting through language, in the direction of the unspeakable, indicated by fantasies and "insight" narratives as well as by symptomatic misspeech (slips of the tongue, illogical statements, etc.).

Such analytic attentiveness to *Einfühlung* through transference speech imposes another status of the psychic *object* on the analyst's attention, one that is different from the metonymic object of desire called "object 'a'" by Lacan.[17]

We are dealing less with a partial object than with a nonobject. As magnet of identification constitutive of identity and condition for that unification, which insures the advent of a subject for an object, the "object" of *Einfühlung* is a *metaphorical* object. Carrying autoerotic motility to the unifying image of One Agency that already sets me up *as* an opposite One is the zero degree of subjectivity. *Metaphor* should be understood as movement toward the discernible, a journey toward the visible. *Anaphora, gesture, indication*, would probably be more adequate terms for this sundered unity, in the process of being set up, which I am at present conjuring. Aristotle refers to an *epiphora*: a generic term for the metaphorical motility previous to any objectivation of *a* figurative meaning. . . . The object of love is a metaphor for the subject—its constitutive metaphor, its "unary feature," which, by having it choose an adored part of the loved one, already locates it within the symbolic code of which this feature is a part.[18] Nevertheless, situating this unifying guideline within an objectality in the process of being established rather than in the absolute of the reference to the Phallus as such has several advantages. It makes the transference relation dynamic, involves to the utmost the interpretative intervention of the analyst, and calls attention to countertransference as identification, this time of the analyst with the patient, along with the entire aura of imaginary formations germane to the analyst that all this entails. Without those conditions, doesn't analysis run the risk of becoming set within the tyranny of idealization, precisely? Of the Phallus or of the superego? A word to wise Lacanians should be enough!

Metonymic object of desire. Metaphorical object of love. The former controls the phantasmatic *narrative*. The latter outlines the *crystallization* of fantasy and rules the poeticalness of the discourse of love . . .

During treatment, the analyst interprets his desire and his love, and that sets him apart from the perverse position of the seducer and from that of a virtuous Werther as well. But he must display himself sometimes as desiring, other times as loving. By ensuring a loving Other to the patient, the analyst (temporarily) allows the Ego in the throes of drive to take shelter in the following fantasy: the analyst is not a dead Father but a living Father; this nondesiring but loving father reconciles the ideal Ego with the Ego Ideal and elaborates the psychic space where, possibly and subsequently, an analysis can take place.

Henceforth, the analyst must in addition let it be known—since he is an analyst and neither a good shepherd nor a father-confessor—that he is a fleeting, failing, or even abject subject of desire. He will then trigger within the psychic space his love has allowed to exist the tragicomedy of life drives and death drives, knowing in his nescience that if Eros opposes Thanatos they are not evenly matched in their struggle. For Thanatos is pure while Eros has, since the beginning, been permeated with Thanatos, the most deep-seated drive being the death drive (Freud).

To say that the analyst handles *love* as a discourse allowing idealizing distance as a condition for the very existence of psychic space is not to assimilate the analytic attitude to that of a *primary love* object, the archaic prototype of the *genital* love, as Balint's work suggests with seductive munificence.[19] Concentrating, *for a while*, one's thoughts on love within analysis actually leads one to scrutinize, in the treatment, not a narcissistic merger with the maternal container but the emergence of a *metaphorical object*—in other words, the very splitting that establishes the psyche and, let us call this splitting "primal repression," bends the drive toward the symbolic of an other. Only the metaphorical dynamics (in the sense of a *heterogeneous* displacement shattering the isotopy of organic needs) justifies that this other be a Great Other. The analyst thus temporarily stands in the place of the Great Other inasmuch as he is a metaphorical object of idealizing identification. It is in knowing this and doing it that he creates the space of transference. If he represses it, on the other hand, the analyst becomes the *Führer* that Freud already loathed in *Group Psychology*—a loathing that showed to what extent analytic practice was not exempt from such hysterical phenomena.

Hate Identification, Love Identification

"It is easy," Freud believed,

> to translate into a phrase the difference between identification with the father and affection for the father as sexual object (*der Unterschied*

einer solchen Vateridentifizierung von einer Vaterobjektwahl): in the first instance the father is what one would want to *be* (*das, was man sein möchte*), in the second he is what one would want to *have* (*das, was man haben möchte*). In the first instance, it is the subject of the *ego* that is concerned, in the second it is its object. That is why identification is possible before any choice of object is made (*Es ist also der Unterschied, ob die Bindung am Subjekt oder am Objekt des Ichs angreift. Die erstere ist darum bereits vor jeder sexuellen Objektwahl möglich*).[20]

It will be noted that the first identification Freud points to in this study is a morbid identification with the mother (for instance, the little girl takes up her mother's cough on account of "a hostile desire to take the mother's place—*ein feindseliges Ersetzenwollen der Mutter*—in which case the symptom expresses the erotic fondness for the father"). Though conceived within the system of the Oedipus complex (*Entweder ist die Identifizierung dieselbe aus dem Ödipuskomplex*), such an identification nevertheless reminds one of Melanie Klein's projective identification, which is sustained by the "hostile" as well as guilt-ridden desire to take the place of a persecuting mother out of envy. Object identification because of hatred for one part of the object and fear of persecution. The second type of identification is revealed by a symptom that apes that of the loved one (the daughter, Dora, catches the father's cough). Here, "identification has taken the place of erotic propensity, and the latter has been changed, through regression, into identification" (*die Identifizierung sei an Stelle der Objektwahl getreten, die Objektwahl sei zur Identifizierung regrediert*). Without hostility in this case, identification coincides with the object of desire through "a kind of insertion of the object into the ego" (*gleichsam durch Introjektion des Objekts ins Ich*). Love, contrary to the morbid identification mentioned above, would be the merging of the identifying ideal with the object of desire. In the third place, libidinal desires can be completely lacking when identification with another person is made on the basis of some common traits.

One is thus led to conceive of at least two identifications, a primal one, resulting from a sentimental (*Gefühlsbindung an ein Objekt*), archaic, and ambivalent affection for the maternal object, more frequently produced by the impetus of guilt-producing hostility, and the other, which underlies the introjection into the ego of an object itself already libidinal (*libidinöse Objektbindung*), providing the dynamics of the pure loving relationship. The first is closer to depersonalization, phobia, and psychosis; the second is closer to hysterical lovehate, taking to itself the phallic ideal that it pursues.

Between Hysteria and Inability to Love

The lover is a narcissist with an *object*. Love involves a sizable *aufhebung* of narcissism; consequently, the relationship established by Freud between love and narcissism must not cause us to forget their essential difference. Is it not true that the narcissist, as such, is precisely someone incapable of love?

The lover, in fact, reconciles narcissism and hysteria. As far as he is concerned, there is an idealizable other who returns his own ideal image (that is the narcissistic moment), but he is nevertheless an other. It is essential for the lover to maintain the existence of that ideal other and to be able to imagine himself similar, merging with him, and even indistinguishable from him. In amorous hysteria the ideal Other is a reality, not a metaphor. The archeology of such an identifying possibility with an *other* is provided by the huge place taken up within narcissistic structure by the vortex of *primary identification* with what Freud called a "father of individual prehistory." Endowed with the sexual attributes of both parents, and by that very token a totalizing, phallic figure, it provides satisfactions that are already psychic and not simply immediate, existential requests; that archaic vortex of idealization is immediately an *other* who gives rise to a powerful, already psychic transference of the previous semiotic body in the process of becoming a narcissistic Ego. Its very existence and my being able to take myself for it—that is what already moves us away from the primal maternal satisfaction and situates us within the hysterical universe of loving idealization.

It is obvious from the behavior of young children that the first love object of boys and girls is the mother. Then where does one fit in this "father of individual prehistory"? Freud's bent perhaps causes him to speak as a Jew, but he speaks primarily as a psychoanalyst. He in fact dissociates idealization (and with it the amatory relationship) from the bodily exchange between mother and child, and he introduces the Third Party as a condition of psychic life, to the extent that it is a loving life. If love stems from narcissistic idealization, it has nothing to do with the protective wrapping over skin and sphincters that maternal care provides for the baby. Worse yet, if that protection continues, if the mother "clings" to her offspring, laying on it the request that originates in her own request as confused neoteinic and hysteric in want of love, the chances are that neither love nor psychic life will ever hatch from such an egg. The loving mother, different from the caring and clinging mother, is someone who has an object of desire; beyond that, she has an Other with relation to whom the child will serve as go-between. She will love her child with respect to that Other, and it is through a discourse aimed at that Third Party that the child will be set up as "loved" for the mother. "Isn't he beautiful," or "I am proud of you," and so forth, are statements of maternal love because they involve a Third Party; it is in the eyes of a Third Party that the baby the mother speaks to becomes a *he*, it is with respect to others that "I am proud of you," and so forth. Against this verbal backdrop or in the silence that presupposes it the bodily exchange of maternal fondness may take on the imaginary burden of representing love in its most characteristic form. Nevertheless, without the maternal "diversion" toward a Third Party, the bodily exchange is abjection or devouring; the eventual schizophrene, whether phobic or borderline, will keep its hot-iron brand against which his only recourse will be hatred. Any borderline person ends up finding a mother who is "loving" for her own sake, but he cannot accept her as loving himself, for she did not love any *other* one. The Oedipal negation of the father is here linked with a complaint against an adhesive maternal wrapping, and it leads the subject toward psychic pain dominated by the inability to love.

If one grants the ternary structure of narcissism and its already harboring the hysterical beginning of an idealizable object (the object of love germane to primary identification), how can one, to the contrary, understand the inability to love? The cold, set, and somewhat false complaint of the borderline person that he is unable to love needs perhaps to be related not to narcissism but to autoeroticism. Previous to the "new psychic action" that includes a third party within narcissism, the autoerotic set-up has neither an other nor an image. All of its figures, all figures disappoint it as much as they fascinate it. The autoerotic person cannot allow himself to be "loved" (no more than he can let himself be lovable), except by a maternal substitute who would cling to his body like a poultice—reassuring balm, asthmogenic perhaps, but nevertheless a permanent wrapping. Such a false mother is the only "farthering" [*père-manence*] tolerated by one who, henceforth, will indolently be able to enjoy his own organs in polymorphous perversity. He is undifferentiated, set within the shattered territories of his parceled body, coiled up about his erogenous zones. He is indifferent to love, withdrawn in the pleasure that a provisionally reassuring diving-suit gives him. The autoerotic person is not, however, autistic: he discovers objects, but they are objects of hatred. Nevertheless, during those moments that have no saving grace and when the subject is deprived of durability, the hatred that an opposite object projects before him works indeed more strongly upon himself, threatening him with decomposition or petrifaction. The autoerotic person who complains or boasts of being unable to love is afraid of going mad—schizophrenia or catatonia . . .

Dynamics of the Ideal

The subject exists only inasmuch as it identifies with an ideal other who is the speaking other, the other insofar as he speaks. A ghost,[21] a symbolic formation beyond the mirror, this Other who is indeed the size of a Master, is a magnet for identification because he is neither an object of need nor one of desire. The Ego ideal includes the Ego on account of the love that this Ego has for it and thus unifies it, restrains its drives, turns it into a *Subject*. An Ego is a body to be put to death, or at least to be deferred, for the love of the Other and so that Myself can be. Love is a death sentence that causes me to be. When death, which is intrinsic to amorous passion, takes place in reality and carries away the body of one of the lovers, it is at its most unbearable; the surviving lover then realizes the abyss that separates the imaginary death that he experienced in his passion from the relentless reality from which love had forever set him apart: saved . . .

The subject's identification with the symbolic Other, with its Ego Ideal, goes through a narcissistic absorption of the mother as object of need, an absorption that sets up the Ideal Ego. The lover is cognizant of the regression that leads him from adoring an ideal ghost to the ecstatic or painful inflating of his own image, his own body.

Such a logic of idealizing identification leads one to posit, as lining of the visual, specular structure of the fantasy ($ \Diamond$a) in search of the ever inadequate image of a desired other, the existence of a preliminary condition. If the object of fantasy is receding, metonymical, it is because it does not correspond to the preliminary ideal that the identification process, $ \varepsilon$ A, has constructed. The subject exists because it belongs to the Other, and it is in proceeding from that symbolic belonging that causes him to be subject to love and death that he will be able to set up for himself imaginary objects of desire. Transferred to the Other ($ \varepsilon$ A) as to the very place from which he is seen and heard, the loving subject does not have access to that Other as to an object, but as to the very possibility of the perception, distinction, and differentiation that allows one to see. That Ideal is nevertheless a blinding, nonrepresentable power— sun or ghost. Romeo says, "Juliet is the sun," and that loving metaphor transfers onto Juliet the glare Romeo experiences in the state of love, dedicating his body to death in order to become immortal within the symbolic community of others restored by his love, precisely.

The ideal identification with the Symbolic upheld by the Other thus activates speech more than image. Doesn't the signifying voice, in the final analysis, shape the visible, hence fantasy? Whenever we observe how young children learn forms, we are led to understand to what extent "sensorimotor spontaneity" is of little avail without the help of language. Poets have known from time immemorial that music is the language of love, and it has led them to suggest that the yearning captured by the loved beauty is nevertheless transcended—preceded and guided—by the ideal signifier: a sound on the fringe of my being, which transfers me to the place of the Other, astray, beyond meaning, out of sight.[22] In short, identification causes the subject to exist within the signifier of the Other. Archaically, primitively, it is not object-oriented but carried out as transference to the place of a captivating and unifying feature, a "unary feature." The analyst is an object (necessarily a partial one) but he also exerts the drawing power of a "unary feature," of a nonobject: the actual drifting of a possible metaphoricity.

Here the term metaphor should not bring to mind the classic rhetorical trope (*figurative* vs. *plain*), but instead, on the one hand, the modern theories of metaphor that decipher within it an indefinite jamming of semantic features one into the other, a meaning being acted out; and, on the other, the drifting of heterogeneity within a heterogeneous psychic apparatus, going from drives and sensations to signifier and conversely.

Since it is not object-oriented, identification reveals how the subject that ventures there can finally find himself a hypnotized slave of his master; how he can turn out to be a nonsubject, the shadow of a nonobject. Nevertheless, it is because identification is not object-oriented that the signifier's nonobject-oriented underlying layer of drives becomes activated during the treatment that is carried out without the *Einfühlung* being repressed. In such a case, therefore, it is possible for transference to gain a hold on nonobject-oriented psychic states such as "false selves," borderline cases, and even psychosomatic symptoms. It is indeed true that one is ill when not loved; this means that a psychic structure that lacks an identifying metaphor or idealization tends to realize it in that embodied nonobject called somatic symptom—illness. Somatic persons are not those who do not verbalize; they are subjects who lack or miscarry the dynamics of metaphoricity, which constitute idealization as a complex process.

Finally, being the magnet for loving identification causes the *Other* to be understood not as a "pure signifier" but as the very space of metaphorical shifting: a condensation of semantic features as well as nonrepresentable drive heterogeneity that subtends them, goes beyond them, and slips away. Actually, by stressing the partiality of the "unary feature" during idealizing identification, Lacan located idealization solely within the field of the signifier and of desire; he clearly if not drastically separated it from narcissism as well as from drive heterogeneity and its archaic hold on the maternal vessel. To the contrary, by emphasizing the *metaphoricity* of the identifying idealization movement, we can attempt to restore to the analytic bond located there (transference and countertransference) its complex dynamic, which includes the narcissistic, drive-animated pre-object-orientation and allows it to be tied down to signifying ideals. From this standpoint, there would be no analytical idealization that did not rest upon sublimation. In other words, psychoanalysis skirts religious faith in order to expend it in the form of literary discourse.

Immediate and Absolute

Freud's definition of "primary identification" as "direct and immediate" (*direkte und unmittelbare*)[23] has not, as far as I know, aroused the attention of analysts. In light of that phrase, let us reflect for a moment on the value that speculative philosophy, particularly that of Hegel, assigns to such *immediacy*.

The immanent presence of the Absolute in Knowing is *immediately* revealed to the Subject as the recognition of that which never left him. More specifically, the Hegelian *immediate* (*Unmittelbare*) is the ultimate disengagement of consistency for the sake of form, the internal overthrow of reflection-in-itself, matter being removed from the self, without yet being for itself and hence for the other. Hegel notes in his *Science of Logic*, "Immediacy, which, as reflection-in-itself, is *consistency* (*Bestehen*) as well as form, reflection on something else, reflection *doing away with itself.*"[24] Heidegger, in his text on Hegel's Introduction to the *Phenomenology of the Spirit* entitled "Hegel and His Concept of Experience," wished to investigate that immediate presence of the Absolute in order to show the a priori or arbitrariness of the "immediate" and reveal, on both its far and near sides, the "blossoming of the Logos," dear to Heideggerian discourse. Within the scope of these reflections, one might maintain that the *immediate*, being the autoseverance of certainty in the self, is at the same time that which severs it from object-relation and bestows on it its power of acquittance (*Absolvenz*) without mediation, without object, but keeping and containing both; hence the immediate is the very logic of *parousia*, that is, the presence of the subject for the object. "It behooves him to keep any relation that merely pertains to the object . . . ," is Heidegger's comment. As the most basic indication of parousia, the immediate also presents itself as the logic of *Absolvenz*, as severance outside of relationship, and constitutes the absoluteness of the absolute. "It is there, in auto-representation, that the parousia of the absolute is displayed."[25]

In other words, the presence of the Absolute in Knowing is *immediately* revealed to the subject; consequently, any other "means" of knowledge is no more than a recognition. "The absolute is from the outset in and for itself beside us and wants to be beside us," Hegel states in his Introduction to the *Phenomenology*. Such a *being-beside-us* would be "the manner in which the light of the truth of the absolute itself enlightens us," as Heidegger says in his commentary. We are immediately within parousia, "always-already," before producing a "relationship" to it.

Let us put aside the visual aspect, be it imagined or imaginary, of that immediacy of the Absolute, which Heidegger enabled us to hear when he unfolded the word for knowledge (*Wissenschaft*) in its sonorousness (*novisse*, to have a knowledge of, *viso*, to look at), and which Lacan emphasized when he placed the *mirror* at the core of the Ego's formation. Let me first stress that specular fascination is a belated phenomenon in the genesis of the Ego. And let us try to think through the philosophical investigation against the backdrop of what the analyst might see in the appearance of the term "immediate" at the heart of primary identification.

With Freud, the arbitrariness of paternal emergence seems undeniable, at any rate absolutely necessary to the interpretative analytic construction. Nevertheless, clinical experience has led us to ascertain that the advent of the *Vater der persönlichen Vorzeit* takes place thanks to the assistance of the so-called pre-Oedipal mother, to the extent that she can indicate to her child that her desire is not limited to responding to her offspring's request (or simply turning it down). This assistance is none other than maternal desire for the Father's Phallus.

Which one? The child's father or her own? For "primary identification" the question is not relevant. If there is an *immediacy* of the child's identification with *that desire* (of the Father's Phallus), it probably comes from the child's not having to elaborate it; rather, he receives it, mimics it, or even sustains it through the mother who offers it to him (or refuses it) as a gift. In a way, such an identification with the father-mother conglomerate, as Freud would have it, or with what we have just called the maternal desire for the Phallus, comes as a godsend. And for a very good reason, since without that disposition of the psyche, the child and the mother do not yet constitute "two" . . .

As for the image making up this "imagination," it should not be conceived as simply visual but as a representation activating various facilitations corresponding to the entire gamut of perceptions, especially the *sonorous* ones; this because of their precocious appearance in the domain of neuropsychological maturation, but also because of their dominant function in speech.

Nevertheless, let us not be mistaken about the ease of such an *immediacy*. It entails an important consequence: within that logic, the word "object," just like the word "identification," becomes *improper*. A not-yet-identity (of the child) is transferred or rather displaced to the site of an Other who is not libidinally cathected as an object but remains an Ego Ideal.

Not I

Let me now point out that the most archaic unity that we thus retrieve—an identity so autonomous that it calls forth displacements—is that of the Phallus desired by the mother. It is the unity of the imaginary father, a coagulation of the mother and her desire. The imaginary father would thus be the indication that the mother is not complete but that she wants . . . Who? What? The question has no answer other than the one that uncovers narcissistic emptiness; "At any rate, not I." Freud's famous "What does a woman want" is perhaps only the echo of the more fundamental "What does a mother want?" It runs up against the same impossibility, bordered on one side by the imaginary father, on the other by a "not I." And it is out of this "not I" (see Beckett's play with that title) that an Ego painfully attempts to come into being . . .

In order to maintain himself in that place, to assume the *leap* that will definitely anchor him in the imaginary father and in language or even in art, the speaking being must engage in a struggle with the imaginary mother, for whom it will eventually constitute an object separated from the Ego. But we are not at that stage yet. The immediate transference toward the imaginary father, who is such a godsend that you have the impression that it is he who is transferred into you, withstands a process of rejection involving what may have been chaos and is about to become an *abject*. The maternal space can come into being as such, before becoming an object correlative to the Ego's desire, only as an *abject*.

In short, primary identification appears to be a transference to (from) the imaginary father, correlative to the establishment of the mother as "ab-jetted." Narcissism would be that correlation (with the imaginary father and the "ab-jetted" mother) enacted around the central emptiness of that transference. This emptiness, which is apparently the primer of the symbolic function, is precisely encompassed in linguistics by the bar separating signifier from signified and by the "arbitrariness" of the sign, or in psychoanalysis by the "gaping" of the mirror.

If narcissism is a defense against the emptiness of separation, then the whole contrivance of imagery, representations, identifications, and projections that accompany it on the way toward strengthening the Ego and the Subject is a means of exorcising that emptiness. Separation is our opportunity to become narcists or narcissistic, at any rate subjects of representation. The emptiness it opens up is nevertheless also the barely covered abyss where our identities, images, and words run the risk of being engulfed.

The mythical Narcissus would heroically lean over that emptiness to seek in the maternal watery element the possibility of representing the self or the other—someone to love. Beginning with Plotinus at least, theoretical thought has forgotten that it rumbled along over emptiness before lovingly springing toward the solar source of representation, the light that enables us to see and with which we aspire to become equal, idealization following upon idealization, perfecting upon perfecting: *In lumine tuo videbimus lumen.* Psychotic persons, however, remind us, in case we had forgotten, that the representational contrivances that cause us to speak, elaborate, or believe rest upon emptiness. Possibly the most radical atheists are those who, not knowing what the ability to represent owes to a Third Party, remain prisoners of the archaic mother, for whom they mourn in the suffering of emptiness.

Within sight of that Third Party I elaborate the narcissistic parry that allows me to block up that emptiness, to calm it and turn it into a producer of signs, representations, and meanings, I elaborate it within sight of the Third Party. I seduce this "father of individual prehistory" because he has already caught me, for he is simple virtuality, a potential presence, a form to be cathected. Always already there, the forming presence that nonetheless satisfies none of my autoerotic needs draws me into the imaginary exchange, the specular seduction. He or I—who is the agent? Or even, is it he or is it she? The immanence of its transcendence, as well as the instability of our borders before the setting of my image as "my own," turn the murky source (*eine neue psychische Aktion*) from which narcissism will flow into a dynamics of confusion and delight. Secrets of our loves.

The Ideal Ego sated with the Ego Ideal will take over from that alchemy and strengthen the defenses of the narcissistic Ego. Consciousness, along with moral conscience (that stern and precious paternal inheritance), will not truly lead us, under the tyrannical protection of the Superego, to forget the narcissistic emptiness and its surface composed of imaginary recognitions and cathexes. At least it will help us block them up; they always remain as more or less painful wounds at the heart of our functions, successes, or failures. Beneath homosexual libido, which our social objectives catch and maintain captive, the chasms of narcissistic emptiness spread out; although the latter can be a powerful motive for ideal or superegotic cathexis, it is also the primary source of inhibition.

In being narcissistic one has already throttled the suffering of emptiness. The fragility, however, of the narcissistic elaboration, underpinning the ego image as well as ideal cathexes, is such that its cracks immediately reveal the negative of our image films to those that others consider to be "narcissistic." More than insane, empty, that lining of our projection and representation devices is yet another defense of the living being. When he succeeds in eroticizing it, when he allows the nonobject-oriented, pre-narcissistic violence of the drive directed toward an abject to run wild, then death triumphs in that strange path. The death drive and its psychological equivalent, hatred, is what Freud discovers after stopping off at Narcissus. Narcissism and its lining, emptiness, are in short our most intimate, brittle, and archaic elaborations of the death drive. The most advanced, courageous, and threatened sentries of primal repression.

In contrast with Melanie Klein's "projective identification," the proposition I am offering here has the advantage of pointing to, even before the Oedipal triangle and within a specific disposition, the place of the Third Party; without the latter, the phase Melanie Klein calls "schizo-paranoid" could not become a "depressive" phase and thus could not carry the "symbolic equivalences" to the level of linguistic "signs." The archaic inscription of the father seems to me a way of modifying the fantasy of a phallic mother playing at the phallus game all by herself, alone and complete, in the back room of Kleinism and post-Kleinism.

As for language, the notion outlined here differs, furthermore, from innatist theories concerning linguistic competence (Chomsky) as well as from Lacanian notions of an always-already-there of language that would be revealed as such in the subject of the unconscious. I of course assume, with respect to the *infans*, that the symbolic function preexists, but also maintain an evolutionary postulate that leads me to seek to elaborate *various dispositions* giving access to that function, and this corresponds as well to various psychic structures.

In the light of the above, what I have called a "narcissistic structuration" appears to be the earliest juncture (chronologically and logically) whose spoors we might detect in the unconscious. Conversely, understanding narcissism as origin or as undecomposable, unanalyzable screen leads the analyst (no matter what theoretical warnings might be given in other respects) to present his interpretative discourse as a haven, either comforting or confrontingly aggressive, for a narcissism that thus finds itself recognized and renewed. Whether comforting or authenticating (by rational criticism, for instance, in interpretations of the "mental process" sort), such a welcome falls into the trap of narcissism and seldom succeeds in leading it through the Oedipal procession on to the topology of a complex subject.

In fact, clinical practicians like Winnicot protected themselves against such a danger, if only by always advocating a mixture of "narcissistic" and "Oedipal" interpretations in so-called psychotic states. Nevertheless, if the dead end that has just been noted can be encountered by others, the reason for it must probably be located in a basic omission— that of the agency of the imaginary father from the start of primary identification, an agency of which "projective identification" is a more belated consequence (logically and chronologically). One may still reach that dead end, by the same token, if one ignores the very concrete and specific structuration required by psychicism within that very elementary disposition, which the term "narcissism" threatens to reduce to a fascination for what is nothing but the mother's phallus.

Persian or Christian

The dynamics of primary identification, which structures *emptiness* and *object* as what may have appeared as a "narcissistic screen," will allow us to examine another enigmatic juncture on the Freudian path.

Freud's uneasiness concerning Christianity is well known, and his rationality would not let him put it into words with respect to revealed religion, but, dazzled and prudent, he did express it when faced with Persian religion. "The sun-drenched face of the young Persian god has remained incomprehensible to us."[26] It is indeed possible to interpret that refulgent jouissance as "direct and immediate" primary identification with the Phallus desired by the mother; this amounts neither to being the mother's Phallus nor entering the Oedipal drama. A certain phantasmatic incestuous potentiality is thus set aside; it works from the place of the imaginary father and constitutes the basis of imagination itself. Moreover, the subsequent naming of that relationship perhaps represents the conditions of sublimation.

In Freud's text, the "refulgent and incomprehensible" face lacking an Oedipal feeling of fault or guilt would be that of the leader of the horde of brothers who kills the father and boasts of his feat (as Ernest Jones suggests).[27] One might, on the other hand, consider a pre- or non-Oedipal disposition of that jouissance; a position of symbolicity that stems from primary identification, coupled with what the latter infers in regard to sexual nondifferentiation (father-and-mother, man-and-woman) and immediate transference to the site of *maternal desire*. That would constitute a fragile inscription of subjecthood, one which, under the subsequent Oedipal sway, would retain no more than a phantasmatic status. In addition, such a warm but dazzling, domesticated paternity includes imaginary exultation as well as a risk of dissolving identities that the Freudian Oedipal process alone ends up strengthening, in the ideal hypothesis of course.

Maintaining against the winds and high tides of our modern civilization the requirement of a stern father who, through his Name, brings about separation, judgment, and identity, constitutes a necessity, a more or less pious wish. But we can only note that jarring such sternness, far from leaving us orphaned or inexorably psychotic, reveals multiple and varied destinies for paternity—notably archaic, imaginary paternity. Those destinies could or can be manifested by the clan as a whole, by the priest, or by the therapist. In all cases, however, we are dealing with a function that guarantees the subject's entry into a disposition, a fragile one to be sure, of an ulterior, unavoidable Oedipal destiny, but one that can also be playful and sublimational.

Seducer or Ideal Father

The tragic dynamic of the Father's idealization is taken up again in *Moses and Monotheism* through the theme of the election of the Jewish people by its God and through the story of Moses. There is nothing to make one conceive this election as a revival of the old idea, subsequently abandoned by Freud, of the father as the hysterical person's first seducer. The father who brings a people into being through his love is perhaps indeed closer to the "father of individual prehistory," and, at any rate, to the idealizing agency that drains early identifications, not as object but as "unary feature." One might nevertheless interpret Freudian thought with respect to this loving father in the following fashion. The hysterical structure of the horde of brothers construes him as a seducer, an agent of the libido, of Eros, and puts him to death; this is Moses' murdered body. Yet there is also a structural necessity for his unique love as symbolic choice; it appears later on as a pressing need to lay down moral rules or a right to the tribe. The father will then be recognized not as seducer but as Law, as an abstract agency of the One that selects our identifying and idealizing power. The Christian trinity, for its part, reconciles the seducer and the legislator by inventing another form of love—*agape*, symbolic (nominal, spiritual) from the very start *and* corporeal, absorbing the acknowledged murder of the erotic body into the universalist profusion of the symbolist distinction for everyone (brother or stranger, faithful or sinner).

What is opposed to the recognition of the imaginary father? What is it that produces its repression, or even its burial? Freud drops the word "character," with its well-known anal connotations. "Whatever resistance character might later be able to bring to bear against the influence of abandoned sexual objects, the effects of earlier identifications, carried out in the most precocious stages of life, will always keep their general, lasting features."[28]

Character is one of the limits to what is analyzable, and that is confirmed by the difficulties encountered in the region we are now investigating. Furthermore, because of the anal character's resistance against primary identification, the advent of the abject during treatment can clearly be seen as the first breach in resistance. . . . Nevertheless and above all it is Oedipal rivalry, which creates mediations, that tragically darkens the dazzlement of primary identification. Within the Oedipus complex, the question is no longer "Who *is* it?" but "Who *has* it?"; the narcissistic question "Am I?" becomes a possessive or attributive question, "Have I?" It is nonetheless true that by starting from Oedipal dramas and their failures—backwards, in other words—one will be able to detect the particulars of primary identification. It is to be noted, however, that "boundary states" lead us there directly, locating the Oedipal conflict as ulterior or secondary.

A boy will have difficulty tearing himself away from the petrifying situation of being his mother's phallus; or if he succeeds, through the maternal grandfather (among others) who has come in between, he will never cease waging war against his brothers in the shadow of an inaccessible father. Only in poetic enunciation will it be possible for him to be son-and-father within the immediate and direct disposition of primary identification, and bypassing sexual difference—witness the troubadours and Joyce. As for the girl, she will retain the traces of that primary transference only if assisted by a father having a maternal character, who nevertheless will not be of much help in her breaking away from the mother and finding a heterosexual object. She will thus tend to bury that primary identification under the disappointed feverishness of the homosexual, or else in abstraction, which, as it flies away from the body, fully constitutes itself as "soul" or fuses with an Idea, a Love, a Self-sacrifice. . . . If ever a jouissance remains, it still seems to partake of that archaic differentiation that Freud so delicately and elliptically touched on under the heading of "primary identification."

"Narcissistic structure" thus remains a permanent fixture in the love grievances that beckon to us . . .

NOTES

1. This corresponds to, although it does not fully render, Kristeva's coinage, *hainamoration*. It was suggested by Margaret Waller (who translated *Revolution in Poetic Language*) to replace one of my own less fortunate neologisms—and I am indebted to her for many other suggestions and corrections as well.—Trans.

2. See *On Narcissism: An Introduction* (1914), in vol. 14 of the *Standard Edition of the Complete Psychological Works of Sigmund Freud*, 24 vols., James Strachey, tr. and ed. (London: Hogarth Press, 1953–1974). This text is doubtless very bound up with the war, Freud's insecurity, and Jung.

Nevertheless, from the time of his earliest works, Freud insisted on a *resistance* that would have been imbedded in the very structure of neurons, as well as on *inhibition* as master faculty of the Ego (*Project for a Scientific Psychology* [895], *Standard Edition* 1). "We must reckon with the possibility that something in the nature of the sexual drive itself is unfavorable to the realization of complete satisfaction," he notes in "The Tendency to Debasement in Love," in *The Psychology of Love*, *Standard Edition* 11:188–89, before discovering narcissism at the same time as the illusion present at the outset of psychicism, as it is at the heart of amatory experience. Next comes what Freud himself called the "strange" postulate of death drive, posited toward the end of an exposition on the impossible in love, on loving hatred, and primary masochism ("Beyond the Pleasure Principle," *Standard Edition* 18:51–61).

3. "Die autoerotischen Triebe sind aber uhrfänglich; es muss also irgend etwas zum Autoerotismus hinzukommen, eine neue psychische Aktion, um den Narzissmus zu gestalten." *Standard Edition* 14:77.

4. Jacques Lacan, *Les Ecrits techniques de Freud*, in *Le Séminaire* (Paris: Seuil, 1975), 1:133.

5. André Green, *Narcissisme de vie, narcissisme de mort* (Paris: Minuit, 1983).

6. See "Being in Love and Hypnosis," in *Group Psychology and the Analysis of the Ego* (1921), *Standard Edition* 18:111ff.

7. Ibid., p. 112.

8. "Identification," in *Group Psychology and the Analysis of the Ego*, *Standard Edition* 18:105.

9. Ibid., p. 105.

10. Ibid., p. 110.

11. Ibid., p. 107.

12. "Diese scheint zunächst nicht Erfolg oder Ausgang einer Objektbesetzung zu sein, sie ist eine *direkte* und *unmittelbare* und frühzeitiger als jede Objektbesetzung." *The Ego and the Id* (1923), *Standard Edition* 19:31. One of the main ideas of Freud's breviary of love amounts to positing that the Oedipus complex's decline (which he calls "natural" but is in fact enigmatic) during the latency period favors the inhibition of partial drives and strengthens ideals—thus making the erotico-ideal cathexis of the love object possible during puberty. "I am in love" is a fact of adolescence when the teenager is capable of partial repression because of difficulties in realizing Oedipal fantasies and can project his idealizing capabilities onto a person toward whom erotic desire can be deferred. See Christian David, *L'Etat amoureux* (Paris: Payot, 1971). Nevertheless, the premises for such a state of love go back to *primary identification* and, before they constitute a lover, they shape psychic space itself.

13. Melanie Klein, *Envy and Gratitude* (London: Hogarth Press, 1957), p. 187. See also Melanie Klein and Jean Rivière, *Love, Hate, and Reparation* (London: Hogarth Press, 1967). On Melanie Klein see Jean-Michel Petot, *Melanie Klein, le moi et le bon object (1932–1960)* (Paris: Dunot, 1982).

14. Melanie Klein, *Envy and Gratitude*, p. 180.

15. Ibid., p. 191.

16. Ibid., p. 193.

17. Recalling that in analytical literature the object is in most instances a partial object (mammilla, scybalum, phallus, urine), Lacan specifies: "This feature, this partial feature, rightly emphasized in objects, is applicable not because these objects are part of a total object, the body, but because they represent only partially the function that produces them." Being a function of separation and of want that found the signifying relationship, these objects, designated by a lower case "a," will be called "objects of want": "These objects have one common feature in my elaboration of them—they have no specular image, or, in other words, alterity. It is what enables them to be the 'stuff,' or rather the lining, though not in any sense the reverse, of the very subject that one takes to be the subject of consciousness. . . . It is to this object that cannot be grasped in the mirror that the specular image lends its clothes." "Subversion of the Subject and Dialectic of Desire," in *Ecrits/A Selection*, Alan Sheridan, tr. (New York: Norton, 1977), pp. 315–16.

Lacan discovered in *fantasy* the exemplary efficacy of the object "a" since in his view the structure of fantasy is linked "to the condition of an object, . . . the moment of a 'fading' or eclipse of the subject that is closely bound up with the *Spaltung* or splitting that it suffers from its subordination to the signifier" (p. 313). That is what is symbolized by the formula, ($ ◊ a) where ◊ indicates desire. Finally, the *metonymical* structure defines the Lacanian object relation to the extent that "it is the connection between signifier and signifier that permits the elision in which the signifier installs the want-of-being in the object relation, using the value of 'reference back' possessed by signification in order to invest it with the desire aimed at the very want it supports." "The Agency of the Letter in the Unconscious" (p. 164).

18. "Take just one signifier as an emblem of this omnipotence [of the other's authority], that is to say of this wholly potential power (*ce pouvoir tout en puissance*), this birth of possibility, and you have the unary feature (*trait unaire*), which, by filling in the invisible mark that the subject derives from the signifier, alienates this subject in the primary identification that forms the ego ideal." "Subversion of the Subject and Dialectic of Desire," in *Ecrits/A Selection*, p. 306.

The unary feature of Lacan goes back to the "unique feature" (*einziger Zug*), to which would be limited the identification that is only partial, according to Freud in *Identification* (das beide Male die Identifizierung eine partielle, höchst beschränkte ist). See the *Seminars on Transference* (1960–1961) and on *Identification* (1961–1962). Lacan takes advantage of that partial status, on the whole rather imprecise with Freud, in order to insist upon the *unique feature* (*einziger Zug*) that establishes identification as intrinsically symbolic, hence subjected to the distinctiveness of signifying traits, and finally ruled by the benchmark of One feature, of the Unique—foundation of my very own unicity. . . . This unary feature is not "in the first field of narcissistic identification" where we have witnessed the emergence of the imaginary Father; Lacan sees it straight off "in the field of desire . . . in the reign of the signifier." *The Four Fundamental Concepts of Psychoanalysis* (New York: Norton, 1978), p. 256.

19. See Michael Balint, *Amour primaire et technique psychanalytique* (Paris: Payot, 1972).

20. See "Identification," in *Group Psychology and the Analysis of the Ego, Standard Edition* 18:105.

21. "Therefore the subject becomes conscious of his desire in the other, by means of the other's image, which presents him with the specter of his own mastery." Lacan, *Les Ecrits techniques de Freud*, in *Le Séminaire*, 1:178.

22. "[The imaginary position of desire] is conceivable only to the extent that a guide may be found beyond the imaginary, at the level of the symbolic plane, the legal exchange that can be embodied only on the basis of verbal exchange among human beings. The guide that rules the subject is the ego ideal" (ibid., p. 162). And this is true even if "love is a phenomenon taking place on the level of the imaginary and provoking a real subduction of the symbolic, a kind of annulment or perturbation of the ego ideal" (ibid.).

23. *The Ego and the Id, Standard Edition* 19:31.

24. G. W. F. Hegel, *Science de la logique* (Paris: Vrin, 1970), pp. 385–86.

25. Ibid.

26. *Totem and Taboo, Standard Edition* 13:153.
27. See *Moses and Monotheism, Standard Edition* 23:110.
28. *The Ego and the Id, Standard Edition* 19:31.

Throes of Love: The Field of the Metaphor

Through the Looking Glass

It may seem paradoxical to be seeking the discourse of amatory relationships in borderline aesthetics. It may seem strange that, instead of bringing to the fore the straightforward language of simple idealization of the love object, one analyzes the painful or ecstatic states where the object slips away. Such a choice is not imposed simply because the staging of amatory capture in a narrative has been more fully investigated. It has been determined essentially by two observations.

The first, psychoanalytic in nature, amounts to asserting that the amatory experience rests on *narcissism* and its aura of emptiness, seeming, and impossibility, which underlies any *idealization* equally and essentially inherent in love. Even more so, when the social consensus gives *little* or *no* support to such an idealizing possibility, as may be observed at the present time (a phenomenon of which the religious and moral crisis is only one aspect), the derealization that underlies amatory idealism shows up with its full power.

In the second place, when one transposes into language the idealization on the edge of primal repression that amatory experience amounts to, this assumes that scription and writer invest in language in the first place precisely because it is a favorite object—a place for excess and absurdity, ecstasy and death. Putting love into words, and this stresses the utterance more than the propositional act ("I must *utter* as close as possible to what I am experiencing with the other"), necessarily summons up not the narcissistic *parry* but what appears to me as narcissistic *economy*. Such and such loving speech that we view as being in a state of uncertainty and metaphorical condensation reveals the continuity of the narcissistic economy, and this includes the "insignificant" love experience that does not dare express itself differently from what is on the surface, does not venture to seek its logic beyond the looking glass where lovers bewitch each other. Because it thus speaks love's painful but also constituent truth, that scription attracts us. We become its readers during the intervals of our own loves when we are able to withstand looking at them beyond the surface, in more fundamental fashion. It is a view that we cannot necessarily share with our partners but to which our dreams, our anguish, and our jouissance bear witness.

On the Referent and Subject of the Metaphor

Let us call metaphor, in the general sense of a *conveyance of meaning*, the economy that modifies language when subject and object of the utterance act muddle their borders. One already senses that one of the purposes of this study is to base a theory of metaphor on a given number of specific states of the subject of the utterance act. My reading of metaphoricalness constitutes neither a philosophical challenge against the metaphor, nor an expansion (conversely symmetrical) of its impact on any language act; it assumes a theoretical distance that is not one of speculative philosophy either. It finds its justification in the ambiguous, loving distance, germane to psychoanalytic transference, and is based on contemporary analyses (semantic, syntactic, discursive) of the metaphorical act.[1] I shall, however, try to understand such broadened metaphoricalness within the amatory economy of the subject of the utterance act, who demonstrates by means of metaphors the complex process of identification (narcissism *and* idealization).

"The metaphorical exists only within the bounds of metaphysics," Heidegger propounds.[2] The assertion is incontrovertible as far as the field of metaphysics itself is concerned, and it suits the metaphoricalness particular to philosophical discourse, which was able to survive because of the very banishment of the metaphor.[3] I shall, nevertheless, in this discussion, go over some points that are essential to my purpose.

We know that, ever since Plato (see *Gorgias*, but also *Phaedrus*), philosophical discourse has been obsessed with setting up the boundary between philosophy and rhetoric, which is the real requirement for its existence.

Eidos, Omoiosis, Analogia

The problematics of *ressemblance*, of the "striking image," worries, as we know, the whole of Platonic thought. It has often been shown, since Heidegger, how light, the "visible," and the "image" conceal themselves in the "idea" and establish thought itself as a lexicalized metaphor, *eidos*. Let us, however, remove from that constituent imagery of the *idea* the portion of resemblance that, for its part, sustains the metaphor. "It is the east, and Juliet is the sun," Romeo tells Juliet, for Juliet and the sun are equally dazzling to him, they are alike in that both are a dazzling light. *Omoioma, atos:* Plato uses those words when discussing love in *Phaedrus,* and he posits that the amorous soul notices an *omoioma,* an *imitation* of celestial things in the things of this world that *resemble* them and for that very reason causes it to fall in love, puts it beside itself. One is in love with what resembles an ideal that is out of sight but present in the memory. The entire motion of metaphorical conveyance is already present in the *omoiosis* relation, which has the advantage, at the very dawn of Greek thought, of placing love in concert with image-making, resemblance, homologation. Greek ontology buried that movement, but we find it again, with the same Platonistic terminology, in the Gospels, where *omoioma* is used to think out the relations between God and his creatures (Romans 6:5). Nevertheless, medieval theology, moving away from the amatory metaphoricalness of the Gospels, became interested in the Aristotelian notion of *analogia,* intent as it was to make the state of shock inherent in amatory *omoiosis* and metaphor thinkable. Aristotle's place is thus fundamental in the "ontologizing of the metaphor" constituted by creating the philosophical category of *analogy.* Torn between ontology and theology, Aristotle's thought keeps aiming for their reconciliation, which, as it is impossible, finally wrecks his ontological design.[4] One of the tokens of this conflict is the effort to elaborate a univocal philosophical language untainted by any poeticalness and yet attentive to some of the signifying effects of the latter.

Having thus expelled metaphorical ambiguity from the field of philosophy, Aristotle kept trying to gain, within that very field, "a scrap of equivocalness."[5] He succeeded in doing so, on the one hand, by gradually blunting the predicative function's preciseness (the predicative copula may be understood as a *being said of*—"Socrates is [said to be] a man"—and as a *being in*—"Socrates is a musician," where "musician" is an accident of the substance). But on the other hand and above all, Aristotle is led to speak of *analogy* (in a different sense from the one he ascribes to this word when he considers it as an instance of metaphor) when discussing aporia in "the multiple meanings of being." There is a being, but this may be said in various ways. How can we reconcile these two assertions if not by *analogy?* Indeed, having inherited from outside his own philosophy a Platonic theology of the being-as-One, Aristotle is forced to reconcile his discourse on the physical world in the diversity of its categorial meanings with the *pros hen, ad unum.* The divine *ousia* constantly underlies the categorial oneness of being. That is precisely what is written in the *Metaphysics* when the word analogy is introduced: "the causes of all are the same. They are the same or analogous," and further on, "the causes of substances may be treated as the causes of all things."[6] The thinkable, the ontological, is based on the theological unthinkable, which, although unthinkable, but perhaps for that very reason, sets the structure of the investigation. The analogy thus introduced was first proportional, hence mathematical, before it was set forth as *attributive* analogy.[7] By breaking with the *Poetics*, Aristotle salvages *some* metaphoricalness for the sake of another no longer metaphorical but transcendental discourse: analogy is witness to this *pros hen, ad unum* in his investigation. And one will have to wait for the whole post-Kantian expansion of positivist logic before Carnap and Russell would define predication as the assignment of something to a class and thus extricate the problem of *attribution* from the sphere of *analogy*. What is nevertheless lost along the way are the other meanings of the predicative copula, notably the function it has to designate the acting being, thereby giving rise in particular to a question concerning the very act of uttering. The philosophical salvaging of analogy by Aristotle had the advantage of opening up the question of *being* as act, and at the same time of raising the problem, if only implicitly, of the *act of naming*. Certain Aristotelian expressions, moreover, state this rather clearly: "The metaphor signifies things in action" (*Rhetoric* III, II, 1411b, 24–25); "the imitators may represent the whole story dramatically, as though they were actually doing the things described" (*Poetics* 1448a, 24); "Now the action is represented in the play by the Fable or Plot" (*Poetics* 1450a, 3).

Let us not forget that advantage, let us not bury it in the simple logical motion of predication or predication as motion. For such a dynamic will enlighten us concerning the significance of the other metaphor, the real one, the poetic one. Let me simply stress here that analogy, even when philosophical, is necessary for thought in order to organize an investigation (not a science) that would be ontotheological (Heidegger's phrase) and dependent on being as *One* and on the *act*.

Furthermore, medieval theology, splitting off in its turn from the poetical metaphoricalness of biblical discourse, postulated with Thomas Aquinas an *analogia entis*. It distinguished first between an analogy of *proportio* (comprising a definite distance and a strict relationship, *determinata habitudo*, between the terms) and an analogy of *proportionalitas*, which is a simple similarity of ratios (for instance, six is to three as four is to two). But in order to imagine the relationship between infinite God and finite creatures Thomas Aquinas posited *causality* itself as *analogy*. What had been a relationship of significance (of creatures by analogy with God) becomes an *efficiency*: one may name God according to creatures only on account of the relationship between creatures and God, their principle and their cause, in whom all the perfections of existing beings preexist excellently.[8] Such an analogy, which has been raised to the level of cause, indeed excludes the strictly poetical metaphor; but, as Paul Ricoeur notes,[9] it also integrates it surreptitiously; this happens when, examining two analogous meanings (for instance, using "wise" in speaking of man and of God), Thomas sees that the *nominis significatio* (germane to the "wise man" and attributed to God by analogy) is exceeded in the *res significata* (God) by a surplus of meaning impossible to circumscribe . . . The surplus of meaning (the *res significata* is richer than the *nominis significatio*) that results from the *new predicative motion* is, properly speaking, the metaphorical effect specific to poetry, which Thomas's logicality wished to contain by means of *analogia entis*.

A final observation concerning the philosophical history of the metaphor as outlined by Paul Ricoeur will bring us closer to my purpose. It is true that a certain conception of the metaphor, itself stemming from a reductive metaphysical interpretation, which moreover is no longer in favor, lends itself to restricting that image to the field of metaphysics. I refer to the interpretation that sees in it a simple shift from *literal* to *figurative*, *primary* to *secondary*, *animate* to *inanimate*, and so on: all such distinctions are indeed metaphysical, they can be upheld only within a naive theory of metaphor dominated by the *word* and insensitive to its syntactical and narrative dissemination. The work done I. A. Richards, Max Black, and, on a different level, by Emile Benveniste, Roman Jakobson, and contemporary semanticists who, in their wake, locate the metaphor in *sentence* and *discourse* bring out a certain potentiality that is specific to the Aristotelian interpretation of the metaphor. The *kurion* ("common" name) or the *idion* (translated as "proper") simply refer to the *starting term* of metaphorical motion and seem not to have had for the Greek philosopher the meaning of a primal, primitive (*etumon*) own. Present day theory of metaphor brings to the fore the interference between two *nonhierarchized semantic fields* and two reference areas also nonhierarchized; it does so by giving greater importance in its analysis to the sentence or discourse context of metaphorical motion as well as to the utterance act as referential and intersubjective act.

"Being Like" or the "Unbeing"

Metaphoricalness consequently appears to me as the utterance not only of a being-as-One and acting, but rather, or even on the contrary, as the indication of uncertainty concerning the reference. *Being like* is not only *being* and *nonbeing*, it is also a longing for *unbeing* in order to assert as only possible "being," not an ontology, that is, something outside of discourse, but the constraint of discourse itself. The "like" of metaphorical conveyance both assumes and upsets that constraint, and to the extent that it probabilizes the identity of signs, it questions the very probability of the reference. Being?—*Unbeing.*

Paul Ricoeur, in his fine study, speaks of an "ontological vehemence" specific to the semantic aim of the metaphor as act, which harbors in itself the premonition of the unknown that the concept is about to take hold of. This is where I part company with him. His interpretation permanently ontologizes the metaphor, which he had yet so strongly reinstated in its possible but not absolute ontotheological scope. By saying that the metaphor signals a new reference to be named, Ricoeur encloses metaphorical dynamics within a speculative philosophy whose plan he explicitly acknowledges, a philosophy subservient to being-as-One, comparable to the process that, besides, we both detected in Aristotle and Thomas Aquinas.

Is there, however, another possibility for thinking out metaphoricalness, without simplifying it in order to reduce it to a metaphysics itself simplified, and without limiting its impact as "premonition of a concept" within the framework of speculative philosophy? It seems so to me. I shall interpret metaphorical dynamics as established not by the designation of a reference inevitably reducible to being, but by the relationship the speaking subject has with the Other during the utterance act. The utterance is precisely what seems to me, from the position of an analyst, the only basis for meaning and significance in discourse.

What I am calling for is not a simple reversal in perspective: setting up an inner foundation, a "mood," a basis for discourse—in place of an outer one, the referent. The *subject* is not simply an inside facing the referential outside. The subjective structure, understood as a specific articulation of the relationship between speaking subject and Other, determines the very situation of reality, its existence or nonexistence, its overturning or hypostasis. In such a perspective, ontology becomes subordinate to the signifying structure that sustains a given subject in its transference upon the Other.

I have observed that the ultimate support of Aristotelian metaphor is a being who acts. The poetic as well as the categorial metaphor merely conveys "motion and life"; yet Aristotle stresses that "act is motion." Nevertheless, in the face of the difficulties that ontology encounters in its attempt to define "strength" and "act," I shall venture the following proposition. The "being who acts" could exist only for a subject in symbolic *contact*, that is to say in motion, in *transference* with another. The being who acts gives its all in subjective experience, and this is even truer in the love between two subjects—that climax of destabilizing-stabilizing identification. There is no act, just as there is no sexual act, outside of love, for it is in the constituent violence of its field that the subject's signifying structure is shaken, drives and ideals included. There, on account of the subject's modification—the questioning of the subject in amatory experience—a modification of its being and of being is carried out; they are opened out, if you will, unfurled. No longer physics but speaking subjectivity will henceforth ask the key epistemological question; what is mobility, what is innovation? "What is" means, in this context, how does one express them? The amatory experience as dynamics of the crisis and of subjective and discursive renewal, along with its linguistic correlative, metaphoricalness, appears to be, from that standpoint, at the core of an essential debate.

The univocity of signs undergoes equivocality and is resolved in a more or less undecidable connotation when the subject of the utterance, in a state of transference (of love) toward the other transposes the same process of identification, of transference, to the units of language—the signs. The undeniable referential effect of this process, which stems from the referent having been made ambiguous, should not conceal its subjective basis. The signifying unit (the "sign") opens up and reveals its components: drives and sensory elements (as in a synesthetic metaphor)—while the subject itself, in a state of loving transference, flares up from sensation to idealization.

If one agrees with that interpretation, one understands why philosophical thought on metaphor is rooted, with Plato, in a reflection on love and on the direction philosophical discourse must take in relation to that reflection: Plato aims at a mastery of *love* and at the same time of *metaphor*, through ontotheology. One also understands why theological discourse alone, concerned with the One and the relationship of the speaking being to that One—hence with faith—was forced to proceed edge-to-edge along the metaphor, which produced a determination of the theory of *analogy* starting from the poetic field but outside of it. Finally, when theology is emptied of its essence and, with Descartes, holds the other in a position of a *causa sive rationem* and seeks the true basis of reason only in the articulation of judgment and no longer in analogy, which, even when preserved, loses its function—we then witness a double banishment. Nascent rationalism brushes aside in the same stroke *analogy*, the scar of metaphoricalness in the specific domain of ontotheology, and its correlative, the *Ego affectus est*: the loving subject. To make possible the advent of *judgment* and the *Ego cogito*.

Psychoanalysis: Poetry and History

The psychoanalytic stance allows one to record a true transformation of Western discourse, in which the metaphor is at stake, accomplished at the expense of the loving subject; it thus determines a position that can only be termed outrageous within the history and typology of interpretative discourse. Functioning under the same amatory conditions that rule the production of metaphoricalness in poetic discourse, psychoanalysis nevertheless keeps a certain distance from it since it produces, with respect to that discourse, a knowledge effect. Does this mean that it produces its concept? If that were true, it would not be distinguishable from speculative philosophy and ontotheology. It might be better to say that it analyzes in precise fashion such a proximity to speculative philosophy. Not in disseminating each concept by way of metaphor or asserting that every sign is necessarily a forgotten metaphor that must be brought to the fore in order to dissolve its idealizing conceptual seizing. Rather, it does so by preserving a *typology of discourses* (for instance, the "poetical" is not the "philosophical" discourse, which is not the "analytical"), and setting for itself the regular task of being, on the one hand, a scene of metaphor production (as in the amatory state or in poetry) and, on the other, a scene of *provisional* interpretation. It is the *provisional* (this means such-and-such, for the *moment*) that inserts *duration* instead of the *absolute* in psychoanalytic interpretation. *Psychoanalysis is the most internalized moment of Western historicality.* The provisional also inserts the *chance* of subjective encounter in the dynamics of transference. If it is the amatory impact that makes me say, and if such saying can have a history, this means there is no absolute that is external to our love, our discourse. Neither your actual history nor anyone else's holds the reference to our discourse's signification. Being in love conveys a throbbing, passionate, unique meaning, but only here and now, and which might, in another juncture, be absurd. For the first time love, and with it metaphoricalness, are removed from the authoritarian domination of a *Res externa*, necessarily divine or deifiable. Love and metaphoricalness, thus deontologized or, in the extreme, dehumanized, henceforth constitute a determination of language with all its resources spread out. The subject himself/herself is merely a subject: a provisional accident, differently renewed within the only *infinite* space where we might unfurl our loves, that is, the infinity of the signifier. *Love is something spoken, and it is only that*: poets have always known it.

From now on amatory styles will be spread out before us like different historical embodiments of the metaphoricalness that is essential to loving states: like stylistic variants of the *cure*, another name for *life*, which the Western subject has experienced for two thousand years through his amorous attitudes, which have been inserted in amatory codes now made official.

NOTES

1. I. A. Richards, *The Philosophy of Rhetoric*, 1936 (London: Oxford University Press, 1965); Max Black, *Models and Metaphors* (Ithaca: Cornell University Press, 1962); Roman Jakobson and Morris Halle, *Fundamentals of Language*, 1956 (The Hague: Mouton, 1962); Jakobson, "La Métaphore," in *Languages* 54 (1979).

2. *Der Satz vom Grund* (Pfullingen: Neske, 1957), pp. 77–90.

3. Paul Ricoeur has lucidly discussed this problem, as well as the ensuing metaphysico-metaphorical deconstruction in the work of Jacques Derrida. See *La Métaphore vive* (Paris: Seuil, 1975), pp. 356ff.

4. As J. Vuillemin has shown in *De la logique à la théologie* (Paris: Flammarion, 1967).

5. Ricoeur, *La Métaphore vive*, p. 344.

6. *Metaphysics*, book XII, ch. 5, 1071a, 33–35.

7. Vuillemin, *De la logique à la théologie*, p. 22.

8. *Summa*, Ia, question 13, art. 5.

9. Ricoeur, *La Métaphore vive*, p. 356.

Extraterrestrials Suffering for Want of Love

The Crisis

The analyst is by definition tuned in to the crisis: the analytical contract issues from an inevitable discontent. The existence of psychoanalysis thus reveals the permanency, the inescapable nature of crisis. The speaking being is a wounded being, his speech wells up out of an aching for love, and the "death drive" (Freud) or the "unbeing" (Lacan) that are coextensive with human nature determine, if they do not justify them, the discontents of civilizations.

Such a view is not necessarily a product of pessimism ("one can do nothing in the face of crisis, that is the way it is") or a disparagement of the present moment ("there is nothing new, things have always been like that"). Psychoanalytic fundamentalism nonetheless shifts the question's viewpoint. On the one hand, periods and societies that believe they are outside the crisis appear, in the psychoanalyst's eyes, symptomatic: through what miracle of repression, idealization, or sublimation has the discontent with "splitting" been stabilized, or even harmonized, within a code of believable, sound, permanent values? On the other hand, in the Jewish and Christian West, the analyst is able to identify a *perpetuum mobile* that, nurturing the crisis basic to the speaking condition and sustained by it, creates the problems the West alone can resolve, although it never succeeds in doing so; and yet, it symbolizes them indefinitely in defilement and by passion, both henceforth universalized. In that case, where is the crisis? What makes up its painful image? Surely not a consciousness shattered by the unconscious, for the former can only recognize itself there, coil up, and speak of it, thus producing a new discourse, baroque or Joycean, witness to an "internal experiment" or to the shaping of a "theater of cruelty." If art may resemble a crisis, it is above all a resurrection. The crisis exists only for mirrors that are enamored of stable images; for calculators that are panic-stricken by swirling markets and currencies, for stabilizing consciences that believe in the contemporary divinity known as a "balance sheet." The analyst is neither an artist nor an accountant. Between the two, he is one of the last images of the fullness of passion.

What are analysands complaining of, dwellers in giant cities who have lost their bearings? Can we isolate *the* contemporary sickness, the one that colors the end of the twentieth century and slips it into the third millennium?

The Abolition of Psychic Space

To say that *hatred* or *death drive* prevails in the complaint more than inhibited desire or a mistreated eros is right but insufficient. Freud already knew it, from *Beyond the Pleasure Principle* (1920) up to *Civilization and Its Discontents* (1929) and *Analysis Terminable and*

Interminable (1937). After him, and independently of him, it is remarkable that women analysts, from Melanie Klein to Sabine Spielrein, have not ceased emphasizing that morbid component of the psyche. Resistant to the notion of castration, a woman perhaps accepts it only when confronted with a dying body (her child's in the worst of cases). Moreover, the dramas of individuation demand of her such a violent rejection of the mother, and by the mother, that in the hatred of the loved object a woman immediately finds herself in a known and intolerable country.

What analysands are henceforth suffering from is *the abolition of psychic space*. Narcissus in want of light as much as of a spring allowing him to capture his true image, Narcissus drowning in a cascade of false images (from social roles to the media), hence deprived of substance or place: these contemporary characters are witnesses to our being unable today to elaborate primary narcissism.

Neither screen nor state, primary narcissism is already a structure, previous to the Oedipus complex, which operates on the basis of three terms. The central node of connection and disconnection, fullness and emptiness, positions and losses represents the instability of the *narcissistic subject*. He remains there, attracted on the one hand by the magnet of *primary identification*, which is a father imagined to be loving, "father of individual prehistory,"[2] the seed of the Ego ideal; and on the other, by a magnet of desire and hatred, fascination and disgust, constituted by the archaic mother who has ceased to be a container of needs but not yet made up into a taboo object of desire: neither subject nor object, an *"abject"-mother*, a place of warding off and differentiation, an infection. The breaking up of Christianity has left those three agencies in suspense.

The image of the Virgin—the woman whose entire body is an emptiness through which the paternal word is conveyed—had remarkably subsumed the maternal "abject," which is so necessarily intrapsychic. Lacking that safety lock, feminine abjection imposed itself upon social representation, causing an actual denigration of women; this in turn gave rise to increased antifeminism but even more so to a strong reaction on the part of women who were unwilling to bear, in narcissistic fashion, the representation of their own rejection of the maternal, which no available secular code could now guarantee. The first feminist generation rejected, through the "women-as-object," the narcissistic wound constituted by maternal sexuality and countered it with the image of the virile activist who was less a libertine than a monitor; the second advocated a centripetal, mitigated, soothed feminine sexuality, before unearthing, quite recently, under the guise of romances among women, sadomasochistic havoc.

In similar fashion, the lack of a secular variant of the loving father makes contemporary discourse incapable of assuming primary identification—the substratum for our idealizing constructions. Thus orphaned, the homosexuality of a man seeking a feminine stance facing the other man encounters only its immediate erotic fulfillment. As to the woman, she lacks a go-between in order to assimilate the supposedly paternal Law and finds herself thrown into paranoia.

Between those two absences in contemporary discourse, Narcissus does not have his own territory. Without a paternal value, he is the negative version of a homosexual, potential but empty of desire. Handed over to an abject mother, he can have no recourse to the holy virgin to liberate himself of her. Worse yet, as an emancipated modern, he does not dare give himself the right to fight her. Like John, he walls himself in, is inhibited, distraught, hermetic, wracked by nightmares, ready to plunge into drugs if he could allow himself to be a happy Narcissus. His thought escapes him, his speech appears to him as empty as his body. "There are blank spaces between each word," he says in sibylline fashion. He specifies that his words do not hold together, for there is a void that breaks them into syllables, purloins them, and blows them up before they settle down between himself and those he speaks with.

As for Juliet, she throws herself into orgies that leave her cold, humiliated, full of rage, and always ready to become ill in order finally to put a stop to the merry-go-round of a life controlled by a perverse father. The latter, a left-wing activist, gave his daughter to understand that stealing was part of the class struggle—until she got caught, thus punished for the father's greatest pleasure (secret, of course) and the mother's greatest shame. "I am trying to write," says Juliet, "but that isn't possible, for I have no place to settle down for that."

It is the paroxysmal consequence of a death drive that no object succeeds in hemming in, no idealization in displacing; the closeness to a psychosis that is more and more perceptible under the appearances of obsessions and hysteria—granted. But the frequency of psychotic symptoms in the area surrounding neuroses and perversions points to a deep challenge to *psychic space*, of which psychoanalysis, its revolutionary explorer, has inherited the whole Western, speculative history.

Narcissus: My Fellow Being, My Brother

At the risk of simplifying, let us consider that this now destroyed *Psychic space* was constituted at the waning of the Ancient world with the advent of the Christian era. The myth of Narcissus and its neo-Platonistic elaborations on the one hand, Christly passion on the other, mark out the outline of that space. Ovid's *Metamorphoses* gave us the first complete version of that myth. Narcissus, that perverse child, appears in it as the first modern antihero, the nongod par excellence. His murky, swampy, invisible drama must have summed up the anguish of a drifting mankind, deprived of stable markers. The imposing body of Greek sculpture becomes scattered at the time of the other crisis constituted by the waning of the Ancient world, which gives rise to the unhealthy and hardly tragic story of an ordinary being who knows neither what he wants nor what he loves. A *novitas furoris* is what we read in Ovid, a new madness. But who is the model for that?

The one in love with his fleeting reflection is in fact someone deprived of his own proper space. He loves nothing because he is nothing. When he realizes that the other, in the spring, is merely an image of himself, Narcissus, unable to withstand such represented property, commits suicide. He is resuscitated, however, and not only as the flower bearing the same name, which takes his body's place. Narcissus is compensated for by the genius of speculative thought, starting with Plotinus and up to the Fathers of the Church who rehabilitate the narcissian concern for one's own proper space, beyond the condemnation of the narcissistic error. Torn away from the Ancient city-state (*polis*) now falling apart, thrown into the civilized world (*oikoumene*)—for which the present-day equivalent would be advanced mass-mediatization—man, seized by an unnamable solitude, was called upon to withdraw into himself and discover himself as a psychic being.

We have seen what efforts were made by Plotinus to build up the dignity inherited from ascetic solitude. His autarkic divinity proceeds by way of *reflections*, it explicitly follows the narcissian dynamic of inessential and yet necessary reverberations and rebounds, for they stem not from Narcissus but from the One. These thoughts then bind together in its unity, through the immanence of transcendence, the very motion of reflection, thus erecting a new psyche. The Western soul is no longer that of a Platonistic "Eros pteros," obsessed with the supralunar world, but that of a thinking space fastened on the same through the intermediary of the One, both origin and light of thought. Western innerness thus asserts itself, *monos pros monon*, establishing the space of psychic solitude. The dismal encounter between Narcissus and his death-bearing because fleeting image has been replaced by hands clasped in prayer—by being *alone-with-oneself*. Mythic tragedy has been changed into meditation and introspection. Henceforth there is an *inside*, an internal life, to be contrasted with the *outside*. Plotinus is on the ridge of that separation, the solar outside of the One making up the contemplative inside of the Wise man, without any otherness.

To Love or to Think

Christly passion, by bringing in the *impossible*, has jolted and opened up narcissism's calm contemplation, neutralized by the autarkic divinity's thought. Sin and passion indicate to Narcissus, who gazes at himself in the Beyond, that everything is not heavenly in this hell, and the son of God himself may be abandoned by his Father. The One is an Other in the agape of the Cross. Theological guile, however, did not forget that salvation, eventually, took over from narcissism. Not only must one love the other as one loves oneself, but God himself is amenable to our love only to the extent that we love our "own and proper" good. In connection with *Amor sui* we have reread Thomas Aquinas, who, in the wake of Augustine, already preaches that the right way to love is "to love oneself," "for and because of God." We have thus noted that without any selfishness, which is indeed a very secondary phenomenon, the Angelic Doctor advocates recognizing one's "own proper good" as the only possible access to the *being good*, which is God. Such an appropriation of God and, conversely, the deification of one's own proper good, is an awesome dialectic, through which, thanks to a creating, donating Third Party, the Church promises salvation to narcissism, which is henceforth entitled, thanks to God, to withdraw into itself.

As long as the Western Self could think of itself as an *Ego affectus est*, with Bernard of Clairvaux for instance, its psychic space—introspective container of primary narcissism—remained safe and was constantly able to integrate crises. The heroism of an *Ego cogito*, which Descartes brought in along Aquinas's whitewashed (i.e., more philosophical than theological) tracks, led to the conquest of the *outside*, neglected in the narcissian salvation device. The outside of nature, to be subjugated by science; the outside of the pleasurable object, to be dominated through the sadomasochistic dynamics of libertine erotics. Galileo and Sade are the heroes of that conquering epic, whose ruin was heralded by Senatspräsident Schreber. In the eyes of this jurist, as interpreted by Freud, a person who, in the wake of humanism and the bourgeois revolution, experienced the impossibility of a stabilized psychic space (his own was shattered by rays and fundamental language), the unbeliever's world is established only through mystical delirium—thus always in a recourse to God, but a recourse that is henceforth devoid of meaning, insane. We have not escaped from the dilemma: Galileo and the revolutionary Sade on one side, the mad legislator Schreber on the other. The discontent always arises out of a repudiation of love—of the *Ego affectus est*.

There has been too much stress on the crisis in paternity as cause of psychotic discontent. Beyond the often fierce but artificial and incredible tyranny of the Law and the Superego, the crisis in the paternal function that led to a deficiency of psychic space is in fact an erosion of the loving father. It is for want of paternal love that Narcissi, burdened with emptiness, are suffering; eager to be others, or women, they want to be loved.

One has wrongly picked a quarrel with Freud in matters of sexuality: he supposedly did not understand women, he repressed his homosexuality, remained a Jewish, "uxorious" bourgeois. . . . Freud's discovery, which opened the royal road of sexuality, actually bears on the unbearable aspect of psychic space—an unbearable psychic space, hence laden with illusions, hallucinations, lies. . . . Let us think once more about all his outlines, sketches, topographies, and territories that he does not cease proposing and renewing, from the *Project for a Scientific Psychology* (1895) to *Moses and Monotheism* (1939). Lacan picked it up again, precisely in that place, to suggest, with the help of Borromean knot and topology, the vistas and infinitudes pertaining to the signifier's experience, which he no longer believes to be internal but wants to maintain amenable to spatialization, totalization, as well as controllable, mathematizeable. Is that possible?

On Eccentric Seeming: Imagination as Process

The stakes of psychoanalysis—but also its crisis—are there. Are we to build a psychic space, a certain mastery of the One, at the very heart of the psychic founderings of anguished, suicidal, and impotent people? Or on the contrary are we to follow, impel, favor breakaways, driftings? Are we concerned with rebuilding their own proper space, a "home," for contemporary Narcissi: repair the father, soothe the mother, allow them to build a solid, introspective inside, master of its losses and wanderings, assuming that such a goal is attainable? Or does not the abundance of sufferers who find their fulfillment, their relaxation, and their satisfaction only in intoxication (from drugs to sacred music, which do away with individuality and sex for the sake of infinity) indicate that a psychic era has come to an end?

I see psychoanalysis rather as the instrument of a departure from that enclosure, not as its warden. Does the old psychic space, the machinery of projections and identifications that relied more or less on neuroses for reinforcement, no longer hold together? Well, it may be because another mode of being, of unbeing, is attempting to take its place. We should not attempt to give it the outlines of the "own proper self" while assuring it of our authority as psychoanalysts and filling it with the psychological meaning of our interpretations. Let it remain floating, empty at times, inauthentic, obviously lying. Let it pretend, let the seeming take itself seriously, let sex be as unessential because as important as a mask or a written sign—dazzling outside, nothing inside.

Am I seeing the European psychic space toppling over into the Japanese?[3] And asking the analyst to be the agent of a new reign of the inauthentic, the promoter of a socialist empire of "false selves"? Has not the art of all periods already blazed that trail?

To the extent that the analyst not only causes truths to emerge but also tries to alleviate the pains of John or Juliet, he is duty bound to help them in building their own proper space. Help them not to suffer from being mere extras in their lives or splinters of parceled out bodies carried along by the spate of their pleasure. Help them, then, to speak and write themselves in unstable, open, undecidable spaces. The free associations of analytic discourse paves the way for the polylogic of such a nomination and such eccentric writing. It is not a matter of filling John's "crisis"— his emptiness—with meaning, or of assigning a sure place to Juliet's erotic wanderings, but to trigger a discourse where his own "emptiness" and her own "out-of-placeness" become essential elements, indispensable "characters" if you will, of a *work in progress*. What is at stake is turning the crisis into a *work in progress*.

Speaking, writing? Is that not again building "one's own," be it polyvalent? While waiting for social institutions to integrate such extraterrestrials, those survivors of primary narcissism, it is still in the imagination and symbolic realizations that their faltering identity will best find a way to construct itself as necessarily false—imaginary. When behaviors and institutions will have integrated the failure of representation not as a misfire on the part of the machine or a suffering of the individual, but as an illusion among others, a new adjustment of narcissism will have been effected. It will remove guilt from the stable image and divest the transcendental Unity that insures its authenticity. It will actualize the seeming, the imagination. For such an open, undecidable psychic space, the crisis will not be a suffering but a sign within a framework whose truth lies in its ability to absorb seemings. I speak in favor of imagination as antidote for the crisis. Not in favor of "power to the imagination," which is the rallying cry of perverts longing for the law. But in favor of saturating powers and counterpowers with imaginary constructions— phantasmatic, daring, violent, critical, demanding, shy. . . Let them speak, the ET's shall live. Imagination succeeds where the narcissist becomes hollowed out and the paranoid fails.

Amatory Discourses and Transferences

Now imagination is a discourse of transference—of love. Through and beyond desire that longs for immediate consummation, love is edged with emptiness and supported by taboos. The fact that today we have no love discourse reveals our inability to respond to narcissism. Indeed, amatory relationship is based on narcissistic satisfaction on the one hand, on idealization on the other. If the "crisis" of psychic space sinks its roots into the "death of God," let us remember that for the West, "God is love." Paul's agape of the cross, John's "God is love," doubtless leave us cold, but empty, too. Freud, the post-Romanticist, was the first to turn love into a cure; he did this, not to allow one to grasp a truth, but to provoke a rebirth—like an amorous relationship that makes us good as new, temporarily and eternally. For transference, like love, is a true process of self-organization, comparable to what contemporary logical and biological theories call "open systems."

   Psychoanalysis thus does not inaugurate a new amatory code, fol- lowing on courtliness, libertine thought, romanticism, and pornography. It asserts the end of codes but also the permanence of love as builder of spoken spaces. If it shows that the transferential or amatory principle is indispensable for a body to be living rather than being a corpse under care, it paradoxically undramatizes the amorous relationship yet cathected in transference. The analytical pact, like Faust's pact with the devil, insures your renewal, your rebirth, your youth; against that back- ground, your necessarily amorous crises might be temporary and un- essential contracts. Freud had considered suggesting, among the power- ful antidotes against the discontents of civilization, the amatory rela- tionship; nevertheless he gave that up very quickly, for, in his view, if love furnishes an overwhelming feeling of fulfilled narcissism, nothing is more hurtful than a breakup. He forgot, however, in that text, to men- tion that the psychoanalytic cure continues to feed on a love that tran- scends the hazards of loves. A transference love that summons that ability to idealize at the very core of desire and hatred—hollowing out and relieving perversion.

John and Juliet precisely come looking for that ability at the analyst's, who is perhaps the only one to allow them to glimpse an abeyance of their narcissistic wounds. Without ideological, moral, or biased suggestions, but through a simple listening, lovingly absent-minded. . .

From Cherubino to ET

Thanks to Christian elaborations, Narcissus was able to rally, give himself musical and pictural dignity, and move generations on account of his metamorphoses. Into Cherubino, for instance. The one who, in Mozart's opera, knowing nothing about love, experiences a tenderness full of desire but does not know what it is.

Today Narcissus is an exile, deprived of his psychic space, an extraterrestrial with a prehistory bearing, wanting for love. An uneasy child, all scratched up, somewhat disgusting, without a precise body or image, having lost his specificity, an alien in a world of desire and power, he longs only to reinvent love. The ET's are more and more numerous. We are all ET's.

The only common ground between the contemporary symptom and Cherubino is that the language that tames and makes us love this being uprooted from psychic space remains always imaginary. Music, film, novel. Polyvalent, undecidable, infinite. A permanent crisis.

NOTES

1. On the topic of narcissism one might read Heinz Kohut, *The Analysis of the Self* (New York: International University Press, 1971) and *The Restoration of the Self* (New York: International University Press, 1977); Otto F. Kernberg, *Borderline Conditions and Pathological Narcissism* (New York: Aronson, 1975); and works by André Green, especially *Narcissisme de vie, narcissisme de mort* (Paris: Minuit, 1983), as well as *La Nouvelle Revue de Psychanalyse* 13 (1976), for an overview and a fuller bibliography.

2. For a psychoanalytic approach to the Japanese world, see Doi Takeo, *The Anatomy of Dependence* (New York: Kodansha International, 1973).

3. Sigmund Freud, *Civilization and Its Discontents* (1930), in *Standard Edition*, vol. 21.

Black Sun (1987)

Psychoanalysis—A Counterdepressant

For those who are racked by melancholia, writing about it would have meaning only if writing sprang out of that very melancholia. I am trying to address an abyss of sorrow, a noncommunicable grief that at times, and often on a long-term basis, lays claims upon us to the extent of having us lose all interest in words, actions, and even life itself. Such despair is not a revulsion that would imply my being capable of desire and creativity, negative indeed but present. Within depression, if my existence is on the verge of collapsing, its lack of meaning is not tragic—it appears obvious to me, glaring and inescapable.

Where does this black sun come from? Out of what eerie galaxy do its invisible, lethargic rays reach me, pinning me down to the ground, to my bed, compelling me to silence, to renunciation?

The wound I have just suffered, some setback or other in my love life or my profession, some sorrow or bereavement affecting my relationship with close relatives—such are often the easily spotted triggers of my despair. A betrayal, a fatal illness, some accident or handicap that abruptly wrests me away from what seemed to me the normal category of normal people or else falls on a loved one with the same radical effect, or yet . . . What more could I mention? An infinite number of misfortunes weigh us down every day . . . All this suddenly gives me another life. A life that is unlivable, heavy with daily sorrows, tears held back or shed, a total despair, scorching at times, then wan and empty. In short, a devitalized existence that, although occasionally fired by the effort I make to prolong it, is ready at any moment for a plunge into death. An avenging death or a liberating death, it is henceforth the inner threshold of my despondency, the impossible meaning of a life whose burden constantly seems unbearable, save for those moments when I pull myself together and face up to the disaster. I live a living death, my flesh is wounded, bleeding, cadaverized, my rhythm slowed down or interrupted, time has been erased or bloated, absorbed into sorrow . . . Absent from other people's meaning, alien, accidental with respect to naive happiness, I owe a supreme, metaphysical lucidity to my depression. On the frontiers of life and death, occasionally I have the arrogant feeling of being witness to the meaninglessness of Being, of revealing the absurdity of bonds and beings.

My pain is the hidden side of my philosophy, its mute sister. In the same way, Montaigne's statement "To philosophize is to learn how to die" is inconceivable without the melancholy combination of sorrow and hatred—which came to a head in Heidegger's *care* and the disclosure of our "being-for-death." Without a bent for melancholia there is no psyche, only a transition to action or play.

Nevertheless, the power of the events that create my depression is often out of proportion to the disaster that suddenly overwhelms me. What is more, the disenchantment that I experience here and now, cruel as it may be, appears, under scrutiny, to awaken echoes of old traumas, to which I realize I have never been able to resign myself. I can thus discover antecedents to my current breakdown in a loss, death, or grief over someone or something that I once loved. The disappearance of that essential being continues to deprive me of what is most worthwhile in me; I live it as a wound or deprivation, discovering just the same that my grief is but the deferment of the hatred or desire for ascendency that I nurture with respect to the one who betrayed or abandoned me. My depression points to my not knowing how to lose—I have perhaps been unable to find a valid compensation for the loss? It follows that any loss entails the loss of my being—and of Being itself. The depressed person is a radical, sullen atheist.

Melancholia—Somber Lining of Amatory Passion

A sad voluptuousness, a despondent intoxication make up the humdrum backdrop against which our ideals and euphorias often stand out, unless they be that fleeting clearmindedness shredding the amorous hypnosis that joins two persons together. Conscious of our being doomed to lose our loves, we grieve perhaps even more when we glimpse in our lover the shadow of a long lost former loved one. Depression is the hidden face of Narcissus, the face that is to bear him away into death, but of which he is unaware while he admires himself in a mirage. Talking about depression will again lead us into the marshy land of the Narcissus myth.[1] This time, however, we shall not encounter the bright and fragile amatory idealization; on the contrary, we shall see the shadow cast on the fragile self, hardly dissociated from the other, precisely by the *loss* of that essential other. The shadow of despair.

Rather than seek the meaning of despair (it is either obvious or metaphysical), let us acknowledge that there is meaning only in despair. The child king becomes irredeemably sad before uttering his first words; this is because he has been irrevocably, desperately separated from the mother, a loss that causes him to try to find her again, along with other objects of love, first in the imagination, then in words. Semiology, concerned as it is with the zero degree of symbolism, is unavoidably led to ponder over not only the amatory state but its corollary as well, melancholia; at the same time it observes that if there is no writing other than the amorous, there is no imagination that is not, overtly or secretly, melancholy.

Thought—Crisis—Melancholia

Nevertheless, melancholia is not French. The rigor of Protestantism or the matriarchal weight of Christian orthodoxy admits more readily to a complicity with the grieving person when it does not beckon him or her into *delectatio morosa*. While it is true that the French Middle Ages rendered sadness by means of delicate tropes, the Gallic, renascent, enlightened tone tended toward levity, eroticism, and rhetoric rather than nihilism. Pascal, Rousseau, and Nerval cut a sorry figure—and they stand as exceptions.

For the speaking being life is a meaningful life; life is even the apogee of meaning. Hence if the meaning of life is lost, life can easily be lost: when meaning shatters, life no longer matters. In his doubtful moments the depressed person is a philosopher, and we owe to Heraclitus, Socrates, and more recently Kierkegaard the most disturbing pages on the meaning or lack of meaning of Being. One must, however, go back to Aristotle to find a thorough reflection on the relationship philosophers have maintained with melancholia. According to the *Problemata* (30, I), attributed to Aristotle, black bile (*melaina kole*) saps great men. The (pseudo-)Aristotelian reflection focuses on the *ethos-peritton*, the exceptional personality, whose distinctive characteristic would be melancholia. While relying on the Hippocratic notions of four humors and temperaments, Aristotle breaks new ground by removing melancholia from pathology and locating it in nature but also and mainly by having it ensue from *heat*, considered to be the regulating principle of the organism, and *mesotes*, the controlled interaction of opposite energies. This Greek notion of melancholia remains alien to us today; it assumes a "properly balanced diversity" (*eukratos anomalia*) that is metaphorically rendered by froth (*aphros*), the euphoric counterpoint to black bile. Such a white mixture of air (*pneuma*) and liquid brings out froth in the sea, wine, as well as in the sperm of man. Indeed, Aristotle combines scientific statement with mythical allusions as he links melancholia to spermatic froth and eroti, with explicit references to Dionysus and Aphrodite (953b, 31–32). The melancholia he evokes is not a philosopher's disease but his very nature, his *ethos*. It is not what strikes the first Greek melancholy hero, Bellerophon, who is thus portrayed in the *Iliad* (VI, 200–203): "Bellerophon gave offense to the gods and became a lonely wanderer on the Aleian plain, eating out his heart and shunning the paths of men." Self-devouring because forsaken by the gods, exiled by divine decree, this desperate man was condemned not to mania but to banishment, absence, void . . . With Aristotle, melancholia, counterbalanced by genius, is coextensive with man's anxiety in Being. It could be seen as the forerunner of Heidegger's anguish as the *Stimmung* of thought. Schelling found in it, in similar fashion, the "essence of human freedom," an indication of "man's affinity with nature." The philosopher would thus be "melancholy on account of a surfeit of humanity."[2]

This perception of melancholia as an extreme state and as an exceptionality that reveals the true nature of Being undergoes a profound transformation during the Middle Ages. On the one hand, medieval thought returned to the cosmologies of late antiquity and bound melancholia to Saturn, the planet of spirit and thought.[3] Dürer's *Melancholia* (1514) was a masterful transposition into graphic art of theoretical speculations that found their highest expression with Marsilio Ficino. Christian theology, on the other hand, considered sadness a sin. Dante set "the woeful people who have lost the good of the intellect" in "the city of grief" (*Inferno*, III). They are "wretched souls" because they have lost God, and these melancholy shadows constitute "the sect of the wicked displeasing both to God and to His enemies"; their punishment is to have "no hope of death." Those whom despair has caused to turn violent against themselves, suicides and squanderers, are not spared either; they are condemned to turn into trees (*Inferno*, XIII). Nevertheless, medieval monks did promote sadness: as mystical ascesis (*acedia*) it became essential as a means toward paradoxical knowledge of divine truth and constituted the major touchstone for faith.

Changing in accordance with the religious climate, melancholia asserted itself, if I may say so, in religious doubt. There is nothing more dismal than a dead God, and Dostoyevsky himself was disturbed by the distressing sight of the dead Christ in Holbein's painting, contrasted with the "truth of resurrection." The periods that witness the downfall of political and religious idols, periods of crisis, are particularly favorable to black moods. While it is true that an unemployed worker is less suicidal than a deserted lover, melancholia does assert itself in times of crisis; it is spoken of, establishes its archeology, generates its representations and its knowledge. A written melancholia surely has little in common with the institutionalized stupor that bears the same name. Beyond the confusion in terminology that I have kept alive up to now (What is melancholia? What is depression?), we are confronted with an enigmatic paradox that will not cease questioning us: if loss, bereavement, and absence trigger the work of the imagination and nourish it permanently as much as they threaten it and spoil it, it is also noteworthy that the work of art as fetish emerges when the activating sorrow has been repudiated. The artist consumed by melancholia is at the same time the most relentless in his struggle against the symbolic abdication that blankets him . . . Until death strikes or suicide becomes imperative for those who view it as final triumph over the void of the lost object . . .

Melancholia/Depression

I shall call *melancholia* the institutional symptomatology of inhibition and asymbolia that becomes established now and then or chronically in a person, alternating more often than not with the so-called manic phase of exaltation. When the two phenomena, despondency and exhilaration, are of lesser intensity and frequency, it is then possible to speak of neurotic depression. While acknowledging the difference between melancholia and depression, Freudian theory detects everywhere the same *impossible mourning for the maternal object*. Question: impossible on account of what paternal weakness? Or what biological frailty? Melancholia—we again encounter the generic term after having demarcated psychotic and neurotic symptomatologies—admits of the fearsome privilege of situating the analyst's question at the intersection of the biological and the symbolical. Parallel series? Consecutive sequences? A dangerous crossing that needs to be clarified, another relationship that needs to be thought up?

The terms melancholia and depression refer to a composite that might be called melancholy/depressive, whose borders are in fact blurred, and within which psychiatrists ascribe the concept of "melancholia" to the illness that is irreversible on its own (that responds only to the administration of antidepressants). Without going into details about various types of depression ("psychotic" or "neurotic," or, according to another classification, "anxious," "agitated," "retarded," or "hostile"), or concerning myself with the promising but still imprecise field in which one studies the exact effects of antidepressants (monoamine oxidase inhibitors, tricyclics, and heterocyclics) or thymic stabilizers (lithium carbonates), I shall examine matters from a *Freudian point of view.* On that basis, I shall try to bring out, from the core of the melancholy/depressive composite, blurred as its borders may be, what pertains to a common experience of *object loss* and of a *modification of signifying bonds.* These bonds, language in particular, prove to be unable to insure, within the melancholy/depressive composite, the autostimulation that is required in order to initiate given responses. Instead of functioning as a "rewards system," language, on the contrary, hyperactivates the "anxiety-punishment" pair, and thus inserts itself in the slowing down of thinking and decrease in psychomotor activity characteristic of depression. If temporary sadness or mourning on the one hand, and melancholy stupor on the other are clinically and nosologically different, they are nevertheless supported by *intolerance for object loss* and *the signifier's failure* to insure a compensating way out of the states of withdrawal in which the subject takes refuge to the point of inaction (pretending to be dead) or even suicide. Thus I shall speak of depression and melancholia without always distinguishing the particularities of the two ailments but keeping in mind their common structure.

The Depressive Person: Full of Hatred or Wounded, Mourned "Object" and Mourned "Thing"

According to classic psychoanalytic theory (Abraham, Freud, and Melanie Klein),[4] depression, like mourning, conceals an aggressiveness toward the lost object, thus revealing the ambivalence of the depressed person with respect to the object of mourning. "I love that object," is what that person seems to say about the lost object, "but even more so I hate it; because I love it, and in order not to lose it, I imbed it in myself; but because I hate it, that other within myself is a bad self, I am bad, I am nonexistent, I shall kill myself." The complaint against oneself would therefore be a complaint against another, and putting oneself to death but a tragic disguise for massacring an other. Such logic presupposes, as one can imagine, a stern superego and a whole complex dialectic of idealization and devalorization of self and other, the aggregate of these activities being based on the mechanism of *identification*. For my identification with the loved-hated other, through incorporation-introjection-projection, leads me to imbed in myself its sublime component, which becomes my necessary, tyrannical judge, as well as its subject component, which demeans me and of which I desire to rid myself. Consequently, the analysis of depression involves bringing to the fore the realization that the complaint against oneself is a hatred for the other, which is without doubt the substratum of an unsuspected sexual desire. Clearly such an advent of hatred within transference entails risks for the analysand as well as the analyst, and the therapy of depression (even the one called neurotic) verges on schizoid fragmentation.

Melancholy cannibalism, which was emphasized by Freud and Abraham and appears in many dreams and fantasies of depressed persons accounts for this passion for holding within the mouth (but vagina and anus also lend themselves to this control) the intolerable other that I crave to destroy so as to better possess it alive. Better fragmented, torn, cut up, swallowed, digested . . . than lost. The melancholy cannibalistic imagination[5] is a repudiation of the loss's reality and of death as well. It manifests the anguish of losing the other through the survival of self, surely a deserted self but not separated from what still and ever nourishes it and becomes transformed into the self—which also resuscitates—through such a devouring.

Nevertheless, the treatment of narcissistic individuals has led modern analysts to understand another form of depression.[6] Far from being a hidden attack on an other who is thought to be hostile because he is frustrating, sadness would point to a primitive self—wounded, incomplete, empty. Persons thus affected do not consider themselves wronged but afflicted with a fundamental flaw, a congenital deficiency. Their sorrow doesn't conceal the guilt or the sin felt because of having secretly plotted revenge on the ambivalent object. Their sadness would be rather the most archaic expression of an unsymbolizable, unnameable narcissistic wound, so precocious that no outside agent (subject or agent) can be used as referent. For such narcissistic depressed persons, sadness is really the sole object; more precisely it is a substitute object they become attached to, an object they tame and cherish for lack of another. In such a case, suicide is not a disguised act of war but a merging with sadness and, beyond it, with that impossible love, never reached, always elsewhere, such as the promises of nothingness, of death.

Thing and Object

The depressed narcissist mourns not an Object but the Thing.[7] Let me posit the "Thing" as the real that does not lend itself to signification, the center of attraction and repulsion, seat of the sexuality from which the object of desire will become separated.

Of this Nerval provides a dazzling metaphor that suggests an insistence without presence, a light without representation: the Thing is an imagined sun, bright and black at the same time. "It is a well-known fact that one never sees the sun in a dream, although one is often aware of some far brighter light."[8]

Ever since that archaic attachment the depressed person has the impression of having been deprived of an unnameable, supreme good, of something unrepresentable, that perhaps only devouring might represent, or an *invocation* might point out, but no word could signify. Consequently, for such a person, no erotic object could replace the irreplaceable perception of a place or preobject confining the libido or severing the bonds of desire. Knowingly disinherited of the Thing, the depressed person wanders in pursuit of continuously disappointing adventures and loves; or else retreats, disconsolate and aphasic, alone with the unnamed Thing. The "primary identification" with the "father in individual prehistory"[9] would be the means, the link that might enable one to become reconciled with the loss of the Thing. Primary identification initiates a compensation for the Thing and at the same time secures the subject to another dimension, that of imaginary adherence, reminding one of the bond of faith, which is just what disintegrates in the depressed person.

With those affected by melancholia, primary identification proves to be fragile, insufficient to secure other identifications, which are symbolic this time, on the basis of which the *erotic Thing* might become a captivating *Object of desire* insuring continuity in a metonymy of pleasure. The melancholy Thing interrupts desiring metonymy, just as it prevents working out the loss within the psyche.[10] How can one approach the place I have referred to? Sublimation is an attempt to do so: through melody, rhythm, semantic polyvalency, the so-called poetic form, which decomposes and recomposes signs, is the sole "container" seemingly able to secure an uncertain but adequate hold over the Thing.

I have assumed depressed persons to be atheistic—deprived of meaning, deprived of values. For them, to fear or to ignore the Beyond would be self-deprecating. Nevertheless, and although atheistic, those in despair are mystics—adhering to the preobject, not believing in Thou, but mute and steadfast devotees of their own inexpressible container. It is to this fringe of strangeness that they devote their tears and jouissance. In the tension of their affects, muscles, mucous membranes, and skin, they experience both their belonging to and distance from an archaic other that still eludes representation and naming, but of whose corporeal emissions, along with their automatism, they still bear the imprint. Unbelieving in language, the depressive persons are affectionate, wounded to be sure, but prisoners of affect. The affect is their thing.

The Thing is inscribed within us without memory, the buried accomplice of our unspeakable anguishes. One can imagine the delights of reunion that a regressive daydream promises itself through the nuptials of suicide.

The looming of the Thing summons up the subject's life force as that subject is in the process of being set up; the premature being that we all are can survive only if it clings to an other, perceived as supplement, artificial extension, protective wrapping. Nevertheless, such a life drive is fully the one that, *at the same time*, rejects me, isolates me, rejects him (or her). Never is the ambivalence of drive more fearsome than in this beginning of otherness where, lacking the filter of language, I cannot inscribe my violence in "no," nor in any other sign. I can expel it only by means of gestures, spasms, or shouts. I impel it, I project it. My necessary Thing is also and absolutely my enemy, my foil, the delightful focus of my hatred. The Thing falls from me along the outposts of significance[11] where the Word is not yet my Being. A mere nothing, which is a cause, but at the same time a fall, before being an Other, the Thing is the recipient that contains my dejecta and everything that results from *cadere* ("to fall")—it is a waste with which, in my sadness, I merge. It is Job's ashpit in the Bible.

Anality is summoned during the process of setting up this Thing, one that is our own and proper Thing as much as it is improper, unclean. The melancholy person who extols that boundary where the self emerges, but also collapses in deprecation, fails to summon the anality that could establish separations and frontiers as it does normally or as a bonus with obsessive persons. On the contrary, the entire ego of those who are depressed sinks into a diseroticized and yet jubilatory anality, as the latter becomes the bearer of a jouissance fused with the archaic Thing, perceived not as a significant object but as the self's borderline element. For those who are depressed, the Thing like the self is a downfall that carries them along into the invisible and unnameable. *Cadere.* Waste and cadavers all.

The Death Drive as Primary Inscription of Discontinuity (Trauma or Loss)

Freud's postulate of a *primary masochism* is consonant with aspects of narcissistic melancholia in which the dying out of all libidinal bonds appears not to be a simple matter of turning aggressiveness toward the object back into animosity against the self but is asserted as previous to any possibility of object positioning.

Brought up by Freud in 1915,[12] the notion of "primary masochism" became established in his work after the "death drive" turned up, particularly in "The Economic Problem of Masochism" (1924).[13] Having observed that living beings appeared later than the nonliving, Freud thought that a specific drive must reside in them, which tended toward "a return to an earlier state."[14] After *Beyond the Pleasure Principle* (1920), which established the notion of the death drive as a tendency to return to the inorganic state and homeostasis, in opposition to the erotic principle of discharge and union, Freud postulated that one part of the death or destructive drive is directed toward the outside world, notably through the muscular system, and is changed into a purely destructive drive, one of ascendency or strong willpower. In the attendance of sexuality it constitutes sadism. Freud points out nevertheless that *"Another portion does not share in this transposition outwards:* it remains inside . . . and becomes libidinally bound there. It is in this portion that we have to recognize the original, erotogenic masochism."[15] Since hatred of the other was already considered "older than love,"[16] would such a masochistic withdrawal of hatred point to the existence of a yet more archaic hatred? Freud seems to imply that: indeed, he considers the death drive as an intrapsychic manifestation of a phylogenetic inheritance going back to inorganic matter. Nevertheless, aside from those conjectures that most analysts since Freud do not endorse, it is possible to note if not the anteriority at least the strength of the disintegration of bonds within several psychic structures and manifestations. Furthermore, the frequency of masochism, the presence of negative therapeutic reaction, and also various pathologies of early childhood that seem to precede the object relation (infantile anorexia, merycism, some forms of autism) prompt one to accept the idea of a death drive that, appearing as a biological and logical inability to transmit psychic energies and inscriptions, would destroy movements and bonds. Freud refers to it thus:

> If we take into consideration the total picture made up of the phenomena of masochism immanent in so many people, the negative therapeutic reaction and the sense of guilt found in so many neurotics we shall no longer be able to adhere to the belief that mental events are exclusively governed by the desire for pleasure. These phenomena are unmistakable evidence of the presence of a power in mental life which we shall call the aggression or destruction drive, and which we trace back to the original death drive of living matter.[17]

Narcissistic melancholia would display such a drive in its state of disunity with the life drive. The melancholy person's superego appears to Freud as "a cultivation of death drive."[18] And yet the problem remains: is this melancholy diserotization opposed to the pleasure principle? Or is it, on the contrary, implicitly erotic? This would mean that the melancholy withdrawal would always be an overturning of the object relation, a metamorphosis of the hatred against the other. The work of Melanie Klein, who attached the greatest importance to the death drive, seems to have it depend, for the most part, on object relation, masochism and melancholia appearing then as imagos of the internalized bad object. Nevertheless, the Kleinian argument acknowledges situations in which erotic bonds are severed, without clearly stating whether they have never existed or have been broken off (in the latter case it would be the projection's introjection that would lead to such a withdrawal of erotic cathexis).

We shall take note particularly of the Kleinian definition of splitting introduced in 1946. On the one hand it moves backward from the depressive position toward a more archaic, paranoid, schizoid position. On the other, it distinguishes a binary splitting (the distinction between "good" and "bad" object insuring the unity of the self) and a parcellary splitting—the latter affecting not only the object but, in return, the very self, which literally "falls into pieces."

Integration/Nonintegration/Disintegration

For our purpose it is absolutely essential to note that such falling into pieces may be caused either by a drive-related *nonintegration* impeding the cohesion of the self or by a disintegration accompanied by anxieties and provoking the schizoid splitting.[19] In the first hypothesis, which seems to have been borrowed from Winnicott, nonintegration results from biological immaturity; if it is possible to speak of Thanatos in this situation, the death drive appears as a biological unfitness for sequentiality and integration (no memory). In the second hypothesis, that of a disintegration of the self consequent to reversing the death drive, we observe "a Thanatic reaction to a threat that is in itself Thanatic."[20] Rather close to Ferenczi's concept, this one emphasizes the human being's tendency toward fragmentation and disintegration as an expression of the death drive. "The early ego largely lacks cohesion, and a tendency towards integration alternates with a tendency towards disintegration, a falling into bits . . . the anxiety of being destroyed from within remains active. It seems to me in keeping with the lack of cohesiveness that under the pressure of this threat the ego tends to fall into pieces."[21] If schizoid fragmentation is a radical, paroxysmal manifestation of parceling, melancholy inhibition (psychomotor retardation, deficiency in sequentiality) can be considered another manifestation of the disintegration of bonds. How so?

Following upon the deflection of the death drive, the *depressive affect* can be interpreted as a defense against parceling. Indeed, sadness reconstitutes an affective cohesion of the self, which restores its unity within the framework of the affect. The depressive mood constitutes itself as a narcissistic support, negative to be sure,[22] but nevertheless presenting the self with an integrity, nonverbal though it might be. Because of that, the depressive affect makes up for symbolic invalidation and interruption (the depressive's "that's meaningless") and at the same time protects it against proceeding to the suicidal act. That protection, however, is a flimsy one. The depressive denial that destroys the meaning of the symbolic also destroys the act's meaning and leads the subject to commit suicide without anguish of disintegration, as a reuniting with archaic nonintegration, as lethal as it is jubilatory, "oceanic."

Hence, schizoid parceling is a defense against death—against somatization or suicide. Depression, on the other hand, does without the schizoid anguish of fragmentation. But if depression is not fortunate enough to rely on a certain *erotization of suffering*, it cannot act as a defense against the death drive. The relief that precedes some suicides perhaps translates the archaic regression by means of which the act of a denied or numbed consciousness turns Thanatos back on the self and reclaims the nonintegrated self's lost paradise, one without others or limits, a fantasy of untouchable fullness.

The speaking subject can thus react to trouble not only through defensive parceling but also through slowing down—inhibition, denial of sequentiality, neutralization of the signifier. Some immaturization or other neurobiological features tending toward nonintegration may condition such behavior. Is it a defensive one? Depressed persons do not defend themselves against death but against the anguish prompted by the erotic object. Depressive persons cannot endure Eros; they prefer to be with the Thing up to the limit of negative narcissism leading them to Thanatos. They are defended against Eros by sorrow but without defense against Thanatos because they are wholeheartedly tied to the Thing. Messengers of Thanatos, melancholy people are witness/accomplices of the signifier's flimsiness, the living being's precariousness.

Less skillful than Melanie Klein in presenting a new repertory of drives, the death drive in particular, Freud nevertheless seems drastic. As he sees it, the speaking being, beyond power, desires death. At this logical extreme, desire no longer exists. Desire becomes dissolved in a disintegration of transmission and a disintegration of bonds. Be it biologically predetermined, following upon preobject narcissistic traumas, or quite simply caused by inversion of aggressiveness, the phenomenon that might be described as a *breakdown of biological and logical sequentiality* finds its radical manifestation in melancholia. Would the death drive be the primary (logically and chronologically) inscription of that breakdown?

Actually, if the death drive remains a theoretical speculation, the experience of depression confronts the observer as much as the patient with the enigma of mood.

Is Mood a Language?

Sadness is the fundamental mood of depression, and even if manic euphoria alternates with it in the bipolar forms of that ailment, sorrow is the major outward sign that gives away the desperate person . Sadness leads us into the enigmatic realm of *affects*—anguish, fear, or joy.[23] Irreducible to its verbal or semiological expressions, sadness (like all affect) is the *psychic representation of energy displacements* caused by external or internal traumas. The exact status of such psychic representations of energy displacements remains, in the present state of psychoanalytic and semiological theories, very vague. No conceptual framework in the relevant sciences (particularly linguistics) has proven adequate to account for this apparently very rudimentary representation, presign and prelanguage. The "sadness" mood triggered by a stimulation, tension, or energy conflict within a psychosomatic organism is not a *specific* answer to a release mechanism (I am not sad as a response to or sign for X and only X). Mood is a "generalized transference" (E. Jacobson) that stamps the *entire* behavior and all the sign systems (from motor functions to speech production and idealization) without either identifying with them or disorganizing them. We are justified in believing that an archaic *energy signal* is involved, a phylogenetic inheritance, which, within the psychic space of the human being, is *immediately* assumed by verbal representation and consciousness. Nevertheless, such an "assumption" is not related to what occurs when the energies that Freud calls "bonded" lend themselves to verbalization, association, and judgment. Let us say that representations germane to affects, notably sadness, are *fluctuating* energy cathexes: insufficiently stabilized to coalesce as verbal or other signs, acted upon by primary processes of displacement and condensation, dependent just the same on the agency of the ego, they record through its intermediary the threats, orders, and injunctions of the superego. Thus moods are *inscriptions*, energy disruptions, and not simply raw energies. They lead us toward a modality of significance that, on the threshold of bioenergetic stability, insures the preconditions for (or manifests the disintegration of) the imaginary and the symbolic. On the frontier between animality and symbol formation, moods—and particularly sadness—are the ultimate reactions to our traumas, they are our basic homeostatic recourses. For if it is true that those who are slaves to their moods, beings drowned in their sorrows, reveal a number of psychic or cognitive frailties, it is equally true that a diversification of moods, variety in sadness, refinement in sorrow or mourning are the imprint of a humankind that is surely not triumphant but subtle, ready to fight, and creative . . .

Literary creation is that adventure of the body and signs that bears witness to the affect—to sadness as imprint of separation and beginning of the symbol's sway; to joy as imprint of the triumph that settles me in the universe of artifice and symbol, which I try to harmonize in the best possible way with my experience of reality. But that testimony is produced by literary creation in a material that is totally different from what constitutes mood. It transposes affect into rhythms, signs, forms. The "semiotic" and the "symbolic"[24] become the communicable imprints of an affective reality, perceptible to the reader (I like this book because it conveys sadness, anguish, or joy) and yet dominated, set aside, vanquished.

Symbolic Equivalents/Symbols

Assuming that affect is the most archaic inscription of inner and outer events, how does one reach the realm of signs? I shall accept Hanna Segal's hypothesis, according to which, beginning with separation (let us note that a "lack" is necessary for the *sign* to emerge), the child produces or uses objects or vocalizations that are the *symbolic* equivalents of what is lacking. Later, and beginning with the so-called depressive position, it attempts to signify the sadness that overwhelms it by producing within its own self elements alien to the outer world, which it causes to correspond to such a lost or shifted outerness; we are then faced with *symbols* properly speaking, no longer with equivalencies.[25]

Let me add the following to Hanna Segal's position: what makes such a triumph over sadness possible is the ability of the self to identify no longer with the lost object but with a third party—father, form, schema. A requirement for a denying or manic position ("no, I haven't lost; I evoke, I signify through the artifice of signs and for myself what has been parted from me"), such an identification, which may be called phallic or symbolic, insures the subject's entrance into the universe of signs and creation. The supporting father of such a symbolic triumph is not the oedipal father but truly that "imaginary father," "father in individual prehistory" according to Freud, who guarantees primary identification. Nevertheless, it is imperative that this father in individual prehistory be capable of playing his part as oedipal father in symbolic Law, for it is on the basis of that harmonious blending of the two facets of fatherhood that the abstract and arbitrary signs of communication may be fortunate enough to be tied to the affective meaning of prehistorical identifications and the dead language of the potentially depressive person can arrive at a live meaning in the bond with others.

Under the totally different circumstances of literary creation, for instance, the manic position as sheathing of depression—an essential moment in the formation of the symbol—can be manifested through the establishment of a symbolic lineage. We may thus find a recourse to proper names linked to a subject's real or imaginary history, with that subject declaring itself their heir or equal; what they truly memorialize, beyond paternal weakness, is nostalgic dedication to the lost mother.

At the outset we have objectal depression (implicitly aggressive) and narcissistic depression (logically previous to the libidinal object relation)—an affectivity struggling with signs, going beyond, threatening, or modifying them. Starting from such a setting, the line of questioning that

I shall pursue could be summed up as follows: aesthetic and particularly literary creation, and also religious discourse in its imaginary, fictional essence, set forth a device whose prosodic economy, interaction of characters, and implicit symbolism constitute a very faithful semiological representation of the subject's battle with symbolic collapse. Such a literary representation is not an *elaboration* in the sense of "becoming aware" of the inter- and intrapsychic causes of moral suffering; that is where it diverges from the psychoanalytic course, which aims at dissolving this symptom. Nevertheless, the literary (and religious) representation possesses a real and imaginary effectiveness that comes closer to catharsis than to elaboration; it is a therapeutic device used in all societies throughout the ages. If psychoanalysts think they are more efficacious, notably through strengthening the subject's cognitive possibilities, they also owe it to themselves to enrich their practice by paying greater attention to these sublimatory solutions to our crises, in order to be lucid counterdepressants rather than neutralizing antidepressants.

Is Death Nonrepresentable?

Having posited that the unconscious is ruled by the pleasure principle, Freud very logically postulated that there is no representation of death in the unconscious. Just as it is unaware of negation, the unconscious is unaware of death. Synonymous with absence of jouissance, imaginary equivalent of phallic dispossession, death could not possibly be seen. It is, perhaps, for that very reason that it opens the way to speculation.

And yet, as clinical experience led Freud to the notion of narcissism, ending in the discovery of the death drive and the second topography,[26] he compelled us to recognize a vision of the psychic apparatus in which Eros is threatened with domination by Thanatos and where, consequently, the possibility of representing death should be examined from a different standpoint.

Castration fear, glimpsed until then as underlying the conscious death anguish, does not disappear but is overshadowed by the *fear of losing the object* or *losing oneself as object* (etiology of melancholia and narcissistic psychoses).

Such an evolution in Freudian thought leaves us with two problems that have been emphasized by André Green.[27]

First, what about the *representation* of the death drive? Unknown to the unconscious, it is, with the "second Freud," a "cultivation of the super-ego," as one might put it in turning Freud's phrase around. The death drive splits the very ego into one component that is unaware of such drive while being affected by it (that is, its unconscious component) and another component that struggles against it (that is, the megalomaniac ego that negates castration and death and fantasizes immortality).

More basically, however, does not such a splitting cut across all discourse? The symbol is established through a negation (*Verneinung*) of the loss, but a disavowal (*Verleugnung*) of the symbol produces a physic inscription as close as one can get to hatred and a hold over the lost object. That is what one deciphers in the blanks of discourse, vocalizations, rhythms, syllables of words that have been devitalized and need to be restored by the analyst on the basis of an apprehended depression.

Thus, if the death drive is not represented in the unconscious, must one invent another level in the psychic apparatus where—simultaneously with jouissance—the being of its nonbeing would be recorded? It is indeed a production of the split ego, made up of fantasy and fiction—in short, the level of the imagination, the level of writing—which bears witness to the hiatus, blank, or spacing that constitutes death for the unconscious.

Dissociations of Forms

Imaginary constructions change the death drive into eroticized aggression against the father or terrified loathing of the mother's body. We know that at the same time as he discovered the power of the death drive Freud shifted his interest not only from the theoretical model of the first topography (conscious/preconscious/unsconscious) toward that of the second topography, but especially, and thanks to the shift, turned toward the analysis of imaginary productions (religions, arts, literature). He found in them a kind of representation of death anxiety.[28] Does this mean that dread of dying—which henceforth is not summed up in castration fear but includes it and adds to it the wounding and perhaps even the loss of integrity of the body and the self—finds its representations in formations that are called "transconscious" in the imaginary constructions of the split subject, according to Lacan? Doubtless so.

The fact remains that another reading of the unconscious itself might locate within its own fabric, such as certain dreams disclose it for us, that nonrepresentative spacing of representation that is not the *sign* but the *index* of death drive. Dreams of borderline patients, schizoid personalities, or those undergoing psychedelic experiments are often "abstract paintings" or cascades of sounds, intricacies of lines and fabrics, in which the analyst deciphers the dissociation—or a nonintegration—of

psychic and somatic unity. Such indices could be interpreted as the ultimate imprint of the death drive. Aside from the images of the death
drive, necessarily displaced on account of being eroticized, the work of
death as such, at the zero degree of psychicism, can be spotted precisely
in the *dissociation of form* itself, when form is distorted, abstracted, dis-
figured, hollowed out: ultimate thresholds of inscribable dislocation and
jouissance . . .

Furthermore, the unrepresentable nature of death was linked with
that other unrepresentable—original abode but also last resting place for
dead souls, in the beyond—which, for mythical thought, is constituted by
the female body. The horror of castration underlying the anguish of
death undoubtedly accounts in large part for the universal partnership
with death of the penis-lacking feminine. Nevertheless, the death drive
hypothesis compels a different reasoning.

Death-Bearing Woman

For man and for woman the loss of the mother is a biological and psychic
necessity, the first step on the way to becoming autonomous. Matricide is
our vital necessity, the sine-qua-non condition of our individuation, provided that it takes place under optimal circumstances and can be eroticized—whether the lost object is recovered as erotic object (as is the case
for male heterosexuality or female homosexuality), or it is transposed by
means of an unbelievable symbolic effort, the advent of which one can
only admire, which eroticizes the *other* (the other sex, in the case of the
heterosexual woman) or transforms cultural constructs into a "sublime"
erotic object (one thinks of the cathexes, by men and women, in social
bonds, intellectual and aesthetic productions, etc.). The lesser or greater
violence of matricidal drive, depending on individuals and the milieu's
tolerance, entails, when it is hindered, its inversion on the self; the maternal object having been introjected, the depressive or melancholic putting
to death of the self is what follows, instead of matricide. In order to protect mother I kill myself while knowing—phantasmatic and protective
knowledge—that it comes from her, the death-bearing she-Gehenna . . .
Thus my hatred is safe and my matricidal guilt erased. I make of Her an
image of Death so as not to be shattered through the hatred I bear against
myself when I identify with Her, for that aversion is in principle meant for
her as it is an individuating dam against confusional love. Thus the feminine as image of death is not only a screen for my fear of castration, but
also an imaginary safety catch for the matricidal drive that, without such

a representation, would pulverize me into melancholia if it did not drive me to crime. No, it is She who is death-bearing, therefore I do not kill myself in order to kill her but I attack her, harass her, represent her . . .

For a woman, whose specular identification with the mother as well as the introjection of the maternal body and self are more immediate, such an inversion of matricidal drive into a death-bearing maternal image is more difficult, if not impossible. Indeed, how can She be that bloodthirsty Fury, since I am She (sexually and narcissistically), She is I? Consequently, the hatred I bear her is not oriented toward the outside but is locked up within myself. There is no hatred, only an implosive mood that walls itself in and kills me secretly, very slowly, through permanent bitterness, bouts of sadness, or even lethal sleeping pills that I take in smaller or greater quantities in the dark hope of meeting . . . no one, unless it be my imaginary wholeness, increased with my death that accomplishes me. The homosexual shares the same depressive economy: he is a delightful melancholy person when he does not indulge in sadistic passion with another man.

The fantasy of feminine immortality perhaps has its basis in the feminine germinal transmission, capable of parthenogenesis. Furthermore, the new techniques of artificial reproduction endow the female body with unsuspected reproductive possibilities. If that feminine "allmightiness" in the survival of the species can be undermined through other technical possibilities that, or so it seems, might make man pregnant as well, it is likely that this latter eventuality could attract only a small minority, even though it fulfills the androgynous fantasies of the majority. Nevertheless, the essential component of the feminine conviction of being immortal in and beyond death (which the Virgin Mary so perfectly embodies) is rooted less in those biological possibilities, where it is hard to discern the "bridge" to the psyche, than in "negative narcissism."

In its climax, the latter weakens the aggressive (matricidal) affect toward the other as well as the despondent affect within oneself and substitutes what one might call an "oceanic void." It is a feeling and fantasy of pain, but anestheticized, of jouissance, but in suspense, of an expectation and a silence as empty as they are fulfilled. In the midst of its lethal ocean, the melancholy woman is the dead one that has always been abandoned within herself and can never kill outside herself. Modest, silent, without verbal or desiring bonds with others, she wastes away by striking moral and physic blows against herself, which, nevertheless, do not give her sufficient pleasures. Until the fatal blow—the definitive nuptials of the Dead Woman with the Same, whom she did not kill.

One cannot overemphasize the tremendous psychic, intellectual, and affective effort a woman must make in order to find the other sex as erotic object. In his philogenetic musings, Freud often admires the intellectual accomplishment of the man who has been (or when he is) deprived of women (through glaciation or tyranny on the part of the father of the primal horde, etc.). If the discovery of her invisible vagina already imposes upon woman a tremendous sensory, speculative, and intellectual effort, shifting to the symbolic order *at the same time* as to a sexual object of a sex other than that of the primary maternal object represents a gigantic elaboration in which a woman cathexes a psychic potential greater than what is demanded of the male sex. When this process is favorably carried out, it is evidenced by the precocious awakening of girls, their intellectual performances often more brilliant during the school years, and their continuing female maturity. Nevertheless, it has its price in the constant tendency to extol the problematic mourning for the lost object . . . not so fully lost, and it remains, throbbing, in the "crypt" of feminine ease and maturity. Unless a massive introjection of the ideal succeeds, at the same time, in satisfying narcissism with its negative side *and* the longing to be present in the arena where the world's power is at stake.

NOTES

Note: All biblical references follow the text of *The Jerusalem Bible*, Reader's Edition (Garden City, N.Y.: Doubleday, 1968)—Trans.

1. See my *Tales of Love* (New York: Columbia University Press, 1987).

2. See *La Melanconia dell'uomo di genio* (Genoa: Enrica Salavaneschi, 1981).

3. On melancholia in the history of art and ideas see the basic work by Raymond Klibanski, Erwin Panofski, and Fritz Saxl, *Saturn and Melancholy* (London: T. Nelson, 1964).

4. See Karl Abraham, "Préliminaires à l'investigation et au traitement psychanalytique de la folie maniaco-depressive et des états voisins" (1912), in *Oeuvres complètes* (Paris: Payot, 1965), 1:99–113; Sigmund Freud, "Mourning and Melancholia" (1917), in *Standard Edition*, 14:237–58; Melanie Klein, "A Contribution to the Psychogenesis of Manic-Depressive States" and "Mourning and Its Relation to Manic-Depressive States," in *Contributions to Psychoanalysis, 1921–1945* (London: Hogarth Press, 1948), pp. 282–338. Klein's "A Contribution" is reprinted in Peter Buckley, ed., *Essential Papers on Object Relations* (New York: New York University Press, 1986).

5. As was stressed in Pierre Fédida's "Le Cannibalisme mélancolique," in *L'Absence* (Paris: Gallimard, 1978), p. 65.

6. See Edith Jacobson, *Depression: Comparative Studies of Normal, Neurotic, and Psychotic Conditions* (New York: International University Press, 1977); B.

Grunberger, "Etude sur la dépression" and "Le Suicide du mélancolique," in *Le Narcissisme* (Paris: Payot, 1975); G. Rosolato, "L'Axe narcissique des dépressions," in *Essais sur le symbolique* (Paris: Gallimard, 1979).

7. Having noted that, from the very dawn of Greek philosophy, holding on to the *thing* is bound up with the utterance of a statement and the assertion of its truth, Heidegger nevertheless throws open the matter of the "historied" aspect of the *thing:* "The question of the thing again comes into motion from its beginning" (*What Is a Thing?* W. B. Barton, Jr., and Vera Deutsch, trs. [Chicago: Henry Regnery, 1967], p. 48). Without going into the history of that conception of the thing but opening it up in the between that extends from the thing to man, Heidegger notes, through a reading of Kant, "that this *between* as an anticipation *(Vorgriff)* reaches beyond the thing and similarly back behind us" (*ibid.*, p. 243).

Through the opening created by Heidegger's question, but also following upon Freud's shaking up rational certainties, I shall speak of the *Thing* as being the "something" that, seen by the already constituted subject looking back, appears as the unspecified, the unseparated, the elusive, even in its determination of actual sexual matter. I shall restrict the term *Object* to the space-time constant that is verified by a statement uttered by a subject in control of that statement.

8. Gérard de Nerval, *Aurelia*, in *Selected Writings*, Geoffrey Wagner, tr. (Ann Arbor: University of Michigan Press, 1957), p. 130.

9. See Sigmund Freud, *The Ego and the Id, Standard Edition*, 19:31.

10. One should differentiate my statement from that of Lacan, who discusses the notion of *das Ding* starting from Freud's *Entwurf*: "*Das Ding* is not involved with what, in a manner somewhat reflexive to the extent that it can be made explicit, leads man to challenge his words as referring to the things they have nevertheless created. There is something else in *das Ding*. What there is is the true secret. . .. Something that wants. *The* need and not just needs, pressure, emergency. The state of *Not des Lebens* is life's state of emergency . . . , the amount of energy preserved by the body considering the response and what is necessary for the preservation of life" (*L'Ethique de la psychanalyse*, seminar of December 9, 1959 [Paris: Seuil, 1986], pp. 58ff.).

This would involve psychic inscriptions (*Niederschrift*) earlier than the fourth year of life, always "secondary" for Lacan but close to "quality," to "effort," to the "endopsychic structure." "The *Ding* as *Fremde*, as an alien and even sometimes hostile place, at any rate as the first outside space . . . is that object, *das Ding*, as the subject's absolute Other that must be recovered. It is recovered, at the most, as regret. . .. It is in the state of hoping and waiting for it that such optimal tension, on this side of which there is no more perception or effort, will be sought after in the name of the pleasure principle" (p. 65). And even more clearly: "*Das Ding* is originally what we therefore call the beyond-the-signified. It is in relation to *that beyond-the-signified and a pathetic link to it that the subject maintains its distance and constitutes itself in such a world of relationships, of primary affect previous to any repression*. The entire first articulation of *Entwurf* is built around that" (pp. 67–68). Nevertheless, while Freud emphasizes that the *Thing* shows up only as a "cry," Lacan translates this as *word*, playing on the ambivalent meaning of the word *mot* in French ("*mot* is that which is silent"). "The things we are dealing with . . . are things insofar as they are silent. And silent things are not quite the same as things that have no connection with words" (pp. 68–69; translation mine.—Trans.).

11. "Significance" refers to semantic operations that are both fluid and archaic—with the latter word restricted to its Freudian sense. It refers to the work performed in language that enables a text to signify what representative and communicative speech does not say.—Trans.

12. See Sigmund Freud, *Papers on Metapsychology, Standard Edition* 14:139.

13. See Sigmund Freud, "The Economic Problem of Masochism," *Standard Edition* 19:159–70.

14. See Sigmund Freud, *An Outline of Psychoanalysis, Standard Edition* 23:139–207.

15. "The Economic Problem of Masochism," *Standard Edition* 19:163.

16. *Papers on Metapsychology, Standard Edition* 14:139.

17. See Sigmund Freud, "Analysis Terminable and Interminable," *Standard Edition* 23:243.

18. *The Ego and the Id, Standard Edition* 19:53.

19. See Melanie Klein, *Developments in Psychoanalysis* (London: Hogarth Press, 1952).

20. See Jean-Michel Petot, *Melanie Klein, le moi et le bon objet* (Paris: Dunod, 1932).

21. Melanie Klein, *Developments in Psychoanalysis*, p. 296.

22. André Green, in *Narcissisme de vie, narcissisme de mort* (Paris: Minuit, 1983), defines the notion of "negative narcissism" thus: "Beyond the parceling that fragments the self and brings it back to autoeroticism, *absolute* primary narcissism demands the mimetic quietness of death. It seeks the non-desire of the other, nonexistence, which is another way of reaching immortality" (p. 278; translation mine.—Trans.).

23. Concerning affect, see Jacobson, *Depression*, and André Green, *Le Discours vivant* (Paris: Presses Universitaires de France, 1971).

24. See my *Revolution in Poetic Language*, Margaret Waller, tr. (New York: Columbia University Press, 1984), ch. 1, secs. 2 and 5: "We understand the term 'semiotic' in its Greek sense: σημεων = distinctive mark, trace, index, precursory sign, imprint, trace, figuration. . . . This modality is the one Freudian psychoanalysis points to in postulating not only the *facilitation* and the structuring *disposition* of drives, but also the so-called primary processes which displace and condense both energies and their inscription. Discrete quantities of energy move through the body of the subject who is not yet constituted as such and, in the course of his development, they are arranged according to the various constraints imposed upon this body—always already involved in a semiotic process—by family and social structures. In this way the drives, which are 'energy' charges as well as 'psychical' marks, articulate what we call a *chora*: a nonexpressive totality formed by the drives and their stases in a motility that is as full of movement as it is regulated" (p. 25). On the other hand, the *symbolic* is identified with judg-

ment and the grammatical sentence: "We shall distinguish the semiotic (drives and their articulation) from the realm of signification, which is always that of a proposition or judgment, in other words, a realm of *positions*. This positionality, which Husserlian phenomenology orchestrates through the concepts of *doxa*, *position*, and *thesis*, is structured as a break in the signifying process, establishing the *identification* of the subject and its object as preconditions of propositionality. We shall call this break, which produces the positing signification, a *thetic* phase. All enunciation, whether of a word or of a sentence, is thetic. It requires an identification; in other words, the subject must separate from and through his image, from and through his objects. This image and objects must first be posited in a space that becomes symbolic because it connects the two separated positions, recording them or redistributing them in an open combinatorial system" (p. 43).

25. See Hanna Segal, "Notes on Symbol Formation," *International Journal of Psychoanalysis* 38 (1957): 391–97.

26. See *On Narcissism* (1914), *Standard Edition* 14:73ff.; *Beyond the Pleasure Principle* (1920), *Standard Edition* 18:3ff.; and *The Ego and the Id* (1923), *Standard Edition* 19:3ff.

27. Green, *Narcissisme de vie, narcissisme de mort*, pp. 255ff.

28. Thus the murder of the father in *Totem and Taboo* (1913) or the deadly threatening vagina in *The Uncanny* (1919).

New Maladies of the Soul

The Clinic: The Soul and the Image

> It is more important that men create the logos of the
> soul than of the body.
> —Democritus

Do you have a soul? This question, which may be philosophical, theological, or simply misguided in nature, has a particular relevance for our time. In the wake of psychiatric medicines, aerobics, and media zapping, does the soul still exist?

Medicine or Philosophy?

Fruitful debates between ancient Greek doctors and philosophers caused the "psyche" to undergo some delicate variations before becoming the "anima" of the Latin Stoics. Doctors of antiquity returned to the metaphysical distinction between the body and the soul and came up with a viable analogy that prefigured modern psychiatry: they spoke of "maladies of the soul" that were comparable to maladies of the body. These maladies of the soul included the passions, from sadness to joy and even delirium. Although some doctors used this parallelism to support a "monistic" conception of human beings, for most of them, the radical difference between the psychic and somatic realms was confirmed by their mutual presence, if not their isomorphy.

Dualisms have prevailed since antiquity, some thought to consist of complementary dynamics of flux and others of troublesome contradictions. Despite scientific efforts that have attempted to reduce it to soma, the psyche, which we have failed to locate (is it in the heart? the humors? the brain?), has remained an implacable enigma. As a structure of meaning, the psyche represents the bond between the speaking being and the other, a bond that endows it with a therapeutic and moral value. Furthermore, by rendering us responsible to our bodies, the psyche shields us from biological fatalism and constitutes us as speaking entities.[1]

Christ's incarnation, that is, the body-and-soul Passion of Man-God, gave momentum to the psychic dynamic that has been nurturing the inner life of Christian humanity for two thousand years. Passionate excesses directed toward the absolute subject—God or Jesus—ceased to be pathological. Instead, they were thought to map out the mystic itinerary of a soul aiming for the Ultimate. Before mental illness could be rethought, however, the dialectic of the Trinity had to be broken, anatomy had to adapt to the body, and the paroxysmal humors had to become objects of observation and surveillance. At that point, mental illness entrenched itself in the sacred space of the insane asylum. Michel Foucault has written a brilliant history of this clinic, which acknowledged the soul, but only as a sign of a sick body.[2] Let us recall, however, that this gesture began well before the Age of Reason, for its roots can be traced to Greek philosophy and medicine, which introduced the distinction and analogy between maladies of the body and maladies of the soul. Like the ancient Greeks, modern psychiatrists—notably Philippe Pinel[3]—have subscribed to physical and moral theories of the origins of mental illness.[4]

Freud can be placed in this tradition, for he explicitly promoted a philosophical dualism[5] that he developed through his conception of the "psychic apparatus"[6]—a theoretical construction that is irreducible to the body, subject to biological influences, yet primarily observable in linguistic structures. Fixed firmly in biology by the drives yet contingent upon an autonomous logic, the soul, as a "psychic apparatus," gives rise to psychological and somatic symptoms and is modified during transference.

By giving priority to the psyche, however, the inventions of the unconscious and of transference do more than resurrect the ancient Greek debate about the soul and the body. What is more important, the Freudian notion of the psyche challenges this formerly presumed dualism and goes beyond the hypertrophy of the psychological that many see as the defining feature of psychoanalysis. In this vein, several aspects of psychoanalysis cross the boundary between body and soul and explore various elements that transcend this dichotomy: for instance, the energy component of drives, the determination of meaning through sexual desire, and the inscription of the treatment within transference, which is understood to be a repetition of prior psychosensory traumas. Nevertheless, the linguistic mechanism remains at the core of treatment: as a signifying construct, the speech of both the analysand and the analyst incorporates different *series of representations.* We recognize the diversity of these series, yet we can rightfully claim that they are primarily "psychic" in origin, irreducible as they are to the biological substrata that contemporary science has more or less categorized for us.

By proposing *different* models of the soul, psychoanalysis expands our notion of the "psyche," acknowledges the peculiarities of our means of signification, and absorbs pathology into specific logical systems. Although the notion of psychological illness does not lose its specific validity, psychoanalysis tends to associate it with one of the logical possibilities inherent in any Freudian "psychic apparatus" or Lacanian "speakbeing" [*parlêtre*]. Although the notions of "norm" and "anomaly" are also challenged, the impact of psychoanalysis is not confined to the ensuing subversion—one that has attracted libertarian spirits for almost a century. The emphasis on *meaning* and the use of *eroticized speech* in transference remain the most important features of the singular adventure of Freud's discovery.

Loyal to the ethics of the person that the West has developed within the folds of its philosophy, religion, and science, psychoanalysis appeals to the life of speaking beings by reinforcing and exploring their *psychic life.* You are alive if and only if you have a psychic life. However distressing, unbearable, deadly, or exhilarating it may be, this psychic life—which combines different systems of representation that involve language—allows you access to your body and to other people. Because of the soul, you are capable of action. Your psychic life is a discourse that acts. Whether it harms you or saves you, you are its subject. Our purpose here is to analyze psychic life, that is, to break it down and to start over. The substantial effects of meaningful representations have never been recognized and put to use with so much precision and force. With Freud, the *psyche* is reborn. Enriched by the Judaic pluralism of its interpretations, the soul has evolved into a multifaceted and polyphonic psyche that is better equipped to serve the "transubstantiation" of the living body. Hence, we can appreciate the powerful synthesis Freud made of the traditions preceding his own, for by assigning a new value to the soul, Freud was able to elaborate a course of action that is at once therapeutic and moral.

Progress in the natural sciences, notably in biology and neurobiology, has enabled us to envision the death of the soul. Since we are continually decoding the secrets of neurons, their tendencies and their electrical dynamics, do we still have a need for this age-old chimera? Have we not come up with cognitive constructs that can account for cellular as well as human behavior?

However that may be, one cannot help noticing that the subject, whose soul was considered banished from the "pure" sciences, is making a triumphant comeback in the most sophisticated biological theories that make up cognitive science. "The image is present in the brain before the object,"[7] claim biologists. "Cognitive architecture is not limited by the nervous system; on the contrary, the nervous system is penetrated by the cognitive architecture that takes place there."[8] "We cannot dispense with a teleonomy here."[9] "I cannot see how we might conceive of mental functioning that did not include a representation of the goal, that is, that did not imply a subject that attempts to represent both itself and its expected goal."[10]

Image before object, subject, teleonomy, representation: where is the soul to be found? If cognitive science is not to lead biology toward a spiritualist rebirth, we must ask how a soul is made. What kinds of representations and which logical varieties constitute the soul? Psychoanalysis does not necessarily have the answers to these questions, but it is the one discipline that is searching for them.

Can We Speak of New Patients?

At the same time, everyday experience points to a spectacular reduction of private life. These days, who still has a soul? We are all too familiar with the sort of emotional blackmail that reminds us of television serials, but this coercion is merely a by-product of the hysterical failure of psychic life that romantic dissatisfaction and middle-class domestic comedy have already depicted for us. As for the renewed interest in religion, we have reason to wonder if it stems from a legitimate quest, or from a psychological poverty that requests that faith give it an artificial soul that might replace an amputated subjectivity. For an affirmation emerges: today's men and women—who are stress-ridden and eager to achieve, to spend money, have fun, and die—dispense with the representation of their experience that we call psychic life. Actions and their imminent abandonment have replaced the interpretation of meaning.

We have neither the time nor the space needed to create a soul for ourselves, and the mere hint of such activity seems frivolous and ill-advised. Held back by his aloofness, modern man is a narcissist—a narcissist who may suffer, but who feels no remorse. He manifests his suffering in his body and he is afflicted with somatic symptoms. His problems serve to justify his refuge in the very problems that his own desire paradoxically solicits. When he is not depressed, he becomes swept away by insignificant and valueless objects that offer a perverse pleasure, but no satisfaction. Living in a piecemeal and accelerated space and time, he often has trouble acknowledging his own physiognomy; left without a sexual, subjective, or moral identity, this amphibian is a being of boundaries, a borderline, or a "false self"—a body that acts, often without even the joys of such performative drunkenness. Modern man is losing his soul, but he does not know it, for the psychic apparatus is what registers representations and their meaningful values for the subject. Unfortunately, that darkroom needs repair.

Of course, the society that shapes modern individuals does not leave them stranded. They can find one possibly effective solution for their problems in neurochemistry, whose methods can often treat insomnia, anxieties, certain psychotic states, and some forms of depression. And who could find fault with that? The body conquers the invisible territory of the soul. Let it stand for the record. There is nothing you can do about it. You are overwhelmed with images. They carry you away, they replace you, you are dreaming. The rapture of the hallucination originates in the absence of boundaries between pleasure and reality, between truth and falsehood. The spectacle is life as a dream—we all want this. Do this "you" and this "we" exist? Your expression is standardized, your discourse becomes normalized. For that matter, do you really have a discourse of your own?

If drugs do not take over your life, your wounds are "healed" with images, and before you can speak about your states of the soul, you drown them in the world of mass media. The image has an extraordinary power to harness your anxieties and desires, to take on their intensity and to suspend their meaning. It works by itself. As a result, the psychic life of modern individuals wavers between somatic symptoms (getting sick and going to the hospital) and the visual depiction of their desires (daydreaming in front of the TV). In such a situation, psychic life is blocked, inhibited, and destroyed.

We see all too easily, however, that this mutation may be beneficial. More than just a commodity or a new variant of the "opium of the people," the current transformation of psychic life may foreshadow a new humanity, one whose psychological conveniences will be able to overcome metaphysical anxiety and the need for meaning. Wouldn't it be great to be satisfied with just a pill and a television screen?

The problem is that the path of such a superman is strewn with traps. A wide variety of troubles can bring new patients to the analyst's couch: sexual and relationship difficulties, somatic symptoms, a difficulty in expressing oneself, and a general malaise caused by a language experienced as "artificial," "empty," or "mechanical." These patients often resemble "traditional" analysands, but "maladies of the soul" soon break through their hysterical and obsessional allure—"maladies of the soul" that are not necessarily psychoses, but that evoke the psychotic patient's inability to symbolize his unbearable traumas.

As a result, analysts must come up with new classification systems that take into account wounded "narcissisms," "false personalities," "borderline states," and "psychosomatic conditions." Whatever their differences, all these symptomatologies share a common denominator—the inability to represent. Whether it takes the form of psychic mutism or adopts various signs experienced as "empty" or "artificial," such a deficiency of psychic representation hinders sensory, sexual, and intellectual life. Moreover, it may strike a blow to biological functioning itself. In a roundabout manner, the psychoanalyst is then asked to restore psychic life and to enable the speaking entity to live life to its fullest.

Are these new patients a product of contemporary life, which exacerbates our familial situations and infantile difficulties and makes them into symptoms of a particular era? If not, are dependence on medicines and refuge in the image merely modern renditions of the narcissistic inadequacies common to all times? Finally, have patients changed or has analytic practice changed, such that analysts have sharpened their interpretations of previously neglected symptomatologies? These questions as well as others will be asked by the readers of this book, just as they are asked by its author. The fact remains, however, that analysts who do not discover a *new malady of the soul* in each of their patients do not fully appreciate the uniqueness of each individual. Similarly, we can place ourselves at the heart of the analytic project by realizing that these new maladies of the soul go beyond traditional classification systems and their inevitable overhaul. What is more important, they embody difficulties or obstacles in psychic representation, difficulties that end up destroying psychic life. Revitalizing grammar and rhetoric, and enriching the style of those who wish to speak with us because they can no longer remain silent and brushed aside: do such projects not mirror the new life and new psyche that psychoanalysis wishes to unearth?

NOTES

1. Jackie Pigeaud's excellent book *La Maladie de l'âme: Etude sur la relation de l'âme et du corps dans la tradition medico-philosophique antique* (Paris: Les Belles Lettres, 1989) retraces the history of these issues and draws some epistemological and moral conclusions that are relevant to the contemporary human sciences. This book has greatly influenced my own thoughts on the subject.

2. See Michel Foucault, *The Birth of the Clinic: An Archaeology of Medical Perception*, A. M. Sheridan Smith, tr. (New York: Pantheon Books, 1973); and his *Madness and Civilization: A History of Insanity in the Age of Reason*, Richard Howard, tr. (New York: Pantheon Books, 1965).

3. See Philippe Pinel, *Treatise on Insanity*, D. D. Davis, tr. (Birmingham, Ala.: Classics of Medicine, 1983); and his *Nosographie philosophique* (Paris, 1813).

4. See Pigeaud, *La Maladie de l'âme*, p. 534.

5. The dualist point of view is sustained throughout Freud's writings. It is most clearly exemplified by his opposition of the life drive and the death drive. "Our views have from the very first been dualistic and today more than ever more definitely dualistic than before—now that we describe the opposition as being not between ego instincts and sexual instincts, but between life instincts and death instincts." *Beyond the Pleasure Principle* (1920), in *The Standard Edition of the Complete Psychological Works of Sigmund Freud*, James Strachey, ed. (London: Hogarth Press, 1953–1974), 18:53.

6. From *Project for a Scientific Psychology* (1895) to *The Interpretation of Dreams* (1900) and *Metapsychology* (1915), this "psychic apparatus" adopts the form of two well-known topographical models (Conscious, Preconscious, Unconscious; and Superego, Ego, and Id). Freud's notion has not ceased to influence the work of his followers (Lacan and Bion have proposed their own variants of the psychic apparatus).

7. Jacques Hochmann and Marc Jeannerot, *Esprit où es-tu? Psychanalyse et neuroscience* (Paris: Odile Jacob, 1991), p. 71.

8. Z. Pylyszyn, "Computation and Cognition: Issues in the Foundation of Cognitive Science," *Behavioural Brain Sciences*, 1980, pp. 111–69. Cited by Hochmann and Jeannerot, *Esprit où es-tu?* p. 81.

9. Hochmann and Jeannerot, *Esprit où es-tu?* p. 129.

10. Hochmann and Jeannerot, *Esprit où es-tu?* p. 53.

In Times Like These, Who Needs Psychoanalysts?

I am picturing a sprawling metropolis with glass and steel buildings that reach to the sky, reflect it, reflect each other, and reflect you—a city filled with people steeped in their own image who rush about with overdone makeup on and who are cloaked in gold, pearls, and fine leather, while in the next street over, heaps of filth abound and drugs accompany the sleep or the fury of the social outcasts.

This city could be New York; it could be any future metropolis, even your own.

What might one do in such a city? Nothing but buy and sell goods and images, which amounts to the same thing, since they both are dull, shallow symbols. Those who can or wish to preserve a lifestyle that downplays opulence as well as misery will need to create a space for an "inner zone"—a secret garden, an intimate quarter, or more simply and ambitiously, a psychic life.

Yet that is where the story gets complicated. The West has been crafting this inner life since the beginning of the Christian era, when Plotinus transformed a Janus-faced Narcissus into two hands joined in prayer. Inner life has been reinforced by the spiritual path and carnival of the Middle Ages, and it has been shaped by Montaigne's fragile ego, Diderot's passions, and the meditations of Hegel and Kant. It has since become a psychic drama, a psychodrama.

Plotinus has degenerated into . . . Dallas. Indeed, the residents of this steel city are not in want of inner drama—in fact, they are as anxious, depressed, neurotic, and psychotic as the Freudian unconscious would wish them to be. If we believe, however, that we can escape from the surface value of our actions, we fall into the trap of psychology. Therefore, psychoanalysis has some work ahead of it, since Freud's doctrine seeks precisely to free us from this suppressed space of psychological ill-being.

The city that I chose as an image of contemporary life encourages us to include *social history* as one of the elements of organization and permanency that constitute psychic life. Using the terminology of our industrial society, one could say that psychoanalysis turns money into time and joins painful affect with language—language that may be listless or indecipherable, but that is always directed toward other people. Such an extraordinary metamorphosis, which goes against the tide of the market economy as well as the neurosis that it patterns, may also shed light on psychosis. Two thousand years of inner experience have built this prison of the soul, a prison that offers psychoanalysis an innocent vulnerability in which it can pierce a hole that will serve to resound the polyphony of our motives.

Proust has accorded us the finest summary of what is becoming (or will soon become) the Freudian psyche: "Those who suffer feel closer to their soul."[1] Or perhaps:

For even if we have the sensation of being always enveloped in, surrounded by our own soul, still it does not seem a fixed and immovable prison; rather do we seem to be borne away with it, and perpetually struggling to transcend it, to break out into the world, with a perpetual discouragement as we hear endlessly all around us that unvarying sound which is not an echo from without, but the resonance of a vibration from within.[2]

Here, Proust evokes the permanency of the psyche and offers a glimpse of its limits. Freud has provided us with a preliminary method for achieving this sort of listening, but we still need to elaborate our approach. Our empathy and familiarity with the malady of the soul will enable us to transcend the psyche—forever.

The psychic realm may be the place where somatic symptoms and delirious fantasies can be worked through and thus eliminated: as long as we avoid becoming trapped inside it, the psychic realm protects us. Yet we must transform it through *linguistic activity* into a form of sublimation or into an intellectual, interpretive, or transformational activity. At the same time, we must conceive of the "psychic realm" as a *speech act*, that is, neither an acting-out nor a psychological rumination within an imaginary crypt, but the link between this inevitable and necessary rumination and its potential for verbal expression.

For this reason, the current onslaught of psychological illness, which takes the form of "soap operas" that inevitably cater to the other side of the society of performance and stress, seems to call out to psychoanalysis. "Tell us the meaning of our inner turmoil, show us a way out of it"— such is the cry of psychological helplessness, of the alter ego of the society, of the spectacle. As a result, psychoanalysis wagers to modify the prison of the soul that the West has made into a means of survival and protection, although this prison has recently been revealing our failings. This wager is therapeutic as well as ethical, and incidentally, political. Yet although we may seek the acceptance and even expansion of psychoanalysis, our wish is coming up against some substantial barriers.

I am not referring to the ever-present danger of transforming psychoanalysis into a normalization that would guide patients toward social success. Such a deterioration of psychoanalytic treatment, traditionally American, is widely known and denounced, and even if it remains a threat, resisting it was primarily a matter for the past that we still must keep in mind.

In my view, psychoanalysis will soon be confronted with two major issues that concern the problem of the organization and permanency of the psyche. The first issue pertains to its competition with the neuro-sciences. From now on, "take a pill or talk" may replace "to be or not to be." The second issue regards the challenge to which psychoanalysis is subject as a result of our desire to *remain in ignorance,* a desire that is in harmony with the apparent simplicity that pharmacology offers, and that also reflects the negative narcissism of modern man.[3]

Biology and Language: Freudian Drives and the Imaginary

The analytic position could be briefly outlined as follows: an uncon-scious psychic life is governed by determinants and restrictions that can be described and modified through an interpretation of the transfer-ence relation.

Some of these determinants and restrictions are *biological* in nature: recent advances in neurobiology and pharmacology have had an impact on our *behavior* and have enabled us to modify certain *fragments* of psychic life. The connection between analytic treatment and these interventions is more topical than ever, and this link is attracting the attention of analysts—who consider each concrete situation to be a singular experience.

The "attack" of the neurosciences is not making psychoanalysis defunct, but it is encouraging us to reconsider the Freudian concept of the *drive*. The drive is a pivot between "soma" and "psyche," between biol-ogy and representation—the highest level of organization and perma-nency to which Freudian listening and theory can aspire—that is, to which analytic construction (or imagination) can aspire. For what we understand by biology is—drives and energy, if you wish, but always already a "carrier of meaning" and a "relation" to another person, even though this person may be yourself.

Owing to its dual nature (biological and energetic/semiotic), the drive is also a structure. Within the space between its source (an organ) and its aim (satisfaction), its strength or weakness governs the restrictions placed on each subject. These restrictions circumscribe relationships that are among the most stubborn, because they are the most archaic (onto- and phylogenetically speaking), and the most discordant in terms of lin-guistic expression. In addition, the ego and its object relation are shaped within this drive framework.

The structure of the subject bases itself upon the different positions of the ego with respect to the different modalities of the object, and we must underscore that egos as well as the types of objects formed within the space between drives and language are *diverse in nature*. Nevertheless, any Freudian analyst would know that these subjective structures are charged with both the fate of drives and their dual nature (one that stems from biology and *non*linguistic representation).

For example, the fantasy, which could be considered a result of the eruption of the drive into the dispassionate logic of judgment—a logic that consequently finds itself transformed into a hallucination or a fit of delirium, reminds us that drives (and by implication, affects) form not only a myth, but also an element of organization and permanency that incites changes in the activity of thinking (as well as of judging and speaking). We also need to analyze the intermingling of drives and language with respect to the dulling of affects, to the disavowal of the object, and to the lifeless speech that characterizes those who suffer from depression.

That depression denies the meaning of discourse—which is to escort eros to the object—implies that the aggressive (or death) drive prevents a separation between the ego and the object. In its place, the death drive ushers in a melancholic subject—a negative Narcissus, an absolute master not of an object, but of a deadly *Thing* that must never be lost.[4]

In short, if we take the "myth" of the drive seriously, we must realize that an *imaginary deployment* reconstructs the logic of the drive in order to free up the linguistic restrictions that ultimately govern our capacities as speaking beings. It does so to show that this element of organization and permanency (discourse) consists not only of myriad significations and logical implications or presuppositions, but also of an interruption of the ability to produce speech (which can be schizophrenic or depressive—the figures vary). This imaginary deployment thereby reveals itself as a privileged witness to the *meaning* of the drive that joins the *signification* of speech.

Once fascinated by linguistics, contemporary psychoanalysis has a growing interest in drives, an interest that stems from Freud's legacy as well as from the daunting impact of the neurosciences. As a result, contemporary psychoanalysis has been attempting to decode the drama of drives while going beyond the *signification of language* that conceals the *meaning of drives*.

Traces of the meaning of drives can be translinguistic. Let us take the example of the voice: vocal stresses and rhythms often harbor the secret eroticism of depressed people who have severed the bond between language and the other, but who have nevertheless buried their affects in the hidden code of their vocalizations—in which the analyst may discover a desire that is not as dead as it may seem.

This brings me to the elements of organization and permanency that are the immediate object of analytic interpretation, insofar as they stem from our relation with others and are manifested through language. In light of what I have said concerning the primacy of drive destiny, these restrictions on signification would appear to constitute a complex, *heterogeneous* structure that is formed from the first years of our lives, grows and develops alongside us, and ultimately determines our symbolic destiny.

As a result of the growth of linguistics and of the other "human sciences" during the 1960s, the notion of *structure* in psychoanalysis (for which we are primarily indebted to Jacques Lacan) has enabled us to surmise more accurately than ever the organization of this *symbolic destiny*, this "being of language" that governs psychic life. Freudian analysts will agree that a discourse or symptom with which someone entrusts us can be taken as a whole, whose parts can only acquire meaning through the relationship between speaking subjects and their addressee, notably their analyst.

What is more, Freudian analyses have already noted that while this network of signifying relations that characterize symptoms, discourses, transference, and subjects is a *theoretical construction,* it is nevertheless the only *reality* in which psychic life can be manifested and developed. A fortiori, it constitutes the sole reality that offers the analyst—to whom someone has made a direct request—the possibility of intervening and modifying it. This aspect of analysis brings up three pressing questions:

1. Can we reduce the fate of speaking beings to *language* and *speech*, or do other *systems of representation* have a bearing on their logical features and on the actual psychic level that encompasses meaning for the subject?
2. Which characteristics of *interpretive language* are able to echo the symbolic fate of subjects, and thus affect and modify their biological substratum?
3. If analytic treatment is capable of such modifications, how might we define its boundaries and its *ethics*?

• The growth of semiology, which has encouraged us to contemplate various signifying systems (the iconic code, the musical code, and so forth) that are irreducible to language (whether language is considered as a specific language or a discourse, a structure or a grammar, an utterance or an enunciation), has shattered "linguistic imperialism." In like manner, the return to Freud, and more specifically to his conception of *representation*, has acknowledged the diversity of psychic representatives: thing-presentation, word-presentation, drive representative, affect representation. This has resulted in a "multi-layered" model of psychic *signifiance*, one that incorporates heterogeneous *marks* and *signs*. Analysts must be aware of this polyphony if they wish to approach the discourse that is addressed to them from different linguistic and translinguistic levels (the voice, movement, and so forth) as well as to identify the levels that reveal the significance that discourse has for transference.

• In an ideal situation, interpretive silence would make these different structures of meaning, which shelter the subject's symptom, reverberate into his conscious. More directly and more frequently, however, analytic *interpretation* is what reveals the diverse linguistic and translinguistic expressions of ill-being and restores them to the subject. How does it do this? By giving a name to the familial determinants that have tainted sexual development with a given symptom or structure. What is more important, though, is that interpretation offers an *appropriate formulation* that is expressed in elliptical, metaphorical, or condensed terms and has a bearing on both the analyst's affects and its own series of psychic representatives (of words, things, and drives).

• A veritable poiesis comes into play here, one that includes the musical qualities of the voice as well as tropes and the rhetorical analysis of mental functioning. As the ultimate reality of transference and countertransference, this poiesis has an effect on conscious listening and exerts an influence on the patient's unconscious psychic representatives, which can be assumed to be closely related to the flux of the neurons that make up subcortical, "electrical," or "humoral" systems. Perhaps there is nothing that would form links between unconscious psychic representatives or separate them from the realm of neurobiology. Yet, while theoreticians and scientists are pondering the relationship between psychoanalysis and neurobiology, interpretive language is producing its own psychosomatic effects.

• If we take this to be true, we cannot help being struck by the violence of analytic interpretation. The mere fact that patients ask us to fulfill their request does not seem to justify such violence. Does their request not constitute an integral part of the symptom as well as the onset of its excess? Consequently, the ethics of psychoanalysis might base itself on two requirements that are characteristic of the Western rationalism from which it stems:

- On the one hand, there is a need to uphold a *single* meaning, a *single* truth that is valid and demonstrable in a given situation. This is the "normative" side of psychoanalysis. Indeed, the norm is dictated by the state of psychoanalytic theory and by any given analyst's position within it.
- On the other hand, there is a need to preserve respect (by way of freedom) for the patient's desire and jouissance, which are what determine his ability to accept our interpretation (since the structure of the patient emerges out of his particular resistance to our interpretation). At the same time, the validity of interpretation itself is challenged, for the analyst's jouissance is revealed, although it is clouded by the "truth" of his interpretive construction.

No other discourse in the history of Western rationalism has wagered to counterbalance truth and jouissance, authority and transgression. The ensuing equilibrium preserves the vitality of this discourse, a vitality that grows out of the immanence of death (the discourse of knowledge) and resurrection (the discourse of desire). As a result, psychoanalysis upsets the social contract, which is founded, according to Freud, on an act of murder. Analysts do not shy away from being dead fathers of knowledge, but they are also subjects of affect, desire, and jouissance. Consequently, they are distanced from schools and institutions and concentrate instead on restructuring other people's psyches.

Each Treatment Is Unique

Two phenomena prompt us to consider each analytic situation to be a specific microcosm: first, the various forms of psychic representation that turn toward language even though they are irreducible to its grammatical and logical structures, and second, the bipolarity of transference and countertransference that cloaks interpretive discourse.

To put it another way, although the psychiatric notions of "structure" (hysterical, obsessional, schizophrenic, paranoid, etc.) can offer an initial and rudimentary outline that the analyst may find useful, these notions are unable to withstand a microanalysis that is attentive to the diversity and polyvalence of psychic representatives. We have a growing interest in structural interferences as well as "borderline states" that go beyond their status as new clinical occurrences indicating the growth of subjectivity and psychic states, for they also have the advantage of challenging the foundation of traditional classification systems.

Hence, although the interest that psychoanalysts have in the linguistic and translinguistic expression of psychic determinants can sometimes make analysis appear abstract, this abstraction ends up personalizing each treatment as much as possible. Each treatment becomes an ideolect, a work of art, as well as a temporary installation of a new theoretical creation within the Freudian world. As a result, we would like to know which features of this discourse can be identified with Freudian thought, as well as where we can draw the line between loyalty, innovation, and dissension.

The history of the analytic movement combined with the current ecumenism of its tenets (Freudian, Kleinian, Winnicottian, Lacanian, and so forth) shows that despite various misunderstandings and impasses, Freud has staked out a path that all innovators must respect if they lay claims to psychoanalysis. It is admittedly a narrow path, one in which sexual experience resists language. This leads to repression and to the related necessity that we use language in order to interpret hidden unconscious signs. But it is also the path through which the eroticization of language within transference allows us to convey sexual experience and to relieve symptoms, which in turn endows us with a greater capacity for signification. Need I emphasize that in proposing that this be the goal of analysis, I am in no way advocating the normalization of the patient?

Two Obstacles to Analytic Speech

I shall briefly outline two examples of analytic treatment, examples that will serve to underscore my remarks and to point out two often-met obstacles to analytic speech.

Depression. Florence, a thirty-year-old woman who suffered from intense bouts of manic-depression, came to see me. She had previously attempted analysis with one of my colleagues, but she stopped going because she felt it was aggravating the intensity and frequency of her cycles. Florence had consulted a psychiatrist before coming to me. He put her on imipramine, but her previous analyst was unwilling to pursue treatment under such conditions.

At first we engaged in psychotherapy. After a while, though, Florence chose to lie down on the couch. She was still taking imipramine at the time. A few months later, she went off antidepressants and continued her analysis without taking any medication. Florence believed that imipramine had diminished her excessive anxiety and had allowed her to speak about the tragic events of her childhood and her life without falling back into the states of serious depression that she had often experienced. Her anxiety threshold seemed rather low, and its stabilization during treatment encouraged drives and their representatives to bond with verbal representations.

It seemed to me, however, that a certain distancing resulted from these chemical interventions—which seemed necessary though provisional. Nevertheless, I believed that in addition to the bonds they supported between drives and words, they offered another advantage. The introduction of a third party (medication, psychiatry) tempered Florence's manic elation—for she was not omnipotent and neither was I; a third party and an alternate reality were involved.

This also enabled us to tackle her narcissism, on the one hand, and its projection onto the exaggerated idealization with which she adorned me, on the other. Hence, a modified anxiety threshold made it possible to confront the manic-depressive devices that Florence had put into place in order to deal with loss and separation. A new object relation was established between us, one that was less catastrophic and less threatened by the unbearable danger of the annihilation she feared might follow a real or imaginary separation. Once this new object relation—which was also a new subjective structure—became stronger, Florence stopped taking imipramine. From that point on, she tried to rely solely on the symbolic and imaginary network that we had built up through the "regional" help of imipramine. She did so without resorting to chemical products, but to the psychic representatives we had restructured and whose disorganization was much less threatening to her than before.

During the portion of the analysis in which she was taking imipramine, I had the impression that the intensity of her drives was in check, but that her discourse was "numbed." My feeling arose primarily from the fact that while taking imipramine, Florence was able to have dreams pertaining to anxiety states that she had previously been unable to represent—the anxiety of being swallowed up and devoured by her mother, and inversely, the anxiety of swallowing up and devouring her mother. Yet even though Florence was able to have and report these dreams (which already was a substantial psychic development as compared to the depressive silence and "blank death" of the depressed signifier that had once characterized her), she approached her dreams with a sense of distance and a defensive lack of understanding. Then, in the second phase of the analysis, we were able to return to these dreams and analyze them.

First dream: A dream about a cannibalistic wedding. The wedding resembles her parents' wedding photo. In this dream, the guests eat each other's body parts and heads. The scene takes place in the staircase of my building.

Second dream: Florence vomits after the sex act, and her mother's head falls into the basin. She has this dream just before becoming pregnant.

In what way were we able to return to these dreams? Florence, who became a mother during her analysis and who continued treatment without the use of medication, had nevertheless developed another symptom. She had become very frightened by her relentless and exhausting fantasies of assassinating her daughter, and she never tired of telling me how preoccupied she was with these obsessions. Florence specified that she did not really feel capable of acting out her fantasies, although she was quite worn out by her phantasmatic ruminations.

I said, "assassin—basin—assimilate." By way of this interpretation—which was highly condensed and which bore witness to a tragic, grotesque poetics—Florence was able to ascertain the meaning of her drives as well as the symbolic signification of her two previous dreams. Then, she could relate them to her current anxieties. Her desire to assassinate her daughter was a by-product of her desire to assimilate (devour) imipramine, and more important, to absorb the head and body parts (breast, basin [*sein, bassin*] of her mother (the cannibal dream) that she chose to spit up into a basin (the vomiting dream) in order to make a place for her own child (to become pregnant, to occupy her own basin).

The meaning of drives in her dreams had already taken effect in her psyche by pushing aside her depressive symptoms, if only because her effort to report her dreams came to replace a melancholic silence. Nevertheless, the meaning of her drives failed to attain the signification of speech, and my interpretations spurred no associations. Eventually, however, the meaning of her drives was able to attain a symbolic signification, a working-out.

Assassin—basin—assimilate. I considered my interpretation to be a "vibration from within" (as Proust would say) that resounded between inexpressible, anxiety-ridden, or depressive drive representatives and an explanation that the patient, with the help of certain aspects of my interpretation, came up with herself—an explanation of her depressive side as well as her manic one. Florence did not wish to assassinate her daughter. She merely wished to reject the image of the daughter that she herself was, the assassin-cannibal daughter that constituted her self-image, a daughter who assimilated, devoured, and "vomited" her mother in order to avenge her infantile paralysis (her immobility from the basin) that had seriously handicapped her when she was very young and had separated her from her mother (orality is often overinvested in order to encompass an object that has eluded a failing motivity).

Like the explanatory, rhetorical work we subsequently engaged in, my transferential word-play resulted from my empathy with my patient's drive economy. I identified with her narcissistic wound and her oral voracity, as well as with her manic attempts to use devouring and evacuation to avenge the depressive *Thing* for which there were no linguistic signs, but only echolalia that bore the intensities of her drives. My interpretation reintroduced this drive economy into the assassin's divested language (Florence wanted to kill, but she felt detached and distanced from her otherwise obsessive desire). What may have appeared to be "word-play" served to revitalize language and transference, on the one hand, and the analysand, on the other. My interpretation accomplished this by recalling infantile time and the history of the archaic fantasy, and by compensating for a narcissistic wound.

I would like to emphasize a few aspects of this analytic fragment that I consider to be of paramount importance for psychoanalysis today and, why not, tomorrow.

- The role that pharmacology played in this treatment leads me to believe that the dialogue between neuroscience and psychoanalysis will follow two basic trends. First, there will be an increasing number of patients who undergo joint treatments (pharmacological and psychoanalytic), and this alliance will require an accurate assessment of the effects of medication as well as of their interaction with transference. Second, the public will need to be made aware of the vast array of psychological illnesses that are not targeted by pharmacology—illnesses that reaffirm the need for traditional psychoanalytic treatment. We require a more precise analysis of the relationship between the psychic apparatus and transference. In other words, our analyses will have to be attentive to the "translatability" of drives into words.
- The "signifier of death" is readily apparent to analysts who are aware of the depressive speech that results from the patient's *disavowal of the signifier* ("lifeless" speech that is painstaking, void, monotonous, accelerated yet self-effacing, "nonexistent"), and from the devalorization of language as an aspect of transference.
- Desire and the determinants of the symptom that are not signified within speech, however, seem to have deposited or coded their mean-

ing in the preverbal register (of voice and intonation) or in a homophony that leads to the play of signifiers, or to an echolalia.

- Analytic interpretation may become a temporary party to regression and stagnation by making itself an echo of such meaning while serving as a bridge to intellectualization and to conscious formations not only of trauma but also of desire that works within a language directed toward the other.
- Depression appears to stem from a relation to the other that is not separated from depressed subjects, but that remains under their grasp in the form of their *Thing*, which is unnameable and deadly (we discovered this symbiotic reunion in the "paradise not lost" of the "suicide wedding"). This particular object relation is clearly embedded in the "form" as well as the "content" of depressive discourse: both object relations and the structure of discourse function at the same level as the determinants of depression. Consequently, the intervention of analysis depends, or should depend (by way of its form and signification), on these two permanent factors of the subject's psyche—the *object* and *discourse*.

Perversion. The following factors have led to my interest in perversion, a disorder that is quite widespread these days and particularly resistant to analysis:

- Narcissistic satisfaction by a part object is supplemented by a fetishist and exhibitionist discourse of someone who is all-knowing and has no desire to learn.
- The overestimation of speech becomes a resistance to analysis: *affects* are split from the *discourse* that recounts the perverse fantasy. This sort of isolation persists even when a fantasy is reported to the analyst with the unconscious intention of including him in the patient's sadomasochistic economy.
- As a result, it may prove necessary to verify that *the image* and *the representations of the perverse act* are *possible* within transference. This sort of actualization of the perverse *scenario* within the treatment mobilizes the intensities of the preverbal affect or drive representatives, and constitutes a precondition for their "translation" into interpretive speech.

Didier entered into analysis with the complaint that he was unable to have any satisfying sexual relations. It soon become apparent that his sexuality was voyeuristic and exhibitionist, masturbatory, and one in which sadomasochistic scenarios gave him the most pleasure. Didier was an amateur painter, though he never showed his paintings to anyone except his mother, while she was still living. Ever since his "audience" had died, his mother's apartment was closed off, and Didier dared not lay a finger on it or sell it.

Didier's discourse remained very fluent throughout his analysis. He knew everything and needed nothing from me. By way of his masturbatory speech, which bore witness to an exorbitant infantile power, Didier described his rituals as if he were reading a film script, coldly exposing the actions of actors whom he directed from afar. I had a feeling—or a countertransferential conviction—that Didier's secret resided in his mother's apartment, as well as in a *secret discourse* that entombed his drives and affects and prevented them from coming forth in his speech. This patient's speech was cut off from his affects; his affects were not to be found in his speech.

As a result, I agreed to look at Didier's artwork, which consisted of collages made of cut-up posters drenched or daubed with colors, of blank pages, and so forth. Didier's voice became increasingly animated. He would explain his paintings to me from the couch, or he would show me a photograph that allowed me to follow his remarks. Nevertheless, his discourse remained neutral, technical, and aesthetic. It was I who had to come up with the perverse signification of his exposition—of the cut-up organs, of the fecal substances. During the treatment, I allotted Didier a certain perverse acting-out—that is, the display of his paintings—and I transplanted onto this demonstration the discourse of the antiperversion that he lacked.

He accepted this perverse fantasy—his or mine?—and his phantasmatic potential was thereby unleashed. Fantasies grew to replace his periods of acting-out without completely eliminating them. Nevertheless, since Didier was able to integrate them and to work them out by way of his discourse, he lost his relentless need to act out. Thus, he was able to create a new and more complex psychic structure.

In the pervert's case, the other is reduced to being the agent of the subject's sadomasochistic pleasure—which also ensures the subject's omnipotence. Although the ensuing discourse displays the logical and grammatical features of normative speech, it holds no heuristic or commutative value. Indeed, the unconscious meaning that it actually conveys resides in the neutralization of the other (the analyst) and in the reduction of a perverse megalomania into an object-fetish. If we wish to be privy to the workings of this unconscious determination, the speech-fetish must be dismantled. The analyst can use words to enrich the scenario-*image*, as well as the *act* that is in fact the pervert's "real language." And it will then become possible to endow speech with the multifaceted, heuristic, and commutative dimension it once had—the dimension in which the subject's complexity will be played out, and not the pervert's repudiation.

Insofar as the onset of transference is contingent upon the desire to know, to know *oneself*, and to transform *oneself* and grow, we have reason to wonder if this subjective pose is not historically determined. This subjective desire can appear in various guises, ranging from the ethical demands of a Jewish God to the Trinitarian mystery of Christian subjectivity and even to the "what do I know?" put forth by Montaigne, whose split ego prefigures in many ways the one that Freud has described. These different forms can be seen as foundations of Western history as well as of psychoanalysis (in the sense of an infinite appropriation of memory into a new history of subjects made ill by their symptoms). On the other hand, satisfying the narcissistic discontent that accompanies the modern crisis of values seems to be at odds with this sort of psychic inquiry, an inquiry that seems necessary for any transformation of subjectivity.

Psychoanalysis goes against the grain of the modern convenience that calls attention not to the end of the Story of Civilization but to end of the possibility of *telling a story*. Nevertheless, this end and this convenience are beginning to overwhelm us, and we have been led to criticize and to reject them.

Be that as it may, psychoanalytic technique cannot ignore this narcissistic withdrawal and decline of desire. Psychoanalysis will need to acknowledge and assimilate these conditions before it can attempt to go further and to strive for a new form of self-knowledge, one that Freud has already outlined by placing the "malady" at the very essence of the psyche and by making psychic life into an interminable construction-destruction. The psychoanalytic approach to depression and perversion, among other "modern" symptoms, shows that the analytic field is reaching out to the very boundaries that offer it the most resistance.

In my view, contemporary psychoanalysis, and especially that of the future, is an art—I admit, an artifice—that may allow the men and women of our modern, sleek, lofty, costly, and profit-bearing cities to preserve a life for themselves. Why? Because the speaking being's life begins and ends with psychic life, a life for which speech is one axis of a heterogeneous dynamic. Freudian psychoanalysis has more to offer than a simple refuge for a society of spectacle and consumption. While acknowledging and assimilating the logic of monetary exchange, it also overthrows our alienating metropolises and incites real change. If it fails to do this, what else will inspire change, faced as we are with the glow of our silver high-rises, the implacable banality of banks, and the fact that destiny is being programmed into the genetic code itself?

Therefore, I suggest that in the future, psychoanalysis may be one of the few remaining endeavors that will allow change and surprise, that is, that will allow life. It will remain cognizant of the elements of psychic permanency (from biology to drives and language), but it will also provide support for those who wish to alter these elements. For by remaining loyal to Freud's skepticism while recognizing the resiliency of psychic discourse, we contend that such a modification is possible.

NOTES

1. Marcel Proust, "Les Plaisirs et les jours," *Jean Santeuil* (Paris: Bibliothèque de La Plèiade, 1971), p. 6.

2. Marcel Proust, *Swann's Way*, in *Remembrance of Things Past*, vol. 1, C. K. Scott Moncrieff and Terence Kilmartin, trs. (New York: Random House, 1981), p. 93.

3. André Green, *Narcissisme de vie, narcissisme de mort* (Paris: Minuit, 1983).

4. Julia Kristeva, *Black Sun: Depression and Melancholia*, Leon S. Roudiez, tr. (New York: Columbia University Press, 1989).

PART 4

Individual and National Identity

Powers of Horror

Pouvoirs de l'horreur was originally published in Paris by Editions du Seuil in 1980. It was translated as *Powers of Horror*, by Leon Roudiez for Columbia University Press in 1982. Part of that translation appears here. In *Powers of Horror*, Kristeva analyzes the separations necessary to set up identity. She applies her analysis of perversion and phobia to the work of Louis-Ferdinand Céline.

In *Powers of Horror*, relying on the work of Mary Douglas in *Purity and Danger* (1969), Kristeva defines a notion of abjection with which she diagnoses separation and identification in both individuals and nations or societies. In the first chapter, "Approaching Abjection," Kristeva suggests that the abject is not, as we might ordinarily think, what is grotesque or unclean; rather it is what calls into question borders and threatens identity. The abject is on the borderline, and as such it is both fascinating and terrifying. Ultimately, the abject is identified with the maternal body since the uncertain boundary between maternal body and infant provides the primary experience of both horror and fascination.

As Kristeva describes the process of separation in *Powers of Horror*, the infant must go through a stage of abjection in which it "abjects," or finds abject, its mother's body. In order to be weaned the infant must find its mother's body both fascinating and horrifying. The (male) infant experiences a horror at its dependence on the maternal body that allows the weaning process; but the (male) infant also experiences a fascination with the maternal body that allows an eroticization of the female body. In a 1980 interview in *Women Analyze Women*, Kristeva suggests that her description of the process of abjection as a splitting of the mother into sublime and terrifying in *Powers of Horror* applies only to males (see part 5 in this volume). Females do not split the mother, but merely try (unsuccessfully) to rid themselves of her. She diagnoses female sexuality as a melancholy sexuality in *Black Sun*.

With her theory of abjection Kristeva challenges Lacan's account of the acquisition of language and onset of self-consciousness through the mirror stage and castration threats. Before the mother or the maternal body becomes an object for the infant, it is an abject. It is neither object nor nonobject, but something in between. Kristeva resists both Freud's and Lacan's identification of the maternal body as the infant's first object. She insists that there is a process of identification and separation that complicates the infant's relation with the maternal body. The maternal body is not simply an object, or the first object, or even a partial object, for the infant. Subjectivity is a process that is set in motion long before Lacan's mirror stage.

In "From Filth to Defilement," Kristeva also challenges Freud's analysis in *Moses and Monotheism* where he maintains that the social is set up against the murder of the father. Here, Kristeva claims that the social is set up against the feminine, specifically the maternal. The social is defined by repressing maternal authority. She emphasizes the shift from matriarchy to patriarchy that accompanies the shift from polytheism to monotheism. Here she extends her analysis of the way in which an individual identity is constructed against the exclusion of the abject maternal body to the way in which a cultural or national identity is constructed against the exclusion of maternity and the feminine.

Strangers to Ourselves

Etrangers à nous-mêmes was originally published in Paris by Fayard in 1988. Leon Roudiez translated *Etrangers à nous-mêmes* as *Strangers to Ourselves* for Columbia University Press in 1991. Part of that translation appears here. In "Toccata and Fugue for the Foreigner," Kristeva describes the experience of the foreigner estranged from his or her homeland. The foreigner experiences a loss of his or her mother, motherland, mother-tongue. Caught between two languages, the foreigner can be reduced to silence. In this text, the foreigner becomes an outward manifestation of the estranged psychic relation between conscious and unconscious. The body of *Strangers to Ourselves* traces the notion of foreigner or stranger from the Ancient Greeks, through the Talmud, the New Testament, the Renaissance, the Enlightenment, to present-day France and the issue of nationalism. She analyzes the rights of citizenship as a paradox that excludes the foreigner in order to protect "the rights of man."

In *Strangers to Ourselves* Kristeva associates the individual struggle to face the return of the repressed unconscious stranger or foreigner that inhabits our psyche with the social struggle to live with foreigners. There she takes up the question "how can I live with others, with otherness, without ostracism but also without leveling difference?" She maintains that encounters with foreigners can help to reacquaint us with the otherness within our own psyches. And, conversely, accepting our unconscious drives, the other within, can help us to accept others within our society. In "Might Not Universality Be . . . Our Own Foreignness?" and "In Practice . . . ," Kristeva maintains that psychoanalysis, with its attempts to embrace the otherness within, becomes a model for an ethics that will embrace difference: "The ethics of psychoanalysis implies a politics: it would involve a cosmopolitanism of a new sort that, cutting across governments, economies, and markets, might work for a mankind whose solidarity is founded on the consciousness of its unconscious— desiring, destructive, fearful, empty, impossible" (*Stranger to Ourselves*, p. 192). Following Montesquieu's notion of cosmopolitanism, Kristeva concludes that we need a new cosmopolitan community that is based on radical strangeness or difference and born out of the individualism of contemporary culture.

Powers of Horror

Approaching Abjection

> *No Beast is there without glimmer of infinity,*
> *No eye so vile nor abject that brushes not*
> *Against lightning from on high, now tender,*
> *now fierce.*
> —*Victor Hugo*, La Légende des siècles

Neither Subject nor Object

There looms, within abjection, one of those violent, dark revolts of being, directed against a threat that seems to emanate from an exorbitant outside or inside, ejected beyond the scope of the possible, the tolerable, the thinkable. It lies there, quite close, but it cannot be assimilated. It beseeches, worries, and fascinates desire, which, nevertheless, does not let itself be seduced. Apprehensive, desire turns aside; sickened, it rejects. A certainty protects it from the shameful—a certainty of which it is proud holds on to it. But simultaneously, just the same, that impetus, that spasm, that leap is drawn toward an elsewhere as tempting as it is condemned. Unflaggingly, like an inescapable boomerang, a vortex of summons and repulsion places the one haunted by it literally beside himself.

When I am beset by abjection, the twisted braid of affects and thoughts I call by such a name does not have, properly speaking, a definable *object*.

The abject is not an ob-ject facing me, which I name or imagine. Nor is it an ob-jest, an otherness ceaselessly fleeing in a systematic quest of desire. What is abject is not my correlative, which, providing me with someone or something else as support, would allow me to be more or less detached and autonomous. The abject has only one quality of the object—that of being opposed to *I*. If the object, however, through its opposition, settles me within the fragile texture of a desire for meaning, which, as a matter of fact, makes me ceaselessly and infinitely homologous to it, what is *abject*, on the contrary, the jettisoned object, is radically excluded and draws me toward the place where meaning collapses. A certain "ego" that merged with its master, a superego, has flatly driven it away. It lies outside, beyond the set, and does not seem to agree to the latter's rules of the game. And yet, from its place of banishment, the abject does not cease challenging its master. Without a sign (for him), it beseeches a discharge, a convulsion, a crying out. To each ego its object, to each superego its abject. It is not the white expanse or slack boredom of repression, not the translations and transformations of desire that wrench bodies, nights, and discourse; rather it is a brutish suffering that "I" puts up with, sublime and devastated, for "I" deposits it to the father's account (*verse au père—père-version*): I endure it, for I imagine that such is the desire of the other. A massive and sudden emergence of uncanniness, which, familiar as it might have been in an opaque and forgotten life, now harries me as radically separate, loathsome. Not me. Not that. But not nothing, either. A "something" that I do not recognize as a thing. A weight of meaninglessness, about which there is nothing insignificant, which crushes me. On the edge of nonexistence and hallucination, of a reality that, if I acknowledge it, annihilates me. There, abject and abjection are my safeguards. The primers of my culture.

The Improper/Unclean

Loathing an item of food, a piece of filth, waste, or dung. The spasms and vomiting that protect me. The repugnance, the retching that thrusts me to the side and turns me away from defilement, sewage, and muck. The shame of compromise, of being in the middle of treachery. The fascinated start that leads me toward and separates me from them.

Food loathing is perhaps the most elementary and most archaic form of abjection. When the eyes see or the lips touch that skin on the surface of milk—harmless, thin as a sheet of cigarette paper, pitiful as a nail paring—I experience a gagging sensation and, still farther down, spasms in the stomach, the belly; and all the organs shrivel up the body, provoke tears and bile, increase heartbeat, cause forehead and hands to perspire. Along with sight-clouding dizziness, *nausea* makes me balk at that milk cream, separates me from the mother and father who proffer it. "I" want none of that element, sign of their desire; "I" do not want to listen, "I" do not assimilate it, "I" expel it. But since the food is not an "other" for "me," who am only in their desire, I expel *myself*, I spit *myself* out, I abject *myself* within the same motion through which "I" claim to establish *myself*. That detail, perhaps an insignificant one, but one that they ferret out, emphasize, evaluate, that trifle turns me inside out, guts sprawling; it is thus that *they* see that "I" am in the process of becoming an other at the expense of my own death. During that course in which "I" become, I give birth to myself amid the violence of sobs, of vomit. Mute protest of the symptom, shattering violence of a convulsion that, to be sure, is inscribed in a symbolic system, but in which, without either wanting or being able to become integrated in order to answer to it, it reacts, it abreacts. It abjects.

The corpse (or cadaver: *cadere*, to fall), that which has irremediably come a cropper, is cesspool, and death; it upsets even more violently the one who confronts it as fragile and fallacious chance. A wound with blood and pus, or the sickly, acrid smell of sweat, of decay, does not *signify* death. In the presence of signified death—a flat encephalograph, for instance—I would understand, react, or accept. No, as in true theater, without makeup or masks, refuse and corpses *show me* what I permanently thrust aside in order to live. These body fluids, this defilement, this shit are what life withstands, hardly and with difficulty, on the part of death. There, I am at the border of my condition as a living being. My body extricates itself, as being alive, from that border. Such wastes drop so that I might live, until, from loss to loss, nothing remains in me and my entire body falls beyond the limit—*cadere*, cadaver. If dung signifies the other side of the border, the place where I am not and which permits me to be, the corpse, the most sickening of wastes, is a border that has encroached upon everything. It is no longer I who expel, "I" is expelled. The border has become an object. How can I be without border? That elsewhere that I imagine beyond the present, or that I hallucinate so that I might, in a present time, speak to you, conceive of you—it is now here, jetted, abjected, into "my" world. Deprived of world, therefore, I *fall in a faint*. In that compelling, raw, insolent thing in the morgue's full sunlight, in that thing that no longer matches and therefore no longer signifies anything, I behold the breaking down of a world that has erased its borders: fainting away. The corpse, seen without God and outside of science, is the utmost of abjection. It is death infecting life. Abject. It is something rejected from which one does not part, from which one does not protect oneself as from an object. Imaginary uncanniness and real threat, it beckons to us and ends up engulfing us.

It is thus not lack of cleanliness or health that causes abjection but what disturbs identity, system, order. What does not respect borders, positions, rules. The in-between, the ambiguous, the composite. The traitor, the liar, the criminal with a good conscience, the shameless rapist, the killer who claims he is a savior. . . . Any crime, because it draws attention to the fragility of the law, is abject, but premeditated crime, cunning murder, hypocritical revenge are even more so because they heighten the display of such fragility. He who denies morality is not abject; there can be grandeur in amorality and even in crime that flaunts its disrespect for the law—rebellious, liberating, and suicidal crime. Abjection, on the other hand, is immoral, sinister, scheming, and shady: a terror that dissembles, a hatred that smiles, a passion that uses the body for barter instead of inflaming it, a debtor who sells you up, a friend who stabs you. . . .

In the dark halls of the museum that is now what remains of Auschwitz, I see a heap of children's shoes, or something like that, something I have already seen elsewhere, under a Christmas tree, for instance, dolls I believe. The abjection of Nazi crime reaches its apex when death, which, in any case, kills me, interferes with what, in my living universe, is supposed to save me from death: childhood, science, among other things.

The Abjection of Self

If it be true that the abject simultaneously beseeches and pulverizes the subject, one can understand that it is experienced at the peak of its strength when that subject, weary of fruitless attempts to identify with something on the outside, finds the impossible within; when it finds that the impossible constitutes its very *being*, that it *is* none other than abject. The abjection of self would be the culminating form of that experience of the subject to which it is revealed that all its objects are based merely on the inaugural *loss* that laid the foundations of its own being. There is nothing like the abjection of self to show that all abjection is in fact recognition of the *want* on which any being, meaning, language, or desire is founded. One always passes too quickly over this word, "want," and today psychoanalysts are finally taking into account only its more or less fetishized product, the "object of want." But if one imagines (and imagine one must, for it is the working of imagination whose foundations are being laid here) the experience of *want* itself as logically preliminary to being and object—to the being of the object—then one understands that abjection, and even more so abjection of self, is its only signified. Its signifier, then, is none but literature. Mystical Christendom turned this abjection of self into the ultimate proof of humility before God, witness Elizabeth of Hungary who "though a great princess, delighted in nothing so much as in abasing herself."[1]

The question remains as to the ordeal, a secular one this time, that abjection can constitute for someone who, in what is termed knowledge of castration, turning away from perverse dodges, presents himself with his own body and ego as the most precious nonobjects; they are no longer seen in their own right but forfeited, abject. The termination of analysis can lead us there, as we shall see. Such are the pangs and delights of masochism.

Essentially different from "uncanniness," more violent, too, abjection is elaborated through a failure to recognize its kin; nothing is familiar, not even the shadow of a memory. I imagine a child who has swallowed up his parents too soon, who frightens himself on that account, "all by himself," and, to save himself, rejects and throws up everything that is given to him—all gifts, all objects. He has, he could have, a sense of the abject. Even before things for him *are*—hence before they are signifiable—he drives them out, dominated by drive as he is, and constitutes his own territory, edged by the abject. A sacred configuration. Fear cements his compound, conjoined to another world, thrown up, driven out, forfeited. What he has swallowed up instead of maternal love is an emptiness, or rather a maternal hatred without a word for the words of the father; that is what he tries to cleanse himself of, tirelessly. What solace does he come upon within such loathing? Perhaps a father, existing but unsettled, loving but unsteady, merely an apparition but an apparition that remains. Without him the holy brat would probably have no sense of the sacred; a blank subject, he would remain, discomfited, at the dump for nonobjects that are always forfeited, from which, on the contrary, fortified by abjection, he tries to extricate himself. For he is not mad, he through whom the abject exists. Out of the daze that has petrified him before the untouchable, impossible, absent body of the mother, a daze that has cut off his impulses from their objects, that is, from their representations, out of such daze he causes, along with loathing, one word to crop up—fear. The phobic has no other object than the abject. But that word, "fear"—a fluid haze, an elusive clamminess—no sooner has it cropped up than it shades off like a mirage and permeates all words of the language with nonexistence, with a hallucinatory, ghostly glimmer. Thus, fear having been bracketed, discourse will seem tenable only if it ceaselessly confronts that otherness, a burden both repellent and repelled, a deep well of memory that is unapproachable and intimate: the abject.

Beyond the Unconscious

Put another way, it means that there are lives not sustained by *desire*, as desire is always for objects. Such lives are based on *exclusion*. They are clearly distinguishable from those understood as neurotic or psychotic, articulated by *negation* and its modalities, *transgression, denial*, and *repudiation*. Their dynamics challenges the theory of the unconscious, seeing that the latter is dependent upon a dialectic of negativity.

The theory of the unconscious, as is well known, presupposes a repression of contents (affects and presentations) that, thereby, do not have access to consciousness but effect within the subject modifications, either of speech (parapraxes, etc.), or of the body (symptoms), or both (hallucinations, etc.). As correlative to the notion of *repression*, Freud put forward that of *denial* as a means of figuring out neurosis, that of *rejection* (*repudiation*) as a means of situating psychosis. The asymmetry of the two repressions becomes more marked owing to denial's bearing on the object whereas repudiation affects desire itself (Lacan, in perfect keeping with Freud's thought, interprets that as "repudiation of the Name of the Father").

Yet, facing the ab-ject and more specifically phobia and the splitting of the ego, one might ask if those articulations of negativity germane to the unconscious (inherited by Freud from philosophy and psychology) have not become inoperative. The "unconscious" contents remain here *excluded* but in strange fashion: not radically enough to allow for a secure differentiation between subject and object, and yet clearly enough for a defensive *position* to be established—one that implies a refusal but also a sublimating elaboration. As if the fundamental opposition were between I and Other or, in more archaic fashion, between Inside and Outside. As if such an opposition subsumed the one between Conscious and Unconscious, elaborated on the basis of neuroses.

Owing to the ambiguous opposition I/Other, Inside/Outside—an opposition that is vigorous but pervious, violent but uncertain—there are contents, "normally" unconscious in neurotics, that become explicit if not conscious in "borderline" patients' speeches and behavior. Such contents are often openly manifested through symbolic practices, without by the same token being integrated into the judging consciousness of those particular subjects. Since they make the conscious/unconscious distinction irrelevant, borderline subjects and their speech constitute propitious ground for a sublimating discourse ("aesthetic" or "mystical," etc.), rather than a scientific or rationalist one.

An Exile Who Asks, "Where?"

The one by whom the abject exists is thus a *deject* who places (himself), *separates* (himself), situates (himself), and therefore *strays* instead of getting his bearings, desiring, belonging, or refusing. Situationist in a sense, and not without laughter—since laughing is a way of placing or displacing abjection. Necessarily dichotomous, somewhat Manichaean, he divides, excludes, and without, properly speaking, wishing to know his abjections is not at all unaware of them. Often, moreover, he includes himself among them, thus casting within himself the scalpel that carries out his separations.

Instead of sounding himself as to his "being," he does so concerning his place: "*Where* am I?" instead of "*Who* am I?" For the space that engrosses the deject, the excluded, is never *one*, nor *homogeneous*, nor *totalizable*, but essentially divisible, foldable, and catastrophic. A deviser of territories, languages, works, the *deject* never stops demarcating his universe whose fluid confines—for they are constituted of a nonobject, the abject—constantly question his solidity and impel him to start afresh. A tireless builder, the deject is in short a *stray*. He is on a journey, during the night, the end of which keeps receding. He has a sense of the danger, of the loss that the pseudo-object attracting him represents for him, but he cannot help taking the risk at the very moment he sets himself apart. And the more he strays, the more he is saved.

Time: Forgetfulness and Thunder

For it is out of such straying on excluded ground that he draws his jouissance. The abject from which he does not cease separating is for him, in short, a *land of oblivion* that is constantly remembered. Once upon blotted-out time, the abject must have been a magnetized pole of covetousness. But the ashes of oblivion now serve as a screen and reflect aversion, repugnance. The clean and proper (in the sense of incorporated and incorporable) becomes filthy, the sought-after turns into the banished, fascination into shame. Then, forgotten time crops up suddenly and condenses into a flash of lightning an operation that, if it were thought out, would involve bringing together the two opposite terms but, on account of that flash, is discharged like thunder. The time of abjection is double: a time of oblivion and thunder, of veiled infinity and the moment when revelation bursts forth.

Jouissance and Affect

Jouissance, in short. For the stray considers himself as equivalent to a Third Party. He secures the latter's judgment, he acts on the strength of its power in order to condemn, he grounds himself on its law to tear the veil of oblivion but also to set up its object as inoperative. As jettisoned. Parachuted by the Other. A ternary structure, if you wish, held in keystone position by the Other, but a "structure" that is skewed, a topology of catastrophe. For, having provided itself with an alter ego, the Other no longer has a grip on the three apices of the triangle where subjective homogeneity resides; and so, it jettisons the object into an abominable real, inaccessible except through jouissance. It follows that jouissance alone causes the abject to exist as such. One does not know it, one does not desire it, one joys in it (*on en jouit*). Violently and painfully. A passion. And, as in jouissance where the object of desire, known as object *a* (in Lacan's terminology), bursts with the shattered mirror where the ego gives up its image in order to contemplate itself in the Other, there is nothing either objective or objectal to the abject. It is simply a frontier, a repulsive gift that the Other, having become alter ego, drops so that "I" does not disappear in it but finds, in that sublime alienation, a forfeited existence. Hence a jouissance in which the subject is swallowed up but in which the Other, in return, keeps the subject from foundering by making it repugnant. One thus understands why so many victims of the abject are its fascinated victims—if not its submissive and willing ones.

We may call it a border; abjection is above all ambiguity. Because, while releasing a hold, it does not radically cut off the subject from what threatens it—on the contrary, abjection acknowledges it to be in perpetual danger. But also because abjection itself is a composite of judgment and affect, of condemnation and yearning, of signs and drives. Abjection preserves what existed in the archaism of preobjectal relationship, in the immemorial violence with which a body becomes separated from another body in order to be—maintaining that night in which the outline of the signified thing vanishes and where only the imponderable affect is carried out. To be sure, if I am affected by what does not yet appear to me as a thing, it is because laws, connections, and even structures of meaning govern and condition me. That order, that glance, that voice, that gesture, which enact the law for my frightened body, constitute and bring about an effect and not yet a sign. I speak to it in vain in order to exclude it from what will no longer be, for myself, a world that can be assimilated. Obviously, *I am* only *like* someone else: mimetic logic of the advent of the ego, objects, and signs. But when I *seek* (myself), *lose* (myself), or experience *jouissance*—then "I" is *heterogeneous*. Discomfort, unease, dizziness stemming from an ambiguity that, through the violence of a revolt *against*, demarcates a space out of which signs and objects arise. Thus braided, woven, ambivalent, a heterogeneous flux marks out a territory that I can call my own because the Other, having dwelt in me as alter ego, points it out to me through loathing.

This means once more that the heterogeneous flow, which portions the abject and sends back abjection, already dwells in a human animal that has been highly altered. I experience abjection only if an Other has settled in place and stead of what will be "me." Not at all an other with whom I identify and incorporate, but an Other who precedes and possesses me, and through such possession causes me to be. A possession previous to my advent: a being-there of the symbolic that a father might or might not embody. Significance is indeed inherent in the human body.

At the Limit of Primal Repression

If, on account of that Other, a space becomes demarcated, separating the abject from what will be a subject and its objects, it is because a repression that one might call "primal" has been effected prior to the springing forth of the ego, of its objects and representations. The latter, in turn, as they depend on another repression, the "secondary" one, arrive only a posteriori on an enigmatic foundation that has already been marked off; its return, in a phobic, obsessional, psychotic guise, or more generally and in more imaginary fashion in the shape of *abjection*, notifies us of the limits of the human universe.

On such limits and at the limit one could say that there is no unconscious, which is elaborated when representations and affects (whether or not tied to representations) shape a logic. Here, on the contrary, consciousness has not assumed its rights and transformed into signifiers those fluid demarcations of yet unstable territories where an "I" that is taking shape is ceaselessly straying. We are no longer within the sphere of the unconscious but at the limit of primal repression that, nevertheless, has discovered an intrinsically corporeal and already signifying brand, symptom, and sign: repugnance, disgust, abjection. There is an effervescence of object and sign—not of desire but of intolerable significance; they tumble over into non-sense or the impossible real, but they appear even so in spite of "myself" (which is not) as abjection.

Premises of the Sign, Linings of the Sublime

Let us pause a while at this juncture. If the abject is already a wellspring of sign for a nonobject, on the edges of primal repression, one can understand its skirting the somatic symptom on the one hand and sublimation on the other. The *symptom*: a language that gives up, a structure within the body, a nonassimilable alien, a monster, a tumor, a cancer that the listening devices of the unconscious do not hear, for its strayed subject is huddled outside the paths of desire. *Sublimation*, on the contrary, is nothing else than the possibility of naming the prenominal, the preobjectal, which are in fact only a transnominal, a transobjectal. In the symptom, the abject permeates me, I become abject. Through sublimation, I keep it under control. The abject is edged with the sublime. It is not the same moment on the journey, but the same subject and speech bring them into being.

For the sublime has no object either. When the starry sky, a vista of open seas or a stained glass window shedding purple beams fascinate me, there is a cluster of meaning, of colors, of words, of caresses, there are light touches, scents, sighs, cadences that arise, shroud me, carry me away, and sweep me beyond the things that I see, hear, or think. The "sublime" object dissolves in the raptures of a bottomless memory. It is such a memory, which, from stopping point to stopping point, remembrance to remembrance, love to love, transfers that object to the refulgent point of the dazzlement in which I stray in order to be. As soon as I perceive it, as soon as I name it, the sublime triggers—it has always already triggered—a spree of perceptions and words that expands memory boundlessly. I then forget the point of departure and find myself removed to a secondary universe, set off from the one where "I" am— delight and loss. Not at all short of but always with and through perception and words, the sublime is a *something added* that expands us, overstrains us, and causes us to be both *here*, as dejects, and *there*, as others and sparkling. A divergence, an impossible bounding. Everything missed, joy—fascination.

Before the Beginning: Separation

The abject might then appear as the most *fragile* (from a synchronic point of view), the most *archaic* (from a diachronic one) sublimation of an "object" still inseparable from drives. The abject is that pseudo-object that is made up *before* but appears only *within* the gaps of secondary repression. *The abject would thus be the "object" of primal repression.*

But what is primal repression? Let us call it the ability of the speaking being, always already haunted by the Other, to divide, reject, repeat. Without *one* division, *one* separation, *one* subject/object having been constituted (not yet, or no longer yet). Why? Perhaps because of maternal anguish, unable to be satiated within the encompassing symbolic.

The abject confronts us, on the one hand, with those fragile states where man strays on the territories of *animal*. Thus, by way of abjection, primitive societies have marked out a precise area of their culture in order to remove it from the threatening world of animals or animalism, which were imagined as representatives of sex and murder.

The abject confronts us, on the other hand, and this time within our personal archeology, with our earliest attempts to release the hold of *maternal* entity even before ex-isting outside of her, thanks to the autonomy of language. It is a violent, clumsy breaking away, with the constant risk of falling back under the sway of a power as securing as it is stifling. The difficulty a mother has in acknowledging (or being acknowledged by) the symbolic realm—in other words, the problem she has with the phallus that her father or her husband stands for—is not such as to help the future subject leave the natural mansion. The child can serve its mother as token of her own authentication; there is, however, hardly any reason for her to serve as go-between for it to become autonomous and authentic in its turn. In such close combat, the symbolic light that a third party, eventually the father, can contribute helps the future subject, the more so if it happens to be endowed with a robust supply of drive energy, in pursuing a reluctant struggle against what, having been the mother, will turn into an abject. Repelling, rejecting; repelling itself, rejecting itself. Ab-jecting.

In this struggle, which fashions the human being, the *mimesis*, by means of which he becomes homologous to another in order to become himself, is in short logically and chronologically secondary. Even before being *like*, "I" am not but do *separate, reject, ab-ject*. Abjection, with a meaning broadened to take in subjective diachrony, *is a precondition of narcissism*. It is coexistent with it and causes it to be permanently brittle. The more or less beautiful image in which I behold or recognize myself rests upon an abjection that sunders it as soon as repression, the constant watchman, is relaxed.

The "Chora," Receptacle of Narcissism

Let us enter, for a moment, into that Freudian *aporia* called primal repression. Curious primacy, where what is repressed cannot really be held down, and where what represses always already borrows its strength and authority from what is apparently very secondary: language. Let us therefore not speak of primacy but of the instability of the symbolic function in its most significant aspect—the prohibition placed on the maternal body (as a defense against autoeroticism and incest taboo). Here, drives hold sway and constitute a strange space that I shall name, after Plato (*Timaeus* 48–53), a *chora*, a receptacle.

For the benefit of the ego or its detriment, drives, whether life drives or death drives, serve to correlate that "not yet" ego with an "object" in order to establish both of them. Such a process, while dichotomous (inside/outside, ego/not ego) and repetitive, has nevertheless something centripetal about it: it aims to settle the ego as center of a solar system of objects. If, by dint of coming back toward the center, the drive's motion should eventually become centrifugal, hence fasten on the Other and come into being as sign so as to produce meaning—that is, literally speaking, exorbitant.

But from that moment on, while I recognize my image as sign and change in order to signify, another economy is instituted. The sign represses the *chora* and its eternal return. Desire alone will henceforth be witness to that "primal" pulsation. But desire ex-patriates the *ego* toward an *other* subject and accepts the exactness of the ego only as narcissistic. Narcissism then appears as a regression to a position set back from the other, a return to a self-contemplative, conservative, self-sufficient haven. Actually, such narcissism never is the wrinkleless image of the Greek youth in a quiet fountain. The conflicts of drives muddle its bed, cloud its water, and bring forth everything that, by not becoming integrated with a given system of signs, is abjection for it.

Abjection is therefore a kind of *narcissistic crisis*: it is witness to the ephemeral aspect of the state called "narcissism" with reproachful jealousy, heaven knows why; what is more, abjection gives narcissism (the thing and the concept) its classification as "seeming."

Nevertheless, it is enough that a prohibition, which can be a superego, block the desire craving an other—or that this other, as its role demands, not fulfill it—for desire and its signifiers to turn back toward the "same," thus clouding the waters of Narcissus. It is precisely at the moment of narcissistic perturbation (all things considered, the permanent state of the speaking being, if he would only hear himself speak) that secondary repression, with its reserve of symbolic means, attempts to transfer to its own account, which has thus been overdrawn, the resources of primal repression. The archaic economy is brought into full light of day, signified, verbalized. Its strategies (rejecting, separating, repeating/abjecting) hence find a symbolic existence, and the very logic of the symbolic—arguments, demonstrations, proofs, etc.—must conform to it. It is then that the object ceases to be circumscribed, reasoned with, thrust aside: it appears as abject.

Two seemingly contradictory causes bring about the narcissistic crisis that provides, along with its truth, a view of the abject. *Too much strictness on the part of the Other*, confused with the One and the Law. The *lapse of the Other*, which shows through the breakdown of objects of desire. In both instances, the abject appears in order to uphold "I" within the Other. The abject is the violence of mourning for an "object" that has always already been lost. The abject shatters the wall of repression and its judgments. It takes the ego back to its source on the abominable limits from which, in order to be, the ego has broken away—it assigns it a source in the non-ego, drive, and death. Abjection is a resurrection that has gone through death (of the ego). It is an alchemy that transforms death drive into a start of life, of new significance.

Perverse or artistic

The abject is related to perversion. The sense of abjection that I experience is anchored in the superego. The abject is perverse because it neither gives up nor assumes a prohibition, a rule, or a law, but turns them aside, misleads, corrupts, uses them, takes advantage of them, the better to deny them. It kills in the name of life—a progressive despot; it lives at the behest of death—an operator in genetic experimentations; it curbs the other's suffering for its own profit—a cynic (and a psychoanalyst); it establishes narcissistic power while pretending to reveal the abyss—an artist who practices his art as a "business." Corruption is its most common, most obvious appearance. That is the socialized appearance of the abject.

An unshakable adherence to Prohibition and Law is necessary if that perverse interspace of abjection is to be hemmed in and thrust aside.

Religion, Morality, Law. Obviously always arbitrary, more or less; unfailingly oppressive, rather more than less; laboriously prevailing, more and more so.

Contemporary literature does not take their place. Rather, it seems to be written out of the untenable aspects of perverse or superego positions. It acknowledges the impossibility of Religion, Morality, and Law—their power play, their necessary and absurd seeming. Like perversion, it takes advantage of them, gets round them, and makes sport of them. Nevertheless, it maintains a distance where the abject is concerned. The writer, fascinated by the abject, imagines its logic, projects himself into it, introjects it, and as a consequence perverts language—style and content. But on the other hand, as the sense of abjection is both the abject's judge and accomplice, this is also true of the literature that confronts it. One might thus say that with such a literature there takes place a crossing over of the dichotomous categories of Pure and Impure, Prohibition and Sin, Morality and Immorality.

For the subject firmly settled in its superego, a writing of this sort is necessarily implicated in the interspace that characterizes perversion; and for that reason, it gives rise in turn to abjection. And yet, such texts call for a softening of the superego. Writing them implies an ability to imagine the abject, that is, to see oneself in its place and to thrust it aside only by means of the displacements of verbal play. It is only after his death, eventually, that the writer of abjection will escape his condition of waste, reject, abject. Then, he will either sink into oblivion or attain the rank of incommensurate ideal. Death would thus be the chief curator of our imaginary museum; it would protect us in the last resort from the abjection that contemporary literature claims to expend while uttering it. Such a protection, which gives its quietus to abjection, but also perhaps to the bothersome, incandescent stake of the literary phenomenon itself, which, raised to the status of the sacred, is severed from its specificity. Death thus keeps house in our contemporary universe. By purifying (us from) literature, it establishes our secular religion.

As Abjection—So the Sacred

Abjection accompanies all religious structurings and reappears, to be worked out in a new guise, at the time of their collapse. Several structurations of abjection should be distinguished, each one determining a specific form of the sacred.

Abjection appears as a rite of defilement and pollution in the paganism that accompanies societies with a dominant or surviving matrilineal character. It takes on the form of the *exclusion* of a substance (nutritive or linked to sexuality), the execution of which coincides with the sacred since it sets it up.

Abjection persists as *exclusion* or taboo (dietary or other) in monotheistic religions, Judaism in particular, but drifts over to more "secondary" forms such as *transgression* (of the Law) within the same monotheistic economy. It finally encounters, with Christian sin, a dialectic elaboration, as it becomes integrated in the Christian Word as a threatening otherness—but always nameable, always totalizable.

The various means of *purifying* the abject—the various catharses—make up the history of religions, and end up with that catharsis par excellence called art, both on the far and near side of religion. Seen from that standpoint, the artistic experience, which is rooted in the abject it utters and by the same token purifies, appears as the essential component of religiosity. That is perhaps why it is destined to survive the collapse of the historical forms of religions.

Outside of the Sacred, the Abject Is Written

In the contemporary practice of the West and owing to the crisis in Christianity, abjection elicits more archaic resonances that are culturally prior to sin; through them it again assumes its biblical status, and beyond it that of defilement in primitive societies. In a world in which the Other has collapsed, the aesthetic task—a descent into the foundations of the symbolic construct—amounts to retracing the fragile limits of the speaking being, closest to its dawn, to the bottomless "primacy" constituted by primal repression. Through that experience, which is nevertheless managed by the Other, "subject" and "object" push each other away, confront each other, collapse, and start again—inseparable, contaminated, condemned, at the boundary of what is assimilable, thinkable: abject. Great modern literature unfolds over that terrain: Dostoyevsky, Lautréamont, Proust, Artaud, Kafka, Céline.

Catharsis and Analysis

That *abjection*, which modernity has learned to repress, dodge, or fake, appears fundamental once the analytic point of view is assumed. Lacan says so when he links that word to the *saintliness* of the analyst, a linkage in which the only aspect of humor that remains is blackness.[2]

One must keep open the wound where he or she who enters into the analytic adventure is located—a wound that the professional establishment, along with the cynicism of the times and of institutions, will soon manage to close up. There is nothing initiatory in that rite, if one understands by "initiation" the accession to a purity that the posture of *death* guaranteed (as in Plato's *Phaedo*) or the unadulterated treasure of the "pure signifier" (as is the gold of truth in *The Republic*, or the pure separatism of the statesman in the *Statesman*). It is rather a heterogeneous, corporeal, and verbal ordeal of fundamental incompleteness: a "gaping," "less One." For the unstabilized subject who comes out of that— like a crucified person opening up the stigmata of its desiring body to a speech that structures only on condition that it let go—any signifying or human phenomenon, insofar as it *is*, appears in its being as abjection. For what impossible *catharsis*? Freud, early in his career, used the same word to refer to a therapeutics, the rigor of which was to come out later.

With Plato and Aristotle

The analyst is thus and forever sent back to the question that already haunted Plato when he wanted to take over where Apollonian or Dionysiac religion left off.[3] Purification is something only the Logos is capable. But is that to be done in the manner of the *Phaedo*, stoically separating oneself from a body whose substance and passions are sources of impurity? Or rather, as in the *Sophist*, after having sorted out the worst from the best; or after the fashion of the *Philebus* by leaving the doors wide open to impurity, provided the eyes of the mind remain focused on truth? In such a case, pleasure, having become pure and true through the harmony of color and form as in the case of accurate and beautiful geometric form, has nothing in common, as the philosopher says, with "the pleasure of scratching" (*Philebus* 51).

Catharsis seems to be a concern that is intrinsic to philosophy, insofar as the latter is an ethics and unable to forget Plato. Even if the *mixture* seems inevitable toward the end of the Platonic course, it is the mind alone, as harmonious wisdom, that insures purity: catharsis has been transformed, where transcendental idealism is concerned, into philosophy. Of the cathartic incantation peculiar to mysteries, Plato has kept only, as we all know, the very uncertain role of poets whose frenzy would be useful to the state only after having been evaluated, sorted out, and purified in its turn by wise men.

Aristotelian catharsis is closer to sacred incantation. It is the one that has bequeathed its name to the common, aesthetic concept of catharsis. Through the mimesis of passions—ranging from enthusiasm to suffering—in "language with pleasurable accessories," the most important of which being *rhythm* and *song* (see the *Poetics*), the soul reaches *orgy* and *purity* at the same time. What is involved is a purification of body and soul by means of a heterogeneous and complex circuit, going from "bile" to "fire," from "manly warmth" to the "enthusiasm" of the "mind." Rhythm and song hence arouse the impure, the other of mind, the passionate-corporeal-sexual-virile, but they harmonize it, arrange it differently from the wise man's knowledge. They thus soothe frenzied outbursts (Plato, in the *Laws*, allowed such use of rhythm and meter only to the mother rocking her child), by contributing an *external* rule, a poetic one, which fills the gap, inherited from Plato, between body and soul. To Platonic *death*, which owned, so to speak, the state of purity, Aristotle opposed the act of *poetic purification*—in itself an impure process that protects from the abject only by dint of being immersed in it. The abject, mimed through sound and meaning, is *repeated*. Getting rid of it is out of the question—the final Platonic lesson has been understood: one does not get rid of the impure; one can, however, bring it into being a second time, and differently from the original impurity. It is a repetition through rhythm and song, therefore through what is not yet, or no longer is "meaning," but arranges, defers, differentiates and organizes, harmonizes pathos, bile, warmth, and enthusiasm. Benveniste translates "rhythm" by "trace" and "concatenation" (*enchaînement*). Prometheus is "rhythmical," and we call him "bound" (*enchaîné*). An attachment on the near and far side of language. Aristotle seems to say that there is a discourse of sex and that is not the discourse of knowledge—it is the only possible catharsis. That discourse is audible, and through the speech that it mimics it repeats on another register what the latter does not say.

Philosophical Sadness and the Spoken Disaster of the Analyst

Poetic catharsis, which for more than two thousand years behaved as an underage sister of philosophy, face to face and incompatible with it, takes us away from purity, hence from Kantian ethics, which has long gov-

erned modern codes and remains more faithful to a certain Platonic stoicism. By means of the "universalizing of maxims," as is well known, the
Kant of the *Foundations of the Metaphysics of Ethics* or of the
Metaphysical Principles of Virtue advocated an "ethical gymnastics" in
order to give us, by means of consciousness, control over our defilements
and, through that very consciousness, making us free and joyous.

More skeptical and, from a certain point of view, more Aristotelian,
Hegel, on the contrary, rejects a "calculation" that claims to eliminate
defilement, for the latter seems *fundamental* to him. Probably echoing
the Greek polis, he conceives of no other ethics than that of the *act*. Also
distrustful, however, of those fine aestheticizing souls who find purity in
the elaboration of empty forms, he obviously does not hold to the
mimetic and orgiastic catharsis of Aristotle. It is in the *historical* act that
Hegel sees fundamental impurity being expended; as a matter of fact, the
latter is a sexual impurity whose historical achievement consists in marriage. But—and this is where transcendental idealism, too, sadly comes
to an end—here it is that desire (*Lust*), thus normalized in order to escape
abject concupiscence (*Begierde*), sinks into a banality that is sadness and
silence. How come? Hegel does not condemn impurity because it is exterior to ideal consciousness; more profoundly—but also more craftily—he
thinks that it can and should get rid of itself through the historico-social
act. If he thereby differs from Kant, he nevertheless shares his condemnation of (sexual) impurity. He agrees with his aim to keep consciousness
apart from defilement, which, nevertheless, dialectically constitutes it.
Reabsorbed into the trajectory of the Idea, what can defilement become
if not the negative side of consciousness—that is, lack of communication
and speech? In other words, defilement as reabsorbed in marriage
becomes sadness. In so doing, it has not strayed too far from its logic,
according to which it is a border of discourse—a silence.[4]

It is obvious that the analyst, from the abyss of his silence, brushes
against the ghost of the sadness Hegel saw in sexual normalization. Such
sadness is the more obvious to him as his ethics is rigorous—founded, as
it must be in the West, on the remains of transcendental idealism. But one
can also argue that the Freudian stance, which is dualistic and dissolving,
unsettles those foundations. In that sense, it causes the sad, analytic
silence to hover above a strange, foreign discourse, which, strictly speaking, shatters verbal communication (made up of a knowledge and a truth
that are nevertheless heard) by means of a device that mimics terror,
enthusiasm, or orgy, and is more closely related to rhythm and song than
it is to the World. There is mimesis (some say identification) in the ana-

lytic passage through castration. And yet it is necessary that the analyst's interpretative speech (and not only his literary or theoretical bilingualism) be affected by it in order to be analytical. As counterpoise to a purity that found its bearings in disillusioned sadness, it is the "poetic" unsettlement of analytic utterance that testifies to its closeness to, cohabitation with, and "knowledge" of abjection.

I am thinking, in short, of the completely mimetic *identification* (transference and countertransference) of the analyst with respect to analysands. That identification allows for securing in their place what, when parcelled out, makes them suffering and barren. It allows one to regress back to the affects that can be heard in the breaks in discourse, to provide rhythm, too, to concatenate (is that what "to become conscious" means?) the gaps of a speech saddened because it turned its back on its abject meaning. If there is analytic jouissance it is there, in the thoroughly poetic mimesis that runs through the architecture of speech and extends from coenesthetic image to logical and phantasmatic articulations. Without, for that matter, biologizing language and while breaking away from identification by means of interpretation, analytic speech is one that becomes "incarnate" in the full sense of the term. On that condition only, it is "cathartic"—meaning thereby that it is the equivalent, for the analyst as well as for the analysand, not of purification but of rebirth with and against abjection.

NOTES

1. Francis de Sales, *Introduction to a Devout Life*, Thomas S. Kepler, tr. (New York: World, 1952), p. 125.
Modified to conform to the French text, which reads, "l'abjection de soy-mesme."—Trans.
2. Jacques Lacan, *Télévision* (Paris: Seuil, 1974), p. 28.
3. In connection with catharsis in the Greek world, see Louis Molinier, *Le Pur et l'impur dans la pensée des Grecs* (Paris: Klincksieck, 1952).
4. See A. Philonenko, "Note sur les concepts de souillure et de pureté dans l'idéalisme allemand," *Les Etudes Philosophiques* 4 (1972): 481–93.

From Filth to Defilement

> *Abjection [. . .] is merely the inability to assume with*
> *sufficient strength the imperative act of excluding*
> *abject things (and that act establishes the foundations*
> *of collective existence).*
> *[. . .] The act of exclusion has the same meaning as*
> *social or divine sovereignty, but it is not located on the*
> *same level; it is precisely located in the domain of*
> *things and not, like sovereignty, in the domain of per-*
> *sons. It differs from the latter in the same way that*
> *anal eroticism differs from sadism.*
> —*Georges Bataille*, Essais de sociologie

Mother-Phobia and the Murder of the Father

In psychoanalysis as in anthropology one commonly links the sacred and the establishment of the religious bond that it presupposes with *sacrifice*. Freud tied the sacred to taboo and totemism,[1] and concluded that, "we consider ourselves justified in substituting the father for the totem animal in the male's formula of totemism."[2] We are all familiar with that Freudian thesis as to the murder of the father and, more specifically, with the one he develops in *Moses and Monotheism*: in connection with Judaic religion the archaic father and master of the primeval horde is killed by the conspiring sons who, later seized with a sense of guilt for an act that was upon the whole inspired by ambivalent feelings, end up restoring paternal authority, no longer as an arbitrary power but as a right; thus renouncing the possession of all women in their turn, they establish at one stroke the sacred, exogamy, and society.

There is nevertheless a strange slippage in the Freudian argument, one that has not been sufficiently noticed. Relying on numerous readings in ethnology and the history of religions, more specifically on Frazer and Robertson Smith, Freud notes that the morality of man starts with "the two taboos of totemism"—*murder* and *incest*.[3] *Totem and Taboo* begins with an evocation of the "dread of incest," and Freud discusses it at length in connection with taboo, totemism, and more specifically with food and sex prohibitions. The woman- or mother-image haunts a large part of that book and keeps shaping its background even when, relying on the testimony of obsessional neurotics, Freud slips from dread (p. 23:

"His incest dread"; p. 24: "the incest dread of savages"; p. 161: "The interpretation of incest dread," "This dread of incest") to the inclusion of dread symptom in obsessional neurosis. At the same time he leaves off speculating on incest ("we do not know the origin of incest dread and do not even know how to guess at it," p. 162) in order to center his conclusion in the second taboo, the one against murder, which he reveals to be the murder of the father.

That such a murderous event could be as much mythical as endowed with founding properties, that it should be both the keystone to the desire henceforth known as Oedipal and a severance that sets up a signifier admitting of logical concatenation, analytic attention now knows only too well. Divergences from and even contradictions of this Freudian thesis[4] are finally no more than variants and confirmations. What will concern me here is not that aspect of the Freudian position, which I shall consider to have been logically established. I shall attempt to question the other side of the religious phenomenon, the one that Freud points to when he brings up dread, incest, and the mother; one that, even though it is presented as the second taboo founding religion, nevertheless disappears during the final elucidation of the problem.

The Two-sided Sacred

Could the sacred be, whatever its variants, a two-sided formation? One aspect founded by murder and the social bond made up of murder's guilt-ridden atonement, with all the projective mechanisms and obsessive rituals that accompany it; and another aspect, like a lining, more secret still and invisible, nonrepresentable, oriented toward those uncertain spaces of unstable identity, toward the fragility—both threatening and fusional—of the archaic dyad, toward the nonseparation of subject/object, on which language has no hold but one woven of fright and repulsion? One aspect is defensive and socializing, the other shows fear and undifferentiation. The similarities that Freud delineates between religion and obsessional neurosis would then involve the defensive side of the sacred. Now, to throw light on the subjective economy of its other side, it is phobia as such, and its drifting toward psychosis, that one would need to tackle head on.

That, at any rate, will be my point of departure. For we shall see, in a large number of rituals and discourses involved in making up the sacred—notably those dealing with *defilement* and its derivations in different religions—an attempt at *coding* the other taboo that the earliest

ethnologists and psychoanalysts viewed as presiding over social formations: beside death, *incest*. Lévi-Strauss's structural anthropology has
shown how all systems of knowledge in so-called primitive societies, and
myths in particular, are a later elaboration, within stages of symbolicity,
of the prohibition that weighs on incest and founds the signifying function as well as the social aggregate. What will concern me here is not the
socially productive value of the son-mother incest *prohibition* but the
alterations, within subjectivity and within the very symbolic competence,
implied by the *confrontation with the feminine* and the way in which
societies code themselves in order to accompany as far as possible the
speaking subject on that journey. Abjection, or the journey to the end of
the night.

Prohibited Incest vs. Coming Face to Face with the Unnameable

What we designate as "feminine," far from being a primeval essence, will
be seen as an "other" without a name, which subjective experience confronts when it does not stop at the appearance of its identity. Assuming
that any Other is appended to the triangulating function of the paternal
prohibition, what will be dealt with here, beyond and through the paternal function, is a coming face to face with an unnamable otherness—the
solid rock of jouissance and writing as well.

I shall set aside in this essay a different version of the confrontation
with the feminine, one that, going beyond abjection and fright, is enun-
ciated as ecstatic. "The light-suffused face of the young Persian god"
Freud refers to, and similarly, in a more secular fashion, Mallarmé's
claim to be that "startled hero," "merry" for having overcome the
"dishevelled tuft"—both point to another manner of coming to terms
with the unnamable. That kind of confrontation appears, where our civilization is concerned, only in a few rare flashes of writing. Céline's
laughter, beyond horror, also comes close to it, perhaps.

Narcissus and Murky Waters

Freud had strongly emphasized, at the outset of *Totem and Taboo*,
"man's deep aversion to his former incest wishes" (p. 24). He had
reminded us of the properties of the taboo: it is "sacred, consecrated; but
on the other hand it means uncanny, dangerous, forbidden and unclean"
(p. 26); as to the object of taboos, "The prohibition mostly concerns mat-

ters that are capable of enjoyment" (*Genussgefähig*) (p. 31), they include the "unclean" (p. 32). The contact avoidance that he observes in it nevertheless makes him think only of compulsion and its rituals, while the ambivalent hostility it harbors suggests to him paranoid projection. The two structures cause the threat that would be hovering over the subject to converge on the paternal apex—the one that prohibits, separates, prevents contact (between son and mother?). This hypothesis would suggest an idyllic dual relationship (mother-child), which, to the extent that the father prevents it, changes into an ulterior aversion to incest. The idea of such a soothing dual relationship crops up again when Freud draws up the hypothesis of a transition between the primeval horde and civilized society, transition in which the sons, out of "maternal love,"[5] and/or supported by "homosexual feelings and activities" (p. 186), would renounce mothers and sisters and set up an organization based at first on matriarchal law, and ultimately on patriarchal law.

Nevertheless there are other thoughts of Freud, from which he will not draw any conclusions, that allow one to progress in another direction. He first appears to refer states of fear and impurity to primary narcissism, a narcissism laden with hostility that does not yet know its limits. For we are dealing with imprecise boundaries in that place, at that moment, where pain is born out of an excess of fondness and a hate that, refusing to admit the satisfaction it also provides, is projected toward an other. Inside and outside are not precisely differentiated here, nor is language an active practice or the subject separated from the other. Melanie Klein will make of this area her privileged field of observation; it is well known that Winnicot found in it a fruitful terrain for the etiology of psychoses and "false selves" as well as for creation and play. But it is Freud indeed who blazes the trail. Let us read more carefully the following passages, which can be understood in another way than as preludes to the obsessional or paranoid structure.

> Under conditions whose nature has not yet been sufficiently established, internal perceptions of emotional and thought processes can be projected outwards in the same way as sense perceptions; they are thus employed for building up the external world, though they should by rights remain part of the internal world. This may have some genetic connection with the fact that the function of attention was originally directed not towards the internal world but towards the stimuli that stream in from the external world, and that that function's only information upon endopsychic processes was received from feelings of pleasure and unpleasure. It was not until a language

of abstract thought had been developed, that is to say, not until the sensory residues of verbal presentations had been linked to the internal processes, that the latter themselves gradually became capable of being perceived. Before that, owing to the projection outwards of internal perceptions, primitive men arrived at a picture of the external world which we, with our intensified conscious perception, have now to translate back into psychology.[6]

And further along, in a footnote:

The projected creations of primitive men resemble the personifications constructed by creative writers; for the latter externalize in the form of separate individuals the opposing instinctual impulses struggling within them.[7]

Incest and the Preverbal

Let me sum up. There would be a "beginning" preceding the word. Freud, echoing Goethe, says so at the end of *Totem and Taboo*: "In the beginning was the deed."[8] In that anteriority to language, the outside is elaborated by means of a projection from within, of which the only experience we have is one of pleasure and pain. An outside in the image of the inside, made of pleasure and pain. The nondistinctiveness of inside and outside would thus be unnamable, a border passable in both directions by pleasure and pain. Naming the latter, hence differentiating them, amounts to introducing language, which, just as it distinguishes pleasure from pain as it does all other oppositions, founds the separation inside/outside. And yet, there would be witnesses to the perviousness of the limit, artisans after a fashion who would try to tap that preverbal "beginning" within a word that is flush with pleasure and pain. They are *primitive man* through his ambivalences and the *poet* through the personification of his opposing states of feeling—but also perhaps through the rhetorical recasting of language that he effects and over which Freud, who says he is heedful and fascinated, never tarries. If the *murder* of the father is that historical event constituting the social code as such, that is, symbolic exchange and the exchange of women, its equivalent on the level of the subjective history of each individual is therefore the *advent of language*, which breaks with perviousness if not with the chaos that precedes it and sets up denomination as an exchange of linguistic signs. Poetic language would then be, contrary to murder and the univocity of verbal message, a reconciliation with what murder as well as names were separated from. It would be an attempt to symbolize the "beginning," an attempt to name the other facet of taboo: pleasure, pain. Are we finally dealing with incest?

Not quite, or not directly. When Freud again speaks, still in *Totem and Taboo*, "of the first beginnings in childhood" of libidinal trends, he asserts that "from the very first" "they are not yet directed toward any external object." As he did in *Three Essays on the Theory of Sexuality*, he calls autoeroticism the phase which gives way to object-choice. Nevertheless he inserts between the two stages a third one that will hold our attention.

> In this intermediary stage [. . .] the sexual impulses which formerly were separate have already formed into a unit and have also found an object; but this object is not external and foreign to the individual, but is his own ego, which is formed at this period.[9]

Fixation at this stage will be called *narcissism*. Let me try to point out the latent meanings of the definition. Narcissism is predicated on the existence of the *ego* but not of an *external object*; we are faced with the strange correlation between an entity (the ego) and its converse (the object), which is nevertheless not yet constituted; with an "ego" in relation to a nonobject.

Two consequences seem necessarily to follow from such a structure. On the one hand, the nonconstitution of the (outside) object as such renders unstable the ego's identity, which could not be precisely established without having differentiated from an other, from its object. The ego of primary narcissism is thus uncertain, fragile, threatened, subjected just as much as its nonobject to spatial ambivalence (inside/outside uncertainty) and to ambiguity of perception (pleasure/pain). On the other hand, one has to admit that such a narcissistic topology has no other underpinning in psychosomatic reality than the mother-child dyad. Now, though that relation has always been immersed in language, it allows the latter's inscription in the future subject only when biophysiological preconditions and the conditions of the Oedipus complex permit the setting up of a triadic relationship. The subject's *active* use of the signifier truly dates only from this moment. By stressing the inherence of language in the human state, by overestimating the subject's having been the slave of language since before his birth, one avoids noting the two moods, active and passive, according to which the subject is constituted in the signifier; by the same token one neglects the economy of narcissism in the elaboration and practice of the symbolic function.

That having been said, the archaic relation to the mother, narcissistic though it may be, is from my point of view of no solace to the protagonists and even less so to Narcissus. For the subject will always be marked by the uncertainty of his borders and of his affective valency as well; these are all the more determining as the paternal function was weak or even nonexistent, opening the door to perversion or psychosis. The edenic image of primary narcissism is perhaps a defensive negation elaborated by the neurotic subject when he sets himself under the aegis of the father. On the other hand, patients who have recently come to the couch (borderline cases, false selves, etc.) reveal the horror of that dual war, its terror, and the ensuing fear of being rotten, drained, or blocked.

Defilement as Ritual Rescue from Phobia and Psychosis

This abjection, which threatens the ego and results from the dual confrontation in which the uncertainties of primary narcissism reside—is it such as to motivate, if not explain, the incest dread of which Freud speaks? I believe so. If it be true, as Claude Lévi-Strauss has demonstrated, that the prohibition of incest has the logical import of founding, by means of that very prohibition, the discreteness of interchangeable units, thus establishing social order and the symbolic, I shall maintain that such a logical operation is carried out owing to a subjective benefit derived from it on the level of libidinal economy. Incest prohibition throws a veil over primary narcissism and the always ambivalent threats with which it menaces subjective identity. It cuts short the temptation to return, with abjection and jouissance, to that passivity status within the symbolic function, where the subject, fluctuating between inside and outside, pleasure and pain, word and deed, would find death, along with nirvana. Phobia alone, crossroad of neurosis and psychosis, and of course conditions verging on psychosis, testify to the appeal of such a risk; as if, with regard to it, the taboo barring contact with the mother and/or primary narcissism suddenly disintegrated.

A whole facet of the sacred, true lining of the sacrificial, compulsive, and paranoid side of religions, assumes the task of warding off that danger. This is precisely where we encounter the rituals of defilement and their derivatives, which, based on the feeling of abjection and all converging on the maternal, attempt to symbolize the other threat to the subject: that of being swamped by the dual relationship, thereby risking the loss not of a part (castration) but of the totality of his living being. The function of these religious rituals is to ward off the subject's fear of his very own identity sinking irretrievably into the mother.

The Poverty of Prohibition: Georges Bataille

The logic of prohibition, which founds the abject, has been outlined and made explicit by a number of anthropologists concerned with defilement and its sacred function in so-called primitive societies. And yet Georges Bataille remains the only one, to my knowledge, who has linked the production of the abject to *the weakness of that prohibition*, which, in other respects, necessarily constitutes each social order. He links abjection to "the inability to assume with sufficient strength the imperative act of excluding." Bataille is also the first to have specified that the plane of abjection is that of the *subject/object relationship* (and not subject/other subject) and that this archaism is rooted in anal eroticism rather than sadism.[10]

In the following, my point will be to suggest that such an archaic relationship to the *object* interprets, as it were, the relationship to the *mother*. Her being coded as "abject" points to the considerable importance some societies attribute to women (matrilineal or related filiation, endogamy, decisive role of procreation for the survival of the social group, etc.). The symbolic "exclusory prohibition" that, as a matter of fact, constitutes collective existence does not seem to have, in such cases, sufficient strength to dam up the abject or demoniacal potential of the feminine. The latter, precisely on account of its power, does not succeed in differentiating itself as *other* but threatens one's *own and clean self*, which is the underpinning of any organization constituted by exclusions and hierarchies.

But before outlining the *weakness of prohibition* and finally the *matrilineal order* that can be perceived in those communities, let us return to the anthropological delineation of the logic of *exclusion* that causes the abject to exist.

The Fundamental Work of Mary Douglas

Anthropologists, since Sir James George Frazer, W. Robertson Smith, Arnold van Gennep, and Alfred Reginald Radcliff-Brown, or Rudolf Steiner, have noted that secular "filth," which has become sacred "defilement," is the *excluded* on the basis of which religious prohibition is made up. In a number of primitive societies religious rites are purification rites whose function is to separate this or that social, sexual, or age group from another one, by means of prohibiting a filthy, defiling element. It is as if dividing lines were built up between society and a certain nature, as well as within the social aggregate, on the basis of the simple logic of *excluding filth*, which, promoted to the ritual level of *defilement*, founded the "self and clean" of each social group if not of each subject.

The purification rite appears then as that essential ridge, which, prohibiting the filthy object, extracts it from the secular order and lines it at once with a sacred facet. Because it is excluded as a possible object, asserted to be a nonobject of desire, abominated as ab-ject, as abjection, filth becomes defilement and founds on the henceforth released side of the "self and clean" the order that is thus only (and therefore, always already) sacred.

Defilement is what is jettisoned from the *symbolic system*. It is what escapes that social rationality, that logical order on which a social aggregate is based, which then becomes differentiated from a temporary agglomeration of individuals and, in short, constitutes a *classification system* or a *structure*.

The British anthropologist Mary Douglas begins by construing the "symbolic system" of religious prohibitions as a reflection of social divisions or even contradictions. As if the social being, coextensive with a "symbolic system," were always present to itself through its religious structures, which transfer its contradictions to the level of rituals. And yet, at a second stage of her thinking, Mary Douglas seems to find in the human body the prototype of that translucid being constituted by society as symbolic system. As a matter of fact, the explanation she gives of defilement assigns in turn different statuses to the human body: as ultimate cause of the socioeconomic causality, or simply as metaphor of that sociosymbolic being constituted by the human universe always present to itself. In so doing, however, Mary Douglas introduces willy-nilly the possibility of a subjective dimension within anthropological thought on religions. Where then lies the subjective value of those demarcations, exclusions, and prohibitions that establish the social organism as a "symbolic system"? The anthropological analysis of these phenomena was for Mary Douglas essentially *syntactic* at first: defilement is an element connected with the boundary, the margin, and the like, of an order. Henceforth she finds herself led to *semantic* problems: what is the *meaning* that such a border element assumes in other psychological, economic, and other, systems? At this moment of her thinking there emerges a concern to integrate Freudian data as semantic values connected with the psychosomatic functioning of the speaking subject. But a hasty assimilation of such data leads Mary Douglas naively to *reject* Freudian premises.

Finally, such a conception disregards both *subjective dynamics* (if one wishes to consider the social set in its utmost particularization) and *lan-*

guage as common and universal code (if one wishes to consider the aggregate and the social aggregates in their greatest generality). Lévi-Strauss's structural anthropology had one advantage among others; it linked a classification system, that is, a symbolic system, within a given society, to the order of language in its universality (binary aspects of phonology, signifier-signified dependencies and autonomies, etc.). In thus attaining universal truth, it nevertheless neglected the subjective dimension and/or the diachronic and synchronic implication of the speaking subject in the universal order of language.

Consequently, when I speak of *symbolic order*, I shall imply the dependence and articulation of the speaking subject in the order of language, such as they appear diachronically in the advent of each speaking being and as analytic listening discovers them synchronically in the speech of analysands. I shall consider as an established fact the analytic finding that different subjective structures are possible within that symbolic order, even if the different types recorded here seem subject to discussion and refinement, if not reevaluation.

One might advance the hypothesis that a (social) symbolic system *corresponds* to a specific structuration of the speaking subject in the *symbolic order*. To say that it "corresponds" leaves out questions of cause and effect; is the social determined by the subjective, or is it the other way around? The subjective-symbolic dimension that I am introducing does not therefore reinstate some deep or primary causality in the social *symbolic system*. It merely presents the *effects* and especially the *benefits* that accrue to the speaking subject from a precise symbolic organization; perhaps it explains what desiring motives are required in order to maintain a given social symbolics. Furthermore, it seems to me that such a statement of the problem has the advantage of not turning the "symbolic system" into a secular replica of the "preestablished harmony" or the "divine order"; rather, it roots it, as a *possible variant*, within the only concrete universality that defines the speaking being—the signifying process.

In the Same Fashion as Incest Prohibition

We are now in a position to recall what was suggested earlier concerning that border of subjectivity where the object no longer has, or does not yet have, a correlative function bonding the subject. On that location, to the contrary, the vacillating, fascinating, threatening, and dangerous object is silhouetted as nonbeing—as the abjection into which the speaking being is permanently engulfed.

Defilement, by means of the rituals that consecrate it, is perhaps, for a social aggregate, only one of the possible foundings of abjection bordering the frail identity of the speaking being. In this sense, abjection is coextensive with social and symbolic order, on the individual as well as on the collective level. By virtue of this, abjection, just like *prohibition of incest*, is a universal phenomenon; one encounters it as soon as the symbolic and/or social dimension of man is constituted, and this throughout the course of civilization. But abjection assumes specific shapes and different codings according to the various "symbolic systems." I shall attempt to examine some of its variants: *defilement, food taboo*, and *sin*.

Sociohistorical considerations can be brought in at a second stage. They will allow us to understand why that demarcating imperative, which is subjectively experienced as abjection, varies according to time and space, even though it is universal. I shall nevertheless stick to a typological argument. Prohibitions and conflicts that are specific to a given subject and ritualized by religion for a given type of body will appear as isomorphic with the prohibitions and conflicts of the social group within which they happen. Leaving aside the question of the priority of one over the other (the social does not represent the subjective any more than the subjective represents the social), I shall posit that they both follow the same logic, with no other goal than the survival of both group and subject.

My reflections will make their way through anthropological domains and analyses in order to aim at a deep psychosymbolic economy: the general, logical determination that underlies anthropological variants (social structures, marriage rules, religious rites) and evinces a specific economy of the speaking subject, no matter what its historical manifestations may be. In short, an economy that analytic listening and semanalytic deciphering discover in our contemporaries. Such a procedure seems to me to be directly in keeping with Freudian utilization of anthropological data. It inevitably entails a share of *disappointment* for the empirical-minded ethnologist. It does not unfold without a share of *fiction*, the nucleus of which, drawn from actuality and the subjective experience of the one who writes, is projected upon data collected from the life of other cultures, less to justify itself than to throw light on them by means of an interpretation to which they obviously offer resistance.

The Margin of a Floating Structure

Taking a closer look at defilement, as Mary Douglas has done, one ascertains the following. In the first place, filth is not a quality in itself, but it applies only to what relates to a *boundary* and, more particularly, represents the object jettisoned out of that boundary, its other side, a margin.

> Matter issuing from them [the orifices of the body] is marginal stuff of the most obvious kind. Spittle, blood, milk, urine, faeces or tears by simply issuing forth have traversed the boundary of the body. [. . .] The mistake is to treat bodily margins in isolation from all other margins.[11]

The potency of pollution is therefore not an inherent one; it is proportional to the potency of the prohibition that founds it.

> It follows from this that pollution is a type of danger which is not likely to occur except where the lines of structure, cosmic or social, are clearly defined.[12]

Finally, even if human beings are involved with it, the dangers entailed by defilement are not within their power to deal with but depend on a power "inhering in the structure of ideas."[13] Let us posit that defilement is an objective evil undergone by the subject. Or, to put it another way, the danger of filth represents for the subject the risk to which the very symbolic order is permanently exposed, to the extent that it is a device of discriminations, of differences. But from where and from what does the threat issue? From nothing else but an equally objective reason, even if individuals can contribute to it, and which would be, in a way, the frailty of the symbolic order itself. A threat issued from the prohibitions that found the inner and outer borders in which and through which the speaking subject is constituted—borders also determined by the phonological and semantic differences that articulate the syntax of language.

And yet, in the light of this structural-functional X-ray of defilement, which draws on the major anthropological works of modern times, from W. Robertson Smith to Marcel Mauss, from Emile Durkheim to Claude Lévi-Strauss, one question remains unanswered. Why does *corporeal waste*, menstrual blood and excrement, or everything that is assimilated to them, from nail-parings to decay, represent—like a metaphor that would have become incarnate—the objective frailty of symbolic order?

One might be tempted at first to seek the answer in a type of society where defilement takes the place of supreme danger or absolute evil.

Between Two Powers

Nevertheless, no matter what differences there may be among societies where religious prohibitions, which are above all behavior prohibitions, are supposed to afford protection from defilement, one sees everywhere the importance, both social and symbolic, of women and particularly the mother. In societies where it occurs, ritualization of defilement is accompanied by a strong concern for separating the sexes, and this means giving men rights over women. The latter, apparently put in the position of passive objects, are, nonetheless, felt to be wily powers, "baleful schemers" from whom rightful beneficiaries must protect themselves. It is as if, lacking a central authoritarian power that would settle the definitive supremacy of one sex—or lacking a legal establishment that would balance the prerogatives of both sexes—two powers attempted to share out society. One of them, the masculine, apparently victorious, confesses through its very relentlessness against the other, the feminine, that it is threatened by an asymmetrical, irrational, wily, uncontrollable power. Is this a survival of a matrilineal society or the specific particularity of a structure (without the incidence of diachrony)? The question of the origins of such a handling of sexual difference remains moot. But whether it be within the highly hierarchical society of India or the Lele in Africa[14] it is always to be noticed that the attempt to establish a male, phallic power is vigorously threatened by the no less virulent power of the other sex, which is oppressed (recently? or not sufficiently for the survival needs of society?). That other sex, the feminine, becomes synonymous with a radical evil that is to be suppressed.[15]

Let us keep that fact in mind; I shall return to it later on for the interpretation of defilement and its rites. In the meantime I turn to the particulars—the prohibited objects and the symbolic devices that accompany those prohibitions.

Excrements and Menstrual Blood

While they always relate to corporeal orifices as to so many landmarks parceling-constituting the body's territory, polluting objects fall, schematically, into two types: excremental and menstrual. Neither tears nor sperm, for instance, although they belong to borders of the body, have any polluting value.

Excrement and its equivalents (decay, infection, disease, corpse, etc.) stand for the danger to identity that comes from without: the ego threatened by the non-ego, society threatened by its outside, life by death. Menstrual blood, on the contrary, stands for the danger issuing from within the identity (social or sexual); it threatens the relationship between the sexes within a social aggregate and, through internalization, the identity of each sex in the face of sexual difference.

Maternal Authority as Trustee of the Self's Clean and Proper Body

What can the two types of defilement have in common? Without having recourse to anal eroticism or the fear of castration—one cannot help *hearing* the reticence of anthropologists when confronted with that explanation—it might be suggested, by means of another psychoanalytic approach, that those *two* defilements stem from the *maternal* and/or the feminine, of which the maternal is the real support. That goes without saying where menstrual blood signifies sexual difference. But what about excrement? It will be remembered that the anal penis is also the phallus with which infantile imagination provides the feminine sex and that, on the other hand, maternal authority is experienced first and above all, after the first essentially oral frustrations, as sphincteral training. It is as if, while having been forever immersed in the symbolics of language, the human being experienced, in addition, an *authority* that was a—chronologically and logically immediate—repetition of the *laws* of language. Through frustrations and prohibitions, this authority shapes the body into a *territory* having areas, orifices, points and lines, surfaces and hollows, where the archaic power of mastery and neglect, of the differentiation of proper-clean and improper-dirty, possible and impossible, is impressed and exerted. It is a "binary logic," a primal mapping of the body that I call semiotic to say that, while being the precondition of language, it is dependent upon meaning, but in a way that is not that of *linguistic* signs nor of the *symbolic* order they found. Maternal authority is the trustee of that mapping of the self's clean and proper body; it is distinguished from paternal laws within which, with the phallic phase and acquisition of language, the destiny of man will take shape.

If language, like culture, sets up a separation and, starting with discrete elements, concatenates an order, it does so precisely by repressing maternal authority and the corporeal mapping that abuts against them. It is then appropriate to ask what happens to such a repressed item when the legal, phallic, linguistic symbolic establishment does not carry out the separation in radical fashion—or else, more basically, when the speaking being attempts to think through its advent in order better to establish its effectiveness.

Defilement Rite—a Social Elaboration of the Borderline Patient?

The structuralist hypothesis is well known. Basic symbolic institutions, such as *sacrifice* or *myths*, expand on logical processes inherent in the economy of language itself; in doing so they realize for the community what makes up in depth, historically and logically, the speaking being as such. Thus *myth* projects on contents that are vitally important for a given community those binary oppositions discovered at the level of phonematic concatenation of language. As for *sacrifice*, it solemnizes the vertical dimension of the sign: the one that leads from the thing that is left behind, or killed, to the meaning of the word and transcendence.

Following that line, one could suggest that the rites surrounding defilement, particularly those involving excremential and menstrual variants, shift the *border* (in the psychoanalytic meaning relating to borderline patients) that separates the body's territory from the signifying chain; they illustrate the boundary between semiotic authority and symbolic law. Through language and within highly hierarchical religious institutions, man hallucinates partial "objects"—witnesses to an archaic differentiation of the body on its way toward ego identity, which is also sexual identity. The *defilement* from which ritual protects us is neither sign nor matter. Within the rite that extracts it from repression and depraved desire, defilement is the translinguistic spoor of the most archaic boundaries of the self's clean and proper body. In that sense, if it is a jettisoned object, it is so from the mother. It absorbs within itself all the experiences of the nonobjectal that accompany the differentiation mother-speaking being, hence all ab-jects (from those the phobic shuns to those that hem in split subjects). As if purification rites, through a language that is already there, looked back toward an archaic experience and obtained from it a partial object, not as such but only as a *spoor* of a preobject, an archaic parceling. By means of the symbolic institution of ritual, that is to say, by means of a system of ritual exclusions, the partial object consequently becomes *scription*—an inscription of limits, an emphasis placed not on the (paternal) Law but on (maternal) Authority through the very signifying order.

NOTES

1. In *Totem and Taboo* (1913), in vol. 13 of *Complete Works*. References will be to the Vintage Book edition published by Random House.

2. Ibid., p. 170.

3. Ibid., p. 185.

4. See René Girard, *Des Choses cachées depuis la fondation du monde* (Paris: Grasset, 1978).

5. Freud quoted from T. W. Atkinson's *Primal Law, Totem and Taboo* (London, 1903); see p. 184n.

6. *Totem and Taboo*, pp. 85–86, although the translation used is that of the *Complete Works*, 13:64.

7. *Totem and Taboo*, p. 86n; quoted from the *Complete Works*, 13:65.

8. *Totem and Taboo*, p. 207.

9. *Totem and Taboo*, pp. 115–16.

10. See Georges Bataille, "L'Abjection et les formes misérables," in *Essais de sociologie, Oeuvres complètes* (Paris: Gallimard, 1970), 2:217ff.

11. Mary Douglas, *Purity and Danger* (London: Routledge & Kegan Paul, 1969), p. 121.

12. Ibid., p. 113.

13. Ibid.

14. See ibid., pp. 149ff.

15. "For the Lele evil is not to be included in the total system of the world, but to be expunged without compromise"; ibid., p. 171.

Strangers to Ourselves

Toccata and Fugue for the Foreigner

Foreigner: a choked up rage deep down in my throat, a black angel clouding transparency, opaque, unfathomable spur. The image of hatred and of the other, a foreigner is neither the romantic victim of our clannish indolence nor the intruder responsible for all the ills of the polis. Neither the apocalypse on the move nor the instant adversary to be eliminated for the sake of appeasing the group. Strangely, the foreigner lives within us: he is the hidden face of our identity, the space that wrecks our abode, the time in which understanding and affinity founder. By recognizing him within ourselves, we are spared detesting him in himself. A symptom that precisely turns "we" into a problem, perhaps makes it impossible, The foreigner comes in when the consciousness of my difference arises, and he disappears when we all acknowledge ourselves as foreigners, unamenable to bonds and communities.

Can the "foreigner," who was the "enemy" in primitive societies, disappear from modern societies? Let us recall a few moments in Western history when foreigners were conceived, welcomed, or rejected, but when the possibility of a society without foreigners could also have been imagined on the horizon of a religion or an ethics. As a still and perhaps ever utopic matter, the question is again before us today as we confront an economic and political integration on the scale of the planet: shall we be, intimately and subjectively, able to live with the others, to live *as others*, without ostracism but also without leveling? The modification in the status of foreigners that is imperative today leads one to reflect on our ability to accept new modalities of otherness. No "Nationality Code" would be practicable without having that question slowly mature within each of us and for each of us.

While in the most savage human groups the foreigner was an enemy to be destroyed, he has become, within the scope of religious and ethical constructs, a different human being who, provided he espouses them, may be assimilated into the fraternities of the "wise," the "just," or the "native." In Stoicism, Judaism, Christianity, and even in the humanism of the Enlightenment, the patterns of such acceptance varied, but in spite of its limitations and shortcomings, it remained a genuine rampart against xenophobia. The violence of the problem set by the foreigner today is probably due to the crises undergone by religious and ethical constructs. This is especially so as the absorption of otherness proposed by our societies turns out to be unacceptable by the contemporary individual, jealous of his difference—one that is not only national and ethical but essentially subjective, insurmountable. Stemming from the bourgeois revolution, nationalism has become a symptom—romantic at first, then totalitarian—of the nineteenth and twentieth centuries. Now, while it does go against universalist tendencies (be they religious or rationalist) and tends to isolate or even hunt down the foreigner, nationalism nevertheless ends up, on the other hand, with the particularistic, demanding individualism of contemporary man. But it is perhaps on the basis of that contemporary individualism's subversion, beginning with the moment when the citizen-individual ceases to consider himself as unitary and glorious but discovers his incoherences and abysses, in short his "strangenesses"—that the question arises again: no longer that of welcoming the foreigner within a system that obliterates him but of promoting the togetherness of those foreigners that we all recognize ourselves to be.

Let us not seek to solidify, to turn the otherness of the foreigner into a thing. Let us merely touch it, brush by it, without giving it a permanent structure. Simply sketching out its perpetual motion through some of its variegated aspects spread out before our eyes today, through some of its former, changing representations scattered throughout history. Let us also lighten that otherness by constantly coming back to it—but more and more swiftly. Let us escape its hatred, its burden, fleeing them not through leveling and forgetting, but through the *harmonious* repetition of the differences it implies and spreads. *Toccatas and Fugues*: Bach's compositions evoke to my ears the meaning of an acknowledged and harrowing otherness that I should like to be contemporary, *because* it has been brought up, relieved, disseminated, inscribed in an original play being developed, without goal, without boundary, without end. An otherness barely touched upon and that already moves away.

Scorched Happiness

Are there any happy foreigners?

The foreigner's face burns with happiness.

At first, one is struck by his peculiarity—those eyes, those lips, those cheekbones, that skin unlike others, all that distinguishes him and reminds one that there is *someone* there. The difference in that face reveals in paroxystic fashion what any face should reveal to a careful glance: the nonexistence of banality in human beings. Nevertheless, it is precisely the commonplace that constitutes a commonality for our daily habits. But this grasping the foreigner's features, one that captivates us, beckons and rejects at the same time. "I am at least as remarkable, and therefore I love him," the observer thinks; "now I prefer my own peculiarity, and therefore I kill him," he might conclude. From heart pangs to first jabs, the foreigner's face forces us to display the secret manner in which we face the world, stare into all our faces, even in the most familial, the most tightly knit communities.

Furthermore, the face that is so *other* bears the mark of a crossed threshold that irremediably imprints itself as peacefulness or anxiety. Whether perturbed or joyful, the foreigner's appearance signals that he is "in addition." The presence of such a border, internal to all that is displayed, awakens our most archaic senses through a burning sensation. Vivid concern or delight, set there in these other features, without forgetfulness, without ostentation, like a standing invitation to some inaccessible, irritating journey, whose code the foreigner does not have but whose mute, physical, visible memory he keeps. This does not mean the foreigner necessarily appears absent, absentminded, or distraught. But the insistent presence of a lining—good or evil, pleasing or death-bearing—disrupts the never regular image of his face and imprints upon it the ambiguous mark of a scar—his very own well-being.

For, curiously, beyond unease, such a doubling imposes upon the other, the observer, the feeling that there is a special, somewhat insolent happiness in the foreigner. Happiness seems to prevail, *in spite of everything*, because something has definitely been exceeded: it is the happiness of tearing away, of racing, the space of a promised infinite. Such happiness is, however, constrained, apprehensively discreet, in spite of its piercing intrusion, since the foreigner keeps feeling threatened by his former territory, caught up in the memory of a happiness or a disaster—both always excessive.

Can one be a foreigner and happy? The foreigner calls forth a new idea of happiness. Between the fugue and the origin: a fragile limit, a temporary homeostasis. Posited, present, sometimes certain, that happiness knows nevertheless that it is passing by, like fire that shines only because it consumes. The strange happiness of the foreigner consists in maintaining that fleeing eternity or that perpetual transience.

The Loss and the Challenge

A secret wound, often unknown to himself, drives the foreigner to wandering. Poorly loved, however, he does not acknowledge it: with him, the challenge silences the complaint. It is a rare person who, like some Greeks (such as Aeschylus' *Suppliants*), the Jews (the faithful at the wall of lamentations), or psychoanalysts, leads the foreigner to avow a humbled entreaty. He is dauntless: "You have caused me no harm," he disclaims, fiercely, "It is I who chose to leave"; always further along, always inaccessible to all. As far back as his memory can reach, it is delightfully bruised: misunderstood by a loved and yet absentminded, discreet, or worried mother, the exile is a stranger to his mother. He does not call her, he asks nothing of her. Arrogant, he proudly holds on to what he lacks, to absence, to some symbol or other. The foreigner would be the son of a father whose existence is subject to no doubt whatsoever, but whose presence does not detain him. Rejection on the one hand, inaccessibility on the other: if one has the strength not to give in, there remains a path to be discovered. Riveted to an elsewhere as certain as it is inaccessible, the foreigner is ready to flee. No obstacle stops him, and all suffering, all insults, all rejections are indifferent to him as he seeks that invisible and promised territory, that country that does not exist but that he bears in his dreams, and that must indeed be called a beyond.

The foreigner, thus, has lost his mother. Camus understood it well: his *Stranger* reveals himself at the time of his mother's death. One has not much noticed that this cold orphan, whose indifference can become criminal, is a fanatic of absence. He is a devotee of solitude, even in the midst of a crowd, because he is faithful to a shadow: bewitching secret, paternal ideal, inaccessible ambition. Meursault is dead unto himself but keyed up with an insipid intoxication that takes the place of passion. Likewise, his father, who started vomiting while watching an execution, understood that being sentenced to death is the only thing a man might truly consider worth bothering with.

Suffering, Ebullience, and Mask

The difficulties the foreigner will necessarily encounter—one mouth too many, incomprehensible speech, inappropriate behavior—wound him severely, but by flashes. They make him turn gray, imperceptibly, he becomes smooth and hard as a pebble, always ready to resume his infinite journey, farther, elsewhere. The (professional, intellectual, affective) aim that some set for themselves in such an unrestrained fugue is already a betrayal of strangeness, for as he chooses a program he allows himself a respite or a residence. On the contrary, according to the utmost logic of exile, all aims should waste away and self-destruct in the wanderer's insane stride toward an elsewhere that is always pushed back, unfulfilled, out of reach. The pleasure of suffering is a necessary lot in such a demented whirl, and amateur *proxeni* know it unconsciously as they choose foreign partners on whom to inflict the torture of their own contempt, their condescension, or, more deceitfully, their heavy-handed charity.

The foreigner is hypersensitive beneath his armor as activist or tireless "immigrant worker." He bleeds body and soul, humiliated in a position where, even with the better couples, he or she assumes the part of a domestic, of the one who is a bother when he or she becomes ill, who embodies the enemy, the traitor, the victim. Masochistic pleasure accounts for his or her submissiveness only in part. The latter, in fact, strengthens the foreigner's mask—a second, impassive personality, an anesthetized skin he wraps himself in, providing a hiding place where he enjoys scorning his tyrant's hysterical weaknesses. Is this the dialectic of master and slave?

The animosity, or at least the annoyance aroused by the foreigner ("What are you doing here, Mac, this is not where you belong!"), hardly surprises him. He readily bears a kind of admiration for those who have welcomed him, for he rates them more often than not above himself, be it financially, politically, or socially. At the same time he is quite ready to consider them somewhat narrow-minded, blind. For his scornful hosts lack the *perspective* he himself has in order to see himself and to see them. The foreigner feels strengthened by the distance that detaches him from the others as it does from himself and gives him the lofty sense not so much of holding the truth but of making it and himself relative while others fall victim to the ruts of monovalency. For they are perhaps owners of things, but the foreigner tends to think he is the only one to have a biography, that is, a life made up of ordeals—neither catastrophes nor adventures (although these might equally happen), but simply a life in which acts constitute events because they imply choice, surprises, breaks, adaptations, or cunning, but neither routine nor rest. In the eyes of the foreigner those who are not foreign have no life at all: barely do they exist, haughty or mediocre, but out of the running and thus almost already cadaverized.

Aloofness

Indifference is the foreigner's shield. Insensitive, aloof, he seems, deep down, beyond the reach of attacks and rejections that he nevertheless experiences with the vulnerability of a medusa. This is because his being kept apart corresponds to his remaining aloof, as he pulls back into the painless core of what is called a soul the humbleness that, when all is said and done, amounts to plain brutality. There, soured of mawkishness, but of sensitivity as well, he takes pride in holding a truth that is perhaps simply a certainty—the ability to reveal the crudest aspects of human relationships when seduction fades out and proprieties give way before the results of confrontations: a clash of bodies and tempers. For the foreigner, from the height of an autonomy that he is the only one to have chosen when the others prudently remain "between themselves," paradoxically confronts everyone with an asymbolia that rejects civility and returns to a violence laid bare. The brutes' encounter.

Not belonging to any place, any time, any love. A lost origin, the impossibility to take root, a rummaging memory, the present in abeyance. The space of the foreigner is a moving train, a plane in flight, the very transition that precludes stopping. As to landmarks, there are none. His time? The time of a resurrection that remembers death and what happened before, but misses the glory of being beyond: merely the feeling of a reprieve, of having gotten away.

Confidence

There remains, however, the self-confidence of being, of being able to settle within the self with a smooth, opaque certainty—an oyster shut under the flooding tide or the expressionless joy of warm stones. Between the two pathetic shores of courage and humiliation, against which he is tossed by the clashes of others, the foreigner persists, anchored in himself, strengthened by such a secret working-out, his neutral wisdom, a pleasure that has been numbed by an unattainable solitude.

Deep-seated narcissism? Blank psychosis beneath the swirl of existential conflicts? In crossing a border (. . . or two) the foreigner has changed his discomforts into a base of resistance, a citadel of life. Moreover, had he stayed home, he might perhaps have become a dropout, an invalid, an outlaw . . . Without a home, he disseminates on the contrary the actor's paradox: multiplying masks and "false selves" he is never completely true nor completely false, as he is able to tune in to loves and aversions the superficial antennae of a basaltic heart. A headstrong will, but unaware of itself, unconscious, distraught. The breed of the tough guys who know how to be weak.

This means that, settled within himself, the foreigner has no self. Barely an empty confidence, valueless, which focuses his possibilities of being constantly other, according to others' wishes and to circumstances. I do what *they* want *me* to, but it is not "me"—"me" is elsewhere, "me" belongs to no one, "me" does not belong to "me," . . . does "me" exist?

Parceling

Nevertheless, such hardness in a state of weightlessness is an absolute that does not last. The traitor betrays himself. Whether a Maghrebian street sweeper riveted to his broom or an Asiatic princess writing her memoirs in a borrowed tongue, as soon as foreigners have an action or a passion, they take root. Temporarily, to be sure, but intensely. For the foreigner's aloofness is only the resistance with which he succeeds in fighting his matricidal anguish. His hardness appears as the metamorphosis of an archaic or potential parceling that runs the risk of bringing his thought and speech down to chaos. Thus does he value that aloofness, his hardness—let us leave it alone.

The flame that betrays his latent fanaticism shows only when he becomes attached—to a cause, to a job, to a person. What he finds there is more than a country; it is a fusion, in which there are not two beings, there is but a single one who is consumed, complete, annihilated.

Social standing or personal talent obviously stamps such a vocation with appreciable variations. Whatever their differences, however, all foreigners who have made a *choice* add to their passion for indifference a fervent extremism that reveals the origin of their exile. For it is on account of having *no one* at home against whom to vent their fury, their conflagration of love and hatred, and of finding the strength not to give in to it, that they wander about the world, neutral but solaced for having developed an interior distance from the fire and ice that had seared them in the past.

A Melancholia

Hard-hearted indifference is perhaps no more than the respectable aspect of nostalgia. We all know the foreigner who survives with a tearful face turned toward the lost homeland. Melancholy lover of a vanished space, he cannot, in fact, get over his having abandoned a period of time. The lost paradise is a mirage of the past that he will never be able to recover. He knows it with a distressed knowledge that turns his rage involving others (for there is always an other, miserable cause of my exile) against himself: "How could I have abandoned them? I have abandoned myself." And even he who, seemingly, flees the slimy poison of depression, does not hold back, as he lies in bed, during those glaucus moments between waking and sleeping. For in the intervening period of nostalgia, saturated with fragrances and sounds to which he no longer belongs and which, because of that, wound him less than those of the here and now, the foreigner is a dreamer making love with absence, one exquisitely depressed. Happy?

Ironists and Believers

Yet, he is never simply torn between here and elsewhere, now and before. Those who believe they are crucified in such a fashion forget that nothing ties them there anymore, and, so far, nothing binds them here. Always elsewhere, the foreigner belongs nowhere. But let there be no mistake about it: there are, in the way one lives this attachment to a lost space, two kinds of foreigners, and this separates uprooted people of all countries, occupations, social standing, sexes . . . into two irreconcilable categories. On the one hand, there are those who waste away in an agonizing struggle between what no longer is and what will never be—the followers of neutrality, the advocates of emptiness; they are not necessarily defeatists, they often become the best of ironists. On the other hand, there are those who transcend: living neither before nor now but beyond, they are bent with a passion that, although tenacious, will remain forever unsatisfied. It is a passion for another land, always a promised one, that of an occupation, a love, a child, a glory. They are believers, and they sometimes ripen into skeptics.

Meeting

Meeting balances wandering. A crossroad of two othernesses, it welcomes the foreigner without tying him down, opening the host to his visitor without committing him. A mutual recognition, the meeting owes its success to its temporary nature, and it would be torn by conflicts if it were to be extended. The foreign believer is incorrigibly curious, eager for meetings: he is nourished by them, makes his way through them, forever unsatisfied, forever the party-goer, too. Always going toward others, always going farther. Invited, he is able to invite himself, and his life is a succession of desired parties, but short-lived, the brilliance of which he learns to tarnish immediately, for he knows that they are of no consequence. "They welcome me, but that does not matter. . . . Next . . . It was only an expenditure that guarantees a clear conscience . . ." A clear conscience for the host as well as the foreigner. The cynic is even more suited for a meeting: he does not even seek it, he expects nothing from it, but he slips in nevertheless, convinced that even though everything melts away, it is better to be with "it." He does not long for meetings, they draw him in. He experiences them as in a fit of dizziness when, distraught, he no longer knows whom he has seen nor who he is.

The meeting often begins with a food fest: bread, salt, and wine. A meal, a nutritive communion. The one confesses he is a famished baby, the other welcomes the greedy child; for an instant, they merge within the hospitality ritual. But this table corner, where they gulp with such pleasure, is covered with the paths of memory: one remembers, makes plans, recites, sings. The nourishing and initially somewhat animal banquet rises to the vaporous levels of dreams and ideas: the hospitality merrymakers also become united for a while through the spirit. A miracle of flesh and thought, the banquet of hospitality is the foreigners' utopia— the cosmopolitanism of a moment, the brotherhood of guests who soothe and forget their differences, the banquet is outside of time. It imagines itself eternal in the intoxication of those who are nevertheless aware of its temporary frailty.

Sole Liberty

Free of ties with his own people, the foreigner feels "completely free." Nevertheless, the consummate name of such a freedom is solitude. Useless or limitless, it amounts to boredom or supreme availability. Deprived of others, free solitude, like the astronauts' weightless state, dilapidates muscles, bones, and blood. Available, freed of everything, the foreigner has nothing, he is nothing. But he is ready for the absolute, if an absolute could choose him. "Solitude" is perhaps the only word that has no meaning. Without other, without guidepost, it cannot bear the difference that, alone, discriminates and makes sense. No one better than the foreigner knows the passion for solitude. He believes he has chosen it for its enjoyment, or been subjected to it to suffer on account of it, and there he is languishing in a passion for indifference that, although occasionally intoxicating, is irreparably without an accomplice. The paradox is that the foreigner wishes to be alone but with partners, and yet none is willing to join him in the torrid space of his uniqueness. The only possible companions would be the members of an affiliation whose uniformity and readiness discourage him, whereas, on the contrary, the lack of accordance on the part of distinguished persons helplessly sends him back to his own distress. Accordance is the foreigner's mirage. More grueling when lacking, it is his only connection—utopic or abortive as it may be. If it appears under the self-satisfying guise of charity or any other right-thinking humanism, he accepts it of course, but in a hard-hearted, unbelieving, indifferent manner. The foreigner longs for affiliation, the better to experience, through a refusal, its untouchability.

A Hatred

"Experiencing hatred": that is the way the foreigner often expresses his life, but the double meaning of the phrase escapes him. Constantly feeling the hatred of others, knowing no other environment than that hatred. Like a woman who, accommodating and conniving, abides by her husband's rebuff as soon as she makes the merest suggestion of a word, gesture, or intention. Like a child that hides, fearful and guilty, convinced beforehand that it deserves its parents' anger. In the world of dodges and shams that make up his pseudo-relationships with pseudo-others, hatred provides the foreigner with consistency. Against that wall, painful but certain, and in that sense familiar, he knocks himself in order to assert, to others and to himself, that he is here. Hatred makes him real, authentic so to speak, solid, or simply existing. Even more so, it causes to resound on the *outside* that other hatred, secret and shameful, apologetic to the point of abating, that the foreigner bears *within himself* against everyone, against no one, and which, in the case of flooding, would cause a serious depression. But there, on the border between himself and others, hatred does not threaten him. He lies in wait, reassured each time to discover that it never misses an appointment, bruised on account of always missing love, but almost pleased with the persistence—real or imaginary?—of detestation.

Living with the other, with the foreigner, confronts us with the possibility or not of *being an other*. It is not simply—humanistically—a matter of our being able to accept the other, but of *being in his place*, and this means to imagine and make oneself other for oneself. Rimbaud's *Je est un autre* ("I is an other") was not only the acknowledgment of the psychotic ghost that haunts poetry. The word foreshadowed the exile, the possibility or necessity to be foreign and to live in a foreign country, thus heralding the art of living of a modern era, the cosmopolitanism of those who have been flayed. Being alienated from myself, as painful as that may be, provides me with that exquisite distance within which perverse pleasure begins as well as the possibility of my imagining and thinking, the impetus of my culture. Split identity, kaleidoscope of identities: can we be a saga for ourselves without being considered mad or fake? Without dying of the foreigner's hatred or of hatred for the foreigner?

Detestation tells you that you are an intruder, that you are irritating, and that this will be shown to you frankly and without caution. No one in this country can either defend or avenge you. You do not count for anyone; you should be grateful for being tolerated among us. Civilized people need not be gentle with foreigners. "That's it, and if you don't like it why don't you go back where you came from!" The humiliation that disparages the foreigner endows his master with who knows what petty grandeur. I wonder if Wanda's husband would have dared to act as brazenly like a Don Juan, to discover libertine bents in himself, to flaunt the girlfriends she, alas, did not have the sense of humor to appreciate—if his wife had not come from Poland, that is from nowhere, without the family or friends that constitute, in spite of what people say, a shelter against narcissism and a rampart against paranoid persecutions. I wonder if his in-laws would have so brutally taken his child away from Kwang, at the time of his separation from Jacqueline, if he did not have such an incomprehensible way of pronouncing words and forgetting verbs, what was called an obsequious way of conducting himself and which was just his own way of being polite, and that inability to strike up a friendship with colleagues at a bar, on the occasion of a fishing trip . . . But perhaps Wanda and Kwang are suffering from something more than being foreign, and Marie or Paul might have the same problems if they were a bit different, a bit special, if they did not play the game, if they were like foreigners from within. Or should one recognize that one becomes a foreigner in another country because one is already a foreigner from within?

The Silence of Polyglots

Not speaking one's mother tongue. Living with resonances and reasoning that are cut off from the body's nocturnal memory, from the bittersweet slumber of childhood. Bearing within oneself like a secret vault, or like a handicapped child—cherished and useless—that language of the past that withers without ever leaving you. You improve your ability with another instrument, as one expresses oneself with algebra or the violin. You can become a virtuoso with this new device that moreover gives you a new body, just as artificial and sublimated—some say sublime. You have a feeling that the new language is a resurrection: new skin, new sex. But the illusion bursts when you hear, upon listening to a recording, for instance, that the melody of your voice comes back to you as a peculiar sound, out of nowhere, closer to the old spluttering than to today's code. Your awkwardness has its charm, they say, it is even erotic, according to womanizers, not to be outdone. No one points out your mistakes, so as not to hurt your feelings, and then there are so many, and after all they don't give a damn. One nevertheless lets you know that it is irritating just the same. Occasionally, raising the eyebrows or saying "I beg your pardon?" in quick succession lead you to understand that you will "never be a part of it," that it "is not worth it," that there, at least, one is "not taken in." Being fooled is not what happens to you either. At the most, you are willing to go along, ready for all apprenticeships, at all ages, in order to reach—within that speech of others, imagined as being perfectly assimilated, *someday*—who knows what ideal, beyond the implicit acknowledgment of a disappointment caused by the origin that did not keep its promise.

Thus, between two languages, your realm is silence. By dint of saying things in various ways, one just as trite as the other, just as approximate, one ends up no longer saying them. An internationally known scholar was ironical about his famous polyglotism, saying that he spoke Russian in fifteen languages. As for me I had the feeling that he rejected speech and his slack silence led him, at times, to sing and give rhythm to chanted poems, just in order to say something.

When Hölderlin became absorbed by Greek (before going back to the sources of German), he dramatically expressed the anesthesia of the person that is snatched up by a foreign language: "A sign, such are we, and of no meaning / Dead to all suffering, and we have almost / Lost our language in a foreign land" (*Mnemosyne*).

Stuck within that polymorphic mutism, the foreigner can, instead of saying, attempt doing—housecleaning, playing tennis, soccer, sailing, sewing, horseback riding, jogging, getting pregnant, what have you. It remains an expenditure, it expends, and it propagates silence even more. Who listens to you? At the most, you are being tolerated. Anyway, do you really want to speak?

Why then did you cut off the maternal source of words? What did you dream up concerning those new people you spoke to in an artificial language, a prosthesis? From your standpoint, were they idealized or scorned? Come, now! Silence has not only been forced upon you, it is within you: a refusal to speak, a fitful sleep riven to an anguish that wants to remain mute, the private property of your proud and mortified discretion, that silence is a harsh light. Nothing to say, nothingness, no one on the horizon. An impervious fullness: cold diamond, secret treasury, carefully protected, out of reach. Saying nothing, nothing needs to be said, nothing can be said. At first, it was a cold war with those of the new idiom, desired and rejecting; then the new language covered you as might a slow tide, a neap tide. It is not the silence of anger that jostles words at the edge of the idea and the mouth; rather, it is the silence that empties the mind and fills the brain with despondency, like the gaze of sorrowful women coiled up in some nonexistent eternity.

"The Former Separations from the Body" (Mallarmé, "Cantique de Saint Jean")

To disagree. Constantly, about nothing, with no one. Coping with that with astonishment and curiosity, like an explorer, an ethnologist. Becoming weary of it and walled up in one's tarnished, neutralized disagreement, through lack of having the right to state it. No longer knowing what one truly thinks, except that "this is not it": that the words, the smiles, the manias, the judgments, the tastes of the native are excessive, faltering, or simply unjust and false, and he cannot imagine—proud as he is of being on his own ground—that one might speak, think, or act differently. In that case, why not tell him so, "argue"? But what right do we have? Perhaps we should ourselves assume that right, challenging the natives' assurance?

No. Those who have never lost the slightest root seem to you unable to understand any word liable to temper their point of view. So, when one is oneself uprooted, what is the point of talking to those who think they have their own feet on their own soil? The ear is receptive to conflicts only if the body looses its footing. A certain imbalance is necessary, a swaying over some abyss, for a conflict to be heard. Yet when the foreigner—the speech-denying strategist—does not utter his conflict, he in turn takes root in his own world of a rejected person whom no one is supposed to hear. The rooted one who is deaf to the conflict and the wanderer walled in by his conflict thus stand firmly, facing each other. It is a seemingly peaceful coexistence that hides the abyss: an abysmal world, the end of the world.

Immigrants, Hence Workers

The foreigner is the one who works. While natives of the civilized world, of developed countries, think that work is vulgar and display the aristocratic manners of offhandedness and whim (when they can . . .), you will recognize the foreigner in that he *still* considers work as a value. A vital necessity, to be sure, his sole means of survival, on which he does not necessarily place a halo of glory but simply claims as a primary right, the zero degree of dignity. Even though some, once their minimal needs are satisfied, also experience an acute pleasure in asserting themselves in and through work: as if *it* were the chosen soil, the only source of possible success, and above all the personal, steadfast, nontransferable quality, but fit to be moved beyond borders and properties. That the foreigner is a worker would seem like a cheap paradox, inferred from the quite controversial existence of "immigrant workers." I have nevertheless come across, in a French village, ambitious farmers who had come from a different region, more hard-working than others and wanting to "make a niche" for themselves by the sweat of their brows, hated as much for being intruders as for being relentless, and who (the worst of insults during demonstrations) heard themselves called Portuguese and Spaniards. Indeed, as they confided, the others (in this case they meant the Frenchmen who were sure of themselves) are never as persistent in their work; you really have to be without anything and thus, basically, to come from somewhere else, to be attached to it to that extent. Now, were they doing the unpleasant work in that village? No, they were simply always doing something, those "foreigners" who had come from another province.

With the second generation, it is true, it happens that these demons for work slacken. As a defiance of industrious parents, or an inevitably excessive aping of native behavior, the children of foreigners are often and from the very start within the code of *dolce vita*, slovenliness, and even delinquency. Many "reasons" are given for that, of course.

But as far as the immigrant is concerned, he has not come here just to waste his time away. Possessed with driving ambition, a pusher, or merely crafty, he takes on all jobs and tries to be tops in those that are scarcest. In those that nobody wants but also in those that nobody has thought of. Man or woman for odd jobs, but also a pioneer in the most up-to-date disciplines, off-the-cuff specialist in unusual or leading occupations, the foreigner devotes himself and exerts himself. If it be true that, in the process, like everyone else he aims at profits and savings for later and for his family, his planning supposes (in order to achieve that aim, and more than with others) an extravagant expenditure of energy and means. Since he has nothing, since he is nothing, he can sacrifice everything. And sacrifice begins with work: the only property that can be exported duty free, a universally tried and tested stock for the wanderer's use. What bitterness then, what disaster it is when one does not obtain one's green card.

Slaves and Master

Dialectics of master and slave? The amount of strength changes the very balance of power. The weight of foreigners is measured not only in terms of greater numbers (from that standpoint did not slaves always constitute an overwhelming majority?) but is also determined by the consciousness of being somewhat foreign as well. On the one hand, because everyone is, in a world that is more open than ever, liable to become a foreigner for a while as tourist or employee of a multinational concern. On the other hand, because the once solid barrier between "master" and "slave" has today been abolished, if not in people's unconscious at least in our ideologies and aspirations. Every native feels himself to be more or less a "foreigner" in his "own and proper" place, and that metaphorical value of the word "foreigner" first leads the citizen to a feeling of discomfort as to his sexual, national, political, professional identity. Next it impels him to identify—sporadically, to be sure, but nonetheless intensely—with the other. Within this motion guilt obviously has its part but it also fades away to the advantage of a kind of underhanded glory of being a little like those other "gooks" (*métèques*), concerning which we now know that, disadvantaged as they may be, they are running before the wind. A wind that jostles and ruffles but bears us toward our own unknown and who knows what future. There is thus set up between the new "masters" and the new "slaves" a secret collusion, which does not necessarily entail practical consequences in politics or the courts (even if they, too, feel its effects progressively, slowly) but, especially with the native, arouses a feeling of suspicion: Am I really at home? Am I myself? Are *they* not masters of the "future"?

Such a habit for suspicion prompts some to reflect, rarely causes humbleness, and even more rarely generosity. But it also provokes regressive and protectionist rage in others: must we not stick together, remain among ourselves, expel the intruder, or at least, keep him in "his" place? The "master" then changes into a slave hounding his conqueror. For the foreigner perceived as an invader reveals a buried passion within those who are entrenched: the passion to kill the *other*, who had first been feared or despised, then promoted from the ranks of dregs to the status of powerful persecutor against whom a "we" solidifies in order to take revenge.

Void or Baroque Speech

To be of no account to others. No one listens to you, you never have the floor, or else, when you have the courage to seize it, your speech is quickly erased by the more garrulous and fully relaxed talk of the community. Your speech has no past and will have no power over the future of the group: why should one listen to it? You do not have enough status—"no social standing"—to make your speech useful. It may be desirable, to be sure, surprising, too, bizarre or attractive, if you wish. But such lures are of little consequence when set against the *interest*—which is precisely lacking—of those you are speaking to. Interest is self-seeking, it wants to be able to use your words, counting on your influence, which, like any influence, is anchored in social connections. Now, to be precise, you have none. Your speech, fascinating as it might be on account of its very strangeness, will be of no consequence, will have no effect, will cause no improvement in the image or reputation of those you are conversing with. One will listen to you only in absentminded, amused fashion, and one will forget you in order to go on with serious matters. The foreigner's speech can bank only on its bare rhetorical strength, and the inherent desires he or she has invested in it. But it is deprived of any support in outside reality, since the foreigner is precisely kept out of it. Under such conditions, if it does not founder into silence, it becomes absolute in its formalism, excessive in its sophistication—rhetoric is dominant, the foreigner is a baroque person. Baltasar Graciàn and James Joyce had to be foreigners.

Orphans

To be deprived of parents—is that where freedom starts? Certainly foreigners become intoxicated with that independence, and undoubtedly their very exile is at first no more than a challenge to parental overbearance. Those who have not experienced the near-hallucinatory daring of imagining themselves without parents—free of debt and duties—cannot understand the foreigners' folly, what it provides in the way of pleasure ("I am my sole master"), what it comprises in the way of angry homicide ("Neither father nor mother, neither God nor master . . . ").

Eventually, though, the time of orphanhood comes about. Like any bitter consciousness, this one has its source in others. When others convey to you that you are of no account because your parents are of no account, that, as they are invisible, they do not exist, you are suddenly aware that you are an orphan, and, sometimes, accountable for being so. A strange light then shines on that obscurity that was in you, both joyful and guilty, the darkness of the original dependency, and transforms it into a solidarity with close relatives of earlier days, henceforth forfeited. How could it possibly not have been understood that you were always with them, dependent on a past that only parents know, on the precious, exquisite pain that you will share with no one else? How is it that they, the others, do not know that your parents are still at your side, unseen witnesses to your problems with the natives? Well, no! They do not, they do not want to know it. They thus reveal your own rejection far from those you have abandoned without really doing so—"I know, but just the same . . ." They thus also reveal your own underhanded perversion. You then experience as murderous those natives who never speak of your close relatives—sure, they were close in the past and elsewhere, unmentionable, buried in another language. Or else they allude to them in such absentminded way, with such offhanded scorn that you end up wondering if those parents truly exist, and in what ghostly world of an underground hell. The pain you feel facing those empty eyes that have never seen *them*. Loss of self in the presence of those distant mouths that do not weigh the artifice of the speech that evokes *them*.

But, by the way, who is the murderer? The one who does not know my relatives, or myself, as I erect my new life like a fragile mausoleum where their shadowy figure is integrated, like a corpse, at the source of my wandering? The indifference of others with respect to my kin makes them at once mine again. The community of my own—translucent, slackened by thousands of kilometers and a near-permanent daytime forgetfulness—is thus created by the scornful absentmindedness of others. In the face of that injustice of which I am both source and victim, a "we" emerges. Certainly not, I do not idealize them! I do not use the indifference of others in order to enhance their merit. I know only too well their insignificancy, and my own . . . And yet there is a fondness that binds to the grave what is beyond the grave, the survivor that I am to my forebears. I hear the sound of bells, a fragrance of warm milk fills my throat: they, the parents from abroad, are those who come to life again in my senses, under the blind stare of scornful paternalism.

And nevertheless, no, I have nothing to say to them, to my parents. Nothing. Nothing and everything, as always. If I tried—out of boldness, through luck, or in distress—to share with them some of the violence that causes me to be so totally on my own, they would not know where I am, who I am, what it is, in others, that rubs me the wrong way. I am henceforth foreign to them. They are my children who do not follow me, sometimes admiring, sometimes fearful, but already bruised, reconciled to being alone in their turn, and doomed not to understand. I must come to terms with it and, with that unassuaged sense of hunger in the body, after having spoken to them, must accept the idea that our "we" is a stirring mirage to be maintained at the heart of disarray, although illusive and lacking real strength. Unless it be precisely the strength of illusion that, perhaps, all communities depend on, and of which the foreigner constantly experiences the necessary, aberrant unreality.

Do You Have Any Friends?

The foreigner's friends, aside from bleeding hearts who feel obliged to do good, could only be those who feel foreign to themselves. Other than that, there are of course paternalists, paranoid and perverse people, who each have the foreigner of their choice, to the extent that they would invent him if he did not exist.

Paternalists: how they understand us, how they commiserate, how they appreciate our talents, provided they can show that they have "more"—more pain, more knowledge, more power, including that of helping us to survive . . .

Paranoid persons: no one is more excluded than they are and, in order to demonstrate that fact, they choose as backdrop to their delirium a basic outcast, the ordinary foreigner, who will be the chosen confidant of the persecutions they themselves suffer even more than he does—until they "discover" in this foreigner in the proper sense of the term a usurper and one of the causes of their misfortune, for if the world does not understand them it is precisely because "foreigners now monopolize public opinion's concern." . .

Perverse people: their jouissance is secret and shameful and, hidden in their shell, they would gladly put up a foreigner within it, who presumably would be happy thus to have a home, even though it might be at the cost of sexual or moral slavery, which is proffered lecherously, innocently . . .

In that case, all that would be left for foreigners would be to join together? Foreigners of the world, unite? Things are not so simple. For one must take into consideration the domination/exclusion fantasy characteristic of everyone: just because one is a foreigner does not mean one is without one's own foreigner, and the faith that abated at the source is suddenly rekindled at the journey's end in order to make up from whole cloth an identity the more exclusive as it had once been lost. In France, Italians call the Spaniards foreigners, the Spaniards take it out on the Portuguese, the Portuguese on the Arabs or the Jews, the Arabs on the blacks, and so forth and vice versa. . . . And even if there are links between one another (are they not on the same side as opposed to the natives?), these unfailingly snap when fanatical bonds fuse together again communities cemented by pure, hard fantasies. Here, on foreign soil, the religion of the abandoned forebears is set up in its essential purity and one imagines that one preserves it better than do the parents who have stayed "back home." As enclave of the other within the other, otherness becomes crystallized as pure ostracism: the foreigner excludes before being excluded, even more than he is being excluded. Fundamentalists are more fundamental when they have lost all material ties, inventing for themselves a "we" that is purely symbolic; lacking a soil it becomes rooted in ritual until it reaches its essence, which is sacrifice.

Might Not Universality Be . . . Our Own Foreignness?

Freud: "Heimlich/Unheimlich"—the Uncanny Strangeness

Explicitly given limited scope, as it was at first connected with aesthetic problems and emphasized texts by E. T. A. Hoffmann, Freud's *Das Unheimliche* (1919) surreptitiously goes beyond that framework and the psychological phenomenon of "uncanny strangeness" as well, in order to acknowledge itself as an investigation into *anguish* generally speaking and, in a fashion that is even more universal, into the *dynamics of the unconscious*. Indeed, Freud wanted to demonstrate at the outset, on the basis of a semantic study of the German adjective *heimlich* and its antonym *unheimlich* that a negative meaning close to that of the antonym is already tied to the positive term *heimlich*, "friendlily comfortable," which would also signify "concealed, kept from sight," "deceitful and malicious," "behind someone's back." Thus, in the very word *heimlich*, the familiar and intimate are reversed into their opposites, brought together with the contrary meaning of "uncanny strangeness" harbored in *unheimlich*. Such an immanence of the strange within the familiar is considered as an etymological proof of the psychoanalytic hypothesis according to which "the uncanny is that class of the frightening which leads back to what is known of old and long familiar,"[1] which, as far as Freud was concerned, was confirmed by Schelling, who said that "everything is *unheimlich* that ought to have remained secret and hidden but has come to light" (p. 225).

Consequently therefore, that which *is* strangely uncanny would be that which *was* (the past tense is important) familiar and, under certain conditions (which ones?), emerges. A first step was taken that removed the uncanny strangeness from the outside, where fright had anchored it, to locate it inside, not inside the familiar considered as one's own and proper, but the familiar potentially tainted with strangeness and referred (beyond its imaginative origin) to an improper past. The other is my ("own and proper") unconscious.

What "familiar"? What "past"? In order to answer such questions, Freud's thought played a strange trick on the aesthetic and psychological notion of "uncanny strangeness," which had been initially posited, and rediscovered the analytical notions of *anxiety*, *double*, *repetition*, and *unconscious*. The uncanny strangeness that is aroused in Nathaniel (in Hoffmann's tale, *The Sandman*) by the paternal figure and its substitutes, as well as references to the eyes, is related to the castration anxiety experienced by the child, which was repressed but surfaced again on the occasion of a state of love.

The Other Is My (Own and Proper) Unconscious

Furthermore, Freud noted that the archaic, narcissistic self, not yet demarcated by the outside world, projects out of itself what it experiences as dangerous or unpleasant in itself, making of it an alien *double*, uncanny and demoniacal. In this instance the strange appears as a defense put up by a distraught self: it protects itself by substituting for the image of a benevolent double that used to be enough to shelter it the image of a malevolent double into which it expels the share of destruction it cannot contain.

The repetition that often accompanies the feeling of uncanny strangeness relates it to the "compulsion to repeat" that is peculiar to the unconscious and emanating out of "drive impulses"—a compulsion "proceeding from the drive impulses and probably inherent in the very nature of the drives—a compulsion powerful enough to overrule the pleasure principle" (p. 238).

The reader is henceforth ready to accept the feeling of uncanny strangeness as an instance of anxiety in which "the frightening element can be shown to be something repressed which *recurs*" (p. 241). To the extent, however, that psychic situations evidencing an absolute repression are rare, such a return of the repressed in the guise of anxiety, and more specifically of uncanny strangeness, appears as a paroxystic metaphor of the psychic functioning itself. The latter is indeed elaborated by repression and one's necessarily going through it, with the result that the builder of the *other* and, in the final analysis, of the *strange* is indeed repression itself and its perviousness. "We can understand why linguistic usage has extended *das Heimliche* into its opposite, *das Unheimliche*; for this uncanny is in reality nothing new or alien, but something which is familiar and old-established in the mind and which has become alienated from it only through the process of repression" (p. 241).

Let us say that the psychic apparatus represses representative processes and contents that are no longer necessary for pleasure, self-preservation, and the adaptive growth of the speaking subject and the living organism. Under certain conditions, however, the repressed "that ought to have remained secret" shows up again and produces a feeling of uncanny strangeness.

While saying that he would henceforth tackle "one or two more examples of the uncanny," Freud in his text actually continues, by means of a subtle, secret endeavor, to reveal the circumstances that are favorable to going through repression and generating the uncanny strangeness. The confrontation with *death* and its representation is initially imperative, for our unconscious refuses the fatality of death: "Our unconscious has as little use now as it ever had for the idea of its own mortality." The fear of death dictates an ambivalent attitude: we imagine ourselves surviving (religions promise immortality), but death just the same remains the survivor's enemy, and it accompanies him in his new existence. Apparitions and ghosts represent that ambiguity and fill with uncanny strangeness our confrontations with the image of death.

The fantasy of being buried alive induces the feeling of uncanny strangeness, accompanied by "a certain lasciviousness—the phantasy, I mean, of intra-uterine existence" (p. 244). We are confronted with a second source of the strange: "It often happens that neurotic men declare that they feel there is something uncanny about the female genital organs. This *unheimlish* place, however, is the entrance to the former *Heim* of all human beings, to the place where each one of us lived once upon a time and in the beginning." "There is a joking saying that 'Love is homesickness'" (p. 245).

The *death* and the *feminine*, the end and the beginning that engross and compose us only to frighten us when they break through, one must add "the living person [. . .] when we ascribe evil intentions to him [. . .] that are going to be carried out with the help of special powers" (p. 243). Such malevolent *powers* would amount to a weaving together of the symbolic and the organic—perhaps *drive* itself, on the border of the psyche and biology, overriding the breaking imposed by organic homeostasis. A disturbing symptom of this may be found in epilepsy and madness, and their presence in our fellow beings worries us the more as we dimly sense them in ourselves.

A Semiology of Uncanny Strangeness

Are death, the feminine, and drives always a pretext for the uncanny strangeness? After having broadened the scope of his meditation, which might have led to seeing in uncanniness the description of the working of the unconscious, which is itself dependant on repression, Freud marked its required limits by stressing a few particularities of the semiology within which it emerges. Magical practices, animism, or, in more down-to-earth fashion, "intellectual uncertainty" and "disconcerted" logic (according to E. Jentsch) are all propitious to uncanniness. Now, what brings together these symbolic processes, quite different for all that, lies in a weakening of the value of signs as such and of their specific logic. The symbol ceases to be a symbol and "takes over the full functions of the thing it symbolizes" (p. 244). In other words, the sign is not experienced as arbitrary but assumes a real importance. As a consequence, the material reality that the sign was commonly supposed to point to crumbles away to the benefit of imagination, which is no more than "the over-accentuation of psychical reality in comparison with material reality" (p.

244). We are here confronted with "the omnipotence of thought," which, in order to constitute itself invalidates the arbitrariness of signs and the autonomy of reality as well and places them both under the sway of fantasies expressing infantile desires or fears.

Obsessional neuroses, but also and differently psychoses, have the distinctive feature of "reifying" signs—of slipping from the domain of "speaking" to the domain of "doing." Such a particularity *also* evinces the fragility of repression and, without actually explaining it, allows the return of the repressed to be inscribed in the reification under the guise of the uncanny affect. While, in another semiological device, one might think that the return of the repressed would assume the shape of the somatic symptom or of the acting out, here the breakdown of the arbitrary signifier and its tendency to become reified as psychic contents that take the place of material reality would favor the experience of uncanniness. Conversely, our fleeting or more or less threatening encounter with uncanny strangeness would be a clue to our psychotic latencies and the fragility of our repression—at the same time as it is an indication of the weakness of language as a symbolic barrier that, in the final analysis, structures the repressed.

Strange indeed is the encounter with the other—whom we perceive by means of sight, hearing, smell, but do not "frame" within our consciousness. The other leaves us separate, incoherent; even more so, he can make us feel that we are not in touch with our own feelings, that we reject them or, on the contrary, that we refuse to judge them—we feel "stupid," we have "been had."

Also strange is the experience of the abyss separating me from the other who shocks me—I do not even perceive him, perhaps he crushes me because I negate him. Confronting the foreigner whom I reject and with whom at the same time I identify, I lose my boundaries, I no longer have a container, the memory of experiences when I had been abandoned overwhelm me, I lose my composure. I feel "lost," "indistinct," "hazy." The uncanny strangeness allows for many variations: they all repeat the difficulty I have in situating myself with respect to the other and keep going over the course of identification-projection that lies at the foundation of my reaching autonomy.

At this stage of the journey, one understands that Freud took pains to separate the uncanniness provoked by aesthetic experience from that which is sustained in reality; he most particularly stressed those works in which the uncanny effect is abolished because of the very fact that the entire world of the narrative is fictitious. Such are fairy tales, in which the generalized artifice spares us any possible comparison between sign, imagination, and material reality. As a consequence, artifice neutralizes uncanniness and makes all returns of the repressed plausible, acceptable, and pleasurable. As if absolute enchantment—absolute sublimation— just as, on the other hand, absolute rationality—absolute repression— were our only defenses against uncanny strangeness . . . Unless, depriving us of the dangers as well as the pleasures of strangeness, they be the instruments of their liquidation.

Subjects, Artists, and . . . a King

Linked to anguish, as we have seen, the uncanny strangeness does not, however, merge with it. Initially it is a shock, something unusual, astonishment; and even if anguish comes close, uncanniness maintains that share of unease that leads the self, beyond anguish, toward depersonalization. "The sense of strangeness belongs in the same category as depersonalization," Freud noted, and many analysts have stressed the frequency of the *Unheimliche* affect in phobia, especially when the contours of the self are overtaxed by the clash with something "too good" or "too bad." In short, if anguish revolves around an *object*, uncanniness, on the other hand, is a *destructuration of the self* that may either remain as a psychotic *symptom* or fit in as an *opening* toward the new, as an attempt to tally with the incongruous. While it surely manifests the return of a familiar repressed, the *Unheimliche* requires just the same the impetus of a new encounter with an unexpected outside element: arousing images of death, automatons, doubles, or the female sex (the list is probably not complete, as Freud's text leaves such an impression of a rather distant reserve—because it is passionate), uncanniness occurs when the boundaries between *imagination* and *reality* are erased. This observation reinforces the concept—which arises out of Freud's text—of the *Unheimliche* as a crumbling of conscious defenses, resulting from the conflicts the self experiences with an other—the "strange"—with whom it maintains a conflictual bond, at the same time "a need for identification and a fear of it" (Maurice Bouvet). The clash with the other, the identification of the self with that good or bad other that transgresses the fragile boundaries of the uncertain self, would thus be at the source of an uncanny strangeness whose excessive features, as represented in literature, cannot hide its permanent presence in "normal" psychical dynamics.

A child confides in his analyst that the finest day in his life is that of his birth: "Because that day it was me—I like being me, I don't like being an other." Now he feels other when he has poor grades—when he is bad, alien to the parents' and teachers' desire. Likewise, the unnatural, "foreign" languages, such as writing or mathematics, arouse an uncanny feeling in the child.[2]

This is where we leave the extraordinary realm of literary uncanniness to find its immanence (a necessary hence commonplace one) in psychism as the experience of otherness. It is possible, as Yvon Brès said, that Freud's recourse to aesthetic works in order to set up the notion of uncanny strangeness was an admission that psychoanalysis could not possibly deal with it. Man would be facing a kind of "existential apriorism," in the presence of which Freudian thought merges with Heidegger's phenomenology.[3] Without going so far as to assume such a link, let us note, however, that Freud picks up the phrase again in *The Future of an Illusion* (1927): civilization humanizes nature by endowing it with beings that look like us—it is such an animistic process that enables us "to breathe freely [and] feel at home in the uncanny [so that we] can deal by psychical means with our [previously] senseless anxiety."[4] Here uncanny strangeness is no longer an artistic or pathological product but a psychic law allowing us to confront the unknown and work it out in the process of *Kulturarbeit*, the task of civilization. Freud, who "must himself plead guilty to a special obtuseness in the matter" of the uncanny,[5] thus opens up two other prospects when confronting the strange, which is related to anguish. On the one hand, the sense of strangeness is a mainspring for identification with the other, by working out its depersonalizing impact by means of astonishment. On the other hand, analysis can throw light on such an affect but, far from insisting on breaking it down, it should make way for esthetics (some might add philosophy), with which to saturate its phantasmal progression and insure its cathartic eternal return, for instance with readers of disturbing tales.

The violent, catastrophic aspect the encounter with the *foreigner* may assume is to be included in the generalizing consequences that seem to stem out of Freud's observations on the activating of the uncanny. As test of our astonishment, source of depersonalization, we cannot suppress the symptom that the foreigner provokes; but we simply must come back to it, clear it up, give it the resources our own essential depersonalizations provide, and only thus soothe it.

And yet, the uncanny strangeness can also be evacuated: "No, that does not bother me; I laugh or take action—I go away, I shut my eyes, I strike, I command . . . " Such an elimination of the strange could lead to an elimination of the psyche, leaving, at the cost of mental impoverishment, the way open to acting out, including paranoia and murder. From another point of view, there is no uncanny strangeness for the person enjoying an acknowledged power and a resplendent image. Uncanniness, for that person, is changed into management and authorized expenditure: strangeness is for the "subjects," the sovereign ignores it, knowing how to have it administered. An anecdote related by Saint-Simon provides a good illustration of that situation.[6] The Sun-King (French psychoanalysts strangely avoid questioning major political and artistic figures of national history, even though the latter is so weighed down with discourse and psychological enigmas as well) erases the uncanny and his fear in order to display the whole of his being exclusively within the law and the pleasure of Versailles' pomp. Disturbed innerness is the courtiers' lot; they were the compost of the psychic subtlety that the brilliant writer of memoirs has handed down to us, often remarkably anticipating Freud's speculations.

Finally, some might change the weird into irony. One imagines Saint-Simon, a shrewd smile on his lips, as far removed from regal censorship as he was from the courtiers' embarrassment: the humorist goes right through uncanny strangeness and—starting from a self-confidence that is his own or is based on his belonging to an untouchable universe that is not at all threatened by the war between same and others, ghosts and doubles—seeing in it nothing more than smoke, imaginary structures, signs. To worry or to smile, such is the choice when we are assailed by the strange; our decision depends on how familiar we are with our own ghosts.

The Strange Within Us

The uncanny would thus be the royal way (but in the sense of the court, not of the king) by means of which Freud introduced the fascinated rejection of the other at the heart of that "our self," so poised and dense, which precisely no longer exists ever since Freud and shows itself to be a strange land of borders and othernesses ceaselessly constructed and deconstructed. Strangely enough, there is no mention of *foreigners* in the *Unheimliche*.

Actually, a foreigner seldom arouses the terrifying anguish provoked by death, the female sex, or the "baleful" unbridled drive. Are we nevertheless so sure that the "political" feelings of xenophobia do not include, often unconsciously, that agony of frightened joyfulness that has been called *unheimlich*, that in English is *uncanny*, and the Greeks quite simply call *xenos*, "foreign"? In the fascinated rejection that the foreigner arouses in us, there is a share of uncanny strangeness in the sense of the depersonalization that Freud discovered in it, which takes up again our infantile desires and fears of the other—the other of death, the other of woman, the other of uncontrollable drive. The foreigner is within us. And when we flee from or struggle against the foreigner, we are fighting our unconscious—that "improper" facet of our impossible "own and proper." Delicately, analytically, Freud does not speak of foreigners: he teaches us how to detect foreignness in ourselves. That is perhaps the only way not to hound it outside of us. After Stoic cosmopolitanism, after religious universalist integration, Freud brings us the courage to call ourselves disintegrated in order not to integrate foreigners and even less so to hunt them down, but rather to welcome them to that uncanny strangeness, which is as much theirs as it is ours.

In fact, such a Freudian distraction or discretion concerning the "problem of foreigners"—which appears only as an eclipse or, if one prefers, as a symptom, through the recall of the Greek word *xenoi*[7]— might be interpreted as an invitation (a utopic or very modern one?) not to reify the foreigner, not to petrify him as such, not to petrify *us* as such. But to analyze it by analyzing us. To discover our disturbing otherness, for that indeed is what bursts in to confront that "demon," that threat, that apprehension generated by the projective apparition of the other at the heart of what we persist in maintaining as a proper, solid "us." By recognizing *our* uncanny strangeness we shall neither suffer from it nor enjoy it from the outside. The foreigner is within me, hence we are all foreigners. If I am a foreigner, there are no foreigners. Therefore Freud does not talk about them. The ethics of psychoanalysis implies a politics: it would involve a cosmopolitanism of a new sort that, cutting across governments, economies, and markets, might work for a mankind whose solidarity is founded on the consciousness of its unconscious—desiring, destructive, fearful, empty, impossible. Here we are far removed from a call to brotherhood, about which one has already ironically pointed out its debt to paternal and divine authority—"In order to have brothers there must be a father," as Louis-François Veuillot did not fail to say when he sharply addressed humanists. On the basis of an erotic, death-bearing unconscious, the uncanny strangeness—a projection as well as a first working out of death drive—which adumbrates the work of the "second" Freud, the one of *Beyond the Pleasure Principle*, sets the difference within us in its most bewildering shape and presents it as the ultimate condition of our being *with* others.

NOTES

1. Sigmund Freud, *The Uncanny*, in *The Standard Edition of the Complete Psychological Works of Sigmund Freud*, 17:220. Page numbers given parenthetically in text refer to this volume.

There are, as usual, discrepancies between the French and English translations of Freud. Here it is especially bothersome because *Das Unheimliche* comes out in French as *l'inquiétante étrangeté*, a phrase that matches Kristeva's vocabulary very neatly but is at a linguistic remove from our "uncanny." While following Strachey's translation, thus letting "the uncanny" stand in all the quotations from Freud's text, I have tried to bridge the gap between French and English words by occasionally rendering the French phrase, *inquiétante étrangeté*, in Kristeva's text, as "uncanny strangeness"—Trans.

2. See Paul Denis, "L'Inquiétante Etrangeté chez l'enfant," *Revue de Psychanalyse* 3 (1981): 503.

3. See Yvon Brès, "Modestie des philosophes: modestie des psychanalystes," *Psychanalyse à l'Université* 11 (October 1986): 585–86. Beyond the frequency of the word *Unheimliche* in German, which removes a bit of spice from the encounter, Brès notes a certain thematic convergence in its use between Freud and Heidegger. With the latter, anguish, which resides in the being-in-the-world, is uncanniness ("In der Angst ist einem 'unheimlich'"—*Sein und Zeit*, section 40): "But this distressing aspect, this strangeness, signifies at the same time the not-being-at-home." Later, *What Is Metaphysics* (1929) clarifies existential anguish as experienced when facing the impossibility of any determination, and it is again described as *Unheimlichkeit*.

4. Freud, *The Future of an Illusion*, *Standard Edition*, 21:17.

5. Freud, *The Uncanny*, *Standard Edition*, 17:220.

6. "Five or six days later I was at the King's supper [. . .]. As sweets were being served, I noticed something or other, rather large, seemingly black, in the air over the table, which I was unable either to make out or point to, so rapidly did this large thing fall at the end of the table [. . .] The noise it made when falling and the weight of the thing nearly caused it to give way and caused the dishes to jump, but without upsetting any [. . .] The King, after the impact, half turned his head and, without being disturbed in any way, I believe, he said, those are my fringes. It was indeed a bundle, larger than the hat of a priest . . . It had been thrown from far behind me [. . .] and a small bit that had come loose in the air had fallen on top of the King's wig; Livry, who was seated to his left, saw it and removed it. He came near the end of the table and saw that they were indeed fringes twisted into a bundle [. . .] Livry, wanting to remove the bundle, found a note attached to it; he took it and left the bundle [. . .]. It contained, in a misshapen, extended writing, like that of a woman, these very words: Take your fringes back, Bontemps; they are more trouble than pleasure. I kiss the King's hands. It was rolled but not sealed. The King again wanted to take it from D'Aquin's hands who stepped back, sniffed it, rubbed it, turned it every which way, and showed it to the King without letting him touch it. The King asked him

to read it aloud, even though he himself read it at the same time. That, said the King, is rather insolent!—but in an even, somewhat statesmanlike tone of voice. After that he asked that the bundle be removed [. . .] Afterwards the King no longer mentioned it and no one dared speak about it, not aloud at any rate; and the remainder of the supper was served as if nothing had happened." Saint-Simon, *Mémoires*, "Bibliothèque de la Pléiade" (Paris: Gallimard, 1983), pp. 632–33. Christian David accompanies this excerpt with a keen commentary in "Irréductible étrangeté," *Revue de Psychanalyse* 3 (1981): 463–71.

    7. Freud, *The Uncanny, Standard Edition*, 17:221.

In Practice . . .

Should nationality be obtained automatically or, on the contrary, should it be chosen by means of a responsible, deliberate act? Is *jus solis* sufficient to erase *jus sanguinis* (when children of immigrants born on French soil are involved), or is it necessary to have an expression of desire from the parties concerned? May foreigners obtain political rights? Subsequent to the right to join labor unions and professional associations, should the very right to vote be granted them within local communities and, eventually, on the national level?

Questions do keep piling up; and the Committee of Wise Men (as it was dubbed by the media) who pondered over the "Nationality Code" has drawn up reasonable suggestions. Having noted that "France has, in both relative and absolute terms, the largest foreign population in its modern history," and that "it is not in the interest of any country to allow excessively large foreign minorities to develop on its soil, minorities that would call attention to themselves through insisting on their difference or through being excluded from social and national life," the Committee on Nationality chaired by Marceau Long advocated "granting French nationality to those foreigners who have settled in France on a long-term basis" and improving the "modalities of acquiring [French nationality] as a result of a conscious choice, which would be advantageous to the individual's integration." It posited "integration as a necessity."[1] Those suggestions will most obviously be discussed, questioned, at least partly adopted, and are necessarily evolutive in nature.

In the kaleidoscope that France is becoming—kaleidoscope first of the Mediterranean and progressively of the third world—the differences between natives and immigrants will never be as clear-cut as before. The homogenizing power of French civilization, which has been able to take in and unify over the course of centuries various influences and ethnic groups, has been tried and tested. Now France today is in the process of welcoming newcomers who do not give up their particularities. The situation is quite different from the one that presided over the beginnings of the United States of America, which offered a new religious and economic faith to uprooted people who all found themselves in the same boat. In France, at the end of the twentieth century, each is fated to remain the same *and* the other—without forgetting his original culture but putting it in perspective to the extent of having it not only exist side by side but also alternate with others' culture. A new homogeneity is not very likely, perhaps hardly desirable. We are called upon, through the pressures of the economy, the media, and history to live together in a single country, France, itself in the process of being integrated into Europe. We already have so many difficulties—but also so many advantages—coexisting in this new multinational (and not supranational) country that Europe has become—even though it is made up of nations whose cultures have been close, religions similar, and economies interdependent for centuries! Consequently one can assess the difficulty presented, in the bosom of the same political entity (even though it might be in the process of being integrated with others), by the cohabitation of people whose considerable ethnic, religious, and economic diversity clashes with the present tradition and mentality of those welcoming them. Are we headed for a jigsaw-puzzle nation made up of various particularities, whose predominant numbers remain French for the time being—but for how long?

A changed attitude of mind is necessary in order to favor the best harmony in such a versatility. What might be involved, in the final analysis, is extending to the notion of *foreigner* the right of respecting our own foreignness and, in short, of the "privacy" that insures freedom in democracies. The access of foreigners to political rights will follow on the heels of that evolution and, necessarily, with adequate legal guarantees. One might imagine, for instance, a "double nationality" statute that would give those "foreigners" who want it a number of rights—but also the political duties specific to natives, with a reciprocity clause giving the latter rights and duties in the countries of origin of those same foreigners. Such a rule, easily applicable within the European Economic Community, could be tempered and adjusted for other countries.

Nevertheless, the fundamental question that slows down such arrangements, which lawyers and politicians are at present working out under the changing constraints of national economic needs, belongs to a more psychological or even metaphysical realm. In the absence of a new community bond—a saving religion that would integrate the bulk of wanderers and different people within a new consensus, other than "more money and goods for everyone"—we are, for the first time in history, confronted with the following situation: we must live with different people while relying on our personal moral codes, without the assistance of a set that would include our particularities while transcending them. A paradoxical community is emerging, made up of foreigners who are reconciled with themselves to the extent that they recognize themselves as foreigners. The multinational society would thus be the consequence of an extreme individualism, but conscious of its discontents and limits, knowing only indomitable people ready to help themselves in their weakness, a weakness whose other name is our radical strangeness.

NOTES

1. See *Etre français aujourd'hui et demain* (Paris: 10/18, 1988), 2:235–36.

PART 5

Maternity, Feminism, and Female Sexuality

Desire in Language

"Motherhood According to Giovanni Bellini"

"Motherhood According to Giovanni Bellini" was first published in *Peinture* in December 1975 (when Kristeva was pregnant with her son who was born in 1976) and was reprinted in *Polylogue* (Paris: Editions de Seuil) in 1977. The first section, "The Maternal Body," first appeared in translation by Claire Pajaczkowska in the journal *m/f* in 1979. It was translated by Thomas Gora, Alice Jardine, and Leon Roudiez in *Desire in Language*, edited by Leon Roudiez (New York: Columbia University Press) in 1980. "The Maternal Body," from *Desire in Language* is reprinted here. In this section, Kristeva sets up a theory of maternity with which she goes on to analyze some of Bellini's paintings of the Madonna and Child.

Kristeva argues that the two discourses of maternity that are currently available, science and Christianity, are inadequate to explain maternity. Science explains maternity as a natural, and therefore presocial, biological process. Yet, where is the mother in this process? Is she the subject of this process or merely subject to it? If the mother is seen as merely subject to this process over which she has no control, then her identity (and subsequently the identity of the infant who identifies with her) as a speaking subject is threatened. If, on the other hand, the mother is seen as the master of this process, then she is the master of something presocial and biological and her identity (and subsequently the identity of the infant) as a speaking subject is once again threatened. Science cannot account for the splitting of subjectivity in the maternal body.

Although Christianity does address the move from nature to culture in the maternal body with the image of the Virgin Mary, in "Stabat Mater" Kristeva suggests that the image of the Virgin does not provide an adequate model of maternity; with the Virgin, the maternal body is reduced to silence. In both "Stabat Mater" and "Motherhood According to Bellini" Kristeva claims that pregnancy and childbirth can be experienced as a reunion with one's own mother. "By giving birth, the woman enters into contact with her mother; she becomes, she is her own mother; they are the same continuity differentiating itself. She thus actualizes the homosexual facet of motherhood." (p. 239). Kristeva's thesis that pregnancy and childbirth reunite a woman and her mother and bring back primal homosexual bonds is radically opposed to Freud's theory that childbirth is motivated by penis envy. Kristeva suggests a notion of the maternal body that locates its *jouissance* in femininity and maternity itself rather than the Freudian notion of the maternal body, which is always defined in relation to masculine sexuality and a phallic economy of desire.

Tales of Love

In *Tales of Love*, Kristeva complicates not only the paternal function but also the maternal function (see part 3 above). Unlike Freud and Lacan, who attribute language acquisition and socialization to the paternal function and ignore the function of the mother as anything other than the primary object or partial object, Kristeva elaborates and complicates the maternal function. She insists that there is regulation and structure in the maternal body and the child's relationship to that body. Before the paternal law is in place, the infant is subject to maternal regulations, what Kristeva calls "the law before the law." While in the womb, the fetus is engaged in processes of exchange with the maternal body that are regulated by that body. After birth, there are further exchanges between the maternal body and the infant. The mother monitors and regulates what goes into, and what comes out of, the infant's body. Language acquisition and socialization, insofar as they develop out of regulations and law, have their foundations in the maternal function prior to the law of the father of traditional psychoanalysis.

In "Stabat Mater," Kristeva suggests that Freud's account of motherhood as either an attempt to satisfy penis envy (baby = penis) or a reactivated anal drive (baby = feces) is merely a masculine fantasy. With regard to the complexities of maternal experience, claims Kristeva, "Freud offers only a massive nothing, which, for those who might care to analyze it, is punctuated with this or that remark on the part of Freud's mother, proving to him in the kitchen that his own body is anything but immortal and will crumble away like dough; or the sour photograph of Marthe Freud, the wife, a whole mute story." (p. 255)

Originally titled "Hérethique de l'amour," "Stabat Mater" was published in *Tel Quel* (Winter 1977) and reprinted in *Histoires d'amour* (1983). "Stabat Mater" was translated by Leon Roudiez as part of *Tales of Love* (New York: Columbia University Press, 1987). "Stabat Mater" is a Latin hymn that begins with the words "Stabat mater dolorosa," "Stood the Mother, full of grief." "Stabat Mater" is written in two columns. In one column Kristeva poetically describes her own experience of motherhood and the birth of her son (1976), and in the other she argues that we need to reconceive maternity. In her interview with Rosalind Coward, Kristeva says that with the split columns she was trying to represent the wound or scar as the place from which the theoretician writes. The theoretician writes a knowing discourse about something, in this case maternity, in which she is deeply and painfully involved. Kristeva uses the scarred text to conjure that pain.

In the theoretical half of the text, Kristeva suggests that we need an image of maternity that can found, rather than threaten, the social relationship. Western images of maternity, especially what she calls the "cult of the Virgin Mary," do not allow for an image of the mother as a speaking social being. "Stabat Mater" is a manifesto of sorts that ends with a call for a reconceived notion of maternity and an heretical ethics, "herethics," based on a reconceived maternity. Insofar as this ethics of maternity would replace the Catholic image of the Virgin bearing her sorrow and baring her breast, it would be a heretical ethics, an ethics that does not reduce women to "milk and tears."

In "Stabat Mater" and "Women's Time" (1979) Kristeva suggests that currently the only way available for women to reestablish their identities with the maternal body is through becoming mothers themselves. Pregnancy allows for an identification with an other: "Pregnancy is a dramatic ordeal: a splitting of the body, the division and coexistence of self and other, of nature and awareness, of physiology and speech" (p. 219). Pregnancy not only identifies a woman with her own mother, but also requires a new notion of identity. As Kristeva argues in "Stabat Mater," neither the mother nor the fetus controls pregnancy. The maternal body operates between nature and culture, between biology and sociology. Neither the mother nor fetus is a unified subject. Rather, the maternal body is the most obvious example of a subject-in-process. Kristeva developed her notion of a subject-in-process in "From One Identity to an Other" and in *Revolution*, where she maintains that we are all subjects-in-process.

Kristeva further delineates the maternal and paternal functions in her interview with Rosalind Coward. There, Kristeva suggests that the distinction between these two necessary functions is breaking down. In this interview, Kristeva makes it clear that maternal and paternal functions can be performed by various people in an infant's development. She also discusses her relationship to feminism. This interview took place at the Institute of Contemporary Arts in London at a conference on Desire in which Kristeva participated. It was published in the *Institute of Contemporary Arts Documents* in 1984 in a special issue on desire.

New Maladies of the Soul

"Women's Time"

"Le Temps des femmes," originally published in *34/44: Cahiers de recherche de sciences des textes et documents*, no. 5, was originally translated by Alice Jardine and Harry Blake as "Women's Time," in *Signs* (Autumn 1981) and reprinted in *Feminist Theory: A Critique of Ideology*, edited by N. Keohane, M. Z. Rosaldo, and B. C. Gelpi (Brighton: Harvester Press, 1982). This translation was also reprinted in *The Kristeva Reader* in 1986, edited by Toril Moi. A slightly updated version of "Le Temps des femmes" was reprinted in *Nouvelles maladies de l'âme* (Paris: Fayard, 1993) and newly translated as "Women's Time" by Ross Guberman in *New Maladies of the Soul* (New York: Columbia University Press, 1994). The new translation by Ross Guberman appears here.

"Women's Time" has had a mixed response from feminists in the United States. In this essay, Kristeva analyzes different tendencies in the women's movement and feminist theory, primarily in Western Europe and also in the United States and Eastern Europe. She identifies what she calls three generations of feminism, which she complicates throughout her analysis. The first (prior to 1968) feminism is the feminism of suffragettes and existentialists. It is a struggle over the identity of woman as rational citizen, deserving of the "rights of man." These feminists maintain that the ideal "woman" contains the same characteristics of the ideal "man" and the struggle is to insert her in man's linear history. The second (after 1968) feminism is the feminism of psychoanalysts and artists. It is a struggle against reducing the identity of woman to the identity of man by inserting her into his linear time. These feminists assert a unique essence of woman or the feminine which falls outside of phallic time and phallic discourse. Kristeva delineates the advantages, advances, and limitations of both of these feminist strategies. Ultimately, she rejects them both for their tendencies to reify and idealize a notion of woman that is homogeneous and does not allow for individual differences. Kristeva identifies herself with a third generation of feminists who challenge notions of seamless identity in general, and notions of man and woman in particular. The last paragraph of "Women's Time," recently added to the essay, points to a post-feminist future.

Interview with Elaine Hoffman Baruch on Feminism in the United States and France

In her interview with Elaine Hoffman Baruch, Kristeva discusses the notion of abjection developed in *Powers of Horror*. She indicates that the abjection of the maternal body that she described in *Powers of Horror* applies only to the experience of the male infant. The female infant has a different relationship to the maternal body. In addition, she discusses her views on feminism in the United States; she is asked to compare her views with those of Dinnerstein, Chodorow, Millett, and Firestone. Also, she addresses issues raised by advances in reproductive technology. This interview took place in Paris in 1980. A translation of the interview by Brom Anderson was first published in *Partisan Review* in 1984. An expanded version of that interview was reprinted in *Women Analyze Women*, edited by Elaine Baruch and Lucienne Serrano, published by New York University Press in 1988. That expanded version is reprinted here.

Black Sun

In her earlier work, *Revolution in Poetic Language*, Kristeva follows Lacan in identifying sexual difference with differing relations to the phallus, in her later work, *Black Sun* (1987), she suggests that sexual difference is a result of differing relations to the maternal body. Although even traditional Freudian theory identifies the phallus and the maternal body in the figure of the phallic mother, in *Black Sun* Kristeva explores a melancholy element of feminine sexuality that cannot be completely explained in terms of either the notion of a phallic mother or the notion of a castrated mother.

In *Black Sun*, Kristeva describes feminine sexuality as a melancholy sexuality because the female infant cannot abject the maternal body without abjecting herself. "Matricide," says Kristeva "is our vital necessity"; the infant must be weaned from the maternal body (p. 27). Weaning requires that the infant abject the maternal body, not as the desiring body of a woman, but as the container that meets its needs. Within a patriarchal and heterosexist culture, however, while males can abject and eroticize the maternal body in order to develop a heterosexual sexuality, females can neither abject nor eroticize the maternal body in order to develop a heterosexual sexuality: "in order to separate from their mother's bodies females must separate from themselves as women; and in order to maintain some identification with their mothers as the bodies of women females carry around the 'corpse' of their mother's bodies locked in the crypt of their psyches" (p. 28–29). Because the girl's first love object is her mother, in a heterosexist culture, this primary homosexual feminine sexuality remains repressed and we lack ways of describing loving relations between women, homosexual or otherwise. Feminine sexuality is melancholic because to identify as women, females must identify with an abject maternal body.

Desire in Language

Motherhood According to Giovanni Bellini

The Maternal Body

Cells fuse, split, and proliferate; volumes grow, tissues stretch, and body fluids change rhythm, speeding up or slowing down. Within the body, growing as a graft, indomitable, there is an other. And no one is present, within that simultaneously dual and alien space, to signify what is going on. "It happens, but I'm not there." "I cannot realize it, but it goes on." Motherhood's impossible syllogism.

This becoming-a-mother, this gestation, can possibly be accounted for by means of only two discourses. There is *science*; but as an objective discourse, science is not concerned with the subject, the mother as site of her proceedings. There is *Christian theology* (especially canonical theology); but theology defines maternity only as an impossible elsewhere, a sacred beyond, a vessel of divinity, a spiritual tie with the ineffable godhead, and transcendence's ultimate support—necessarily virginal and committed to assumption. Such are the wiles of Christian reason (Christianity's still matchless rationalism, or at least its rationalizing power, finally become clear); through the maternal body (in a state of virginity and "dormition"[1] before Assumption), it thus establishes a sort of subject at the point where the subject and its speech split apart, fragment, and vanish. Lay humanism took over the configuration of that subject through the cult of the mother; tenderness, love, and seat of social conservation.

And yet, if we presume that *someone* exists throughout the process of cells, molecules, and atoms accumulating, dividing, and multiplying without any *identity* (biological or socio-symbolical) having been formed so far, are we not positing an animism that reflects the inherent psychosis of the speaking Being? So, if we suppose that a *mother* is the subject of gestation, in other words the *master* of a process that science, despite its effective devices, acknowledges it cannot now and perhaps never will be able to take away from her; if we suppose her to be *master* of a process that is prior to the social-symbolic-linguistic contract of the group, then we acknowledge the risk of losing identity at the same time as we ward it off. We recognize on the one hand that biology jolts us by means of unsymbolized instinctual drives and that this phenomenon eludes social intercourse, the representation of preexisting objects, and the contract of desire. On the other hand, we immediately deny it; we say there can be no escape, for mamma is there, she embodies this phenomenon; she warrants that *everything is*, and that it is representable. In a double-barreled move, psychotic tendencies are acknowledged, but at the same time they are settled, quieted, and bestowed upon the mother in order to maintain the ultimate guarantee: symbolic coherence.

This move, however, also reveals, better than any mother ever could, that the maternal body is the place of a splitting, which, even though hypostatized by Christianity, nonetheless remains a constant factor of social reality. Through a body, destined to insure reproduction of the species, the woman-subject, although under the sway of the paternal function (as symbolizing, speaking subject and like all others), more of a *filter* than anyone else—a thoroughfare, a threshold where "nature" confronts "culture." To imagine that there is *someone* in that filter—such is the source of religious mystifications, the font that nourishes them: the fantasy of the so-called "Phallic" Mother. Because if, on the contrary, there were no one on this threshold, if the mother were not, that is, if she were not phallic, then every speaker would be led to conceive of its Being in relation to some void, a nothingness asymmetrically opposed to this Being, a permanent threat against, first, its mastery, and ultimately, its stability.

The discourse of analysis proves that the *desire* for motherhood is without fail a desire to bear a child of the father (a child of her own father) who, as a result, is often assimilated to the baby itself and thus returned to its place as *devalorized man*, summoned only to accomplish his function, which is to originate and justify reproductive desire. Only through these phantasmatic nuptials can the father-daughter incest be carried out and the baby come to exist. At that, the incest is too far removed, bringing peace only to those who firmly adhere to the paternal symbolic axis. Otherwise, once the object is produced, once the fruit is detached, the ceremony loses its effect unless it be repeated forever.

And yet, through and with this desire, motherhood seems to be impelled *also* by a nonsymbolic, nonpaternal causality. Only Ferenczi, Freud, and, later, Marie Bonaparte, have spoken about this, evoking the biological destiny of each differentiated sex. Material compulsion, spasm of a memory belonging to the species that either binds together or splits apart to perpetuate itself, series of markers with no other significance than the eternal return of the life-death biological cycle. How can we verbalize this prelinguistic, unrepresentable memory? Heraclitus' flux, Epicurus' atoms, the whirling dust of cabalic, Arab, and Indian mystics, and the stippled drawings of psychedelics—all seem better metaphors than the theories of Being, the logos, and its laws.

Such an excursion to the limits of primal regression can be phantasmatically experienced as the reunion of a woman-mother with the body of *her* mother. The body of her mother is always the same Master-Mother of instinctual drive, a ruler over psychosis, a subject of biology, but also, one toward which women aspire all the more passionately simply because it lacks a penis: that body cannot penetrate her as can a man when possessing his wife. By giving birth, the woman enters into contact with her mother; she becomes, she is her own mother; they are the same continuity differentiating itself. She thus actualizes the homosexual facet of motherhood, through which a woman is simultaneously closer to her instinctual memory, more open to her own psychosis, and consequently, more negatory of the social, symbolic bond.

The symbolic paternal facet relieves feminine aphasia present within the desire to bear the father's child. It is an appeasement that turns into melancholy as soon as the child becomes an object, a gift to others, neither self nor part of the self, an object destined to be a subject, an other. Melancholy readjusts the paranoia that drives to action (often violent) and to discourse (essentially parental, object-oriented, and pragmatic discourse) the feminine, verbal scarcity so prevalent in our culture.

The homosexual-maternal facet is a whirl of words, a complete absence of meaning and seeing; it is feeling, displacement, rhythm, sound, flashes, and fantasied clinging to the maternal body as a screen against the plunge. Perversion slows down the schizophrenia that collapsing identities and the delights of the well-known and oft-solicited (by some women) pantheist fusion both brush up against.

Those afflicted or affected by psychosis have put up in its place the image of the Mother: for women, a paradise lost but seemingly close at hand; for men, a hidden god but constantly present through occult fantasy. And even psychoanalysts believe in it.

Yet, swaying between these two positions can only mean, for the woman involved, that she is within an *enceinte* separating her from the world of everyone else.[2] Enclosed in this "elsewhere," an *enceinte* woman loses communital meaning, which suddenly appears to her as worthless, absurd, or at best, comic—a surface agitation severed from its impossible foundations. Oriental nothingness probably better sums up what, in the eyes of a Westerner, can only be regression. And yet it is jouissance, but like a negative of the one, tied to an object, that is borne by the unfailingly masculine libido. Here, alterity becomes nuance, contradiction becomes a variant, tension becomes passage, and discharge becomes peace. This tendency toward equalization, which is seen as a regressive extinction of symbolic capabilities, does not, however, reduce differences; it resides within the smallest, most archaic, and most uncertain of differences. It is powerful sublimation and indwelling of the symbolic within instinctual drives. It affects this series of "little differences-resemblances" (as the Chinese logicians of antiquity would say). Before founding society in the same stroke as signs and communication, they are the precondition of the latter's existence, as they constitute the living entity within its species, with its needs, its elementary apperceptions and communication, distinguishing between the instinctual drives of life and death. It affects primal repression. An ultimate danger for identity, but also supreme power of symbolic instance thus returning to matters of its concern. Sublimation here is both eroticizing without residue and a disappearance of eroticism as it returns to its source.

The speaker reaches this limit, this requisite of sociality, only by virtue of a particular, discursive practice called "art." A woman also attains it (and in our society, *especially*) through the strange form of split symbolization (threshold of language and instinctual drive, of the "symbolic" and the "semiotic") of which the act of giving birth consists. As the archaic process of socialization, one might even say civilization, it causes the childbearing woman to cathect, immediately and unwittingly, the physiological operations and instinctual drives dividing and multiplying her, first, in a biological, and finally, a social teleology. The maternal body slips away from the discursive hold and immediately conceals a cipher that must be taken into account biologically and socially. This ciphering of the species, however, this pre- and transsymbolic memory, makes the mother mistress of neither begetting nor instinctual drive (such a fantasy underlies the cult of any ultimately feminine deity); it does make of the maternal body the stakes of a natural and "objective" control, independent of any individual consciousness; it inscribes both biological operations and their instinctual echoes into this necessary and hazardous *program* constituting every species. The maternal body is the module of a biosocial program. Its jouissance, which is mute, is nothing more than a recording, on the screen of the preconscious, of both the messages that consciousness, in its analytical course, picks up from this ciphering process and their classifications as empty foundation, as a-subjective lining of our rational exchanges as social beings. If it is true that every national language has its own dream language and unconscious, then each of the sexes—a division so much more archaic and fundamental than the one into languages—would have its own unconscious wherein the biological and social program of the species would be ciphered in confrontation with language, exposed to its influence, but independent of it. The symbolic destiny of the speaking animal, which is essential although it comes second, being superimposed upon the biological—this destiny *seals off* (and in women, in order to preserve the homology of the group, it *censures*) that archaic basis and the special jouissance it procures in being transferred to the symbolic. Privileged, "psychotic" moments, or whatever induces them naturally, thus become necessary. Among such "natural" inducements, maternity is needed for this sexual modality to surface, this fragile, secretly guarded and incommunicable modality, quickly stifled by standard palliatives (by virile and "rational" censorship, or by the sentimentality of "maternal" tenderness toward a substitute-object for everything). This process is quite rightly understood as the demand for a penis. Fantasy indeed has no other sign, no other way to imagine that the speaker is capable of reaching the Mother, and thus, of unsettling its own limits. And, as long as there is language-symbolism-paternity, there will never be any other way to represent, to objectify, and to explain this unsettling of the symbolic stratum, this nature/culture threshold, this instilling the subjectless biological program into the very body of a symbolizing subject, this event called motherhood.

In other words, from the point of view of social coherence, which is where legislators, grammarians, and even psychoanalysts have their seat; which is where every body is made homologous to a male speaking body, motherhood would be nothing more than a phallic attempt to reach the Mother who is presumed to exist at the very place where (social and biological) identity recedes. If it is true that idealist ideologies develop along these lines, urging women to satisfy this presumed demand and to maintain the ensuing order, then, on the other hand, any negation of this utilitarian, social, and symbolic aspect of motherhood plunges into regression—but a particular regression whose currently recognized manifestations lead to the hypostasis of blind substance, to the negation of symbolic position, and to a justification of this regression under the aegis of the same Phallic Mother-screen.

The language of art, too, follows (but differently and more closely) the other aspect of maternal jouissance, the sublimation taking place at the very moment of primal repression within the mother's body, arising perhaps unwittingly out of her marginal position. At the intersection of sign and rhythm, of representation and light, of the symbolic and the semiotic, the artist speaks from a place where she is not, where she knows not. He delineates what, in her, is a body rejoicing [*jouissant*]. The very existence of aesthetic practice makes clear that the Mother as subject is a delusion, just as the negation of the so-called poetic dimension of language leads one to believe in the existence of the Mother, and consequently, of transcendence. Because, through a symbiosis of meaning and nonmeaning, of representation and interplay of differences, the artist lodges into language, and through his identification with the mother (fetishism or incest), his own specific jouissance, thus traversing both sign and object. Thus, before all other speakers, he bears witness to what the unconscious (through the screen of the mother) records of those clashes that occur between the biological and social programs of the species. This means that through and across secondary repression (founding of signs), aesthetic practice touches upon primal repression (founding biological series and the laws of the species). At the place where it obscurely succeeds within the maternal body, every artist tries his hand, but rarely with equal success.

Nevertheless, craftsmen of Western art reveal better than anyone else the artist's debt to the maternal body and/or motherhood's entry into symbolic existence—that is, translibidinal jouissance, eroticism taken over by the language of art. Not only is a considerable portion of pictorial art devoted to motherhood, but within this representation itself, from Byzantine iconography to Renaissance humanism and the worship of the body that it initiates, two attitudes toward the maternal body emerge, prefiguring two destinies within the very economy of Western representation. Leonardo Da Vinci and Giovanni Bellini seem to exemplify in the best fashion the opposition between these two attitudes. On the one hand, there is a tilting toward the body as fetish. On the other, a predominance of luminous, chromatic differences beyond and despite corporeal representation. Florence and Venice. Worship of the figurable, representable man; or integration of the image accomplished in its truth-likeness within the luminous serenity of the unrepresentable.

A unique biographical experience and an uncommon, historical inter-section of pagan-matriarchal Orientalism with sacred Christianity and incipient humanism were perhaps needed for Bellini's brush to retain the traces of a marginal experience, through and across which a maternal body might recognize its own, otherwise inexpressible in our culture.

NOTES

1. "Dormition" refers to the period of the Virgin Mary's death, which is viewed merely as a period of sleep, before she was carried to heaven (Assumption). The word originated in the *Transitus Maria*, a fifth-century Byzantine apocrypha. —Trans.

2. The French word *enceinte* has been kept as the only way to preserve the pun: *enciente* is a protective wall around a town; *femme enceinte* is a pregnant woman.—Trans.

Tales of Love

Stabat Mater

The Paradox: Mother or Primary Narcissism

If it is not possible to say of a *woman* what she *is* (without running the risk of abolishing her difference), would it perhaps be different concerning the *mother*, since that is the only function of the "other sex" to which we can definitely attribute existence? And yet, there, too, we are caught in a paradox. First, we live in a civilization where the *consecrated* (religious or secular) representation of femininity is absorbed by motherhood. If, however, one looks at it more closely, this motherhood is the *fantasy* that is nurtured by the adult, man or woman, of a lost territory; what is more, it involves less an idealized archaic mother than the idealization of the *relationship* that binds us to her, one that cannot be localized—an idealization of primary narcissism. Now, when feminism demands a new representation of femininity, it seems to identify motherhood with that idealized misconception and, because it rejects the image and its misuse, feminism circumvents the real experience that fantasy overshadows. The result?—a negation or rejection of motherhood by some avant-garde feminist groups. Or else an acceptance—conscious or not—of its traditional representations by the great mass of people, women and men.

I

FLASH—instant of time or of dream without time; inordinately swollen atoms of a bond, a vision, a shiver, a yet formless, unnameable embryo. Epiphanies. Photos of what is not yet visible and that language necessarily skims over from afar, allusively. Words that are always too distant, too abstract for this underground swarming of seconds, folding in unimaginable spaces. Writing them down is an ordeal of discourse, like love. What is loving, for a woman, the same thing as writing. Laugh. Impossible. Flash on the unnameable, weavings of abstractions to be torn. Let a body venture at last out of its shelter, take a chance with meaning under a veil of words. WORD FLESH. From one to the other, eternally, broken up visions, metaphors of the invisible.

II

Christianity is doubtless the most refined symbolic construct in which femininity, to the extent that it transpires through it—and it does so incessantly—is focused on *Maternality*.[1] Let us call "maternal" the ambivalent principle that is bound to the species, on the one hand, and on the other stems from an identity catastrophe that causes the Name to topple over into the unnameable that one imagines as femininity, nonlanguage, or body. Thus Christ, the Son of man, when all is said and done, is "human" only through his mother—as if Christly or Christian humanism could only be a maternalism (this is, besides, what some secularizing trends within its orbit do not cease claiming in their esotericism). And yet, the humanity of the Virgin mother is not always obvious, and we

shall see how, in her being cleared of sin, for instance, Mary distinguishes herself from mankind. But at the same time the most intense revelation of God, which occurs in mysticism, is given only to a person who assumes himself as "maternal." Augustine, Bernard of Clairvaux, Meister Eckhart, to mention but a few, played the part of the Father's virgin spouses, or even, like Bernard, received drops of virginal milk directly on their lips. Freedom with respect to the maternal territory then becomes the pedestal upon which love of God is erected. As a consequence, mystics, those "happy Schrebers" (Sollers) throw a bizarre light on the psychotic sore of modernity: it appears as the incapability of contemporary codes to tame the maternal, that is, primary narcissism. Uncommon and "literary," their present-day counterparts are always somewhat oriental, if not tragical— Henry Miller, who says he is pregnant; Artaud, who sees himself as "his daughters" or "his mother" . . . It is the orthodox constituent of Christianity, through John Chrysostom's golden mouth, among others, that sanctioned the transitional function of the Maternal by calling the Virgin a "bond," a "medium," or an "interval," thus opening the door to more or less heretical identifications with the Holy Ghost.

This resorption of femininity within the Maternal is specific to many civilizations, but Christianity, in its own fashion, brings it to its peak. Could it be that such a reduction represents no more than a masculine appropriation of the Maternal, which, in line with our hypothesis, is only a fantasy masking primary narcissism? Or else, might one detect in it, in other respects, the workings of enigmatic sublimation? These are perhaps the workings of masculine sublimation, a sublimation just the same, if it be true that for Freud picturing Da Vinci, and even for Da Vinci himself, the taming of that economy (of the Maternal or of primary narcissism) is a requirement for artistic, literary, or painterly accomplishment?

Within that perspective, however, there are two questions, among others, that remain unanswered. What is there, in the portrayal of the Maternal in general and particularly in its Christian, virginal, one, that reduces social anguish and gratifies a male being; what is there that also satisfies a woman so that a commonality of the sexes is set up, beyond and in spite of their glaring incompatibility and permanent warfare? Moreover, is there something in that Maternal notion that ignores what a woman might say or want—as a result, when women speak out today it is in matters of conception and motherhood that their annoyance is basically centered. Beyond social and political demands, this takes the well-known "discontents" of our civilization to a level where Freud would not follow—the discontents of the species.

A Triumph of the Unconscious in Monotheism

It would seem that the "virgin" attribute for Mary is a translation error, the translator having substituted for the Semitic term that indicates the sociolegal status of a young unmarried woman the Greek word *parthenos*, which on the other hand specifies a physiological and psychological condition: virginity. One might read into this the Indo-European fascination (which Dumézil analyzed)[2] with the virgin daughter as guardian of paternal power; one might also detect an ambivalent conspiracy, through excessive spiritualization, of the mother-goddess and the underlying matriarchy with which Greek culture and Jewish monotheism kept struggling. The fact remains that western Christianity has organized that "translation error," projected its own fantasies into it, and produced one of the most powerful imaginary constructs known in the history of civilizations.

The story of the virginal cult in Christianity amounts in fact to the imposition of pagan-rooted beliefs in, and often against, dogmas of the official Church. It is true that the Gospels already posit Mary's existence. But they suggest only very discreetly the immaculate conception of Christ's mother, they say nothing concerning Mary's own background and speak of her only seldom at the side of her son or during crucifixion. Thus Matthew 1:20 (". . . the angel of the Lord appeared to him in a dream and said, 'Joseph, son of David, do not be afraid to take Mary home as your wife, because she has conceived what is in her by the Holy Spirit'"), and Luke 1:34 ("Mary said to the angel, 'But how can this come about since I do not know man?'") open a door, a narrow opening for all that, but one that would soon widen thanks to apocryphal additions, on impregnation without sexuality; according to this notion a woman, preserved from masculine intervention, conceives alone with a "third party," a nonperson, the Spirit. In the rare instances when the Mother of Jesus appears in the Gospels, she is informed that filial relationship rests not with the flesh but with the name or, in other words, that any possible matrilinearism is to be repudiated and the symbolic link alone is to last. We thus have Luke 2:48–49 (". . . his mother said to him, 'My child, why have you done this to us? See how worried your father and I have been, looking for you.' 'Why were you looking for me?' he replied. 'Did you not know that I must be busy with my father's affairs?'"), and also John 2:3–5 (". . . the mother of Jesus said to him, 'They have no wine.' Jesus said, 'Woman, why turn to me?[3] My hour has not come yet.'") and 19:26–27 ("Seeing his mother and the disciple he loved standing near her, Jesus said to his mother, 'Woman, this is your son.' Then to the disciple he said, 'This is your mother.' And from that moment the disciple made a place for her in his home.")

Starting from this programmatic material, rather skimpy nevertheless, a compelling imaginary construct proliferated in essentially three directions. In the first place, there was the matter of drawing a parallel between Mother and Son by expanding the theme of the immaculate conception, inventing a biography of Mary similar to that of Jesus, and, by depriving her of sin to deprive her of death. Mary leaves by way of Dormition or Assumption. Next, she needed letters patent of nobility, a power that, even though exercised in the beyond, is nonetheless political, since Mary was to be proclaimed queen, given the attributes and paraphernalia of royalty and, in parallel fashion, declared Mother of the divine institution on earth, the Church. Finally, the relationship with Mary and from Mary was to be revealed as the prototype of a love relationship and followed two fundamental aspects of western love: courtly love and child love, thus fitting the entire range that goes from sublimation to asceticism and masochism.

Neither Sex nor Death

Mary's life, devised on the model of the life of Jesus, seems to be the fruit of apocryphal literature. The story of her own miraculous conception, called "immaculate conception," by Ann and Joachim, after a long, barren marriage, together with her biography as a pious maiden, show up in apocryphal sources as early as the end of the first century. Their entirety may be found in the *Secret Book of James* and also in one of the pseudepigrapha, the Gospel according to the Hebrews (which inspired Giotto's frescoes, for instance). Those "facts" were quoted by Clement of Alexandria and Origen but not officially accepted; even though the Eastern Church tolerated them readily, they were translated into Latin only in the sixteenth century. Yet the West was not long before glorifying the life of Mary on its own but always under orthodox guidance. The first Latin poem, "Maria," on the birth of Mary was written by the nun Hrotswith von Gandersheim (who died before 1002), a playwright and poet.

Fourth-century asceticism, developed by the Fathers of the Church, was grafted on that apocryphal shoot in order to bring out and rationalize the immaculate conception postulate. The demonstration was based on a simple logical relation: the intertwining of sexuality and death. Since they are mutually implicated with each other, one cannot avoid the one without fleeing the other. This asceticism, applicable to both sexes, was vigorously expressed by John Chrysostom (*On Virginity*: "For where there is death there is also sexual copulation, and where there is no death there is no sexual copulation either"); even though he was attacked by Augustine and Aquinas, he nonetheless fueled Christian doctrine. Thus, Augustine condemned "concupiscence" (*epithumia*) and posited that Mary's virginity is in fact only a logical precondition of Christ's chastity. The Orthodox Church, heir no doubt to a matriarchy that was more intense in eastern European societies, emphasized Mary's virginity more boldly. Mary was contrasted with Eve, life with death (Jerome, *Letter 22*, "Death came through Eve but life came through Mary"; Irenaeus, "Through Mary the snake becomes a dove and we are freed from the chains of death"). People even got involved in tortuous arguments in order to demonstrate that Mary remained a virgin after childbirth (thus the second Constantinople council, in 381, under Arianistic influence, emphasized the Virgin's role in comparison to official dogma and asserted Mary's perpetual virginity; the 451 council called her *Aeiparthenos*—ever virgin). Once this was established, Mary, instead of being referred to as Mother of man or Mother of Christ, would be proclaimed Mother of God: *Theotokos*. Nestorius, patriarch of Constantinople, refused to go along; Nestorianism, however, for all practical purposes died with the patriarch's own death in 451, and the path that would lead to Mary's deification was then clear.

I

Head reclining, nape finally relaxed, skin, blood, nerves warmed up, luminous flow: stream of hair made of ebony, of nectar, smooth darkness through her fingers, gleaming honey under the wings of bees, sparkling strands burning bright . . . silk, mercury, ductile copper: frozen light warmed under fingers. Mane of beast—squirrel, horse, and the happiness of a faceless head, Narcissuslike touching without eyes, sight dissolving in muscles, hair, deep, smooth, peaceful colors. Mamma: anamnesis.

Taut eardrum, tearing sound out of muted silence. Wind among grasses, a seagull's faraway call, echoes of waves, auto horns, voices, or nothing? Or his own tears, my newborn, spasm of syncopated void. I no longer hear anything, but the eardrum keeps transmitting this resonant vertigo to my skull, the hair. My body is no longer mine, it doubles up, suffers, bleeds, catches cold, puts its

teeth in, slobbers, coughs, is covered with pimples, and it laughs. And yet, when its own joy, my child's, returns, its smile washes only my eyes. But the pain, its pain—it comes from inside, never remains apart, other, it inflames me at once, without a second's respite. As if that was what I had given birth to and, not willing to part from me, insisted on coming back, dwelled in me permanently. One does not give birth in pain, one gives birth to pain: the child represents it and henceforth it settles in, it is continuous. Obviously you may close your eyes, cover up your ears, teach courses, run errands, tidy up the house, think about objects, subjects. But a mother is always branded by pain, she yields to it. "And a sword will pierce your own soul too . . ."

Dream without glow, without sound, dream of brawn. Dark twisting, pain in the back, the arms, the thighs—pincers turned into fibers, infernos bursting veins, stones breaking bones: grinders of volumes, expanses, spaces, lines, points. All those words, now, ever visible things to register the roar of a silence that hurts all over. As if a geometry ghost could suffer when collapsing in a noiseless tumult . . . Yet the eye picked up nothing, the ear remained deaf. But everything swarmed, and crumbled, and twisted, and broke—the grinding continued . . . Then, slowly, a shadowy shape gathered, became detached, darkened, stood out: seen from what must be the true place of my head, it was the right side of my pelvis. Just bony, sleek, yellow, misshapen, a piece of my body jutting out unnaturally, asymmetrically, but slit: severed scaly surface, revealing under this disproportionate pointed limb the fibers of a marrow . . . Frozen placenta, live limb of a skeleton, monstrous graft of life on myself, a living dead. Life . . . death . . . undecidable. During delivery it went to the left with the afterbirth . . . My removed marrow, which nevertheless acts as a graft, which wounds but increases me. Paradox: deprivation and benefit of childbirth. But calm finally hovers over pain, over the terror of this dried branch that comes back to life, cut off, wounded, deprived of its sparkling bark. The calm of another life, the life of that other who wends his way while I remain henceforth like a framework. Still life. There is him, however, his own flesh, which was mine yesterday. Death, then, how could I yield to it?

II

Very soon, within the complex relationship between Christ and his Mother where relations of God to mankind, man to woman, son to mother, and the like, are hatched, the problematics of *time* similar to that of cause loomed up. If Mary preceded Christ and he originated in her if only from the standpoint of his humanity, should not the conception of Mary herself have been immaculate? For, if that were not the case, how could a being conceived in sin and harboring it in herself produce a God? Some apocryphal writers had not hesitated, without too much caution, to suggest such an absence of sin in Mary's conception, but the Fathers of the Church were more careful. Bernard of Clairvaux is reluctant to extol the conception of Mary by Anne, and thus he tries to check the homologation of Mary with Christ. But it fell upon Duns Scotus to change the hesitation over the promotion of a mother goddess within Christianity into a logical problem, thus saving them both, the Great Mother as well as logic. He viewed Mary's birth as a *praeredemptio*, as a matter of congruency: if it be true that Christ alone saves us through his redemption on the cross, the Virgin who bore him can but be preserved from sin in "recursive" fashion, from the time of her own conception up to that redemption.

For or against, with dogma or logical shrewdness, the battle around the Virgin intensified between Jesuits and Dominicans, but the Counter-Reformation, as is well known, finally ended the resistance: henceforth, Catholics venerated Mary in herself. The Society of Jesus succeeded in completing a process of popular pressure distilled by patristic asceticism, and in reducing, with neither explicit hostility nor brutal rejection, the share of the Maternal (in the sense given above) useful to a certain balance between the two sexes. Curiously and necessarily, when that balance began to be seriously threatened in the nineteenth century, the Catholic Church—more dialectical and subtle here than the Protestants who were already spawning the first suffragettes—raised the Immaculate Conception to dogma status in 1854. It is often suggested that the blossoming of feminism in Protestant countries is due, among other things, to the greater initiative allowed women on the social and ritual plane. One might wonder if, in addition, such a flowering is not the result of a *lack* in the Protestant religious structure with respect to the Maternal, which, on the contrary, was elaborated within Catholicism with a refinement to which the Jesuits gave the final touch, and which still makes Catholicism very difficult to analyze.

The fulfillment, under the name of Mary, of a totality made of woman and God is finally accomplished through the avoidance of death. The Virgin Mary experiences a fate more radiant than her son's: she undergoes no calvary, she has no tomb, she doesn't die and hence has no need to rise from the dead. Mary doesn't die but, as if to echo oriental beliefs, Taoists' among others, according to which human bodies pass from one place to another in an eternal flow that constitutes a carbon copy of the maternal receptacle—she is transported.

Her transition is more passive in the Eastern Church: it is a Dormition (*Koimesis*) during which, according to a number of iconographic representations, Mary can be seen changed into a little girl in the arms of her son who henceforth becomes her father; she thus reverses her role as Mother into a Daughter's role for the greater pleasure of those who enjoy Freud's "Theme of the Three Caskets."

Indeed, *mother* of her son and his *daughter* as well, Mary is also, and besides, his *wife*: she therefore actualizes the threefold metamorphosis of a woman in the tightest parenthood structure. From 1135 on, transposing the Song of Songs, Bernard of Clairvaux glorifies Mary in her role of beloved and wife. But Catherine of Alexandria (said to have been martyred in 307) already pictured herself as receiving the wedding ring from Christ, with the Virgin's help, while Catherine of Siena (1347–80) goes through a mystical wedding with him. Is it the impact of Mary's function as Christ's beloved and wife that is responsible for the blossoming out of the Marian cult in the West after Bernard and thanks to the Cistercians? *Vergine Madre, figlia del tuo Figlio,* Dante exclaims, thus probably best condensing the gathering of the three feminine functions (daughter-wife-mother) within a totality where they vanish as specific corporealities while retaining their psychological functions. Their bond makes up the basis of unchanging and timeless spirituality; "the set time limit of an eternal design," *Termine fisso d'eterno consiglio,* as Dante masterfully points out in his *Divine Comedy.*

The transition is more active in the West, with Mary rising body and soul toward the other world in an *Assumption.* That feast, honored in Byzantium as early as the fourth century, reaches Gaul in the seventh under the influence of the Eastern Church; but the earliest Western visions of the Virgin's assumption, women's visions (particularly that of Elizabeth von Schönau, who died in 1164) date only from the twelfth century. For the Vatican, the Assumption became dogma only in 1950. What death anguish was it intended to soothe after the conclusion of the deadliest of wars?

Image of Power

On the side of "power," *Maria Regina* appears in imagery as early as the sixth century in the church of Santa Maria Antiqua in Rome. Interestingly enough, it is she, woman and mother, who is called upon to represent supreme earthly power. Christ is king but neither he nor his father are pictured wearing crowns, diadems, costly paraphernalia, and other external signs of abundant material goods. That opulent infringement to Christian idealism is centered on the Virgin Mother. Later, when she assumed the title of *Our Lady,* this would also be an analogy to the earthly power of the noble feudal lady of medieval courts. Mary's function as guardian of power, later checked when the Church became wary of it, nevertheless persisted in popular and pictorial representation, witness Piero della Francesca's impressive painting, *Madonna della Misericordia,* which was disavowed by Catholic authorities at the time. And yet, not only did the papacy revere more and more the Christly mother as the Vatican's power over cities and municipalities was strengthened, it also openly identified its own institution with the Virgin: Mary was officially proclaimed Queen by Pius XII in 1954 and *Mater Ecclesiae* in 1964.

Eia Mater, Fons Amoris!

Fundamental aspects of Western love finally converged on Mary. In a first step, it indeed appears that the Marian cult homologizing Mary with Jesus and carrying asceticism to the extreme was opposed to courtly love for the noble lady, which, while representing social transgression, was not at all a physical or moral sin. And yet, at the very dawn of a "courtliness" that was still very carnal, Mary and the Lady shared one common trait: they are the focal point of men's desires and aspirations. Moreover, because they were unique and thus excluded all other women, both the Lady and the Virgin embodied an absolute authority the more attractive as it appeared removed from paternal sternness. This feminine power must have been experienced as denied power, more pleasant to seize because it was both archaic and secondary, a kind of substitute for effective power in the family and the city but no less authoritarian, the underhand double of explicit phallic power. As early as the thirteenth century, thanks to the implantation of ascetic Christianity and especially, as early as 1328, to the promulgation of Salic laws, which excluded daughters from the inheritance and thus made the loved one very vulnerable and colored one's love for her with all the hues of the impossible, the Marian and courtly streams came together. Around the time of Blanche of Castile, (who died in 1252), the Virgin explicitly became the focus of courtly love, thus gathering the attributes of the desired woman and of the holy mother in a totality as accomplished as it was inaccessible. Enough to make any woman suffer, any man dream. One finds indeed in a *Miracle de Notre Dame* the story of a young man who abandons his fiancee for the Virgin: the latter came to him in a dream and reproached him for having left her for an "earthly woman."

Nevertheless, besides that ideal totality that no individual woman could possibly embody, the Virgin also became the

I

Scent of milk, dewed greenery, acid and clear, recall of wind, air, seaweed (as if a body lived without waste): it slides under the skin, does not remain in the mouth or nose but fondles the veins, detaches skin from bones, inflates me like an ozone balloon, and I hover with feet firmly planted on the ground in order to carry him, sure, stable, ineradicable, while he dances in my neck, flutters with my hair, seeks a smooth shoulder on the right, on the left, slips on the breast, swingles, silver vivid blossom of my belly, and finally flies away on my navel in his dream carried by my hands. My son.

Nights of wakefulness, scattered sleep, sweetness of the child, warm mercury in my arms, cajolery, affection, defenseless body, his or mine, sheltered, protected. A wave swells again, when he goes to sleep, under my skin—tummy, thighs, legs: sleep of the muscles, not of the brain, sleep of the flesh. The wakeful tongue quietly remembers another withdrawal, mine: a blossoming heaviness in the middle of the bed, of a hollow, of the sea . . . Recovered childhood, dreamed peace restored, in sparks, flash of cells, instants of laughter, smiles in the blackness of dreams, at night, opaque joy that roots me in her bed, my mother's, and projects him, a son, a butterfly soaking up dew from her hand, there, nearby, in the night. Alone: she, I, and he.

He returns from the depths of the nose, the vocal chords, the lungs, the ears, pierces their smothering stopping sickness swab, and awakens in his eyes. Gentleness of the sleeping face, contours of pinkish jade—forehead, eyebrows, nostrils, cheeks, parted features of the mouth, delicate, hard, pointed chin. Without fold or shadow, neither being nor unborn, neither present nor absent, but real, real inaccessible innocence, engaging weight and seraphic lightness. A child?—An angel, a glow on an Italian painting, impassive, peaceful dream—dragnet of Mediterranean fishermen. And then, the mother-of-pearl bead awakens: quicksilver. Shiver of the eyelashes, imperceptible twitch of the eyebrows, quivering skin, anx-

ious reflections, seeking, knowing, casting their knowledge aside in the face of my nonknowledge: fleeting irony of childhood gentleness that awakens to meaning, surpasses it, goes past it, causes me to soar in music, in dance. Impossible refinement, subtle rape of inherited genes: before what has been learned comes to pelt him, harden him, ripen him. Hard, mischievous gentleness of the first ailment overcome, innocent wisdom of the first ordeal undergone, yet hopeful blame on account of the suffering I put you through, by calling for you, desiring, creating . . . Gentleness, wisdom, blame: your face is already human, sickness has caused you to join our species, you speak without words but your throat no longer gurgles—it harkens with me to the silence of your born meaning that draws my tears toward a smile.

The lover gone, forgetfulness comes, but the pleasure of the sexes remains, and there is nothing lacking. No representation, sensation, or recall. Inferno of vice. Later, forgetfulness returns but this time as a fall—leaden—grey, dull, opaque. Forgetfulness: blinding, smothering foam, but on the quiet. Like the fog that devours the park, wolfs down the branches, erases the green, rusty ground, and mists up my eyes.

Absence, inferno, forgetfulness. Rhythm of our loves.

A hunger remains, in place of the heart. A spasm that spreads, runs through the blood vessels to the tips of the breasts, to the tips of the fingers. It throbs, pierces the void, erases it, and gradually settles in. My heart: a tremendous pounding wound. A thirst.

Anguished, guilty. Freud's *Vaterkomplex* on the Acropolis? The impossibility of being without repeated legitimation (without books, man, family). Impossibility—depressing possibility—of "transgression."

Either repression in which *I* hands the Other what I want from others.

Or this squalling of the void, open wound in my heart, which allows me to be only in purgatory.

I yearn for the Law. And since it is not made for me alone, I venture to desire outside the law. Then, narcissism thus awakened—the narcissism that wants to be sex—roams, astonished. In sensual rapture I am distraught. Nothing reassures, for only the law sets anything down. Who calls such a suffering jouissance? It is the pleasure of the damned.

II

fulcrum of the humanization of the West in general and of love in particular. It is again about the thirteenth century, with Francis of Assisi, that this tendency takes shape with the representation of Mary as poor, modest, and humble—madonna of humility at the same time as a devoted, fond mother. The famous nativity of Piero della Francesca in London, in which Simone de Beauvoir too hastily saw a feminine defeat because the mother kneeled before her barely born son, in fact consolidates the new cult of humanistic sensitivity. It replaces the high spirituality that assimilated the Virgin to Christ with an earthly conception of a wholly human mother. As a source for the most popularized pious images, such maternal humility comes closer to "lived" feminine experience than the earlier representations did. Beyond this, however, it is true that it integrates a certain feminine masochism but also displays its counterpart in gratification and jouissance. The truth of it is that the lowered head of the mother before her son is accompanied by the immeasurable pride of the one who knows she is also his wife and daughter. She knows she is destined to that eternity (of the spirit or of the species), of which every mother is unconsciously aware, and with regard to which maternal devotion or even sacrifice is but an insignificant price to pay. A price that is borne all the more easily since, contrasted with the love that binds a mother to her son, all other "human relationships" burst like blatant shams. The Franciscan representation of the Mother conveys many essential aspects of maternal psychology, thus leading up to an influx of common people to the churches and also a tremendous

increase in the Marian cult—witness the building of many churches
dedicated to her ("Notre Dame").
Such a humanization of Christianity through the cult of the mother

also led to an interest in the
humanity of the father-man: the
celebration of "family life" showed
Joseph to advantage as early as the
fifteenth century.

What Body?

We are entitled only to the ear of the virginal body, the tears, and the
breast. With the female sexual organ changed into an innocent shell,
holder of sound, there arises a possible tendency to eroticize hearing,
voice, or even understanding. By the same token, however, sexuality is
brought down to the level of innuendo. Feminine sexual experience is thus
rooted in the universality of sound, since wit is distributed *equally* among
all men, all women. A woman will only have the choice to live her life
either *hyperabstractly* ("immediately universal," Hegel said) in order thus
to earn divine grace and homologation with symbolic order; or merely
different, other, fallen ("immediately particular," Hegel said). But she will
not be able to accede to the complexity of being divided, of heterogeneity, of the catastrophic fold-of-"being" ("never singular," Hegel said).

Under a full, blue gown, the maternal, virginal body allowed only the
breast to show, while the face, with the stiffness of Byzantine icons gradually softened, was covered with tears. Milk and tears became the privileged signs of the *Mater Dolorosa* who invaded the West beginning with
the eleventh century, reaching the peak of its influx in the fourteenth. But
it never ceased to fill the Marian visions of those, men or women (often
children), who were racked by the anguish of a maternal frustration.
Even though orality—threshold of infantile regression—is displayed in
the area of the breast, while the spasm at the slipping away of eroticism
is translated into tears, this should not conceal what milk and tears have
in common: they are the metaphors of nonspeech, of a "semiotics" that
linguistic communication does not account for. The Mother and her
attributes, evoking sorrowful humanity, thus become representatives of a
"return of the repressed" in monotheism. They reestablish what is nonverbal and show up as the receptacle of a signifying disposition that is
closer to so-called primary processes. Without them the complexity of
the Holy Ghost would have been mutilated. On the other hand, as they
return by way of the Virgin Mother, they find their outlet in the arts—
painting and music—of which the Virgin necessarily becomes both
patron saint and privileged object.

The function of this "Virginal Maternal" may thus be seen taking shape in the Western symbolic economy. Starting with the high Christly sublimation for which it yearns and occasionally exceeds, and extending to the extralinguistic regions of the unnameable, the Virgin Mother occupied the tremendous territory on this and that side of the parenthesis of language. She adds to the Christian trinity and to the World that delineates their coherence the heterogeneity they salvage.

The ordering of the maternal libido reached its apotheosis when centered in the theme of death. The *Mater Dolorosa* knows no masculine body save that of her dead son, and her only pathos (which contrasts with the somewhat vacant, gentle serenity of the nursing Madonnas) is her shedding tears over a corpse. Since resurrection there is, and, as Mother of God, she must know this, nothing justifies Mary's outburst of pain at the foot of the cross, unless it be the desire to experience within her own body the death of a human being, which her feminine fate of being the source of life spares her. Could it be that the love, as puzzling as it is ancient, of mourners for corpses relates to the same longing of a woman whom nothing fulfills—the longing to experience the wholly masculine pain of a man who expires at every moment on account of jouissance due to obsession with his own death? And yet, Marian pain is in no way connected with tragic outburst: joy and even a kind of triumph follow upon tears, as if the conviction that death does not exist were an irrational but unshakeable maternal certainty, on which the principle of resurrection had to rest. The brilliant illustration of the wrenching between desire for the masculine corpse and negation of death, a wrenching whose paranoid logic cannot be overlooked, is masterfully presented by the famous *Stabat Mater*. It is likely that all beliefs in resurrections are rooted in mythologies marked by the strong

I

Belief in the mother is rooted in fear, fascinated with a weakness—the weakness of language. If language is powerless to locate myself for and state myself to the other, I assume—I want to believe—that there is someone who makes up for that weakness. Someone, of either sex, *before* the id speaks, before language, who might make me be by means of borders, separations, vertigos. In asserting that "in the beginning was the Word," Christians must have found such a postulate sufficiently hard to believe and, for whatever it was worth, they added its compensation, its permanent lining: the maternal receptacle, purified as it might be by the virginal fantasy. Archaic maternal love would be an incorporation of my suffering that is unfailing, unlike what often happens with the lacunary network of signs. In that sense, any belief, anguished by definition, is upheld by the fascinated fear of language's impotence. Every God, even including the God of the Word, relies on a mother Goddess. Christianity is perhaps also the last of the religions to have displayed in broad daylight the bipolar structure of belief: on the one hand, the difficult experience of the Word—a passion; on the other, the reassuring wrapping in the proverbial mirage of the mother—a love. For that reason, it seems to me that there is only one way to go through the religion of the Word, or its counterpart, the more or less discreet cult of the Mother; it is the "artists"' way, those who make up for the vertigo of language weakness with the oversaturation of sign systems. By this token, all art is a kind of counter reformation, an accepted baroqueness. For is it not true that if the Jesuits finally did persuade the official Church to accept the cult of the Virgin, following the puritanical wave of the Reformation, that dogma was in fact no more than a pretext, and its efficacy lay elsewhere. It did not become the opposite of the cult of the mother but its inversion through expenditure in the wealth of signs that constitutes the baroque. The latter renders belief in the Mother useless by overwhelming the symbolic weakness where she takes refuge, withdrawn from history, with an overabundance of discourse.

The immeasurable, unconfinable maternal body.

First there is the separation, previous to pregnancy, but which pregnancy brings to light and imposes without remedy.

On the one hand—the pelvis: center of gravity, unchanging ground, solid pedestal, heaviness and weight to which the thighs adhere, with no promise of agility on that score. On the other—the torso, arms, neck, head, face, calves, feet: unbounded liveliness, rhythm and mask, which furiously attempt to compensate for the immutability of the central tree. We live on that border, crossroads beings, crucified beings. A woman is neither nomadic nor a male body that considers itself earthly only in erotic passion. A mother is a continuous separation, a division of the very flesh. And consequently a division of language—and it has always been so.

Then there is this other abyss that opens up between the body and what had been its inside: there is the abyss between the mother and the child. What connection is there between myself, or even more unassumingly between my body and this internal graft and fold, which, once the umbilical cord has been severed, is an inaccessible other? My body and . . . him. No connection. Nothing to do with it. And this, as early as the first gestures, cries, steps, long before *its* personality has become my opponent. The child, whether *he* or *she*, is irremediably an other. To say that there are no sexual relationships constitutes a skimpy assertion when confronting the flash that bedazzles me when I confront the abyss between what was mine and is henceforth but irreparably alien. Trying to think through that abyss: staggering vertigo. No identity holds up. A mother's identity is maintained only through the well-known closure of consciousness within the indolence of habit, when a woman protects herself from the borderline that severs her body and expatriates it from her child. Lucidity, on the contrary, would restore her as cut in half, alien to its other—and a ground favorable to delirium. But also and for that very reason, motherhood destines us to a demented jouissance that is answered, by chance, by the nursling's laughter in the sunny waters of the ocean. What connection is there between it and myself? No connection, except for that overflowing laughter where one senses the collapse of some ringing, subtle, fluid identity or other, softly buoyed by the waves.

Concerning that stage of my childhood, scented, warm, and soft to the touch, I have only a spatial memory. No time at all. Fragrance of honey, roundness of forms, silk and velvet under my fingers, on my cheeks. Mummy. Almost no sight—a shadow that darkens, soaks me up, or vanishes amid flashes. Almost no voice in her placid presence. Except, perhaps, and more belatedly, the echo of quarrels: her exasperation, her being fed up, her hatred. Never straightforward, always held back, as if, although the unmanageable child deserved it, the daughter could not accept the mother's hatred—it was not meant for her. A hatred without recipient or rather whose recipient was no "I" and which, perturbed by such a lack of recipience, was toned down into irony or collapsed into remorse before reaching its destination. With others, this maternal aversion may be worked up to a spasm that is held like a delayed orgasm. Women doubtless reproduce among themselves the strange gamut of forgotten body relationships with their mothers. Complicity in the unspoken, connivance of the inexpressible, of a wink, a tone of voice, a gesture, a tinge, a scent. We are in it, set free of our identification papers and names, on an ocean of preciseness, a computerization of the unnameable. No communication between individuals but connections between atoms, molecules, wisps of words, droplets of sentences. The community of women is a community of dolphins. Conversely, when the other woman posits herself as such, that is, as singular and inevitably in opposition, "I" am startled, so much that "I" no longer know what is going on. There are then two paths left open to the rejection that bespeaks the recognition of the other woman as such. Either, not wanting to experience her, I ignore her and, "alone of my sex," I turn my back on her in friendly fashion. It is a hatred that, lacking a recipient worthy enough of its power, changes to unconcerned complacency. Or else, outraged by her own stubbornness, by that other's belief that she is singular, I unrelentingly let go at her claim to address me and find respite only in the eternal return of power strokes, bursts of hatred—blind and dull but obstinate. I do not see her as herself but beyond her I aim at the claim to singularity, the unacceptable ambition to be something other than a child or a fold in the plasma that constitutes us, an echo of the cosmos that unifies us. What an inconceivable ambition it is to aspire to singularity, it is not natural, hence it is inhuman; the mania smitten with Oneness ("There is only One woman") can only impugn it by condemning it as "masculine" . . . Within this strange feminine see-saw that makes "me" swing from the unnameable community of women over to the war of individual singularities, it is unsettling to say "I." The languages of the great formerly matriarchal civilizations must avoid, do avoid, personal pronouns: they leave to the context the burden of distinguishing protagonists and take refuge in

tones to recover an underwater, transverbal communication between bodies. It is a music from which so-called oriental civility tears away suddenly through violence, murder, blood baths. A woman's discourse, would that be it? Did not Christianity attempt, among other things, to freeze that see-saw? To stop it, tear women away from its rhythm, settle them permanently in the spirit? Too permanently . . .

II

dominance of a mother goddess. Christianity, it is true, finds its calling in the displacement of that biomaternal determinism through the postulate that immortality is mainly that of the name of the Father. But it does not succeed in imposing *its* symbolic revolution without relying on the feminine representation of an immortal biology. Mary defying death is the theme that has been conveyed to us by the numerous variations of the *Stabat Mater*, which, in the text attributed to Jacopone da Todi, enthralls us today through the music of Palestrina, Pergolesi, Haydn, and Rossini.

Let us listen to the baroque style of the young Pergolesi (1710–36), who was dying of tuberculosis when he wrote his immortal *Stabat Mater*. His musical inventiveness, which, through Haydn, later reverberated in the work of Mozart, probably constitutes his one and only claim to immortality. But when this cry burst forth, referring to Mary facing her son's death, *Eia Mater, fons amoris!* ("Hail mother, source of love!")—was it merely a remnant of the period? Man overcomes the unthinkable of death by postulating maternal love in its place—in the place and stead of death and thought. This love, of which divine love is merely a not always convincing derivation, psychologically is perhaps a recall, on the near side of early identifications, of the primal shelter that insured the survival of the newborn. Such a love is in fact, logically speaking, a surge of anguish at the very moment when the identity of thought and living body collapses. The possibilities of communication having been swept away, only the subtle gamut of sound, touch, and visual traces, older than language and newly worked out, are preserved as an ultimate shield against death. It is only "normal" for a maternal representation to set itself up at the place of this subdued anguish called love. No one escapes it. Except perhaps the saint, the mystic, or the writer who, through the power of language, nevertheless succeeds in doing no better than to take apart the fiction of the mother as mainstay of love, and to identify with love itself and what he is in fact—*a fire of tongues*, an exit from representation. Might not modern art then be, for the few who are attached

to it, the implementation of that maternal love—a veil over death, in death's very site and with full knowledge of the facts? A sublimated celebration of incest . . .

Alone of Her Sex

Freud collected, among other objects of art and archeology, countless statuettes representing mother goddess. And yet his interest in them comes to light only in discreet fashion in his work. It shows up when Freud examines artistic creation and homosexuality in connection with Leonardo da Vinci and deciphers there the ascendancy of an archaic mother, seen therefore from the standpoint of her effects on man and particularly on this strange function of his sometimes to change languages. Moreover, when Freud analyzes the advent and transformations of monotheism, he emphasizes that Christianity comes closer to pagan myths by integrating, through and against Judaic rigor, a preconscious acknowledgment of a maternal feminine. And yet, among the patients analyzed by Freud, one seeks in vain for mothers and their problems. One might be led to think that motherhood was a solution to neurosis and, by its very nature, ruled out psychoanalysis as a possible other solution. Or might psychoanalysis, at this point, make way for religion? In simplified fashion, the only thing Freud tells us concerning motherhood is that the desire for a child is a transformation of either penis envy or anal drive, and this allows her to discover the neurotic equation child-penis-feces. We are thus enlightened concerning an essential aspect of male phantasmatics with respect to childbirth, and female phantasmatics as well, to the extent that it embraces, in large part and in its hysterical labyrinths, the male one. The fact remains, as far as the complexities and pitfalls of maternal experience are involved, that Freud offers only a massive *nothing*, which, for those who might care to analyze it, is punctuated with this or that remark on the part of Freud's mother, proving to him in the kitchen that his own body is anything but immortal and will crumble away like dough; or the sour photograph of Marthe Freud, the wife, a whole mute story . . . There thus remained for his followers an entire continent to explore, a black one indeed, where Jung was the first to rush in, getting all his esoteric fingers burnt, but not without calling attention to some sore points of the imagination with regard to motherhood, points that are still resisting analytical rationality.[4]

There might doubtless be a way to approach the dark area that motherhood constitutes for a woman; one needs to listen, more carefully than ever, to what mothers are saying today, through their economic difficulties and, beyond the guilt that a too existentialist feminism handed down, through their discomforts, insomnias, joys, angers, desires, pains, and pleasures . . . One might, in similar fashion, try better to understand the incredible construct of the Maternal that the West elaborated by means of the Virgin, and of which I have just mentioned a few episodes in a never-ending history.

What is it then in this maternal representation that, alone of her sex, goes against both of the two sexes,[5] and was able to attract women's wishes for identification as well as the very precise interposition of those who assumed to keep watch over the symbolic and social order?

Let me suggest, by way of hypothesis, that the virginal maternal is a way (not among the less effective ones) of dealing with feminine paranoia.

—The Virgin assumes her feminine denial of the other sex (of man) but overcomes him by setting up a third person: *I* do not conceive with *you* but with *Him*. The result is an immaculate conception (therefore with neither man nor sex), conception of a God with whose existence a woman has indeed something to do, on condition that she acknowledge being subjected to it.

—The Virgin assumes the paranoid lust for power by changing a woman into a Queen in heaven and a Mother of the earthly institutions (of the Church). But she succeeds in stifling that megalomania by putting it on its knees before the child-god.

—The Virgin obstructs the desire for murder or devouring by means of a strong oral cathexis (the breast), valorization of pain (the sob), and incitement to replace the sexed body with the ear of understanding.

—The Virgin assumes the paranoid fantasy of being excluded from time and death through the very flattering representation of Dormition and Assumption.

—The Virgin especially agrees with the repudiation of the other woman (which doubtless amounts basically to a repudiation of the woman's mother) by suggesting the image of A woman as Unique: alone among women, alone among mothers, alone among humans since she is without sin. But the acknowledgment of a longing for uniqueness is immediately checked by the postulate according to which uniqueness is attained only through an exacerbated masochism: a concrete woman, worthy of the feminine ideal embodied by the Virgin as an inaccessible goal, could only be a nun, a martyr, or, if she is married, one who leads a life that would remove her from that "earthly" condition and dedicate her to the highest sublimation alien to her body. A bonus, however: the promised jouissance.

A skillful balance of concessions and constraints involving feminine paranoia, the representation of virgin motherhood appears to crown the efforts of a society to reconcile the social remnants of matrilinearism and the unconscious needs of primary narcissism on the one hand, and on the other the requirements of a new society based on exchange and before long on increased production, which require the contribution of the superego and rely on the symbolic paternal agency.

While that clever balanced architecture today appears to be crumbling, one is led to ask the following: what are the aspects of the feminine psyche for which that representation of motherhood does not pro-vide a solution or else provides one that is felt as too coercive by twentieth-century women?

The unspoken doubtless weighs first on the maternal body: as no signifier can uplift it without leaving a remainder, for the signifier is always meaning, communication, or structure, whereas a woman as mother would be, instead, a strange fold that changes culture into nature, the speaking into biology. Although it concerns every woman's body, the heterogeneity that cannot be subsumed in the signifier nevertheless explodes violently with pregnancy (the threshold of culture and nature) and the child's arrival (which extracts woman out of her oneness and gives her the possibility—but not the certainty—of reaching out to the other, the ethical). Those particularities of the maternal body compose woman into a being of folds, a catastrophe of being that the dialectics of the trinity and its supplements would be unable to subsume.

Silence weighs heavily nonetheless on the corporeal and psychological suffering of childbirth and especially the self-sacrifice involved in becoming anonymous in order to pass on the social norm, which one might repudiate for one's own sake but within which *one must* include the child in order to educate it along the chain of generations. A suffering lined with jubilation—ambivalence of masochism—on account of which a woman, rather refractory to perversion, in fact allows herself a coded, fundamental, perverse behavior, ultimate guarantee of society, without which society will not reproduce and will not maintain a constancy of standardized household. Feminine perversion does not reside in the parceling or the Don Juan–like multiplying of objects of desire; it is at once legalized, if not rendered paranoid, through the agency of masochism: all sexual "dissoluteness" will be accepted and hence become insignificant, provided a child seals up such outpourings. Feminine perversion [*père-version*] is coiled up in the desire for law as desire for reproduction and continuity, it promotes feminine masochism to the rank of structure stabilizer (against its deviations); by assuring the mother that she may thus enter into an order that is above humans' will it gives her her reward of pleasure. Such coded perversion, such close combat between maternal masochism and the law have been utilized by totalitarian powers of all times to bring women to their side, and, of course, they succeed easily. And yet, it is not enough to "declaim against" the reactionary role of mothers in the service of "male dominating power." One would need to examine to what extent that role corresponds to the biosymbolic latencies of motherhood and, on that basis, to try to understand, since the myth of the Virgin does not subsume them, or no longer does, how their surge lays women open to the most fearsome manipulations, not to mention blinding, or pure and simple rejection by progressive activists who refuse to take a close look.

Among things left out of the virginal myth there is the war between mother and daughter, a war masterfully but too quickly settled by promoting Mary as universal and particular, but never singular—as "alone of her sex." The relation to the other woman has presented our culture, in massive fashion during the past century, with the necessity to reformulate its representations of love and hatred—inherited from Plato's

Symposium, the troubadours, or Our Lady. On that level, too, mother-hood opens out a vista: a woman seldom (although not necessarily) experiences her passion (love and hatred) for another woman without having taken her own mother's place—without having herself become a mother, and especially without slowly learning to differentiate between same beings—as being face to face with her daughter forces her to do.

Finally, repudiation of the other sex (the masculine) no longer seems possible under the aegis of the third person, hypostatized in the child as go-between: "neither me, nor you, but him, the child, the third person, the nonperson, God, which I still am in the final analysis . . ." Since there is repudiation, and if the feminine being that struggles within it is to remain there, it henceforth calls for, not the deification of the third party, but countercathexes in strong values, in strong *equivalents of power.* Feminine psychosis today is sustained and absorbed through passion for politics, science, art . . . The variant that accompanies motherhood might be analyzed perhaps more readily than the others from the standpoint of the rejection of the other sex

I

The love of God and for God resides in a gap: the broken space made explicit by sin on the one side, the beyond on the other. Discontinuity, lack, and arbitrariness: topography of the sign, of the symbolic relation that posits my otherness as impossible. Love, here, is only for the impossible.

For a mother, on the other hand, strangely so, the other as arbitrary (the child) is taken for granted. As far as she is concerned—impossible, that is just the way it is: it is reduced to the implacable. The other is inevitable, she seems to say, turn it into a God if you wish, it is nevertheless natural, for such an other has come out of myself, which is yet not myself but a flow of unending germinations, an eternal cosmos. The other goes much without saying

and without my saying that, at the limit, it does not exist for itself. The "just the same" of motherly peace of mind, more persistent than philosophical doubt, gnaws, on account of its basic disbelief, at the symbolic's allmightiness. It bypasses perverse negation ("I know, but just the same") and constitutes the basis of the social bond in its generality, in the sense of "resembling others and eventually the species." Such an attitude is frightening when one imagines that it can crush everything the other (the child) has that is specifically irreducible: rooted in that disposition of motherly love, besides, we find the leaden strap it can become, smothering any different individuality. But it is there, too, that the speaking being finds a refuge when his/her symbolic shell cracks and a crest emerges where speech causes biology to show through: I am thinking of the time of illness, of sexual-intellectual-physical passion, of death . . .

II

that it comprises. To allow what? Surely not some understanding or other on the part of "sexual partners" within the preestablished harmony of primal androgyny. Rather, to lead to an acknowledgment of what is irreducible, of the irreconcilable interest of both sexes in asserting their differences, in the quest of each one—and of women, after all—for an appropriate fulfillment.

These, then, are a few questions among others concerning a motherhood that today remains, after the Virgin, without a discourse. They suggest, all in all, the need of an ethics for this "second" sex, which, as one asserts it, is reawakening.

Nothing, however, suggests that a feminine ethics is possible, and Spinoza excluded women from his (along with children and the insane). Now, if a contemporary ethics is no longer seen as being the same as morality,; if ethics amounts to not avoiding the embarrassing and inevitable problematics of the law but giving it flesh, language, and jouissance—in that case its reformulation demands the contribution of women: Of women who harbor the desire to reproduce (to have stability). Of women who are available so that our speaking species, which knows it is mortal, might withstand death. Of mothers. For an heretical ethics separated from morality, an *herethics*, is perhaps no more than that which in life makes bonds, thoughts, and therefore the thought of death, bearable: herethics is undeath (*a-mort*), love . . . *Eia mater, fons amoris* . . . So let us again listen to the *Stabat Mater*, and the music, all the music . . . it swallows up the goddesses and removes their necessity.

NOTES

1. Between the lines of this section one should be able to detect the presence of Marina Warner, *Alone of All Her Sex: The Myth and Cult of the Virgin Mary* (New York: Knopf, 1976) and Ilse Barande, *Le Maternel singulier* (Paris: Aubier-Montaigne, 1977), which underlay my reflections.

2. Georges Dumézil, *La Religion romaine archaïque* (Paris: Payot, 1974).

3. The French version quoted by Kristeva ("Woman, what is there in common between you and me?") is even stronger than the King James translation, "Woman, what have I to do with thee?"—Trans.

4. Jung thus noted the "hierogamous" relationship between Mary and Christ as well as the overprotection given the Virgin with respect to original sin, which places her on the margin of mankind; finally, he insisted very much on the Vatican's adoption of the Assumption as dogma, seeing it as one of the consider-

able merits of Catholicism as opposed to Protestantism. C. G. Jung, *Answer to Job* (Princeton: Princeton University Press, 1969).

5. As Caelius Sedulius wrote, "She. . . had no peer / Either in our first mother or in all women / Who were to come. But alone of all her sex / She pleased the Lord" ("Paschalis Carminis," Book II, lines 68ff. of *Opera Omnia* [Vienna, 1885]). Epigraph to Marina Warner, *Alone of All Her Sex*.

Julia Kristeva in Conversation with Rosalind Coward

ROSALIND COWARD: Could you say something more about your notion of transference in the book [*Tales of Love*]. At one point you say that almost all of human history and human philosophy around the subject of love could be described as a transference. Could you explain that a bit more?

KRISTEVA: The word transference is a technical word, it comes from psychoanalysis. I think it was a great discovery by Freud to consider that what happens between the patient and the analyst is a sort of love which is a displacement of love-traumatism or love-disappointments from the past reality through the actual cure. And from that point on it was possible to remember what happened in the personal history. But also Freud tried to extrapolate this notion of transference from the cure itself to the whole field of human creativity: art, history, and the like. This extrapolation was not done very explicitly: when he analyzes religion, for instance, or some works of art by Michelangelo, he doesn't speak about transference, but I think it's implicit in his vision. There is something very romantic in Freud's vision of human relationships. His device, which is psychoanalysis, has always been analyzed in comparison with the development of scientific thought, and in comparison with religion. Maybe it will be necessary to compare it with the development of romanticism as well. His romantic death instinct. Eros and so on are a constant from romantic literature. He always said that the great artists preceded him in this way, by analyzing the human psyche. So transference is a therapeutic device but also something that has always operated in creation. And the Freudian view of symbolic creations allows us now to view it in a different way perhaps.

COWARD: Correct me if I'm wrong but my understanding of what you mean by transference is that the analytic process, in going back to the earliest stages of the child's life, reactivates the first form of love the child achieved or failed to achieve.

KRISTEVA: Yes, and he places this onto the analyst. It is a very dangerous moment because in a special article about identification Freud
speaks about love and compares it with hypnosis. And he says that
in this situation the person is really submitted to the beloved who can
be a tyrant which is very often noticeable not only in relations but
also in mass history—the Führer and so on. So there can be a submission from the person to the beloved and it can also happen in the
psychoanalytic cure. And unfortunately there are psychoanalysts in
psychoanalytic movements who use this kind of submission. And
people are right to be afraid of this.

For the psychoanalyst the problem is he knows what kind of dangerous weapon he has . . . to make this person go through this danger and to give to the person the whole range of his symbolic and
imaginary capacity in order not to be submitted in other experiences
but instead of this to be alive and perfectly present.

COWARD: You seem to be saying that in analysis that relationship of love
that the analyst has with the analysand is one that to some extent
goes back over the primary construction of identification. In the
book you do relate to that and this is where you draw on the myth
of Narcissus: you feel that psychoanalysis has shown us how the subject is actually constituted in its first identifications. And that the
whole history of love has been one or other form of demonstrating
that process of primary identification. Is that right?

KRISTEVA: What happens in psychoanalysis is the discovery of some substantial points in the human development, psychic development. The
first essential point that Freud made was narcissism. We know that
when he began psychoanalysis he found a hysterical desire which was
masculine as well as feminine. And then he was aware of the fact that
this desire is limited and the transference which we spoke about is not
endless and there are cases in which transference doesn't work. And
then he discovered that there was an organization of the psychic
space that he called narcissism. It was a word already used by psychiatrists, but Freud used it in a different way in order to stress the
organization which is universal for every person, which is not symptomatic, in the sense that a symptom may be considered as an illness
or something which is pejorative, but which is universal in the organization of every psychic space. This means that at some point of his
life the human being is fascinated by his image. But it is possible only
if this human being is capable of some separation from his mother
and is capable of grasping some imaginary forms, which is the zero

degree of the third between the infant and the mother. And this zero degree is not a word used by Freud; I use the word, Freud speaks about the father of pre-individual history, which is not grasped as a real person by the infant but like a sort of symbolic instance; something that is here that cannot be here—the possibility of absence, the possibility of love, the possibility of interdiction but also a gift. And this is something different from the overwhelming presence of the mother which is loving but which is also too much desiring, too much in close proximity with the child, and in this way she perhaps cannot give enough space for this symbolic elaboration. That's why he stressed the necessity, even for the narcissistic organization which is the primary one, the necessity for the existence of this third position.

COWARD: How do those ideas about narcissism relate to Lacan's notion of the mirror phase, because it seems to me that you talk of this first experience of love as almost being the first experience of the self, or the first grasp of the self—it's an identification built on a void where before there was only fragmentation and drives, and that the child identifies with an imaginary Other who is the speaking subject and who introjects the words of the speaking subject and has an imaginary sense of its own unity. I wanted to know how that relates to Lacan's notion of the mirror phase, where he seems to be talking about the same thing. Is yours an extension of that, or a kind of criticism of that?

KRISTEVA: Lacan is a very important figure, everyone agrees with that, though he may be a very controversial one. The point of the mirror stage in his work was very important, because he drew back the consideration of the psychic space precisely to the archaic stages which were not well observed or analyzed by analysts of his time. Afterwards different works have been written in this field and about this stage. And I think some parts of Winnicott's work, even though he doesn't mention the mirror stage, do deal with this stage or the very early stages of infant play.

What I wanted to do was two things. First, to make more detailed the archaic stages preceding the mirror stage because I think that the grasping of the image by the child is a result of a whole process. And this process can be called *imaginary*, but not in the specular sense of the word, because it passes through voice, taste, skin and so on, all the senses yet doesn't necessarily mobilize sight. That's why I think it is an attempt to elaborate the early development in a more precise and a nonspecular way.

And this is important with regard to art. Because I think in modern art there is this so-called crisis of representation which is a crisis generally, and more commonly of visual representation—the breaking of the image, abstract art, and so on. From this point of view you could say that modern art is a sort of elaboration of this narcissistic and prenarcissistic dynamic, where the figure is not yet constituted as one, as a coherent figure, where hearing, skin, taste, and so on enter into account. That's why it is important for me to stress the previous-to-the-mirror-stage development, that I called in different elaborations that are not in this book but other books, the *semiotic* variety of meaning in order to differentiate it from the *symbolic* variety of meaning which will be more connected to a coherent and full image, and to the verbal sign which always refers to objects which are total and not split.

The second point, which is perhaps different from Winnicott's, is the accent put on the third position, the so-called father of the prehistory. Because if I have read Winnicott well, he always talks about the child and the good-enough mother, which is an enigma, nobody knows what the good-enough mother is. I wouldn't try to explain what that is, but I would try to suggest that maybe the good-enough mother is the mother who has something else to love besides her child; it could be her work, her husband, her lovers, etc. If for a mother the child is the meaning of her life, it's too heavy. She has to have another meaning in her life. And this other meaning in her life is the father of prehistory. And it's the guarantee of a love relationship between the mother and the child. If it doesn't exist it produces a clash which produces all sorts of inhibitions, and also difficulty to even accede to language.

COWARD: I understand that you use the term 'the imaginary father' or the 'father of the individual prehistory' as the third term, but before the actual symbolic triangle.

KRISTEVA: Yes, exactly, some sort of archaic occurrence of the symbolic.

COWARD: You say in your book and you've just repeated that you're not referring to a real father or a real man. You're actually referring to the mother's desire being elsewhere as a necessary precondition for that kind of primary separation to take place. At the same time I did find it slightly worrying reading the book that it seemed to repeat some of those classic Freudian divisions of father and mother, even in maintaining those terms, even in maintaining the paternal metaphor which is something that very much comes from Freud and

Lacan. And there were for me very strong echoes of nineteenth-century philosophy, twentieth-century philosophy, the division between the maternal too-close, too-natural bond that's undifferentiated, and the paternal, which is the intellectual, the altruistic love . . . it's very like Bachofen. And in your instance, the paternal metaphor stands for the sense of positions of speaking. But I wondered what you felt about the kinds of criticisms that we have now become familiar with from feminism. And someone like Irigary, say, with that criticism that the paternal metaphor is itself a problem because it reproduces ideologies about women and men, even in attempts to talk symbolically.

KRISTEVA: I think I understand your preoccupation. It's true that feminism has been very much against these sharp distinctions. I have two things to say. First, for me it is not absolutely necessary to call them mother or father—what is necessary is to have three terms, if you prefer call them X and Y, why not? But I'm not sure that changes much. What is necessary for what I call the psychic space to accede to language is the existence of this distance and I cannot imagine another organization but the one of the three terms.

The second thing is that this is only a basic condition which I think is a kernel one in every civilization, which is a universal one for the symbolic acquisition. But there are ideological changes and historical differences and I think maybe the time we're going through now is more perverse, or if you like more baroque, a play with the psychic space, which supposes that these distinctions between X and Y are not so sharp, and which supposes that there are contaminations between them. This gives to the modern psychic space something that resembles the medieval, the fact that people don't have fixed identities but have the impression to bring masks, to have looks and not essential authenticities. This is due to the crisis of the paternal function and the rendering of my 'X' and 'Y' ambiguous. This is a contemporary fact.

For me the feminist movement has several positive points, particularly on the liberation of women. But maybe one of its most unexpected achievements at the moment will be to contribute to the creation of this baroque space, which is not now perceived in this way. What is perceived by the feminist movement now is mainly the rigor or the constraints: for instance in France, the aspect the feminist movement gives is the interdiction on sexist publicity and so on. Public opinion recently has a very problematic idea of the feminist movement as a movement more capable of interdiction than invention. But I think it is a momentary phenomenon. What will be retained from this contribution, and particularly in the field of ideas, will be this ambiguization of identities that goes in the sense of a new baroquism. Maybe we have lived too long in a postwar climate which was the climate of militancy and it was necessary for several reasons: political and economic, as well as sexual. I am under the impression, from my patients and also from my students that there is a desire for a "belle époque," for a new turn of the century, which doesn't mean that demands of militants should be put aside. But we have to add to them something more subtle, and more linked with desire, love, and so on. I think the success of different discourses particularly on desire and love is due to this need, which is a modern one, which maybe characterizes the end of the twentieth century.

COWARD: I'm not sure that I share your view of feminism as being something that is mainly about prohibitions at this stage. This relates to one of the points I wanted to make. For me one of the transforming aspects of feminism has been precisely its recasting of notions of love from the couple toward the friendship, from the sexual, erotic, idealizing love—I'm not saying that feminism is not erotic and not sexual—but for me that's been one of the positive recastings, almost in the way that you talk of psychoanalysis actually, as being an investigation of love as well as a cure for it. I think a lot of feminists would be critical of the notion of love that you talk about. You start the book by saying you think there is something, an *absolute* state of love, that can be described. And I think that a lot of feminists would say this is a particular historical state which contains as many problems as pleasures.

KRISTEVA: It is very difficult when we want to describe something essentially, not to generalize. If you want to generalize you might appear to be schematic although that is not the intention. For instance, if you take the configuration of love, it's true that there are different historically based amorous forms—that's what I try to examine from some point of view. But it's true also that there is a situation which is differently organized in different historical spaces, but which nevertheless has some essential points that last in every time, in every space. For me this is essential. And this allows for scientific investigation. There are some universals and that's why we can investigate them. Otherwise everything is different and nothing can be investigated scientifically or theoretically. Then everything could only be described poetically or literarily or in an individual manner.

What is universal in the love situation is, on the one hand, for me, the narcissistic investment which is a necessity for the living being to last, to stay alive, to preserve itself. And on the other hand, the idealization. The possibility for this living being to project himself through an ideal instance and to identify with it. And this can be found in different kinds of friendship, sympathy, love, homosexual, erotic—differently orchestrated. The emphasis may be put in this situation more on violence, or more on narcissism, or more on idealization, or more or the erotic, and so on. But the two components: narcissism and idealization will last, will endure.

COWARD: So would you say that those universal aspects are more significant, than the particular forms as expressed over history on the one hand, and on the other, the particular object choices. For example, about homosexuality and heterosexuality—are you more interested in the similarities or in the differences. You make some fairly tantalizing remarks about homosexuality throughout the book. I'd be interested to know whether you do actually see there being significant differences and if so what would they be for you?

KRISTEVA: I think that every difference is significant. But what I would like to consider is the very particularity of the love experience of every person. I would say even that what interests me when I listen to someone in a psychoanalytic session is not to know that Jean is homosexual and Marie is not, but what kind of particular homosexuality he is living, not to put an etiquette on it, homosexual or heterosexual. Because there are sometimes more resemblances between one homosexual and one heterosexual than the people considered to belong to the same group. I'm not interested in groups. I am interested in individuals. And it's true that homosexual particularities can be apparent in the amorous behavior of a person who claims to be in this group. But it's not this main purpose that interests me.

I think that one of the negative points of the feminist movement, of all movements, is to consider that we can exhaustively understand a human being by classifying him somehow. First we had different economic classes; now in a more subtle way we have different sexual classes, which is perhaps a step forward because it's more deeply interested in the developments of the psychic experience. But it's not enough. I have the deep conviction that every person has a very particular sexuality. This sexuality and this kind of love organization is

what interests me and not the group of *the* homosexuals, *the* hetero-
sexuals, and so on.

COWARD: It seems to me that you're maintaining a kind of dual position
by saying that on the one hand it's the individual, the particularities
of the individual that gives significance, meaning to that individual.
On the other hand, there are generalities in the process of love if not
the object choices of love. I wonder how you would classify the more
historical approach that would err toward the former I suppose, that
meaning is given to sexuality by different situations and different histories. I'm thinking of Foucault's *History of Sexuality,* which had a
big impact here. This book would absolutely refuse your generalities.

KRISTEVA: And the reverse is true also! It's a field I'm not investigating,
you can't do everything.

It's very legitimate to put some historical questions about why and
for what historical reasons, for instance a Plotinian discourse has
been organized, or a narcissist's discourse has been organized, but it
is not the question I have analyzed.

If I understand your question correctly, it's about the legitimacy of
this separation, of the psychoanalytical investigation from the historical one. I think it's possible to support this separation when we
want to go as deeply as possible into the psychic particularity of sexual and love organization. If you stress the social conditions of these
amorous discourses, for instance, you can very quickly disregard the
particularity of what happens in the inner life. Your other question
was about how to put together the tendency to generalize on the one
hand and the tendency to individualize on the other. This is a problem for every human scientist. For instance, if you take linguistics,
we try to describe what is the deep structure and then to individualize, if you can say that, the surface structure. You put some universal components on the basis and try to see developments of the universal components on the surface structure. You always have a subject and a predicate but you have different phrases on the surface.

In this type of investigation, which I would say is more difficult
than linguistics, the problem is even more complicated because the
neutrality of the theoretician is put into question. I cannot have a neutral position when I speak about love. And this is one of the reasons
why I cannot involve myself in a so-called neutral historical discourse.

I think when a theoretician speaks about love, he or she is too
much involved, and honestly he or she has to take account and tell
people why he or she, in what way they are involved and not to block

this involvement by a neutral historical discourse about classes, the economy, and the like. It can be done but it doesn't interest me.

I wanted to give an image of this contradiction which is, on the one hand, a description of the universal and the individual and, on the other hand, the involvement of the author. I tried to give an image of this in the chapter of *Histoires d'amour,* which is about maternal love and is presented in two kinds of typeface: on the left you have a sort of literary poetic text and on the right, a more theoretical or academic discourse. And for me it's not a coherent text. I didn't want to give an impression of coherence, on the contrary I wanted to give an impression of a sort of wound, a scar. In the field of social sciences, human sciences, particularly psychoanalysis, the theoretician is posited precisely on this place of the scar, because we are holding a knowing discourse, a discourse that pretends to some objectivity and at the same time we elaborate this discourse through what is often painful involvement in the observation. We have to exhibit this contradiction, this pain. Maybe it's a point which may appear too literary and not scientific, but I think this is the point that many human sciences and philosophy particularly (which is not a human science but is a discourse on meaning and psychic space) have reached. It is more and more difficult to have a sort of mastered academic neutral discourse. It is possible for academic or deductive purposes and so on. But the very point human sciences have achieved is this one—because we are aware of the transference that links the author and his object.

COWARD: I think we in England have been very attracted to French thought. For left-wing intellectuals, our "other" has been France and we've had an idealizing relationship to France. So for many of us some of your more recent statements about politics have been bewildering.

I wondered, particularly, given what you've just said about not being able to take a neutral position—that you are involved yourself in any utterance you make—whether you'd accept a comment that perhaps some of the political metaphors you use seem very much like the subject of this book, in that they seem to be about an idealized love, this time a political love. I'll explain what I mean. Like many people in England you passed through a phase of seeing in China the embodiment of the kind of ideal socialist society. Recently you made a statement in a piece called *Mémoires* that it was your disillusionment with China that ended your involvement with socialism, and feminism. And now you've published a number of things which make it clear, for example, that you see a lot more freedom within America than in China, and perhaps more than anywhere else. Don't these extremes of idealized love and disillusionment show the dangers of not being critical of love?

KRISTEVA: It's a point of personal history, I suppose from different people here in this room, having different histories, the appreciation of political actuality would be different. I will speak briefly about my history through politics. I come from a socialist country and my natural way would be, as most dissidents have done, to move to the Right, as has been said in a schematic way. But nevertheless these two realities exist. What I did was something else—I went to the Left because I was under the impression, and I still am, that socialist ideas and Marxist ideas understood in particular ways, are the more generous ideas of our time; and that different, positive social transformations, can be done with this, besides the despotism and totalitarianism of Eastern countries. This is one point.

Second, I had the impression that because of the Western tradition—which is more democratic than the East European tradition—the communist movements could be more liberal and could allow a richer development of individuals' art and creativity without dogmatism.

I have never been a member of a Communist Party but we tried with *Tel Quel* and others to organize meetings and discussions with Communist intellectuals. My experience didn't confirm my initial impression. The French Communist Party, particularly, is very strongly dependent on the Soviet one and it gives a different problematic, different colorations of the ideological development of Marxism within the research institutes of the French Communist Party. In the meantime we went to China and for me it was more a cultural interest than a political one. There were both interests. But I wanted to see what can be done when Marxism is developed in a country that possessed a different cultural background, that doesn't have a monolithic religion, that thinks in a particular way, that speaks in a particular way because I think the Chinese character and language indicate not a particular mentality, which would be a racist position, but a different logic of organization. I wanted to see what could be the difference of a society organized on the basis of the meeting of these two components. And what I saw was very problematic, particularly in the situation of women. Several positive things have been done and said, but I couldn't discover any liberation of women in the sense of the Western movements, and of course in different fields, as well. So this was for me a point of a reevaluation of the whole problematic of political involvement. And personally from the point of view of my own development I thought that it would be more honest for me not to engage politically but to try to be helpful or useful in a narrow field, where the individual life is concerned, where the individual way of expression is concerned, and where I can do something more objective and maybe more sharp, and more independent of different political pressures.

I also have the impression that in our modern society, and it's a sort of heritage from the eighteenth-century French Revolution I suppose, we have a new religion which is not only sex—which may be important but also very pleasant and not dangerous—we have a religion which is politics. We think that everything is political. When we say political we say something which cannot be analyzed, it's the final act. This is political . . . stop. It's tremendously important, this final enigma, which is politics. We can say that different social sciences try to analyze it, but nevertheless it's there, it's present even in the questions, even in the objections when people say why don't you consider political events. Because it's considered as the most important. And what is interesting now in the new French government is that they try to develop some ideological fields, cultural fields, and so on, and this puts the stress, the dominance on the fact that politics is not the only, the dominant important phenomenon, that there are other expressions within human society that can be taken into consideration. And it's done by a political regime—that's what is happening now and the future will show the consequences. The political regime shows that politics is not the only thing that's important. That's what interests me.

When I spoke about love and stressed Christianity, for me that's not nostalgia. It's more a questioning about the discourse that can take the place of this religious discourse which is cracking now. And I don't think political discourse can take its place. The political discourse, the political causality which is dominant even in human sciences in universities and everywhere is too narrow and too feeble in comparison with St. Bernard and St. Thomas. If we stay with only a political explanation of human phenomena we will be overwhelmed by the so-called mystical crisis, or spiritual crisis—that happens, it's a reality. Every bourgeois family has a son or daughter who has a mys-

tical crisis—it's understandable because of this very schematic explanation of such phenomenon as love or desire simply by politics. So my
problem is: how, through psychoanalysis or something else like art,
through such discourses can we try to develop a more complicated
elaboration, discourse, sublimation of these critical points of the
human experience, which cannot be reduced to a political causality.

COWARD: If you love yourself through another, what kind of love is that?
Is that agape or eros?

KRISTEVA: The differentiation between agape and eros has been done by
a scholar called Nigren in the thirties—he wrote a book about it, and
I used this a lot, this research. The difference between the two is that
eros is a sort of ascendant movement, it tries to achieve something
that is placed above, it tries to go beyond the possibilities of the person he loves; it aspires to power and it's compared to an erection in
an organic sense of the word. Agape is something else, it's a sort of
gift, it comes to you from outside, you don't need to merit it, it's a
sort of profusion, it's the love of parents for their children, for
instance, when it happens which is not very often.

Both phenomenon happen in analysis. We can observe also erotic
movements but in this sense they will be more connected with desire
and violence and sado-masochistic dynamics. While in agape the
phenomenon is more sublimated, for me, it is more related to an
ideal instance and in this case the analyst is considered as a sort of
ideal, an ideal I.

AUDIENCE: It is somewhat strange that the inability to love or be loved
makes somebody a patient. If that's the area where trouble lies and
if love is the remedy . . . you seem to describe the love that takes place
in an analytic situation as simply a reactivated early infantile love.

KRISTEVA: Partly.

AUDIENCE: But surely there's something that happens, a step further
than that that is necessary for a successful cure, that is entirely new,
that is specific to that situation and it is actually taking place in the
reality of that relationship.

KRISTEVA: You are right. Maybe I expressed myself in a very inexact
way, if I said that what is actualized in transference is only the infantile love. I think it's one of the aspects of the human experience that
is actualized but it's not the only one. Also, we can bring in the cure,
in the transference different events that happen in your actual life,
not only the past one but the current one. That's why it's a laboratory of different events, past or present.

What I wanted to say is that through this reactualization you can render your love affairs more vivid in the cure, reelaborate them and be able to displace them and to pass through the suffering, for instance all different amorous pains.

AUDIENCE: But isn't it a different kind of love, neither a reenactment of either past or present other love affairs, but one that goes on between therapist and patient, analyst and patient, which has its own specific character that is not a repetition.

KRISTEVA: I would call it a reelaboration. There is a part of repetition and there is a new part which is added and which makes this transference a sort of innovation. That's why it's not a mere repetition. If it were only a repetition it would be something morbid. It's a point which is very important for me because you know generally people imagine a psychoanalyst as a sort of obsessional person, very rigid who doesn't say anything, is dark and silent and so on. That's important perhaps because it's a way that Freud and psychoanalysts invented to resist the seduction of the patient. But it's of no use with narcissistic patients and I think modern patients are more and more narcissistic for different, perhaps sociological, reasons, because of the family, different difficulties of child-mother relationship, different causes. The fact is that, here, with more and more narcissistically suffering people, the psychoanalyst should not behave as if he were an obsessional or morbid person. I think that we have to construct something, not only to analyze, but to give something new. From this point of view the simple repetition which never occurs because in every transference there is something new that happens, it's particularly true with a narcissistic person—to give them something new, something that they have never experienced. That's why the imaginary and the symbolic possibilities of the analyst are very important. People come to you because they know that you can give them something that they have never had. This is important and this is dangerous because of the sort of victim position that can be developed in such situations. And if the analyst doesn't know this, if he can't get rid of this overwhelming domination it's very dangerous. But I think it's an important point with the new kind of patients we have now.

BARBARA TAYLOR: I may have misunderstood you but there appears to be an elision between love and desire in the way you're describing transference love. Would it not be correct to say that, for Freud, in fact, transference love is profoundly defensive in character, and one of the things it defends the analyst against is desire, that is the fantasy which is in the gap between need and demand, which is often extremely hostile in character, as you say violent, sadistic. So that the feeling of being in love and being loved is a way of delegitimizing the hostile character of desire itself.

KRISTEVA: I think Freud was right to first of all stress the hostile component of desire and also the erotic one. He speaks of Eros and Thanatos, but this is an essential part of erotic ways and that's what happens with neurotic patients. What I wanted to stress is something else which is not elaborated by Freud very much because he didn't work with psychotics, he didn't like them and he was right, it is very difficult. But it is a problem which is more and more an actual problem. You have the impression that the patient who is coming is a neurotic and very quickly it appears that he has some psychotic margins. From this point of view you have to construct something and to stress the idealizing part of the transference, which can be a resistance and you are right that Freud described it like this. But it is not only a resistance. You have to work with this as far as the cure is concerned. On the other hand, as far as the social field is concerned, and I persist in thinking that the social field is concerned through psychoanalysis, art as well as politics—the idealization is a very essential part of creation, of the possibility of innovation, as well as style movements and desire.

In this book I stressed more idealization and love and it can appear that I have in mind only this part of the cure. But I have already written another book called *The Powers of Horror* where the problem of negativity, rejection, hostility has been the dominant problem. So in order to have a complete image of what happens in the cure we have to read the two books.

I want to stress again that this book was purposely partial. I had the impression that in modern human sciences literature there were few elaborations of what is faith, what is idealization, what is positive, what is value, on what grounds are they based? I wanted in a sort of polemical way to stress this part of the human psyche, the idealization, love, the positive. My previous book was concerned with rejection and hate, particularly in different phobias but also in the psychotic stages and psychotic situations where the rejection of the other and the hate for the other become predominant, in desire, but also in murder. The problematic of this book was to describe how in different religions and literary elaborations people tried to defend against these negative impulses, negative drives, through different rituals, for instance, of catharsis, purification, and so on.

My last point has to do with a French writer very much compromised during Nazism, Céline, who was a violent anti-Semite. I am not sure the book answered all the questions about hatred and values but I think it shed some light on them. So then it was necessary for me, and again I think it is a lack in human sciences, to try to show what happens in other kinds of cultural elaborations which are not elaborations about evil, about the negative but that are preoccupied with the sublime.

COWARD: Do you draw a distinction between love and desire?

KRISTEVA: Yes. For me desire doesn't involve idealization. Idealization is a level which concerns the symbolic elaboration, while desire is deeply involved in passion and depends on the symbolic imaginary. For me desire is more dominated by passion, by drives, instinct.

COWARD: One of the points that puzzle me is your assertion about the crisis of idealization in love. Is psychoanalysis really the only code that is investigating that process, because it seems to me that to some extent we're swamped with it rather than there being an absence of it.

KRISTEVA: I would ask what other codes are there that elaborate idealization.

COWARD: I know they're not art or religion but in popular culture for example there is a massive representation of narcissistic love.

KRISTEVA: Yes there are works, there are productions . . . It is unimaginable that a society could exist without different fields where such kinds of idealization exist. And popular art, different kinds of art, go in this direction. But what I wanted to say is that in the psychoanalytical field you have at the same time the practice and the attempt to think about it, to elaborate a discourse about not the surface of idealization, not of the external aspects of what *is* idealized but of what are the dynamic causes of the idealization. For me the psychoanalytic field has the advantage of being at the same time the practice and the attempt to think about it, to elaborate a coherent discourse about not the surface of idealization, not of the external aspects of what is idealized but of what are the dynamic causes of idealization. For me the psychoanalytic field has the advantage of being at the same time the practice and the metalanguage of idealization, the metalanguage which is not only description but which gives, not the final because I hope there will be other propositions, but some causes of this idealization and the ideal state. I don't think it happens in theology—it doesn't exist anymore—or in philosophy.

In art criticism, classical art describes different forms of idealization but it doesn't say what happens in the subjectivity of the artist when he does this.

JACQUELINE ROSE: At the risk of fulfilling a stereotype I want to say that I think that everything you've said is very political and what you're saying is political. And that's what's at stake in the discussion that has just taken place. The way I would like to pose the question is to bring it back to what I see as a very significant change in your work. It came out a bit earlier when you talked about the carnivalesque in relation to feminism and your earlier work on what you used to call, and perhaps still call, the semiotic moment, the moment of the before, of the presymbolic. In your earlier work it seemed very much as if the celebration was of the possibility of that presymbolic expression and of the necessity of it, whereas now it seems that in relation to psychoanalysis you're talking about the necessity of the symbolic and the need to move out of those fragmented forms of expression and experience. And I think that's the point at which a political problem emerges for many people, especially for feminists, because the discourse of love and idealization, of which you're talking this evening, and the discourse of relations in what is after all still a family unit between father, mother, and child, may well be seen by feminists as discourses of which they have been victims in some sense. Now in your work there seems to be a move toward a celebration of that and a loss of that earlier emphasis on what can't be spoken with them. I know that's a very serious psychoanalytic problem because I know what it means to construct *another* idealization of those presymbolic moments, it also has its dangers. But nonetheless there seems to be a move across from one side of your division to another, and in a sense that seems to lead to almost what you concluded with, which would I know pose a problem for many people here, which is that only in love and art are we living beings. And your account of the political, which seems to be a consequence of what you are doing, is a relegation of the political to a marginal and inadequate arena of work. And in a sense your personal history, which I'm sure we've all responded to, has a classical ring about it. It's the story of somebody who became disillusioned with politics and those very big desires for change—which I would want to argue are also based on love, for example, love of the victim of exploitation—leads to a move into a more personal, more individualized sphere because of a kind of giving-up of those larger questions in which I'd want to say the question of love is at least as important, and perhaps more importantly important.

KRISTEVA: I agree with you that this interest for the love discourse and for psychoanalysis and art even can be considered as political in the deeper and larger sense of the word, social and the like. What I wanted to say is that it seems to me that if artists or psychoanalysts act politically they act politically through an intervention on an individual level. And it can be a main political concern to give value to the individual. My reproach to some political discourses with which I am disillusioned is that they don't consider the individual as a value.

ROSE: That's what is special about feminism . . . it brings subjectivity . . .

KRISTEVA: Well I am involved in different feminist movements and I dare say from time to time it does, and from time to time it does not, because there are dangers. . . . We are not preserved from what happened to different political groups, the sort of dogmatism and also violence and the annihilation of some personal particularities. It has happened also to feminist movements and to feminist groups—I have seen that. I suppose that honestly women will recognize that it can also happen in feminist groups. That's why I say that, of course, political struggles for people that are exploited will continue, they have to continue, but they will continue perhaps better if the main concern remains the individuality and the particularity of the person.

ROSE: I agree with a lot of what you've just said. But what I wanted to say about feminism was that for many people in England, the reason many feminists have such a hard time in relationship to certain dogmatisms of say the Marxist Left is precisely because of their insistence on bringing into the political arena the questions of subjectivity and sexuality.

KRISTEVA: It is true. That's why feminist movements have had so much difficulty with leftist movements for some time. Now it seems to be accepted but I think it's only a very surface acceptance. It's a question also to be put to feminists themselves. I think we now have sufficient strength to be able to criticize ourselves; we have passed the point when everything that was done by feminists was fine and we have to applaud. We can now, without fearing a collapse of the movement, criticize the movement. I remember that we elaborated some time ago in France an article about the feminist movement, a sort of *compte rendu* of what has been done before, and we put this as *unes femmes* (instead of *une femme*) in order to stress that there is a group, a plurality, but that this plurality is composed of different individuals, unities. And if the feminist movement is a movement of individuals I think it's a good political answer to what I called the political religion which can erase the individual.

AUDIENCE: I would just like to say that perhaps you need a third book which combines the issues of hate with the issues of love. I am not very familiar with the works of the early Church Fathers. Their discussions of evil involve a sort of transcendence of that to the good, whereas I think psychoanalysis has introduced a kind of wicked, witty, mischievous mix of the way to understand that love and hate are always tangled up together.

KRISTEVA: This is true. It happens that in my presentation, I stressed the love situation and I still think that I was right. Because it's very disturbing to speak about love. People think that either you are a little bit ethereal or that you are not aware that there are struggles and hate and violence in the world and so on. Or that you are a little bit religious or something like that. Love has become the modern obscenity, it's more obscene than sex, you can talk about sex and violence and that's OK; everybody knows that exists, but love is too strange. So I just tried to stress this in my presentation. But if you read the book, you will find that I begin by speaking of love and end up by speaking of hate. I can't finish the paragraph without speaking about hate because they are so mingled.

New Maladies of the Soul

Women's Time

National and European Women

The nation, which was the dream and the reality of the nineteenth century, seems to have reached both its peak and its limit with the 1929 crash and the National Socialist apocalypse. We have witnessed the destruction of its very foundation—economic homogeneity, historical tradition, and linguistic unity. World War II, which was fought in the name of national values, brought an end to the reality of the nation, which it turned into a mere illusion that has been preserved for ideological or strictly political purposes ever since. Even if the resurgence of nations and nationalists may warrant hope or fear, the social and philosophical coherence of the nation has already reached its limit.

The search for economic *homogeneity* has given way to *interdependence* when it has not yielded to the economic superpowers of the world. In like manner, *historical* tradition and *linguistic* unity have been molded into a broader and deeper denominator that we might call a *symbolic denominator*: a cultural and religious memory shaped by a combination of historical and geographical influences. This memory generates national territories determined by the ever diminishing but still widespread conflicts between political parties. At the same time, this common "symbolic denominator" is a means not only to globalization and economic standardization but also to entities that are greater than any one nation and that *sometimes* embrace the boundaries of an entire continent.

In this way, a "common symbolic denominator" can lead to a new social grouping that is greater than the nation, though it enables the nation to retain and build upon its characteristics instead of losing them. This transformation occurs, however, within a paradoxical temporal structure, a sort of "future perfect" in which the most deeply repressed and transnational past gives a distinctive character to programmed uniformity. For the memory in question (the common symbolic denominator) is linked to the solution that spatially and temporally united human groupings have offered less for the problems of the *production* of material goods (which is the domain of economics, human relations, and politics) than of *reproduction*—the survival of the species, life and death, the body, sex, and the symbol. If it is true, for instance, that Europe represents this sort of sociocultural grouping, its existence stems more from its "symbolic denominator" of art, philosophy, and religion than from its economic profile. Of course, economics is a function of collective memory, but its characteristics are easily modified by pressures from one's partners in the world.

Therefore, we see that this sort of social grouping is endowed with a *solidity* rooted in the various modes of reproduction and its representations by which the biological species is placed within a temporally determined humanity. Yet, it is also tainted with a certain *fragility*, for the symbolic denominator can no longer aspire to universality and endure the influences and assaults inflicted by other sociocultural memories. Hence, Europe, which is still fairly inconstant, is obliged to identify with the cultural, artistic, philosophical, and religious manifestations of other supranational groupings. Such identifications are of no surprise when the entities in question share a historical connection, like Europe and North America, or Europe and Latin America. They also occur, however, when the universality of this symbolic denominator juxtaposes two modes of production and reproduction that may seem incongruous, like those of Europe and the Arab world, Europe and India, Europe and China, and so forth.

In short, when dealing with the sociocultural groupings of the "European" type, we are forever faced with two major issues: first, that of *identity*, which is brought about by historical sedimentation, and second, the *loss of identity*, which is caused by memory links that bypass history in favor of anthropology. In other words, we are confronted with two temporal dimensions: the time of linear, *cursive* history, and the time of another history, that is, another time, a *monumental* time (the nomenclature comes from Nietzsche) that incorporates these supranational sociocultural groupings within even larger entities.

I would like to draw attention to certain formations that seem to embody the dynamics of this sort of sociocultural organism. I am speaking of groups we call "sociocultural" because they are defined by their role in production, but also (and especially) because of their role in the mode of reproduction and its representations. Although these groups share all the traits of the sociocultural formation in question, they *transcend* it and link it to other sociocultural formations. I am thinking specifically of sociocultural groups that we summarily define according to age categories (for instance, "European youth"), or gender divisions (for instance, "European women"), and so forth. Clearly, European youth and European women have a particularity of their own, and it is no less obvious that what defines them as "youth" or "women" is concomitant with their "European" origin and shared by their counterparts in North America and China, among others. Insofar as they participate in "monumental history," they are not merely European "youth" or "women." In a most specific way, they will mirror the universal features of their structural position with regard to reproduction and its representations.

In the pages that follow, I would like to place the problematics of European women in the context of an inquiry into time, that is, the time that the feminist movement has not only inherited but altered. Then, I shall delimit two phases or two generations of women, whose respective demands cause them to be directly universalist or cosmopolitan, though they still can be distinguished from each other. The first generation is particularly linked to national concerns, and the second, which tends to be determined by the "symbolic denominator," is European and trans-European. Finally, I shall attempt to use the problems I am addressing and the type of analysis I am proposing to show that against the backdrop of what has become a global generality, a European stance (or at least a stance taken by a European woman) has emerged.

Which Time?

Joyce said "Father's time, mother's species," and it seems indeed that the evocation of women's name and fate privileges the *space* that *generates* the human species more than it does *time*, destiny, or history. Modern studies of subjectivity—of its genealogy or its accidents—have reaffirmed this separation, which may result from sociohistorical circumstances.

After listening to his patients' dreams and fantasies, Freud grew to believe that "hysteria was linked to place."[1] Subsequent studies on children's acquisition of the symbolic function have shown that the permanency and quality of maternal love pave the way for the earliest spatial references, which give rise to childhood laughter and then prepare the whole array of symbolic manifestations that permit sign and syntax.[2]

Before endowing the patient with a capacity for transference and communication, do not both anti-psychiatry and applied psychoanalysis (when applied to the treatment of psychoses) purport to mark out new places that serve as gratifying and healing substitutes for long-standing deficiencies of maternal space? The examples of this are many, but they all converge upon the problematics of space, which so many religions with a matriarchal bent attribute to "the woman" and which Plato, who echoed the atomists of antiquity within his own system, referred to as the aporia of the *chora*, a matrixlike space that is nourishing, unnameable, prior to the One and to God, and that thus defies metaphysics.[3]

As for time, female subjectivity seems to offer it a specific concept of measurement that essentially retains *repetition* and *eternity* out of the many modalities that appear throughout the history of civilization. On the one hand, this measure preserves cycles, gestation, and the eternal return of biological rhythm that is similar to the rhythm of nature. Its predictability can be shocking, but its simultaneity with what is experienced as extra-subjective and cosmic time is a source of resplendent visions and unnameable jouissance. On the other hand, it preserves a solid temporality that is faultless and impenetrable, one that has so little to do with linear time that the very term "temporality" seems inappropriate. All-encompassing and infinite, like imaginary space, it reminds us of Hesiod's Kronos, the incestuous son who smothered Gaea with his entire being in order to take her away from Ouranos the father. It also recalls the myths of resurrection in the various traditions that have perpetuated the trace of a maternal cult through its most recent manifestation within Christianity. In Christianity, the body of the Virgin Mother does not die, but travels from one space to another within the same time frame, whether by dormition (according to the Orthodox faith) or assumption (according to Catholicism).[4]

These two types of temporality—cyclical and monumental—are traditionally associated with female subjectivity, when female subjectivity is considered to be innately maternal. We must not forget, however, that repetition and eternity serve as fundamental conceptions of time in numerous experiences, notably mystical ones.[5] That the modern feminist movement has identified with these experiences suggests that it is not intrinsically incompatible with "masculine" values.

On the other hand, female subjectivity poses a problem only with respect to a certain conception of time, that of time as planning, as teleology, as linear and prospective development—the time of departure, of transport and arrival, that is, the time of history. It has been amply demonstrated that this sort of temporality is inherent in the logical and ontological values of any given civilization. We can assume that it explains a rupture, a waiting period, or an anxiety that other temporalities hide from our view. This sort of time is that of language, of the enunciation of sentences (noun phrase and verb phrase, linguistic topic and comment, beginning and end), and it is maintained through its outer limit—death. A psychoanalyst would call it obsessional time, for the very structure of the slave can be found within the mastery of this time. A male or female hysteric (who suffers from reminiscences, according to Freud) would identify, rather, with prior temporal modalities—the cyclical, the monumental.

Within the bounds of a given civilization, however, this antinomy of psychic structures becomes an antinomy among social groups and ideologies. Indeed, the radical viewpoints of certain feminists are akin to the discourse of marginal spiritual or mystic groups, as well as, interestingly enough, to the concerns of modern science. Is it not true that the problematics of a time indissociable from space—of a space-time placed in an infinite expansion or articulated by accidents and catastrophes—are of great interest to space science as well as genetics? And in a different way, is it not true that the media revolution that has manifested itself as the information age suggests that time is frozen or exploded according to the fortuity of demand? Is it a time that returns to its source but cannot be mastered, that inexorably overwhelms its subject and restricts those who assimilate it to only two concerns: who will wield power over the origin (its programming) and the end (its use)?

The reader may be struck by these fluctuating points of reference—mother, woman, hysteric. Although the seemingly coherent use of the word "woman" in current ideology may have a "popular" or "shock" effect, it eradicates the differences among the various functions and structures that operate beneath this word. The time may have come, in fact, to celebrate the *multiplicity* of female perspectives and preoccupations. In a more accurate, honest, and less self-serving way, we must guarantee that the *fundamental difference* between the sexes arises out of the network of these differences. Feminism has accomplished a formidable task by making this difference a *painful* one, which means it is able to generate contingency and symbolic life in a civilization that has nothing to do besides playing the stock market and waging war.

We cannot speak about Europe or about "women in Europe" without defining the history that encompasses this sociocultural reality. It is true that a feminine sensibility has been in existence for more than a century now, but it is likely that by introducing its notion of time, it clashes with the idea of an "Eternal Europe," or perhaps even a "Modern Europe." Feminine sensibility, rather, would look for its own trans-European temporality by way of the European past and present as well as the European "ensemble," defined as the storehouse of memory. We can contend, however, that European feminist movements have displayed three attitudes toward this conception of linear temporality—a temporality that we readily deem to be masculine, and that is as "civilizational" as it is obsessional.

Two Generations

When the women's movement began as the struggle of suffragists and existential feminists, it sought to stake out its place in the linear time of planning and history. As a result, although the movement was universalist from the start, it was deeply rooted in the sociopolitical life of nations. The political demands of women, their struggles for equal pay for equal work and for the right to the same opportunities that men have, as well as the rejection of feminine or maternal traits considered incompatible with participation in such a history all stem from the *logic of identification* with values that are not ideological (such values have been rightly criticized as too reactionary) but logical and ontological with regard to the dominant rationality of the nation and the state.

It is unnecessary to enumerate all the benefits that this logic of identification and spirited protest have offered and still offer to women (abortion rights, contraception, equal pay, professional recognition, and more). These benefits have had or will soon prove to have even more significant effects than those of the Industrial Revolution. This current of feminism, which is universalist in scope, *globalizes* the problems of women of various social categories, ages, civilizations, or simply psychic structures under the banner of Universal Woman. In this world, a reflection about *generations* of women could only be conceived of as a succession, a progression that sought to implement the program set out by its founding members.

A second phase is associated with women who have come to feminism since May 1968 and who have brought their aesthetic or psychoanalytic experiences with them. This phase is characterized by a quasi-universal rejection of linear temporality and by a highly pronounced mistrust of political life. Although it is true that this current of feminism still has an allegiance to its founding members and still focuses (by necessity) on the struggle for the sociocultural recognition of women, in a *qualitative* sense, it sees itself in a different light from the prior generation of feminists.

The "second phase" women, who are primarily interested in the specificity of feminine psychology and its symbolic manifestations, seek a language for their corporeal and intersubjective experiences, which have been silenced by the cultures of the past. As artists or writers, they have undertaken a veritable exploration of the *dynamics of signs*. At least on the level of its intentions, their exploration is comparable to the most ambitious projects for religious and artistic upheaval. Attributing this experience to a new generation does not merely imply that new concerns have been added to the earlier demands of sociopolitical identity, for it also means that by requiring that we recognize an irreducible and self-sufficient singularity that is multifaceted, flowing, and in some ways nonidentical, feminism is currently situated outside the linear time of identities that communicate through projections and demands. Today, feminism is returning to an archaic (mythic) memory as well as to the cyclical or monumental temporality of marginal movements. It is clearly not by chance that the European and trans-European problem has manifested itself at the same time as this new phase of feminism.

What sociopolitical processes or events have led to this mutation? What are its problems, its contributions, its limits?

Socialism and Freudianism

It could be maintained that this new generation of women has a more pronounced presence in Western Europe than in the United States, which may be attributed to the *rupture* in social relations and attitudes that has been caused by socialism and Freudianism. Although *socialism* as an egalitarian doctrine is now experiencing a profound crisis, it still requires that governments and political parties of all persuasions expand solidarity by redistributing wealth and allowing free access to culture. *Freudianism*, which serves as an internal mechanism of the social realm, challenges egalitarianism by exploring sexual difference as well as the singularity of subjects who preserve their individuality.

Western socialism, shaken from its beginnings by the egalitarian or differential demands made by its women (Flora Tristan, for instance), has not hesitated to rid itself of those women who want us to recognize the specificity of the female role in culture and society. In the spirit of the egalitarian and universalist context of Enlightenment humanism, the only idea that socialism has held to is the notion that identity between the sexes is the only way to liberate the "second sex." For the moment, I shall refrain from pursuing the fact that this "ideal of equality" has not really been adopted by the actual movements and political parties that lay claims to socialism, and that since May 1968, the new generation of Western European women has been inspired, to some extent, by a revolt against the reality of the situation. Let me simply note that in theory (and in practice, in the case of Eastern Europe), socialist ideology, which is founded on the idea that human beings are determined by their relation to *production*, has ignored the role of the human being in *reproduction* and the *symbolic order*. As a result, socialist ideology has been compelled, in its totalizing, if not totalitarian, spirit,[6] to believe that the specific nature of women is unimportant, if not nonexistent. We have begun to realize, moreover, that Enlightenment humanism and even socialism have imposed this same egalitarian and censuring treatment onto individual religious groups, especially Jewish ones.[7]

Nevertheless, the effects of this attitude are of paramount importance for women. Let us take the example of the evolution of women's destiny in the socialist countries of Eastern Europe. It would only be a slight exaggeration to say that in these countries, the demands of the suffragists and existential feminists have been met, at least to a large degree. What is more, in Eastern Europe, various blunders and vacillations have not prevented three of the most important demands of the early feminist movement from being answered to: the demands of economic, political, and professional equality. The fourth demand, sexual equality, which would require permissiveness in sexual relationships as well as abortion and contraceptive rights, remains inhibited by a certain Marxist ethics as well as by the reason of state. Thus, it is the fourth equal right that poses a problem and seems *vital* to the struggle of the new generation. This may be true, but because of the successful socialist agenda (which has been quite disappointing, in reality), this struggle will no longer aim specifically for equality. At this point in its journey, the new generation is coming up against what I have called the *symbolic* question.

Sexual, biological, physiological, and reproductive difference reflects a difference in the relation between subjects and the symbolic contract—

that is, the social contract. It is a matter of clarifying the difference between men and women as concerns their respective relationships to power, language, and meaning. The most subtle aspects of the new generation's feminist subversion will be directed toward this issue in the future. This focus will combine the sexual with the symbolic in order to discover first the specificity of the feminine (*le féminin*) and then the specificity of each woman.

The saturation of socialist ideology and the exhaustion of its plan in favor of a new social contract has made way for Freudianism. I am not unaware, however, that militant women have seen Freud as an annoying male chauvinist from a Vienna that was at once puritanical and decadent, as someone who believed women were submen, castrated men.

Castrated or Subject to Language

Before we bypass Freud in order to propose a more accurate vision of women, let us first attempt to understand his notion of castration. The founder of psychoanalysis posited a castration *anxiety* or *fear* and a correlative penis *envy*, both of which are *imaginary* constructs peculiar to the *discourse* of neurotic *men as well as women*. A close reading of Freud that goes beyond the biological and mechanical models of his day enables us to delve into these issues more deeply.

First, the castration fantasy and its correlative penis envy are like the "primal scene" in that they are all *hypotheses, a priori* judgments intrinsic to psychoanalytic theory itself. These notions represent logical necessities that are relegated to the "origin" in order to explain that which never fails to function in neurotic discourse. In other words, neurotic discourse (in men as well as women) can only be understood in terms of its own logic if we acknowledge its fundamental sources—the primal scene and castration fantasy—even if these are never present in reality itself. The reality of castration is as real as the supposed "big bang" at the origin of the universe, yet we are much less shocked when this sort of intellectual process concerns inanimate matter than when it is applied to our own subjectivity and to the fundamental mechanism of our epistemic thought.

Furthermore, certain Freudian texts (like *The Interpretation of Dreams*, but especially those of the second topology, in particular the *Metapsychology*) as well as their recent elaborations (notably by Jacques Lacan), suggest that castration is an imaginary construction stemming from a psychic mechanism that constitutes the symbolic field as well as anyone who enters it. Castration, then, would be the advent of sign and of syntax, that is, of language as a *separation* from a fusion state of pleasure. In this way, the institution of an *articulated network* of *differences*, which refers to objects separated from a subject, forms *meaning*. This logical operation of separation, which has been described by child psychology and psycholinguistics, anticipates the syntactic links of language for boys as well as girls. Freud offers a new approach to this notion by postulating that certain biological or familial conditions prompt some women (notably hysterics) to deny this logical operation of separation and the language that ensues, whereas some men (notably obsessional neurotics) glorify this separation and language while trying, petrified as they are, to master them.

Analytic practice has shown that in fantasies, the penis becomes the primary referent of this operation of separation and gives full meaning to the *lack* or *desire* that constitutes subjects when they join the order of language. In order for this operation, which constitutes the symbolic and social orders, to reveal its truth and be accepted by both sexes, it would be wise to add to it the entire series of deprivations and exclusion that accompany the fear of losing one's penis and impose the loss of wholeness and completeness. Castration, then, would be the ensemble of "cuts" that are indispensable to the advent of the symbolic.

Living the Sacrifice

Whether or not women are aware of the mutations that have generated or accompanied their awakening, the question they are asking themselves today could be formulated as follows: *what is our place in the social contract?* If this contract, whose terms do not treat everyone in an equal fashion, bases itself upon an ultimately sacrificial relationship of separation and articulation of differences that serves to create a meaning that can be communicated, what is our place in the order of sacrifice and/or language? Since we no longer wish to be excluded from this order, and we are no longer satisfied with our perpetually assigned role of maintaining, developing, and preserving this sociosymbolic contract as mothers, wives, nurses, doctors, teachers, and so forth, how might we appropriate our own space, a space that is passed down through tradition and that we would like to modify?

It is difficult to enumerate with certainty the aspects of the current relationship between women and the symbolic that stem from sociohistorical circumstances (including patriarchal, Christian, humanist, and socialist ideologies, among others), or from a structure. We can only speak of a structure observed in a sociohistorical context, that of Western Christian civilization and its secular ramifications. At the interior of this psychosymbolic structure, women feel rejected from language and the social bond, in which they discover neither the affects nor the meanings of the relationships they enjoy with nature, their bodies, their children's bodies, another woman, or a man. The accompanying frustration, which is also experienced by some men, is the quintessence of the new feminist ideology. Consequently, it is difficult, if not impossible, for women to adhere to the sacrificial logic of separation and syntactic links upon which language and the social code are based, and this can eventually lead to a rejection of the symbolic that is experienced as a rejection of the paternal function and may result in psychosis.

Faced with this situation, some women have sought to develop a new perspective—through new objects and new analyses—for anthropology, psychoanalysis, linguistics, and other disciplines that explore the symbolic dimension.[8] Other, more subjective women, who have come forth in the wake of contemporary art, have attempted to modify language and other codes of expression through a style that remains closer to the body and to emotion. I am not referring here to "female language,"[9] whose existence as a particular syntactic style is problematic, and whose apparent lexical specificity may be less a product of sexual difference than of social marginality. I am also not speaking of the aesthetic value of creations by women, most of which mirror a more or less euphoric and depressed romanticism, on the one hand, and stage an explosion of an ego that lacks narcissistic gratification, on the other. This leads me to believe that the primary focus of the new generation of women has become the sociosymbolic contract as a sacrificial contract.

For more than a century, anthropologists and sociologists have attracted our attention to the society-sacrifice that works behind "savage thought," wars, dream discourse, or great writers. In so doing, these scholars have reformulated and analyzed the metaphysical question of evil. If society is truly founded on a communal murder, the realization that castration provides the basis for the sociosymbolic is what will enable human beings to postpone murder. We symbolize murder (and ourselves) and thus have an opportunity to transform baleful chaos into an optimal sociosymbolic order.

Today's women have proclaimed that this sacrificial contract imposes itself against their will, which has compelled them to attempt a revolt that they perceive to be a resurrection. Society as a whole, however, considers this revolt to be a refusal and it can result in violence between the sexes (a murderous hatred, the breakup of the couple and the family) or in cultural innovation. In fact, it probably leads to them both. In any event, that is where the stakes are, and they are of enormous consequence. By fighting against evil, we reproduce it, this time at the core of the social bond—the bond between men and women.

The Terror of Power or the Power of Terrorism

First in the former socialist countries (such as the former Soviet Union and China) and later, increasingly, in Western democracies, feminist movements have enabled women to attain positions of leadership in the worlds of business, industry, and culture. Even if various forms of unfair discrimination and persecution continue to hold sway, the struggle against these is a struggle against the ways of the past. Even if the cause has been made known and the principles accepted, there still are obstacles that need to be overcome. Thus, although the ensuing struggle remains one of the major *preoccupations* of the new generation, in a strict sense of the word, it is no longer its primary *problem*. With respect to *power*, however, its problem could be stated as follows: What occurs when women attain power and identify with it? What occurs when they reject power but create an analogous society, a counterpower that ranges from a coterie of ideas to terrorist commandos?

That women have assumed commercial, industrial, and cultural power has not changed the nature of this power, which can be clearly seen in the case of Eastern Europe. The women who have been promoted to positions of leadership and who have suddenly obtained economic (as well as narcissistic) advantages that had been refused to them for thousands of years are the same women who become the strongest supporters of the current regimes, the guardians of the status quo, and the most fervent protectors of the established order.[10] This identification between women and a power that they once found frustrating, oppressive, or unattainable has often been used to the advantage of such totalitarian regimes as the German National Socialists or the Chilean junta.[11] One possible explanation of this troubling phenomenon might be that it results from a paranoid counterinvestment (in the psychoanalytic sense) of an initially denied symbolic order. Even so, this does not prevent its massive propagation around the world, sometimes in more subtle forms than the totalitarian ones I have mentioned. In any event, all these forms share an interest in equalization, stability, and conformity, though this comes at a cost: the eradication of each individual's uniqueness, of personal experiences, and of the vagaries of life.

Some may regret that the rise of a libertarian movement such as feminism may wind up reinforcing conformity, and others will celebrate this consequence and use it to their advantage. Electoral campaigns and political life never fail to bet on the latter alternative. Experience has shown that even the antiestablishment or innovative initiatives led by women dragged in by power (when they do not readily submit to it) are quickly attributed to "the system." The self-proclaimed democratization of institutions that pride themselves on accepting women most often means that they simply add a few female "bosses" to their ranks.

The various feminist currents, which tend to be more radical in approach, reject the powers that be and make the second sex into a *countersociety*, a sort of alter ego of official society that harbors hopes for pleasure. This female society can be opposed to the sacrificial and frustrating sociosymbolic contract: a countersociety imagined to be harmonious, permissive, free, and blissful. In our modern societies, which do not acknowledge an afterlife, the countersociety is the only refuge for jouissance, for it is precisely an anti-utopia, a place outside the law, yet a path to utopia.

Like all societies, the countersociety bases itself upon the expulsion of an already excluded element. The scapegoat deemed responsible for evil thus keeps it away from the established community,[12] which is thereby exonerated of any responsibility for it. Modern protest movements have often reproduced this model by designating a guilty party that shields them from criticism, whether it be the foreigner, money, another religion, or the other sex. If we take this logic at face value, does feminism not become a sort of reverse sexism?

In our world, the various marginal groups of sex, age, religion, ethnic origin, and ideology represent a refuge of hope, that is, a secular transcendence. All the same, insofar as the number of women affected by these problems has increased (albeit in a less dramatic way than was the case a few years ago), the problem of the countersociety is becoming an enormous one, no more and no less important than "half the sky."

It is not the case that protest movements, including feminism, are "libertarian at first" and then dogmatic only later. They do not fall into the abyss of defeated models through the fault of some internal deviation or external maneuver. The particular structure of the logic of counterpower and countersociety is what lies behind its essence as an image of defeated society or power. In such a perspective, which is most likely too Hegelian, modern feminism would be a single moment in an ongoing process—the process of becoming aware of the implacable violence (of separation and castration) that underlies *any* symbolic contract.

The large number of women participating in terrorist groups like the Palestinian commandos, the Baader-Meinhoff Gang, and the Red Brigades, has been noted. Exploitation of women is still far too frequent, and the traditional prejudices against women are so fierce that we cannot evaluate this phenomenon in an objective manner, though we may rightfully claim that it stems from a negation of the sociosymbolic contract as well as its counterinvestment. This paranoid mechanism is at the base of all forms of political commitment and it can generate various humanizing attitudes. Yet when a woman feels ruthlessly isolated and becomes aware of her affective experience as a woman or her status as a social being who remains unknown to the discourse and the powers that be (everything from her own family to the social institutions of the world), she can make herself into a "possessed" agent through the counterinvestment of the violence she encounters. She fights against her frustration, then, with weapons that may appear extreme at first glance, but that are justifiable and understandable once the narcissistic suffering that elicits their use is recognized.

This terrorist violence, which is inevitably directed against the regimes of current bourgeois democracies, assigns itself a program of liberation that consists of an order even more repressive and sacrificial than the one it is fighting. Indeed, the object of female terrorists groups' aggression is not the various totalitarian regimes, but the liberal regimes that are becoming increasingly democratic. Their mobilization comes about in the name of a nation, an oppressed group, or what is believed to be a good and sound human essence, that is, the fantasy of an archaic fulfillment that would be disturbed by an arbitrary, abstract, and thus undesirable order. Although this order has been accused of being oppressive, is our primary criticism not that it is weak? That it does not stand up to a substance believed to be pure and good but that is lost forever, a substance that the marginalized woman hopes to recover?

Anthropologists have affirmed that the social order is a sacrificial one, yet sacrifice stops violence and develops into its own order (through prayer or social well-being). If we reject it, we subject ourselves to the explosion of the so-called good substance that uncontrollably erupts outside the bounds of law and rights, like an absolute arbitrariness.

As a result of the crisis of monotheism, two centuries of revolutions (most recently materialized as Fascism and Stalinism) have staged the tragedy of the logic of oppressed goodwill that winds up as a massacre. Are women more able than other social groups to invest in the implacable terrorist mechanism? Perhaps one might merely note that ever since the dawn of feminism (and even before), women who fall outside the norm have often gained power through murder, conspiracy, or assassination. Eternal debt toward the mother has made her more vulnerable to the symbolic order, more fragile when she suffers from it, and more virulent when she protects herself. If the archetypal belief in a good and sound chimerical substance is essentially a belief in the omnipotence of an archaic, fulfilled, complete, all-encompassing mother who is not frustrated, not separated, and who lacks the "cut" that permits symbolism (that is, who lacks castration), the ensuing violence would be impossible to defuse without challenging the very myth of the archaic mother. It has been noted that feminist movements have been invaded by paranoia,[13] and we may remember Lacan's scandalous pronouncement that "There is no such thing as Woman." Indeed, she does not exist with a capital "W," as a holder of a mythical plenitude, a supreme power upon which the terror of power as well as terrorism as the desire for power base themselves. All the same, talk about a forceful subversion! Talk about playing with fire!

Creators: Male and Female

The desire to be a mother, which the previous generation of feminists held to be alienating or reactionary, has not become a standard for the current generation. Nevertheless, there is a growing number of women who find maternity to be compatible with their professional careers (this is also due to such improvements in living conditions as the increase of daycare centers and nursery schools, the more active participation of men in domestic life, and so forth). Furthermore, women are finding that maternity is vital to the richness of female experience, with its many joys and sorrows. This trend is illustrated to its fullest extent in lesbian mothers or in certain single mothers who reject the paternal function. The latter cases exemplify one of the most dramatic examples of the rejection of the symbolic order to which I referred earlier on, and they also exhibit an ardent deification of maternal power.

Hegel distinguishes between female right (familial and religious) and male law (civil and political). Although our societies are very well acquainted with the uses and abuses of this male law, we must admit that for the moment, female right appears to be a void. If these practices of fatherless maternity were to become the norm, it would become absolutely necessary to develop appropriate laws that could diminish the violence that might be inflicted on the child and the father. Are women equipped for this psychological and legal responsibility? That is one of the most profound questions that the members of this new generation of women are coming up against, especially when they refuse to confront such questions because they are gripped with a rage against the order and its law that victimizes them.

Faced with this situation, feminist groups are becoming increasingly aware (especially when they try to broaden their audience) that refusing maternity cannot be their primary political approach. The majority of women today feel that they have a mission to put a child into the world. This brings up a question for the new generation that the preceding one repudiated: what lies behind this desire to be a mother? Unable to answer this question, feminist ideology opens the door to a return of religion, which may serve to pacify anxiety, suffering, and maternal expectations. Although we can only offer a partial adherence to Freud's belief that the desire to have a child is the desire to have a penis, and is thus a replacement for phallic and symbolic power, we still must pay close attention to what today's women have to say about this experience. Pregnancy is a dramatic ordeal: a splitting of the body, the division and coexistence of self and other, of nature and awareness, of physiology and speech. This fundamental challenge to identity is accompanied by a fantasy of wholeness of narcissistic self-containment. Pregnancy is a sort of institutionalized, socialized, and natural psychosis. The arrival of the child, on the other hand, guides the mother through a labyrinth of a rare experience: the love for another person, as opposed to love for herself, for a mirror image, or especially for another person with which the "I" becomes merged (through amorous or sexual passion). It is rather a slow, difficult, and delightful process of becoming attentive, tender, and self-effacing. If maternity is to be guilt-free, this journey needs to be undertaken without masochism and without annihilating one's affective, intellectual, and professional personality, either. In this way, maternity becomes a true *creative act*, something that we have not yet been able to imagine.

At the same time, women's desire for affirmation has emerged as a longing for artistic and especially literary creation. Why the emphasis on literature? Is it because when literature is in conflict with social norms, it diffuses knowledge and occasionally the truth about a repressed, secret, and unconscious universe? Is it because literature intensifies the social contract by exposing the uncanny nature of that which remains unsaid?

Is it because it plays with the abstract and frustrating order of social signs, of the words of everyday communication, and thus creates a place for fantasy and pleasure?

Flaubert said, "Madame Bovary, c'est moi." These days, some women think, "Flaubert, c'est moi." This claim points not only to an identification with the power of the imaginary, but also to women's desire to lift the sacrificial weight of the social contract and to furnish our societies with a freer and more flexible discourse that is able to give a name to that which has not yet been an object of widespread circulation: the mysteries of the body, secret joys, shames, hate displayed toward the second sex.

For this reason, women's writing has recently attracted a great deal of attention from "specialists" as well as the media. Nevertheless, the stumbling blocks that it must overcome are not inconsequential. Does women's writing not consist of a morose rejection of the very "male literature" that serves as a model for so much of women's writing? Thanks to the stamp of feminism, do we not sell many books whose naïve whining or commercialized romanticism would normally be scoffed at? Do female writers not make phantasmatic attacks against Language and the Sign, which are accused of being the ultimate mainstays of male chauvinist power, in the name of a body deprived of meaning and whose truth would only be "gestural" or "musical"?

Nevertheless, however questionable the results of women's artistic productions may be, the symptom has been made clear: women *are* writing. And we are eagerly waiting to find out what *new material* they will offer us.

In the Name of the Father, the Son—and the Woman?

These few characteristic features of the new generation of women in Europe show that these women are placed within the same framework as the religious crisis of contemporary civilization. In my view, religion is our phantasmatic necessity to procure a *representation* (which could be animal, feminine, masculine, or parental, among others) that replaces the element that makes us what we are—our capacity to form symbols. Feminism today seems to constitute exactly this sort of *representation*, one that complements the frustration that women feel when faced with the Christian tradition and its variation—secular humanism. That this new ideology has some affinities with so-called matriarchal beliefs does not obliterate its radical innovation, for it participates in the antisacrificial trend that drives our culture. Although this ideology contests these

constraints, it still remains vulnerable to the hazards of violence and terrorism. When radicalism goes this far, it challenges the very notion of
social exchange.

Some contemporary thinkers maintain that modernity is the first era
in human history in which human beings have attempted to live without
religion. As it stands today, is feminism not about to become a sort of
religion? Or will it manage to rid itself of its belief in Woman, Her power,
and Her writing and support instead the singularity of each woman, her
complexities, her many languages, at the cost of a single horizon, of a single perspective, of faith?

Is it a matter of ultimate solidarity, or a matter of analysis?

Is it an imaginary support in a technocratic era that frustrates narcissistic personalities, or a measurement of the time in which the cosmos,
atoms, and cells—our true contemporaries—call for the formation of a
free and flowing subjectivity?

Another Generation Is Another Space

It is now becoming possible to have a more objective perspective on the
two preceding generations of women. I am suggesting, then, that a *third
one* is taking shape, at least in Europe. I am thinking neither of a new age
group (although its importance is far from negligible) nor of a new "mass
feminist movement" that would follow in the footsteps of the second
generation. The meaning I am attributing to the word "generation" suggests less a chronology than a *signifying* space, a mental space that is at
once corporeal and desirous.

For this third generation, which I strongly support (which I am imagining?), the dichotomy between man and women as an opposition of two
rival entities is *a problem for metaphysics*. What does "identity" and
even "sexual identity" mean in a theoretical and scientific space in which
the notion of "identity" itself is challenged?[14] I am not simply alluding to
bisexuality, which most often reveals a desire for totality, a desire for the
eradication of difference. I am thinking more specifically of subduing the
"fight to the finish" between rival groups, not in hopes of reconciliation—since at the very least, feminism can be lauded for bringing to light
that which is irreducible and even lethal in the social contract—but in the
hopes that the violence occurs with the utmost mobility within individual and sexual identity, and not through a rejection of the other.

As a result, both individual equilibrium and social equilibrium (which
emerges through the homeostasis of aggressive forces typical of social,

national, and religious groups) are made vulnerable. All the same, does not the unbearable tension that underlies this "equilibrium" lead those who suffer from it to avoid it, to seek another way of regulating *difference?*

Despite the apparent indifference that has been shown toward the militancy of the first and second generations of women, I have generally found sexism to be less pronounced than before.

With the exception of the proclaimed rights of male and female homosexuals, sex has an ever shrinking hold on subjective interest. This "desexualization" goes as far as challenging not only humanism, but also the anthropomorphism that serves as a basis for our society. For this reason, "the man and the woman" are less of a fulcrum for social interest than they once were. The paroxysmal narcissism and egoism of our contemporaries only seem to contradict the retreat from anthropomorphism, for when anthropomorphism does not fall into technological supremacy or a general state of automation, it is forced to look to spirituality. Could the sexual revolution and feminism have merely been transitions into spiritualism?

That spiritualism turns to evasion or to conformist repression should not obscure the radical nature of the process, which comes forth as an *interiorization of the fundamental separation of the sociosymbolic contract.* From that point on, the other is neither an evil being foreign to me nor a scapegoat from the outside, that is, of another sex, class, race, or nation. I am *at once the attacker and the victim,* the same *and* the other, identical *and* foreign. I simply have to analyze incessantly the fundamental separation of my own untenable identity.

Religion is willing to accept this European awareness of *intrinsic evil,* which emerges from the ideological accomplishments and impasses of the feminist experience. Is any other discourse able to support it? Along with psychoanalysis, the role of aesthetic practices needs to be augmented, not only to counterbalance the mass production and uniformity of the information age, but also to demystify the idea that the community of language is a universal, all-inclusive, and equalizing tool. Each artistic experience can also highlight the diversity of our identifications and the relativity of our symbolic and biological existence.

Understood as such, aesthetics takes on the question of morality. The imaginary helps to outline an ethics that remains invisible, as the outbreak of the imposture and of hatred wreaks havoc on societies freed from dogmas and laws. As restriction and as play, the imaginary enables us to envision an ethics aware of its own sacrificial order and that thus retains part of the burden for each of its adherents, whom the imaginary pronounces guilty and responsible, though it offers them the direct possibility of jouissance, of various aesthetic productions, of having a life filled with trials and differences. This would be a utopian ethics, but is any other kind possible?

In this sense, we might return to Spinoza's question: are women subject to ethics? Women are probably not subject to the ethics laid out by classical philosophy, with which generations of feminists have had a dangerously precarious relationship. Nevertheless, do women not participate in the upheaval that our society is experiencing on several levels (war, drugs, artificial insemination), an upheaval that will require a new ethics? If we consider feminism to be a *moment* in the thought pertaining to the anthropomorphic identity that has diminished the freedom of our species, we will only be able to answer this question in the affirmative once this moment has come to a close. And what is the meaning of the current "politically correct" movement that has swept across the United States? European consciousness has surpassed such concerns, thanks, in some respects, to the dissatisfaction and creativity of its women.

NOTES

1. See *The Freud/Jung Letters*, Ralph Manheim and R. F. C. Hull, tr. (Princeton, N.J.: Princeton University Press, 1974).

2. See René Spitz, *The First Year of Life: A Psychoanalytic Study of Normal and Deviant Development of Object Relations* (New York: International Universities Press, 1966); D. W. Winnicott, *Playing and Reality* (New York: Basic Books, 1971); Julia Kristeva, "Place Names," *Desire in Language: A Semiotic Approach to Literature and Art*, Thomas Gora, Alice Jardine, Leon S. Roudiez, tr. (New York: Columbia University Press, 1980), pp. 271–95.

3. See Plato, *Timaeus*, Francis M. Cornford, tr. (New York: Harcourt, Brace, 1937): "Space, which is everlasting, not admitting destruction; providing a situation for all things that come into being but itself apprehended without the senses by a sort of bastard reasoning, and hardly an object of belief. This, indeed, is that which we look upon as in a dream and say that anything that is must needs be in some place and occupy some room" (52a–52b). See my remarks on the *chora* in *Revolution in Poetic Language*, Margaret Waller, tr. (New York: Columbia University Press, 1984).

4. See Julia Kristeva, "Stabat Mater," in *Tales of Love*, Léon S. Roudiez, tr. (New York: Columbia University Press, 1983).

5. See H. C. Puech, *La Gnose et le temps* (Paris: Gallimard, 1977).

6. See D. Desanti, "L'autre sexe des bolcheviks," *Tel Quel* 76 (1978); and Julia Kristeva, *About Chinese Women*, Anita Barrows, tr. (London: Marion Boyars, 1977).

7. See Arthur Hertzberg, *The French Enlightenment and the Jews* (New York: Columbia University Press, 1968); and *Les Juifs et la révolution française*, B. Blumenkranz and A. Soboul, ed. (Paris: Editions Privat, 1976).

8. From time to time, this work is published in various academic women's journals, one of the most prestigious being *Signs: Journal of Women in Culture and Society*, University of Chicago Press. Also of note are the special issue of the *Revue des sciences humaines* 4 (1977) entitled "Ecriture, féminité, féminisme" and "Les femmes et la philosophie" in *Le Doctrinal de sapience* 3 (1977).

9. See the various linguistic studies on "female language," such as Robin Lakoff, *Language and Women's Place* (New York: Harper & Row, 1974); Mary R. Key, *Male/Female Language* (Metuchen, N.J.: Scarecrow Press, 1973); and A. M. Houdebine, "Les femmes et la langue," *Tel Quel* 74 (1977): 84–95.

10. See Julia Kristeva, *About Chinese Women*.

11. See M. A. Macciocchi, *Eléments pour une analyse du fascisme* (Paris: 10/18, 1976); Michèle Mattelart, "Le Coup d'état au féminin," *Les Temps modernes* (January 1975).

12. The principles of a "sacrificial anthropology" have been laid out by René Girard in *Violence and the Sacred*, Patrick Gregory, tr. (Baltimore: Johns Hopkins University Press, 1977); and especially in *Things Hidden Since the Foundation of the World*, Stephen Bann and Michael Metteer, tr. (Palo Alto: Stanford University Press, 1987).

13. See Micheline Enriquez, "Fantasmes paranoïaques: Différences de sexes, homosexualité, loi du père," *Topiques* 13 (1974).

14. See Claude Lévi-Strauss et al., *L'Identité: séminaire interdisciplinaire* (Paris: Grasset & Fasquelle, 1977).

Interview with Elaine Hoffman Baruch on Feminism in the United States and France

BARUCH: In an interview that you had done once for *Psych et Po*, which was translated in an anthology edited by Elaine Marks and Isabelle de Courtivron called *New French Feminisms,* you said, and here is the translation: "There can be no sociopolitical transformation without a transformation of subjects, in other words, in our relation to social constraints, to pleasure and, more deeply, to language." Elsewhere you have spoken about the importance of language for structuring experience, and so have other French theorists. American feminists speak about the importance of language also, but they are talking about something quite different from what you are talking about. How could we go about changing our relation, particularly women's relation, to social constraints, to pleasure, and, especially, to language?

KRISTEVA: When I spoke the sentence you have quoted, it had to do with the following: very often, in France, a certain sort of feminism had posed itself solely as a movement of sociological protest, which consisted in making of women a sort of social force or motor which would ultimately take on the role played in Marxist theory by the proletariat. Here is a class or social group which is oppressed, which is not paid well enough, which does not have its proper place in production and in political representation, and this oppressed class, this oppressed social stratum, should fight, essentially, to obtain this recognition—economic, political, and ideological. I, on the other hand—and I am not alone in this; a large part of the French feminist movement, I think, is aware of this problematic—think that women's protest is situated at an altogether different level. It is not first of all a social protest, although it is also that. It is a protest which consists in demanding that attention be paid to the subjective particularity which an individual represents, in the social order, of course, but also and above all in relation to what essentially differentiates that individual, which is the individual's sexual difference. Well then: how can one define this sexual difference? It is not solely biological; it is, above all, given in the representations which we make ourselves of this difference, and we have no other means of constructing this representation than through language, through tools for symbolizing. Now these tools for symbolizing are common to the two sexes. Everyone speaks English if you're English; everyone speaks French if you're French, whether we are men or women. So how do we situate ourselves in relation to these universal tools in order to try to mark our difference?

Here the position of some feminists has seemed to me rather strange and regressive. Certain feminists, in France, particularly, say that whatever is in language is of the order of strict designation, of understanding, of logic, and is male. Ultimately, theory, science, is phallic, is male. On the other hand, that which in language, according to the same feminists, is feminine, is whatever has to do with the imprecise, with the whisper, with impulses, perhaps with primary processes, with rhetoric—in other words, speaking roughly, the domain of literary expression, the region of the tacit, the vague, and where one would escape from the too-tight tailoring of the linguistic sign and of logic. I think that this is, so to speak, a Manichean position which consists in designating as feminine a phase or a modality in the functioning of language. And if one assigns to women that phase alone, this in fact amounts to maintaining women in a position of inferiority, and in any case of marginality, to reserving them the place of the childish, of the unsayable, or of the hysteric.

That the valorization of this modality of expression can have a critical, if not a subversive function, is obvious; but I think that it is not sufficient either. On the other hand, other women say that we must equip ourselves with or appropriate the logical, mastering, scientific, theoretical apparatus. They consider it as an extremely gratifying promotion that there are women physicists, theorists, and philosophers. In saying this, they preserve for women an extremely important place in the domain of culture. But these attitudes can be accompanied by a denial of two things; on the one hand, of the question of power and, on the other, of the particularity of women. One can be a theoretician and a woman, or only a theoretician and not a woman. In other words one can fit oneself to the dominant discourse—theoretical discourse, scientific discourse—and on the basis of that find an extremely gratifying slot in society, but this to the detriment of the expression of the particularity belonging to the individual as a woman.

On the basis of this fact, it seems to me that what one must try to do is not to deny these two aspects of linguistic communication, the mastering aspect and the aspect which is more of the body and of the impulses, but to try, in every situation and for every woman, to find a proper articulation of these two elements. What does "proper" mean? That which best fits the specific history of each woman, which expresses her better. So you see that I would be just as much against the slogan, "All women should master the dominant discourse." I am also against the position which asserts that all that is part of the game of power and that women must express themselves in literature. I think that the time has come when we must no longer speak of "all women." We have to talk in terms of individual women and that each should try to find her place inside these two poles. I gave a talk on this some time ago which appeared in *Les Cahiers du Grif,* which is the Belgian women's paper, and it was called "Unes Femmes," spelled "unes" with an "s" on the end and "femmes" with an "s." What I meant by that is that there is a community of women, but what seemed to me important is that this community should be made up of particularities and that it not be a uniform mass. And one of the gravest dangers that now presents itself in feminism is the impulse to practice feminism in a herd. I think that at first this was perhaps something important because people cried out, "We demand abortion," "We demand the social advantages we have been denied," but now this "we" is becoming troublesome. There have to be "I's" and women have to become authors, actors, not to hypostasize or overvalue those particular kinds of work, but I say this so that this perspective will push each one of us to find her own individual language.

BARUCH: Would you say something about your concept of "abjection" in your book *Powers of Horror*?

KRISTEVA: The term in French has a much more violent sense than in English. It means something disgusting.

BARUCH: *Abasement* perhaps? *Degradation*? It doesn't quite cover it but are these terms closer?

KRISTEVA: Yes, there is all that; there is also the aspect of nausea, of wanting to vomit. *L'abjection* is something that disgusts you. For example, you see something rotting and you want to vomit. It's "abject" on the level of matter. It can also be a notion that concerns moral matters—an *abjection* in the face of crime, for example. But it is an extremely strong feeling which is at once somatic and symbolic, and which is above all a revolt of the person against an external menace from which one wants to keep oneself at a distance, but of which one has the impression that it is not only an external menace but that it may menace us from the inside. So it is a desire for separation, for becoming autonomous and also the feeling of an impossibility of doing so—whence the element of crisis which the notion of abjection carries within it. Taken to its logical consequences, it is an impossible assemblage of elements, with a connotation of a "fragile limit."

BARUCH: Would you say that women's experience of abjection, to use the English word for a moment, is the same as men's, or is it different? Is there a sexual differentiation?

KRISTEVA: To tell the truth, I did that work without asking myself that question. I wanted first of all to scan the notion in a more general way. But obviously I did it also on the basis of my own experience, because it is mainly a psychoanalytical book, but which like all psychoanalytical books is somewhat self-analytical, like—I am going to make a pretentious comparison—Freud's *Interpretation of Dreams*, which was based essentially on his dreams—and so this book is in great measure based on my own experience. I would say that abjection is a category which cuts across the two sexes, as one can be phobic whether one is a man or a woman or as one can be schizophrenic whether one is a man or a woman. On the other hand I have asked myself whether men and women behave in the same way when abjection becomes a source of pleasure. When, in other words, there are eroticizations of abjection, as for example one finds in the case of perversions: sexual pleasure in the face of disgusting things or in the face of disgusting actions. And in fact I think that here I can say that there is a difference in the relations of man and woman in this regard. I think that a woman does not eroticize abjection or the abject by herself. She does it if she is in a relationship with a man. In other words, if she does it, it is to carry out the desire of a man.

I do not think that there is a propensity to perversion in women. Cases of feminine perversion are very rare, and are above all perversions which are meant to satisfy the perversion of a man. Why? Because this relation to abjection is finally rooted in the combat which every human being carries on with one's mother. In order that we become autonomous it is necessary that one cut the instinctual dyad of the mother and the child and that one become something other.

Now a woman gets rid of her mother in a much more complex way than a man. Either we don't succeed in doing so, and we carry with us this living corpse—but in that case we women (and, once again, it's very difficult to generalize) close our eyes: that is to say, we don't want to know, we don't eroticize this relationship. There is, as it were, a veil, like the hysterical veil which one sees in the gaze, very often, of the hysterical woman, which is extremely brilliant but sees nothing—a veiled gaze at a region of forgetfulness, which is the archaic relationship with the mother. Or one recognizes this relationship with the archaic mother, but in this case there are different forms of defense, of which feminism can be one, or again, if one enters the combat, this gives rise to fairly serious forms of psychosis. And this retreat, the eroticization of the mother, which produces abjection as a source of pleasure, does not seem to me something built in.

BARUCH: Is what you have said about the eroticization of abjection connected with Freud's theory of the splitting of the sexual object into the degraded and the exalted?

KRISTEVA: Yes. Exactly.

BARUCH: And would you agree that women do not split the sexual object in the same way that men do?

KRISTEVA: Exactly. They don't have to divide the object—the feminine sexual object has only to be abandoned: one abandons the mother for the father. And therefore the cleavage happens differently.

BARUCH: That's the cleavage.

KRISTEVA: Right. The question of the eroticization of abjection—it's interesting, what you asked—can present itself in another form as well, not only that of the desire which a woman can have for a man but also in the case of female homosexuality. That is, when one has not made the move to a male object but chooses as an erotic object an object of the same sex. Thus, inside a certain sort of female homosexuality one can find an eroticization of "abjection." This is not the case for all female homosexuality, for here we have a rather interesting range of variations.

BARUCH: There are two rather well-known books in the United States: one by Dorothy Dinnerstein, called *The Mermaid and the Minotaur,* and the other by Nancy Chodorow called *The Reproduction of Mothering,* whose thesis is that the exaltation and the degradation of the woman stem from the fact that it is mothers who rear children, and that if fathers or men were to have equal responsibility for the rearing of infants, this would eliminate all of our sexual malaise and end all of the problems having to do with women's inaccessibility to culture.

KRISTEVA: I don't think so. Because if there is a sort of rage against mothers it is not only because they take care of the child, it's because they carry it in their bodies. And that is something which men, even if they handle the diapers, can't do. I think that there is rooted a negative desire, a certain rejection of the maternal function—a fascinated rejection. Moreover the fact that men do the same work as women with regard to the education of children or their early upbringing will certainly change things in the psychic functioning of children. But I don't know if it will do so in the way foreseen by these feminists. In fact it will first displace and then decimate the paternal function. It will render ambiguous the paternal role. Up to the present, in the division of sexual roles, the mother takes care of the child, the father is farther away. The father represents the symbolic moment of separation.

BARUCH: And you feel that that should be retained?

KRISTEVA: If we do what they call for, that is, if the fathers are always present, if fathers become mothers, one may well ask, who will play the role of separators?

BARUCH: Couldn't they both be? Couldn't both sexes be nurturers and differentiators somehow?

KRISTEVA: I would like to think so. But it would be very difficult. What seems more likely is just that there will be many borderline children produced, and it will become necessary to find a third party, for example, the child psychotherapist, the school, all those medical sectors of the different "psy's": psychoanalysts, psychiatrists, psychotherapists, et cetera, who will play the paternal role. The number of helping institutions for early childhood, for school children, that are forming now in our society, is extraordinary, and one may well ask oneself what their function is. Well, every time I have looked closely at what these people do, it is, of course, to replace a failed mother, as is remarked only too often. But it is above all to replace a nonexistent father: to play the role of the separator, to play the role of someone who comforts the mother in order to permit her to take her role in hand, but at the same time the role is one of a third party. The question I think one ought to ask is not so much what must be done in order that women be happy, it is: what is to be done in order that children have a development—not a normal development—but let us say a development which permits them to accede to the various elements of human culture? And I think that what interferes with that access is the underestimation of the paternal function.

BARUCH: Nancy Chodorow would say that the function of the father has nothing to do with his sex, and that someone female could play the same role of separator.

KRISTEVA: Yes, certainly; that's why I say "a third party"—who could be the woman psychotherapist of the hospital where one can go with the child. In the family, the mother can be this third party, in relation to the father, or further, to a symbolic institution (religion, morality, social and professional goal). But how can a mother gain access to this third or symbolic function? That is the problem.

BARUCH: To return to that problem of not being able to overcome the biological fact of the mother carrying the child, never mind rearing it. How would you feel if the biological revolution were to go so far that the reproduction of the infant would take place outside the womb? Would you welcome that possibility, which is no longer quite so much of a fantasy as we had considered it even five years ago?

KRISTEVA: It's a very grave question and in fact I think about it often. We are all caught up in moral scruples, and we tell ourselves that in the near future such a prospect is to be avoided for ontological and ethical reasons, for the various experiments which could be done in this area should have guarantees. People have the impression that they are exposing themselves to kinds of arbitrariness which are not very far from the experiments of the Nazis, which hover on the horizon. This is a defensive attitude, which I cannot keep myself from having. But I think that nothing will stop "progress" and that, as you say, this will be the case some day. Assuming that, the question to ask ourselves is, how will sexual roles be distributed? What will fathers do and what will mothers do, when the child is no longer carried in the uterus?

Here we are in the face of a humanity whose character is completely unforeseeable. In the present state of things, there are two attitudes one might have. One, a defensive one, would consist in saying: there must be preserved, along a straight Freudian line, the distribution of the paternal function on the one side and the maternal function on the other, so that the speaking subjects who are constructed, psychically and not just biologically, can have the "normality" which we think of as theirs; and what is this normality? It is that which succeeds in getting along, surviving, in the Oedipal triangle, that is, the defensive position. It seems to be more and more untenable. Hence the interest that I have in the cases of "borderlines." For I think that we will not be able to hold on for very long to this position—the fathers on one side, the mothers on the other. There will be mixtures of these two functions, which will give rise to a very different psychic map of humanity. One will no longer see, or very rarely—we are daydreaming, but perhaps it is not altogether a mere daydream, that hypothesis of which you spoke—if the production of children outside the uterus were to be realized, the good neurotic caught between Daddy and Mommy. One will have a psychic structure much closer to what is now seen as borderline, I suppose. Which does not necessarily mean that it will be outside the social order.

For a modern individual, who has had to manage the array of information of our times, which is scientific information, which is the mixture of the media—along with television, there are ten thousand sorts of information which bombard us constantly—if an individual wants to be, not someone who lives in the middle of the seventeenth, eighteenth, or nineteenth century, but contemporary with that information, one should be an individual who is not individual, but an explosion of either polyvalence or polymorphism. Well, that is someone of whom one cannot yet have the map, the precise representation. But I think that what some are trying to address today starting from these cases of borderlines, or indeed what a certain sort of modern art today displays as subjectivity, will approach that sort of individual. So what I can say is that the interest which the psy-choanalyst can bring at the present moment to subjectivities which are not neurotic, but which have something to do with what is called psychosis, well, that interest will permit us to address with more assurance the psychic problems that will pose themselves in the face of this new, artificially manufactured humanity. For the moment, this is, again, a dream.

BARUCH: Or a nightmare.

KRISTEVA: Or a nightmare. It is fairly terrifying. But perhaps one must not close one's eyes to it. There is going to be a great battle around this; the opposite attitude will be taken by the moral authorities: the Church, a certain part of the psychoanalytic profession, which will fight for the classic Oedipus, and initially this will be a safety belt—perhaps a saving one—which will permit us to push away this exper-iment or at least to protect humanity from a certain number of moral risks which this experiment implies. But I think that if one calculates over the long term, if science were capable of what you say, the moral authorities would not be able to resist very long. And at that moment it would be necessary to have a knowledge of the human psychic structure in order to have a response or a way of acting toward those individuals. And for the moment I don't know what means we can have for knowing what problems these people can pose, except for these cases of borderlines and even psychosis.

BARUCH: Do you feel that desire between the sexes depends on differ-ence, on differentiation? Could it possibly be founded on some-thing else?

KRISTEVA: I don't think that it's founded only on difference; it's also founded on sameness. Anyway, one must know what one means by "desire." If you mean a desire as Freud defined it or as it functions in Western literature, for example, or when one takes the texts of Hegel, desire is founded on the notion of negativity, of lack, and therefore always on difference. But if you mean by desire, the attrac-tion of the sexes to each other or of individuals to each other, which makes it possible for the sexual act to take place, that, I think, in great part, functions on the basis of identification. For example, all homosexuality (but not only homosexuality, also the attraction of many men to women) has arisen on the basis of the similarity or identification which one may feel with another. This is not necessar-ily desire in the Hegelian sense of the term, but it is an attraction in the sense of the Freudian eros.

BARUCH: What do you see as the place of love in the new conservatism of the family?

KRISTEVA: It's the only thing which can save us. My seminar, this year, at Paris VII University, is on the "Love object." One would have to try, in this situation, to save some territories of freedom. What is a territory of freedom? It is, in what concerns affective work, let us say, a place where people could explore the limits of their discourse, of their thought, of their manipulation of colors and sounds, of words, whatever you like. But the space of freedom for the individual is love—it is the only place, the only moment in life, where the various precautions, defenses, conservatism break down and one tries to go to the limit of one's being, so it's fundamental. The love relation is a situation where the limits between the *Ego* and the *Other* are constantly abolished and established.

BARUCH: Well, that is an assumption that many women today would not accept at all.

KRISTEVA: Yes. An assumption, yes.

BARUCH: People like Kate Millett in *Sexual Politics,* or Shulamith Firestone in the *Dialectic of Sex* say that love is a myth propagated by men for the control of women, that, in effect, what it has done is to perpetuate the hierarchy of the sexes and make women accept their oppressive place within the family. Firestone has said that men don't really know how to love at all—it's only women who know how to love. So this would seem totally opposed to your point of view, which is that love can be a species of freedom, the only means of defense against an oppressive state.

KRISTEVA: There are many things to be said about that. First of all, love is not something fixed; there is a history of love. When one takes the evolution of this concept in the West, one realizes that love for the Greeks was not the same thing as medieval love—courtly love— Romantic love, and existentialist love. So there is an evolution which is not necessarily progress. I would call it a recreation, but in any case a movement in what is called love, and it is obvious that in certain situations and some of the time, it has been possible that it is a means of blackmail by one sex of the other—and essentially by the male in the history of humanity as we have experienced it in relation to the female. But that is a vision, perhaps, through the wrong end of the telescope, which doesn't interest me very much because if you look at things that way, the whole of culture oppresses women—a madrigal or Shakespeare is antiwoman. Fine, if one wants to put it that way, but, on that basis, long live genetic manipulation or whatever. What is one supposed to do about it? What does one suggest as an alternative? It doesn't seem to me a very exalted view of things. On the contrary, I am not in favor of decimating men or of believing that patriarchy is a horror. I think that culture—in particular Occidental culture, which is founded on patriarchy and expressed in the great religions which were—which still are—Judaism and Christianity—has produced profoundly true visions of the human being as the symbolical being, as the being who lives in language and who is not reduced just to the womb and to reproduction. Now love is a moment in the life of a speaking being who, all the while caught in the body, opens oneself to the symbolic dimension. I love the other, who is not necessarily me, and who gives me the possibility of opening myself to something other than myself. This can take place through an imaginary fusion with this outer body, but if it is experienced not in a merely narcissistic way but as the governing principle of my whole subsequent existence, what I call love is openness to the other, and it is what gives me my human dimension, my symbolic dimension, my cultural and historical dimension. So if one says that it's patriarchy which produces that, long live patriarchy.

I for my part say that the love relation is the only chance to go through narcissism toward the recognition of the symbolic moment. And I would look with horror on a humanity that would decapitate or wipe out this symbolic moment. If that's what some feminists propose, I don't want any of it.

BARUCH: Well, I guess that some of them, at least, would say that what they propose is a different form of love from what has existed in the past. As you point out there is a history of love, there are changes, and no doubt there will be transformations.

KRISTEVA: As you say, they will probably say that there are forms of love, but I don't know if they would recognize that love is a relation not merely to another self (*moi*) as we come together in order to get ourselves narcissistic gratifications, but it is also, by means of that, an *opening of my self* toward a symbolic dimension. Love is not simply when you give pleasure to each other, it can even be very different; it's above all when I am able to listen to Gesualdo, or to see a Rothko painting. Those can be moments of love. I am not capable of seeing them or of hearing those objects if I am caught in an essentially biological dimension or the dimension of protest. And I think that the feminists now, after a phase which was essentially critical or protesting, are trying to find a way of talking to people—to women—about that opening, the symbolic dimension where women ought to place themselves, and not to shut themselves up in wombs, or in machines which make children outside wombs. Can you imagine a humanity having as an objective or as sole horizon the reproduction of the species? The symbolic is a matter for speaking beings, and we women are first of all speaking beings. That must not be left to the patriarchy alone.

Illustrations of Feminine Depression

The following fragments do not open up the universe of clinical melancholia; rather, they lead us into neurotic regions of the melancholy/depressive set. What one notices there is the alternation between depression and anxiety, depression and perverse action, loss of object and meaning of speech and sadomasochistic domination over them. Being caught in woman's speech is not merely a matter of chance that could be explained by the greater frequency of feminine depressions—a sociologically proven fact. This may also reveal an aspect of feminine sexuality: its addiction to the maternal Thing and its lesser aptitude for restorative perversion.

Cannibalistic Solitude

The Body as Tomb or the Omnipotent Devouring. From the time of her birth Helen suffered from serious motor problems that had required several surgical operations and confined her to bed until she was three. The little girl's brilliant intellectual development, however, enabled her to have an equally brilliant professional career, all the more so since nothing remains of her earlier motor deficiencies or of the family context that, quite obviously, fostered them.

Nothing, that is, aside from frequent instances of serious depression that did not seem triggered by the current reality, a rather prosperous one, of Helen's life. A number of situations (speaking with more than one person, being in a public place, defending a position shared by none of the people present) produced in her a state of stupor. "I find myself glued to the spot, as if paralyzed, I lose the ability to speak, my mouth fills with chalk, my mind is completely empty." She was overcome with a sense of total incapacity, quickly followed by utter dejection that separated Helen from the world, caused her to withdraw into her room, dissolve into tears, and remain speechless, thoughtless for days on end. "As if I were dead but I do not even think of killing myself, nor do I desire to do so, it is as if it had already been done."

In such circumstances, "being dead" meant a physical experience for Helen, an unspeakable one at first. When she later tried to find words to describe it, she spoke of states of artificial weightiness, of swept-out dryness, of absence against a backdrop of dizziness, of emptiness cut out into black lightning . . . But those words still seemed to her too imprecise for what she experienced as a total paralysis of psyche and body, an irremediable dissociation between herself and everything else, and also within what should have been "she." An absence of sensations, a loss of pain or hollowing out of sorrow—an absolute, mineral, astral numbness, which was nevertheless accompanied by the impression, also an almost physical one, that this "being dead," physical and sensory as it might be, was also a thought nebula, an amorphous imagination, a muddled representation of some implacable helplessness. The reality and fiction of death's being. Cadaverization and artifice. An absolute impotence that was, nevertheless, secretly all powerful. The artifice of maintaining herself alive, but . . . "beyond it all." Beyond castration and disintegration; being *as if* she were dead, *playing* dead seemed for Helen when she could talk about it, therefore after the event, like a "poetics" of survival, an inverted life, coiled around imaginary and real disintegration to the extent of embodying death *as if* it were real. In that worldview, swallowing a vial of barbiturates is not a choice but a gesture that is imperative on the basis of an elsewhere—a non-act, or rather a sign of completion, a near-aesthetic harmonization of its fictitious fullness, "beyond."

A total oceanic death would engulf the world and Helen's being in a prostrate, mindless, motionless passivity. Such a lethal flood could settle down for days and weeks on end, allowing neither interest in nor access to any exteriority. When an object's image or a person's face managed to crystallize in it, they were at once perceived as precipitates of hatred, as hurtful or hostile elements, both disintegrating and agonizing, which she could face in no other way except by killing them. Putting those aliens to death was then a substitute for being dead, and the lethal flood changed into torrents of anguish. Nevertheless, it was anguish that kept Helen alive. It was her vital dance, following and in addition to morbid stupor. Certainly painful and insufferable, anguish just the same gave her access to an extent of reality. The faces to be killed were mainly the faces of children. That unbearable temptation horrified her and gave her the impression of being monstrous, and yet *being*—emerging out of nothingness.

Faces of the disabled child that she was and henceforth wanted to be finished with? It would seem, rather, that the desire to kill was triggered only when the world of others, previously taken over by the lethal self in its almighty helplessness, succeeded in becoming free from the confinement where dreamlike melancholia had trapped her. Then confronted with others without seeing them as such, the depressed Helen continued to project onto them: "I am not killing my frustraters or my tyrants, I am killing *their* baby, which they have dropped."

Like an Alice in distressland, the depressed woman cannot put up with mirrors. Her image and that of others arouse within her wounded narcissism, violence, and the desire to kill—from which she protects herself by going through the looking glass and settling down in that other world where, by limitlessly spreading her constrained sorrow, she regains a hallucinated completeness. Beyond the grave, Proserpina survives as a blind shade. Her body is already elsewhere, absent, a living corpse. It often happens that she does not feed it or else, on the contrary, she stuffs it the better to get rid of it. Through her fuzzy, tear-misted gaze that sees neither you nor herself, she savors the bitter sweetness of being forsaken by so many absent ones. Concerned with brooding, within her body and her psyche, over a physical and moral distress, Helen nevertheless strolls among the others—when she leaves her graveyard bed—like an extraterrestrial, the inaccessible citizen of the magnificent land of Death, of which no one could ever deprive her.

At the start of her analysis Helen was warring with her mother—inhuman, artificial, nymphomaniac, incapable of any feeling, and having thoughts only, so said the patient, for money or for seduction. Helen remembered her mother's "bursting into" her room as "a desecration, a forcible entry, a rape," or her overly intimate, overly explicit remarks— "in fact, I thought them obscence"—made in the presence of friends, which made her blush with shame . . . and pleasure.

Behind that veil of erotic aggressiveness, however, we uncovered another relationship between the handicapped child and her mother. "As much as I try to imagine her face, now or at the time of my childhood, I don't see it. I am sitting on someone who holds me, perhaps on her lap, but actually it isn't anybody. A person would have a face, a voice, a glance, a head. The fact is that I perceive nothing of the sort, merely a support, that's all, nothing else." I venture an interpretation: "As to the other, you have perhaps assimilated her into yourself, you wanted her support, her legs, but as for everything else, *she* was perhaps *you*." "I had a dream," Helen went on, "I was climbing your stairs, they were covered with bodies that looked like the people on my parents' wedding photo. I myself had been invited to that wedding, it was a cannibalistic meal, I was supposed to eat those bodies, those scraps of bodies, those heads, my mother's head also. It was ghastly."

Orally assimilating the mother who gets married, who has a man, who flees. Possessing her, holding her within oneself so as never to be separated from her. Helen's almightiness shows through the mask of aggressiveness and shores up the other's nonexistence in her daydream as well as the difficulty she experiences in deciding who she is when facing a person different from herself, separated from herself, in actual life.

The thought of a minor surgical operation distresses Helen so much that she is willing to run the risk of aggravating her condition rather than confronting anesthesia. "It's too dismal, being put to sleep, I don't think I could stand it. They are going to go through me, of course, but that isn't what frightens me. It's strange, I have the feeling that I'm going to end up being frightfully alone. Even so, that's preposterous, because in fact, people will never have taken care of me so much." She perhaps feels that the surgical "operation" (I refer to my own interpretational "operations") will take away someone close, some indispensable person, whom she imagines she has locked up within herself and constantly keeps her company? "I don't see who that might be. I've already told you, I think of no one, for me there is no other one, I see no one by my side as far back as I can remember . . . I forgot to tell you, I've had sex and I was nauseated. I vomited and I saw, as if I were in between sleep and wakefulness, something like the head of a child falling into the washbasin while a voice called me from a distance, but mistakenly calling me by my mother's name." Helen thus confirmed my interpretation—she had locked up a fantasy, the representation of her mother, within her body. And she reeled as she spoke of it, as if she were disconcerted by having to relinquish, if only by words, the object that was imprisoned within herself, and which, if she happened to miss it, would plunge her into a bottomless grief. Punctual and remarkably regular, she forgot, for the first time during her analysis, the time of her ensuing appointment. At the next meeting, she confessed that she remembered nothing about the meeting previous to the one she missed: everything was void, blank, she felt drained and frightfully sad, nothing meant anything, she was once more back in those states of stupor that are so painful . . . Had she tried to lock me within herself instead of the mother we had flushed out? To confine me in her body so that, the one blended with the other, we could no longer meet, since she had for a time incorporated, ingested, buried me in her imaginary tomb-like body, as she had done with her mother?

Perverse and Frigid. Helen often complained that her words, with which she hoped to "touch" me, were actually hollow and dry, "far removed from true feeling": "It is possible to say anything, it may be a piece of information, but it has no meaning, at any rate not for me." That description of her speech reminded her of what she called her "orgies." Beginning with her teens and up to the start of her analysis she alternated between states of prostration and "erotic feasts": "I did everything and anything, I was man, woman, beast, whatever was called for, it created a sensation, and me, it made me come, I think, but it wasn't really me. It was pleasant, but it was someone else."

Omnipotence and disavowal of loss led Helen on a feverish quest for gratification: she could do everything, she was almightiness. A narcissistic and phallic triumph, such a maniacal attitude finally turned out to be exhausting, since it blocked all possibility of symbolization for the negative affects—fear, sorrow, pain . . .

Nonetheless, when the analysis of omnipotence gave those affects access to speech, Helen went through a period of frigidity. The maternal object, necessarily erotic, which had first been captured in order to be annihilated in Helen, once it was recovered and named during the course of analysis did probably, and for a time, fulfill the patient. "I have her within me," the frigid woman seemed to say, "she doesn't leave me, but no one else can take her place, I am impenetrable, my vagina is dead." Frigidity, which is essentially vaginal and can be partly compensated for with clitoral orgasm, betrays an imaginary capture by the frigid woman of a maternal figure anally imprisoned and transferred to the cloaca-vagina. Many women know that in their dreams their mothers stand for lovers or husbands and vice versa, and they keep settling with them, without satisfaction, accounts of anal possession. Such a mother, who is imagined as indispensable, fulfilling, intrusive, is for that very reason death-bearing: she devitalizes her daughter and leaves her no way out. What is more, since she has been imagined as monopolizing the jouissance her daughter had given her, but without returning anything in its stead (without getting her pregnant), such a mother cloisters the frigid woman in an imaginary solitude that is affective as well as sensory. The partner would need to be imagined, in turn, as "more-than-a-mother," in order to act the part of both "Thing" and "Object," in order not to fall short of the narcissistic request, but also and foremost in order to dislodge that request and lead the woman to cathex her autoeroticism in a jouissance of the other (separate, symbolic, phallic).

Two forms of jouissance thus seem possible for a woman. On the one hand there is phallic jouissance—competing or identifying with the partner's symbolic power—which mobilizes the clitoris. On the other hand, there is an *other jouissance* that fantasy imagines and carries out by aiming more deeply at psychic space, and the space of the body as well. That other jouissance requires that the melancholy object blocking the psychic and bodily interior literally be liquefied. Who is capable of doing it? An imagined partner able to dissolve the mother imprisoned within myself by giving me what she could and above all what she could not give me, while remaining in a different place—no longer the mother's but that of the person who can obtain for me the major gift she was never able to offer: a new life. A partner who acts neither the father's part, ideally rewarding his daughter, nor the symbolic stallion's that one is supposed to obtain through a manly competition.

The feminine interior (meaning the psychic space and, at the level of bodily experience, the vagina-anus combination) can then cease being the crypt that encloses the dead woman and conditions frigidity. Putting to death the death-bearing mother within me endows the partner with the appeal of a life-giver, precisely of one who is "more-than-a-mother." He is not a phallic mother but rather a restoration of the mother by means of a phallic violence that destroys the bad but also bestows and honors. The so-called vaginal jouissance that follows is symbolically dependent, as can be seen, on a relation to the Other no longer imagined as part of a phallic outbidding, but as an invigorator of the narcissistic object and able to insure its *outward* displacement—by giving a child, by himself becoming the link between the mother-child bond and phallic power, or else by furthering the beloved woman's symbolic life.

There is no evidence that the other jouissance is absolutely necessary for a woman's psychic fulfillment. Very often, either phallic, professional, or maternal compensation, or else clitoral pleasure are frigidity's hermetic veil. Just the same, if men and women endow the *other jouissance* with nearly sacred value, it is perhaps because it is the language of the female body that has temporarily triumphed over depression. It is a triumph over death, surely not as the individual's ultimate fate, but over the imaginary death where the premature human being is permanently at stake if abandoned, neglected, or misunderstood by the mother. Within feminine fantasy such a jouissance assumes a triumph over the death-bearing mother, in order for the interior to become a source of rewards while eventually becoming a source of biological life, childbearing, and motherhood.

To Kill or to Kill Oneself: The Enacted Wrongdoing

The Act Would Be Merely Reprehensible. Feminine depression is occasionally concealed by a feverish activity that gives the depressed person the appearance of a practical woman, at ease with herself, who thinks only of being useful. To such a mask, which many women wear either deceitfully or unwittingly, Marie-Ange adds a cold urge for revenge, a true death-bearing plot, of which she herself is surprised to be the brain and the weapon, and which brings her suffering because she experiences it as a serious wrongdoing. Having discovered that her husband deceived her, Marie-Ange succeeds in identifying her rival and indulges in a series of more or less childish or diabolical schemings in order simply to eliminate the intruder, who happens to be a friend and colleague. It mainly amounts to pouring sleeping drugs and other harmful products into coffee, tea, and other drinks that Marie-Ange offers her freely. But it also goes as far as slashing her car's tires, disabling the brakes, and so forth.

A kind of rapture seizes Marie-Ange when she undertakes such retaliations. She forgets her jealousy and her wound and, even though ashamed of what she is doing, she comes close to feeling gratified. To be at fault causes her to suffer because being at fault gives her joy, and vice versa. Hurting her rival, disorienting her, or even killing her, does that not also amount to inserting herself into the other woman's life, giving her jouissance unto death? Marie-Ange's violence endows her with a phallic power that makes up for humiliation and, even more so, gives her the feeling of being more powerful than her husband—more authoritative, so to speak, over his mistress' body. The complaint against the husband's adultery is but a trivial coating. While wounded by her spouse's "wrongdoing," what rouses Marie-Ange's suffering and avenging mood is neither moral castigation nor the complaint about the narcissistic wound inflicted by her guilty husband.

In more primary fashion, *any possibility for action* would appear to be seen by her fundamentally as a transgression, as a wrongdoing.

Acting would amount to compromising herself, and when the depressive retardation underlying inhibition hampers any other possibility of realization, the only act that is possible for such a woman becomes the major wrongdoing—to kill or to kill oneself. One may imagine an intense oedipal jealousy with respect to the parents' "primal act," doubtless perceived and thought of always as reprehensible; or a precocious harshness on the part of the superego, a fierce hold on the Thing-Object of archaic homosexual desire . . . "I do not act, or if I do it is abominable, it must be reprehensible."

In the manic phase, the paralysis of action takes on the appearance of insignificant activity (and for that very reason hardly culpable), hence possible, or else it aspires to the major wrongdoing.

A Blank Perversion. Loss of the erotic object (unfaithfulness or desertion by the lover or husband, divorce, etc.) is felt by the woman as an assault on her genitality and, from that point of view, amounts to castration. At once, such a castration starts resonating with the threat of destruction of the body's integrity, the body image, and the entire psychic system as well. As a result, feminine castration, rather than being diseroticized, is concealed by narcissistic anguish, which masters and protects eroticism as a *shameful secret.* Even though a woman has no penis to lose, it is her entire being—body and especially soul—that she feels is threatened by castration. *As if her phallus were her psyche,* the loss of the erotic object breaks up and threatens to empty her whole psychic life. The outer loss is immediately and depressively experienced as an inner void.

This means that the psychic void[1] and the painful affect that constitutes its minute yet intense expression settle in place instead of the shameful loss. Depressive behavior develops on the basis of and within such a void. Blank activity, lacking meaning, may just as well follow a death-bearing course (killing the rival who steals the partner) or an innocuous one (wearing herself out doing housework or checking the children's homework). She remains constantly restrained by an aching psychic wrapping, anesthetized, as if "dead."

In the early stages of analysis for depressive women their emptiness as living dead is honored and respected. Only through friendly collusion, free from superego tyranny, does analysis allow shame to be spoken out and death to find its orbit as the death wish. Marie-Ange's desire to cause (the other's) death so as not to pretend to be dead (herself) can then be narrated as a sexual desire to joy in her rival or to give her jouissance.

For that reason, depression appears as the veil of a *blank perversion*—one that is dreamed of, desired, even thought through, but unmentionable and forever impossible. The depressive course precisely avoids carrying out the perverse act: it hollows out the painful psyche and stands in the way of experienced sex as shameful. Melancholia's unbounded activity, which is somewhat hypnoidal, secretely cathexes perversion in the most inflexible feature of the law—constraint, duty, destiny, and even the fatality of death.

By revealing the sexual (homosexual) secret of the depressive course of action that causes the melancholy person to *live with death,* analysis gives back its place to desire within the patient's psychic territory (the death drive is not the death wish). It thus marks off a psychic territory that becomes able to integrate *loss* as signifiable as well as erogenetic. The separation henceforth appears no longer as a threat of disintegration but as a *stepping stone* toward some other—conflictive, bearing Eros and Thanatos, open to both meaning and nonmeaning.

Don Juan's Wife—Sorrowful or Terrorist. Marie-Ange has an elder sister and several younger brothers. She has always been jealous of that elder sister, the father's favorite, but she retains from her childhood the certainty that she was abandoned by her mother, whose many successive pregnancies claimed all her attention. No hatred toward her sister or her mother seems to have been shown in the past, any more than at present. Marie-Ange, on the contrary, comported herself like a well-behaved child, sad, always withdrawn. She was afraid of going out, and when her mother went shopping she would wait for her by the window, worried. "I stayed in the house as if I were there in her stead, I preserved her fragrance, I imagined her presence, I kept her with me." Her mother deemed that such sadness was not normal. "That nun's expression is deceitful, she is hiding something," the matriarch would say disapprovingly, and those words would discourage the little girl even more as she withdrew to her inner hiding place.

It took Marie-Ange a long time to talk of her present depressive states. Under the surface of the always punctual, busy, and faultless teacher, a woman showed up who sometimes took extended sick leaves because she did not want to, could not, leave her house; in order to imprison what fleeing presence?

Nevertheless, she managed to control her states of total dereliction and paralysis by identifying with the maternal figure: either with the superactive housewife, or even—and this is how she came to take action against her rival—with a desired phallic mother whose homosexual passive partner she would like to be or, conversely, whose body she herself would like to arouse by putting her to death. So, Marie-Ange told me a dream that enabled her to glimpse the kind of passion that nourished her hatred for her rival. She manages to open the door of her husband's mistress' car to hide an explosive in it. But in fact it is not a car, it is her mother's bed; Marie-Ange is huddled against her, and she suddenly notices that this mother, who so generously breast-fed the swarm of little boys who came after Marie-Ange, owned a penis.

The heterosexual partner of a woman, when the relationship is satisfying from her point of view, often bears the attributes of her mother. The depressive woman goes against this rule only indirectly. Her favorite partner or her husband is a fulfilling although unfaithful mother. The desperate woman can then be dramatically, painfully, attached to her Don Juan. For, beyond the fact that he gives her the possibility of enjoying an unfaithful mother, Don Juan satisfies her eager thirst for other women. His own mistresses are her own mistresses. His exploits satisfy her own erotomania and provide her with an antidepressive, a feverish excitement beyond pain. If the sexual desire underlying that passion were repressed, murder might take the place of embrace and the depressed woman might change into a terrorist.

Taming sorrow, not fleeing sadness at once but allowing it to settle for a while, even to blossom, and in this way to wear itself out: that is what one of the temporary and yet indispensable phases of analysis might be. Could the wealth of my sadness be my way of protecting myself against death—the death of the desired/rejected other, the death of myself?

Marie-Ange had muffled within herself the distress and devalorization where the real or imaginary maternal neglect had left her. The idea of her being ugly, useless, and insignificant did not leave her, but it was more of an ambiance than an idea, nothing obvious, just the glum coloring of a dull day. On the other hand, the desire for death, for her own death (for want of avenging herself on the mother) filtered into her phobias: fear of falling out the window, from the elevator, off a rock, or off the slope of a mountain. Fear of finding herself in a void, of dying of the void. A permanent vertigo. Marie-Ange protected herself from it for the time being by displacing it onto her rival, who was supposed to be drowned in poison or vanish in a car going at breakneck speed. Her life was unharmed at the price of the other's sacrificed life.

The terrorism of such depressive hysteria is often expressed by aiming for the mouth. Many stories involving harems and other feminine jealousies have established the image of the poisoner as a privileged image of feminine Satanism. Poisoning drink or food nevertheless reveals, beyond the raging sorceress, a little girl deprived of the breast. And if it is true that little boys are also deprived, everyone knows that man recovers his lost paradise in the heterosexual relationship, but also and mainly through various roundabout means that lavish oral satisfactions on him or do so by means of orality.

Acting out, where a woman is concerned, is more inhibited, less developed, and consequently it can be, when it takes place, more violent. For the loss of the object seems beyond remedy for a woman and its mourning more difficult, if not impossible. So, substitutive objects, perverse objects that should lead her to the father, seem derisory to her. She often reaches heterosexual desire by repressing archaic pleasures, even pleasure itself—she yields to heterosexuality in frigidity. Marie-Ange wants to keep her husband to herself, for herself but not for sexual pleasure. Access to jouissance is then effected only through man's perverse object: Marie-Ange's pleasure comes from the mistress, and when her husband does not have one he no longer interests her. The depressive woman's perversion is deceitful, it needs the go-between and screen of man's object-woman in order to seek the other sex. But once settled on that path, the tired-out desire of the melancholy woman knows no bounds: it wants everything, to the end, until death.

The sharing of that death-bearing secret with analysts is not merely a test of their reliability or of the difference between their discourse and the domain of law, condemnation, or repression. Such a trust ("I am having you share in my crime") is an attempt to win over the analyst into a common jouissance—the one that the mother declined, that the mistress steals. By pointing out that the trust is an attempt to gain ascendency over the analyst as erotic object, the interpretation maintains the patient in the truth of her desire and her attempts at manipulation. But in abiding by an ethics that does not merge with that of punitive legislation the analyst recognizes the reality of the depressive stance, and asserting the symbolic legitimacy of its distress, allows the patient to seek out other means, symbolic or imaginary, of working out her suffering.

A Virgin Mother

"Black Hole". To her it seemed as if conflicts with, desertions by, separations from her lovers did not affect her, she experienced no grief. No

more than when her mother died . . . This did not imply an indifference that would be based on self-control and mastery of the situation or else (and this is most frequently the case) on hysterical repression of sadness and desire. When Isabel, during sessions, attempted to piece together such states, she would speak of "anesthetized wounds," "numbed sorrow," or "a blotting out that holds everything in check." I had the impression that she had fitted in her psychic space one of those "crypts" Maria Torok and Nicolas Abraham talk about, in which there was nothing, but the whole depressive identity was organized around this nothingness. Such nothingness was an absolute. Grief, humiliating by dint of having been kept secret, unnameable, and unspeakable, had turned into a *psychic silence* that did not repress the wound but took its place and, what is more, by condensing it, gave it back an exorbitant intensity, imperceptible by sensations and representations.

Melancholy mood, with her, amounted only to mental blanks, evasiveness, distraught and seemingly hallucinated gazings on what may have been grief, but which Isabel's superego dignity at once transformed into inaccessible hypertrophy. A nothingness that is neither repression nor simply the mark of the affect but condenses into a *black hole*—like invisible, crushing, cosmic antimatter—the sensory, sexual, fantasy-provoking ill-being of abandonments and disappointments. Narcissistic wounds and castration, sexual dissatisfaction and fantasy-laden dead-ends become telescoped into a simultaneously killing and irretrievable burden that organizes her subjectivity; within, she is nothing but bruises and paralysis; outside, all that was left to her was acting out or sham activism.

Isabel needed that "black hole" of her melancholia in order to construct her living motherhood and activities outside it, just as others organize themselves around repression or splitting. It was her own thing, her home, the narcissistic center where she foundered as much as she replenished herself.

Isabel decided to have a child at the darkest moment of one of her depressive periods. Disappointed by her husband, distrustful of what appeared to be her lover's "childish inconsistency," she wanted to have her child "for herself." Knowing who fathered it mattered little to her. "I want the child, not the father," the "virgin mother" reflected. She had to have a "reliable companion," "Someone who would need me, we would be accomplices, we would never leave each other, well, almost never . . ."

The child conceived as antidote against depression is destined to bear a heavy burden. The indeed virginal calmness of the pregnant Isabel—no period in her life had ever seemed so euphoric to her as her pregnancy—

concealed a bodily tension that any heedful observer would have detected at the beginning of this analysis. Isabel did not manage to relax on the couch but, her neck muscles tensed and her feet on the ground ("so as not to damage your belongings," she said), she seemed ready to leap forward and confront some threat or other. That of being made pregnant by the analyst? Some unweaned babies' hyperkinesia no doubt conveys their mothers' unnamed, unconscious, utmost physical and psychic tension.

Living for the Sake of Dying. Anxiety over deformity in the fetus, common in most pregnant women, reached a suicidal peak with Isabel. She imagined that her baby would die during delivery or be born with a serious congenital defect. She would then kill it, before killing herself, mother and child becoming united again, inseparable in death as in pregnancy. The much hoped for birth changed into a burial, and the vision of the funeral exalted the patient, as if she had desired her child for death alone. She would give birth for death's sake. The brutal stopping of the life she was preparing to give, and of her own as well, was destined to spare her all worry, to relieve her of the troubles of life. Birth destroyed the future and the project.

Desire for a child was revealed as narcissistic desire for lethal fusion—it was a death of desire. Thanks to her child Isabel would elude the risks of erotic ordeals, the surprises of pleasure, the uncertainties of the other's discourse. Once she had become a mother she would be able to remain a virgin. Deserting the child's father in order to live as a single woman (or else as an imaginary couple with her analyst?), alone with her daydreams, needing no one and threatened by none, she entered motherhood as one enters a convent. Isabel was getting ready to gaze upon herself complacently in that living being destined for death that her child was to be, like a painful shadow of herself that she would at last be able to care for and bury, whereas no one would be capable of doing it "properly" for herself. The depressive mother's selflessness is not without a modicum of paranoid smugness.

When little Alice was born, Isabel felt as if she were bombarded by reality. The baby's neonatal jaundice and the first childhood illnesses that were inordinately serious threatened to change the death fantasy into an unbearable fact. Undoubtedly with the help of analysis, Isabel was not swallowed up by postpartum blues. Her depressive inclination was transformed into a fierce struggle to save the life of her daughter, whose development she henceforth followed with great tenderness, albeit with the temptation to be overprotective.

Smug Abnegation. The initial melancholia was devoured by "Alice's problems." Nevertheless, without disappearing, it acquired another aspect. It was transformed into total ascendancy, both oral and anal, over the girl's body, and her development was thus set back. Feeding Alice, controlling her meals, weighing her, weighing her again, supplementing the diet prescribed by some doctor or other by drawing from the advice found in such-and-such a book . . . Checking Alice's stools until she started school and afterward, her constipations, her diarrheas, giving her enemas . . . Watching over her sleep—what is the normal length of sleep for a two-year-old? And a three-year-old? A four-year-old? And is not this babble rather an abnormal cry? The obsessive anxiety of the "typical" worried mother was multiplied by Isabel. As an unwed mother wasn't she responsible for everything? Wasn't she all that this "poor Alice" had in the world? Her mother, father, aunt, grandfather, grandmother? The grandparents, having deemed that this birth was not very orthodox, had stood aloof from the "virgin mother" and unwittingly given Isabel an additional excuse in her need to be all-powerful.

A depressive person's pride is immeasurable, and this is something one must take into account. Isabel is ready to take on any labor, worry, duty, trouble, even defect (if someone chanced to find any), rather than to admit her suffering. Alice has become a new speech inhibitor in the already not-so-talkative world of her mother. For the sake of the daughter's well-being, the mother had to "hold out": facing up to things, not appearing to be an inadequate person or a loser.

How long can this last, this delightful, smug imprisonment by the sadness of being alone, the sorrow *of not being?* With some women, it lasts until the child no longer needs her, has sufficiently grown up, and leaves her. They then find themselves abandoned once more, downcast, this time without being able to resort to another childbirth. Pregnancy and motherhood turned out to be a parenthesis within the depression, a new negation of that impossible loss.

Isabel, for her part, did not wait that long. She had the verbal and erotic recourse of transference. She could cry and break down before her analyst, trying to come to life again not beyond but this time *through* the mourning of the analysis, ready to hear a wounded speech. Once solitude has been named, we are less alone if words succeed in infiltrating the spasm of tears—provided they can find an addressee for an overflow of sorrow that had up to then shied away from words.

Aroused Father and Ideal Father. Isabel's dreams and fantasies might suggest that she had been the victim of a precocious seduction on the part of her father or some other adult among their acquaintances. No precise memory clearly surfaced from Isabel's discourse, either to confirm or deny it; the hypothesis was suggested by an oneiric, repetitive sequence where Isabel is alone in a closed room with an older man who is irrationally pushing her against the wall; or one in her father's office where again the two of them are alone, with her shaking less from fear than from emotion, blushing and perspiring, such an incomprehensible state filling her with shame. Was this true seduction or a desire to be seduced? Isabel's father appears to have been an uncommon character. A poor farmer who became the manager of a firm, he aroused the admiration of his employees, friends, and children, and particularly that of Isabel. And yet this man, aiming at success, had frightful, sudden changes of mood, especially under the influence of alcohol, which he indulged in more and more as he grew older. Isabel's mother would conceal that emotional instability; at the same time she compensated for it and held it in contempt. As far as the child was concerned, such contempt meant that mother disapproved of the father's sexuality, his excessive fire, his lack of composure. A father, in short, who was both desired and condemned. He might have been, to a certain extent, an identifying solution for his daughter, a support in her rivalry with and disappointment in the mother, the genitor who was always distracted by another baby. But beyond an intellectual and social attraction, that father was also a disappointing figure. "From my point of view he was immediately demystified, I could not believe in him as outsiders did, he was my mother's creation, her biggest baby. . . ."

Her father's symbolic existence doubtless helped Isabel in erecting her professional armor, but the erotic man, the imaginary father, the loving, giving, and gratifying one had become unbelievable. He displayed emotions, passions, and pleasures from the angle of crisis and anger—fascinating, but how dangerous and destructive. The link between pleasure and symbolic dignity that is insured by an imaginary father, as he leads his child from primary to secondary identification, no longer existed for Isabel.

She then had a choice between a paroxysmal sexual life and . . . "virginity"—between perversion and abnegation. The experience of the former had filled her years as a teenager and a young woman. Such excesses, or "overflows" as she called them, punctuated the end of her depressive episodes. "It was as if I were drunk, and afterwards I ended up vacuous. Perhaps I am like my father. But his constant fluctuation between high and low—that, I don't want. I prefer serenity, stability, sacrifice if you wish. The sacrifice for my daughter, however, is it really a sacrifice? It is a moderate joy, a permanent joy. . . . Well, a well-tempered joy, like the clavier."

Isabel gave a child to her ideal father—not the father who displayed a drunken body but the father with the absent body, therefore a dignified father, a master, a leader. The masculine body, the aroused and drunken body, that is the mother's object: Isabel leaves it to that deserting rival, for in the competition with her mother's presumed perversion, the daughter at once admitted she was a minor, a loser. As for her, she chose the prestigious name, and it is precisely as a celibate, unwed mother that she will succeed in preserving it in its untouchable perfection, dissociating it from the "overly" aroused masculine body, which is manipulated by the other woman.

If it be true that such a paternity largely conditions Isabel's depression, forcing her back toward the mother from whom she could not be separated without risks (of stimulation, of imbalance), it is also true that, through his ideal aspect, his symbolic success, such a father also provides his daughter with a few means, admittedly ambiguous, to pull herself through. In becoming the mother *and* the father Isabel has finally reached an absolute. But does the ideal father exist anywhere other than in the abnegation of his own daughter as celibate, unwed mother?

When all is said and done, however, and even if it is only with one child, Isabel manages much better than her mother. For is it not true that if she does not produce many children, she does everything for a single one? Nevertheless, that overtaking the mother in the imagination is only a temporary solution to depression. Mourning still remains impossible under the guise of a masochistic triumph. The real work remains to be done, through separation from the child and, finally, through separation from the analyst, so that a woman might try to face the void within the meaning that is produced and destroyed in all its connections and all its objects . . .

NOTES

1. One is particularly indebted to the works of André Green for having developed the notion of "psychic void." See, among others, "L'Analyste, la symbolisation et l'absence dans la cure analytique," at the Twenty-ninth International Psychoanalytic Congress, 1975, and *Narcissisme de vie, narcissisme de mort* (Paris: Minuit, 1983).

Bibliography

Books by Kristeva

1969. *Semeiotiké: Recherches pour une sémanalyse.* Paris: Editions du Seuil.

1970. *Le Texte du roman.* The Hague: Mouton.

1974. *La Révolution du langage poétique.* Paris: Editions du Seuil. Translated by Margaret Waller as *Revolution in Poetic Language.* New York: Columbia Press, 1984.

1974. *Des Chinoises.* Paris: Editions des Femmes. Translated by Anita Barrows as *About Chinese Women.* London: Marion Boyars, 1977.

1977. *Polylogue.* Paris: Editions du Seuil.

1980. *Desire in Language.* Translated by Thomas Gora, Alice Jardine, and Leon Roudiez and edited by Leon Roudiez. New York: Columbia Press.

1980. *Pouvoirs de l'horreur.* Paris: Editions du Seuil, 1980. Translated by Leon Roudiez as *Powers of Horror.* New York: Columbia University Press, 1982.

1981. *Le langage, cet inconnu.* Paris: Editions du Seuil. Translated by Anne Menke as *Language, the Unkown.* New York: Columbia University Press, 1989.

1983. *Histoires d'amour.* Paris: Editions Denoël. Translated by Leon Roudiez as *Tales of Love.* New York: Columbia University Press, 1987.

1985. *Au commencement etait l'amour.* Paris: Hachette. Translated by Author Goldhammer as *In the Beginning Was Love: Psychoanalysis and Faith.* New York: Columbia Press, 1988.

1986. *The Kristeva Reader.* Edited by Toril Moi. New York: Columbia Press, 1986.

1987. *Soleil noir: Depression et mélancolie.* Paris: Gallimard. Translated by Leon Roudiez as *Black Sun.* New York: Columbia University Press, 1989.

1989. *Etrangers à nous-mêmes.* Paris: Fayard. Translated by Leon Roudiez as *Strangers to Ourselves.* New York: Columbia University Press, 1991.

1990. *Lettre ouverte à Harlem Désir.* Paris: Editions Rivages.

1990. *Les Samouraïs*. Paris: Fayard. Translated by Barbara Bray as *The Samurai*. New York: Columbia University Press, 1992.

1991. *Le vieil homme et les loups*. Paris: Fayard. Translated by Barbara Bray as *The Old Man and the Wolves*. New York: Columbia University Press, 1994.

1993. *Proust and the Sense of Time*. Translated by Stephen Bann. New York: Columbia University Press.

1993. *Les Nouvelles maladies de l'ame*. Paris: Fayard. Translated by Ross Guberman as *New Maladies of the Soul*. Columbia University Press, 1995.

1993. *Nations Without Nationalism*. Partly translated from *Lettre ouverte à Harlem Désir* (1990) by Leon Roudiez. New York: Columbia University Press.

1994. *Le temps sensible: Proust et l'experience litteraire*. Paris: Gallimard. Translated as by Ross Guberman *Time and Sense: Proust and the Experience of Literature*. New York: Columbia University Press, 1996.

Books on Kristeva in English

Crownfield, David, ed. *Body/Text in Julia Kristeva: Religion, Women, and Psychoanalysis*. Albany: SUNY Press, 1992.

Fletcher, John, and Andrew Benjamin, eds. *Abjection, Melancholia and Love*. New York: Routledge Press, 1990.

Grosz, Elizabeth. *Sexual Subversions*. Boston: Allen & Unwin, 1989.

Lechte, John. *Julia Kristeva*. New York: Routledge Press, 1990.

Oliver, Kelly. *Reading Kristeva: Unraveling the Doublebind*. Bloomington: Indiana University Press, 1993.

——, ed. *Ethics, Politics and Difference in Kristeva's Writing*. New York: Routledge Press, 1993.

Index